lonely planet

Best Road Trips USA

MARGOT BIGG, KATE ARMSTRONG, CAROLYN BAIN, AMY C BALFOUR, RAY BARTLETT, LOREN BELL, ANDREW BENDER, SARA BENSON, ALISON BING, CRISTIAN BONETTO, CELESTE BRASH, JADE BREMNER, GREGOR CLARK, MICHAEL GROSBERG, ANTHONY HAM, ASHLEY HARRELL, MARK JOHANSON, ADAM KARLIN, BRIAN KLUEPFEL, STEPHEN LIOY, VESNA MARIC, CAROLYN MCCARTHY, HUGH MCNAUGHTAN, BECKY OHLSEN, CHRISTOPHER PITTS, KEVIN RAUB, SIMON RICHMOND, BRENDAN SAINSBURY, ANDREA SCHULTE-PEEVERS, REGIS ST LOUIS, RYAN VER BERKMOES, MARA VORHEES, BENEDICT WALKER, KARLA ZIMMERMAN

CONTENTS

ALASKA
CANADA
ROCKY MOUNTAINS, p241
THE PACIFIC NORTHWEST, p371
GREAT PLAINS, p209
GREAT LAKES, p185
NEW YORK & THE MID-ATLANTIC, p59
NEW ENGLAND, p95
FLORIDA & THE SOUTH, p139
CALIFORNIA & NEVADA, p315
THE SOUTHWEST, p273
PACIFIC OCEAN
ATLANTIC OCEAN
Gulf of Mexico
MEXICO
Mexico City
GUATEMALA
BELIZE
BAHAMAS
CUBA
CAYMAN IS
HAITI
JAMAICA
Vancouver
Victoria
Olympia
Seattle
WASHINGTON
Salem
Albany
OREGON
IDAHO
Boise
Helena
MONTANA
WYOMING
Winnipeg
NORTH DAKOTA
Bismarck
SOUTH DAKOTA
Pierre
MINNESOTA
St Paul
WISCONSIN
Madison
MICHIGAN
Lansing
Lake Superior
Lake Michigan
Lake Huron
Lake Ontario
Lake Erie
Ottawa
Toronto
Québec City
Fredericton
NEW YORK
MAINE
Augusta
Montpelier
Concord
Boston
Providence
Albany
PENNSYLVANIA
New York
Harrisburg
Trenton
Dover
WASHINGTON, DC
Richmond
VIRGINIA
WEST VIRGINIA
NORTH CAROLINA
Raleigh
SOUTH CAROLINA
Columbia
Jacksonville
Sacramento
San Francisco
NEVADA
Salt Lake City
UTAH
CALIFORNIA
Los Angeles
San Diego
Mexicali
ARIZONA
Phoenix
NEW MEXICO
Santa Fe
Cheyenne
Denver
COLORADO
NEBRASKA
Lincoln
Des Moines
IOWA
Chicago
INDIANA
Indianapolis
Columbus
OHIO
ILLINOIS
MISSOURI
Topeka
KANSAS
Jefferson City
Frankfort
KENTUCKY
Nashville
TENNESSEE
Oklahoma City
OKLAHOMA
ARKANSAS
Little Rock
ALABAMA
Atlanta
GEORGIA
Columbus
LOUISIANA
Jackson
MISSISSIPPI
TEXAS
Dallas
Austin
Baton Rouge
New Orleans
Tallahassee
Jacksonville
Tampa
Orlando
FLORIDA
Miami
Rocky Mountains
1000 km
500 miles

WELCOME TO THE USA

There is nothing more American than a road trip. From the Florida coast to the Pacific Northwest, from the Great Plains to the Rockies, and from the Grand Canyon to the Great Smokies, the 52 road trips in this book are like a road map to the very soul of America. You'll get to know some of the country's most dramatic natural wonders and the national parks that protect them. Just as often, you'll find yourself on a journey of discovery through small-town America. There will be times when the unfolding journey's the thing: a road trip that teaches you something about this remarkable country from the drive alone. At other times, the drive is a starting point – to a trailhead for a hike where no vehicle can travel or to a city where you have to get out and walk. Either way, this book will take you there.

Monument Valley (p52), Utah
CHRISTOPHER M HALL/SHUTTERSTOCK

MY PERFECT ROAD TRIP

MARGOT BIGG

HIGH & LOW ROADS TO TAOS, p296

This small but mighty itinerary travels from Santa Fe, one of the most beautiful cities in the US, up to historic Taos, home to a magnificent – and still inhabited – pueblo, with stops in historic towns and artistic communities along the way. I love that it showcases New Mexico's highlights and a few of its lesser-known haunts, making it easy to check out the must-sees while still having time to slow down and connect to local culture.

Taos Pueblo (p300), New Mexico

BEST SCENIC DRIVES

1. **Fall Foliage Tour** See New England's famously colorful autumnal foliage as you travel from Connecticut to Vermont.
2. **Going-to-the-Sun-Road** Drive into the wilds of Glacier National Park on this National Historic Route.
3. **Zion & Bryce National Parks** Gawp at towering cliffs and otherworldly hoodoos at Utah's most picturesque parks.
4. **Pacific Coast Highways** From sunny San Diego to misty redwoods, this trip displays the best of coastal California.
5. **Crater Lake Circuit** Waterfalls, hot springs and the deepest lake in the US showcase the beauty of Oregon's waters.

BEST URBAN DRIVES

1. **Maryland's National Historic Road** Visit significant cities and mind-blowing museums.

2. **Coastal New England** Visit the Atlantic Seaboard cities that helped shape US history.

3. **Highway 1** Stop by lively cities and chilled-out beach towns as you drive along Florida's Atlantic Coast.

4. **The Great River Road** Let the Mississippi lead you through gritty towns and museum-filled cities.

5. **California's Greatest Hits & Las Vegas** From SF to Las Vegas, this trip pulls out all the stops.

Leavenworth (p365), Washington

BEST FAMILY DRIVES

1. **The Jersey Shore** Busy boardwalks and amusement rides make this stretch a hit with intergenerational groups.

2. **Oklahoma's Tribal Trails** Immerse yourself, and your kids, in Indigenous history on this eye-opening journey.

3. **Grand Canyon Voyage** Learn about the Wild West and see the Grand Canyon as you zip through Arizona.

4. **Disneyland & Orange County Beaches** Watch the glee on your kiddos' faces at Disneyland. After all, it is 'the Happiest Place on Earth.'

5. **Cascade Drive** The faux-Bavarian town of Leavenworth and Chelan's Slidewaters Water Park are a hit with kids.

COASTAL JOURNEYS

With 5000-plus miles of coastline along two oceans and the Gulf of Mexico, there's enough sand and coastal driving – from the rugged, wild shores of New England to the sunny, surfable coasts of Florida and Southern California – to satisfy all kinds of beach lovers. There are so many classic summer drives, taking you from one beach to the next, but these are beautiful road trips at any time of year.

① COASTAL CALIFORNIA

Drive from one end of California to the other, along an incredibly varied coastline. p326

② HIGHWAY 1

Miami to Amelia Island showcases Florida in all its beach and historic-town Atlantic glory. p142

③ HIGHWAY 101 OREGON COAST

Drive the length of spectacular Oregon with its cliffs, beaches and lighthouses. p390

④ COASTAL NEW ENGLAND

Wind along New England's delightful shore with superb scenery and charming villages. p98

⑤ THE JERSEY SHORE

Beaches and boardwalks dominate this road trip along New Jersey's Atlantic rim. p66

Left: Sand Beach (p135), Acadia National Park, Maine; Right: Pacific Coast (p34), California

DRIVER'S LICENSE

Foreign visitors can legally drive a car in the USA for up to 12 months using their home license.

WINTER TIRES

Where winter driving is an issue, many cars are fitted with steel-studded snow tires, while snow chains are sometimes required.

NATIONAL PARK PICKS

They don't call national parks 'America's Best Idea' for nothing. From the tall trees, Rockies and great canyons of the west to the forest-clad hills and stunning islands of the east, America's parks protect some of the most beautiful landscapes in the country. And for many parks, the drives are just the beginning: get out and hike or paddle from where the paved road ends.

① GRAND TETON TO YELLOWSTONE

The Rockies unfold on this glorious Wyoming road trip with plenty of wildlife en route. p244

② THE GREAT SMOKIES

Spot wildlife, hike past waterfalls and take in the views in Great Smoky Mountains National Park. p176

③ YOSEMITE, SEQUOIA & KINGS CANYON NATIONAL PARKS

California's giant trees, chiseled cliffs and deep canyons make this one for the ages. p336

④ GOING-TO-THE-SUN ROAD

Watch the Great Plains unfurl from the high Rockies on this astonishing Glacier National Park drive. p252

⑤ ACADIA NATIONAL PARK

The most beautiful island road trip in America through a New England summer. p132

LEFT TO RIGHT: ANH LUU/SHUTTERSTOCK, ERIC URQUHART/SHUTTERSTOCK

Left: Going-to-the-Sun Road (p252), Glacier National Park, Montana; Above: Acadia National Park (p132), Maine

LAKE & RIVER EXCURSIONS

CREDIT CARDS & INSURANCE

Many credit cards offer free collision damage coverage for rental cars if you rent for 15 days or fewer and charge it to your card.

America's lakes and rivers have always been focal points for great American journeys. Great cities grew up around the lakes and the big rivers served as ways to travel from one world to another. Today is no different. These routes follow the shores of some of the country's iconic waterways. From a volcanic crater lake in the Pacific Northwest to the Great Lakes, the Mississippi, the Missouri and rural New York, these are America's best drives.

1 CRATER LAKE CIRCUIT

Explore America's most beautiful (and deepest) lake in south-central Oregon. p406

2 FINGER LAKES LOOP

Follow lakeshores past vineyards and deep gorges through rural New York State. p62

3 MICHIGAN'S GOLD COAST

Drive along a Great Lakes Michigan shore, past cool towns and even cooler sand dunes. p188

4 THE GREAT RIVER ROAD

Head south with the Mississippi from northern pine forests to America's musical heartland. p194

5 THE MIGHTY MO

Follow the Missouri River on its journey from St Louis to North Dakota. p232

Crater Lake (p407), Oregon
ALLARD SCHAGER/GETTY IMAGES

STEPHEN MOEHLE/SHUTTERSTOCK

The Narrows, Zion National Park (p285), Utah

WILD WEST DRIVES

If one vast landscape has come to define the way we see America, then the country's Southwest (especially Utah, New Mexico, Arizona, California, Texas and Nevada) would surely be a prime candidate. Home to some of the most beautiful (and hottest) deserts on earth, the Southwest is where you can draw near the incredibly scenic Grand Canyon, Monument Valley, Zion and Bryce Canyon National Parks and more.

① GRAND CANYON VOYAGE

Take a road trip through Arizona's Wild West heartland to the incomparable Grand Canyon. p276

HANDS-FREE

In many states, it's illegal to talk on a handheld cell phone while driving; use a hands-free device instead.

WATCH FOR LIVESTOCK

In deserts and range country, livestock sometimes graze next to unfenced roads. These areas are signed as 'Open Range.'

② ZION & BRYCE NATIONAL PARKS

The Wild West as it once was and where glorious nature still holds sway on this trip across Utah. p284

③ MONUMENT VALLEY & TRAIL OF THE ANCIENTS

Red-rock sandstone buttes shelter cliff ruins and astonishing desert views in this Western classic. p290

④ EASTERN SIERRA SCENIC BYWAY

Experience one of California's more picturesque routes with plenty of Old West relics to enjoy. p354

⑤ BIG BEND SCENIC LOOP

Drop off the map and into Big Bend's ghost towns and West Texas magnificence. p304

STAY ON THE ROAD

Driving off-road, or on dirt roads, is often forbidden by car-rental companies; insurance won't cover you in case of accident.

INTERSECTIONS

At four-way stop signs, cars should proceed in order of arrival; when two cars arrive simultaneously, the one on the right has the right of way.

HISTORY'S STORY

America's rich historical story takes many forms, from historic towns to great trails across the West left by Native American peoples. These drives take you deep into the many facets of this story, often laced along the way with beautiful scenery that's ripe for exploration, both on foot and four wheels. It all began out east before moving west along trails that came to define the story of a nation.

① OKLAHOMA'S TRIBAL TRAILS

Trace the poignant Trail of Tears and Native American history on this Oklahoma traverse. p212

② RHODE ISLAND: EAST BAY

Return to the dawn of America at Little Compton on this Rhode Island road trip. p112

③ MARYLAND'S NATIONAL HISTORIC ROAD

History lingers in New Market and Frederick, charming poster children for the American past. p80

④ ON THE PIONEER TRAILS

See where pioneers and Native American peoples clashed on America's westward march. p218

⑤ NATCHEZ TRACE PARKWAY

Take a journey south from Nashville that stuns with natural beauty and American history. p160

LEFT TO RIGHT: DAVID SUCSY/GETTY IMAGES, JORDAN HILL PHOTOGRAPHY/SHUTTERSTOCK

Left: Scotts Bluff National Monument (p221), Nebraska;
Above: Natchez Trace Parkway (p160), Mississippi

WHEN TO GO

Local conditions can make or break a trip. But summer road trips are an American rite of passage.

Summer is best for most road trips: it's when all roads are open (and mountain roads are cleared of snow), and it's also when visitor centers, accommodations and all attractions are open.

In some areas, however, especially some national parks, roads can be unpleasantly crammed, procession-like, with vehicles. Where that's the case, consider late spring (when wildflowers often bloom) or early fall. Spring and fall can also be good for local festivals. An exception to the summer-is-best mantra is also found in the Southwest, especially in Utah, New Mexico and Nevada where summer temperatures can be brutal.

I LIVE HERE

BIG CYPRESS NATIONAL PRESERVE IN SUMMER

Tim L Tetzlaff, Director of Conservation at Naples Zoo @TimTetzlaff

A late-afternoon drive in the South Florida wilderness frequently offers the widest screen show of nature at its most magnificent. US 41's two lanes of civilization give you safe passage through hundreds of thousands of acres of Big Cypress National Preserve, where the horizon is a thin line of earthbound prairies, waterways and cypress domes, like an American Serengeti of endless wet plains. In contrast, the sky is consumed by magnificent, shaded clouds billowing with rounded immensity as they bring life to alligators, otters, deer, wood storks and Florida panthers.

Bison, Firehole River, Yellowstone National Park (p246), Wyoming

YEGOROV/SHUTTERSTOCK

WEATHER WATCH: NEW YORK CITY

JANUARY
Avg. daytime max: **39°F**
Days of rainfall: **7**

FEBRUARY
Avg. daytime max: **43°F**
Days of rainfall: **7**

MARCH
Avg. daytime max: **50°F**
Days of rainfall: **8**

APRIL
Avg. daytime max: **61°F**
Days of rainfall: **9**

MAY
Avg. daytime max: **72°F**
Days of rainfall: **10**

JUNE
Avg. daytime max: **79°F**
Days of rainfall: **10**

VEZZANI PHOTOGRAPHY / SHUTTERSTOCK

Death Valley National Park, California

ACCOMMODATIONS

Prices vary considerably by season, but festivals are one example where otherwise innocuous dates can see hotels, motels and RV parks booked out months in advance for sky-high prices. The same applies to most national parks in summer. Moving your trip even a few weeks either side of the logjam can make all the difference.

A CLIMATE OF EXTREMES

The world's hottest-ever air temperature was recorded at Furnace Creek, in Death Valley in the Mojave Desert on July 10, 1913: 134°F (57°C). At the other extreme, the coldest-ever recorded temperature for the lower 48 states was on January 20, 1954, at Rogers Pass, Montana: -69.7°F (-56.5°C).

QUIRKY FESTIVALS

Mermaid Festival
Summer craziness takes over Brooklyn, NY, with the Mermaid Parade, when Coney Island celebrates summer's steamy arrival with a kitsch-loving parade led by colorfully attired mermaids and horn-blowing mermen. **June**

Oregon Country Fair
Since the summer of '69, the Oregon Country Fair has been bringing flower-powered craft vendors and live entertainment to the Pacific Northwest. **July**

Iowa State Fair
This celebration is a refreshing throwback with country crooning, wondrous butter carvings, livestock shows, food stalls and a down-home good time in America's heartland. **August**

Fantasy Fest
Key West's answer to Mardi Gras is Fantasy Fest. It brings some 75,000 revelers to the subtropical enclave in the 10 days leading up to Halloween. Expect parades, colorful floats, costume parties, the selection of a conch king and queen, and much merriment. **October**

JULY
Avg. daytime max: **84°F**
Days of rainfall: **10**

AUGUST
Avg. daytime max: **82°F**
Days of rainfall: **10**

SEPTEMBER
Avg. daytime max: **75°F**
Days of rainfall: **8**

OCTOBER
Avg. daytime max: **64°F**
Days of rainfall: **7**

NOVEMBER
Avg. daytime max: **54°F**
Days of rainfall: **8**

DECEMBER
Avg. daytime max: **54°F**
Days of rainfall: **8**

GET PREPARED FOR THE USA

Useful things to load in your bag, your ears and your brain

WATCH

- **North by Northwest** *(Alfred Hitchcock; 1959)* Thriller with Cary Grant on the run across America.
- **The Muppet Movie** *(James Frawley; 1979)* Kermit and the gang take to the road on their way to Hollywood in this road movie–lite.
- **National Lampoon's Vacation** *(Harold Ramis; 1983)* Chevy Chase and Goldie Hawn on a classic, hilarious summer road trip holiday.
- **Rain Man** *(Barry Levinson; 1988)* Dustin Hoffman and Tom Cruise take a journey together across the country.
- **Thelma & Louise** *(Ridley Scott; 1991)* America's favorite road movie with two suburban women on a road trip across America.

CLOTHING

In America just about anything goes, and you'll rarely feel uncomfortable because of what you're wearing. But knowing the kind of trip you're planning will help in preparing the wardrobe. Will you be hiking? Are you traveling in summer or winter? Will you be eating in nice restaurants? Do you plan to go to the beach?

If you're traveling in mountain regions, especially the Rockies, you should always carry some warm clothes. In winter (when many mountain roads are closed), this may mean a full set of ski gear. In high summer, take a warm jacket for cooler high-altitude temperatures. If you're in the deserts of the Southwest, don't forget sunglasses and a broad-brimmed sun hat. In the Pacific Northwest, you should always carry a raincoat. You'll need a wetsuit if you want to take a dip in the chilly Pacific Ocean.

Many upmarket restaurants, and certainly most upscale bars and clubs, have quite strict dress codes. It's worth bringing along dressier attire (smart casual) for those times when you decide to go somewhere nice.

If you're hiking, especially in the mountains, make that jacket waterproof, and make sure you're wearing proper hiking boots. Otherwise, good walking shoes should be fine for most walks.

FROM LEFT TO RIGHT: LILKIN/SHUTTERSTOCK, DRPNNCPPTAK/SHUTTERSTOCK, DZHA33/SHUTTERSTOCK, HURST PHOTO/SHUTTERSTOCK, PICCHU PRODUCTIONS/SHUTTERSTOCK

Rafting, Colorado River, Grand Canyon (p276), Arizona

WORDS

to ride shotgun To travel in the passenger seat.
BLM The acronym for Bureau of Land Management, the government department responsible for public lands where you can park with an RV.
SP Stands for 'State Park' (just as 'NP' stands for 'National Park').
Airstream A specific kind of travel trailer that looks like an expensive metal tube.
RV Stands for 'Recreation Vehicle' and refers to a motor home or caravan.
KOA A popular chain of family-friendly campgrounds.
rig Another way of saying motor home or RV.
hit the road To start driving or get back on the move.
fender bender A minor accident that usually only involves some scratches or bumper dents.
zipper merge When one lane ends, drivers are forced to merge.
wallydocking Refers to the practice of parking overnight in a Walmart parking lot to avoid paying for camping.

LISTEN

- **America** *(Simon & Garfunkel; 1968)* Young lovers hitchhiking in search of America.
- **The Freewheelin' Bob Dylan** *(Bob Dylan; 1963)* Early classic from this Nobel Prize–winner.
- **Born in the USA** *(Bruce Springsteen; 1984)* Classic rock from the Boss.
- **Smells Like Teen Spirit** *(Nirvana; 1991)* The Gen-X grunge-rock anthem.

READ

- **On the Road** *(Jack Kerouac; 1957)* A journey through post–WWII America.
- **The Adventures of Huckleberry Finn** *(Mark Twain; 1884)* A moving tale of journey and self-discovery.
- **Blue Highways** *(William Least Heat-Moon; 1982)* A classic of American travel writing and the ultimate road trip.
- **The Longest Road** *(Philip Caputo; 2013)* From Florida's Key West to Alaska's Arctic shore, this is a road trip through many different Americas.

ROAD TRIPS

Bixby Bridge, Big Sur (p42), California
JAY CHEN/GETTY IMAGES

CONTENTS

01

EPIC TRIP: ROUTE 66

It's a lonely road – a ghost road really – that appears for a stretch and then disappears, gobbled up by the interstate. You know you've found it again when a 20ft lumberjack holding a hot dog rises from the roadside, or a sign points you to the 'World's Largest Covered Wagon,' driven by a giant Abe Lincoln. And that's just Illinois – the first of eight states on the nostalgic, kitschy, slowpoke drive west.

BY RYAN VER BERKMOES

Route 66 sign, Illinois

PHOTO.ECCLES/SHUTTERSTOCK

HISTORICAL ROUTE 66
ILLINOIS
US
66
"GET YOUR KICKS ON ROUTE 66"

EPIC TRIP

★ BEST TWO DAYS

California's stretch of road offers tumbleweed landscapes and Hollywood glitz.

Route 66, Mojave Desert, California

DURATION: 14 DAYS

DISTANCE: 2400 MILES / 3862KM

GREAT FOR: HISTORY & CULTURE, FOOD & DRINK

BEST TIME TO GO: MAY TO SEPTEMBER FOR BALMY WEATHER THAT'S IDEAL FOR CRUISING IN A CONVERTIBLE.

LINK YOUR TRIP

23 The Great River Road
The epic roadway (actually a series of roads) traces the meanderings of the Mississippi River. Pick it up in St Louis.

40 Coastal California
This route along the edge of the continent cruises an equally iconic numbered route: Hwy 1. When you finish Route 66, follow Hwy 1 north or south.

01 Chicago

Route 66 kicks off in downtown Chicago on Adams St just west of Michigan Ave. Before you snap the obligatory photo with the 'Route 66 Begin' sign (on the northern side of Adams, FYI), spend some time exploring the Windy City. Wander through the **Art Institute of Chicago** *(artic.edu)* – literally steps from the Mother Road's launching point – and ponder Edward Hopper's *Nighthawks* (a diner scene) and Grant Wood's *American Gothic* (a farmer portrait) to set the scene for what you'll see en route. Nearby historic and elegant **Grant Park** includes soaring Buckingham Fountain, which Route 66 drivers once saw in their rearview mirrors as they started west.

THE DRIVE: Stay on Adams St for 1.5 miles until you come to Ogden Ave. Go left, and continue through the old suburbs of Cicero and Berwyn. At Harlem Ave, turn left (south) and stay on it briefly until you jump onto Joliet Rd. Soon Joliet Rd joins southbound I-55 (at exit 277), and you're funneled onto the interstate.

02 Wilmington & the Gemini Giant

Our first stop rises from the cornfields 60 miles south of Chicago. Leave I-55 at exit 241, and follow Hwy 44 south a short distance to Hwy 53, which rolls into the town of Wilmington. Here the **Gemini Giant** – a 28ft fiberglass spaceman – stands guard outside the Launching Pad Drive-In.

THE DRIVE: Get back on I-55. Take exit 154 for Funks Grove, a 19th-century maple-sirup farm (yes, that's sirup with an 'i'). Get on Old Route 66 (a frontage road that parallels the interstate), and in 10 miles you'll reach Atlanta and its sky-high statue of Paul Bunyan clutching a hot dog (at 112 SW Arch St). Springfield is 50 miles southwest.

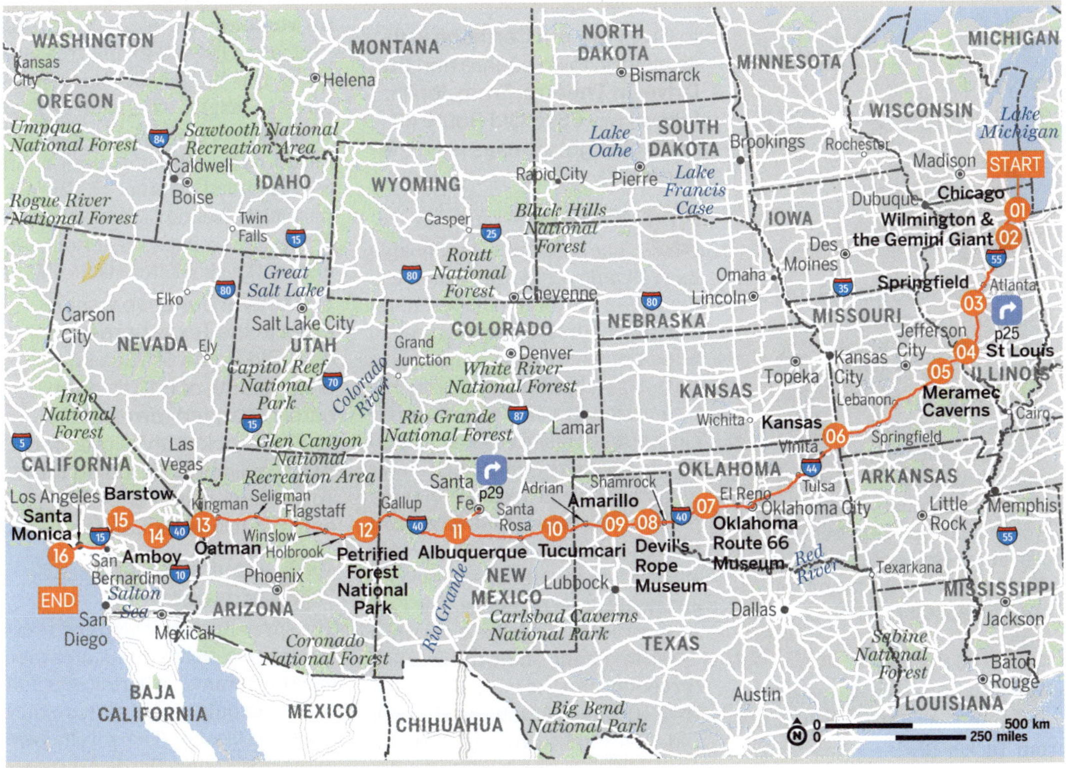

TREKANDSHOOT/SHUTTERSTOCK

03 Springfield

Illinois is the Land of Lincoln, according to local license plates, and the best place to get your Honest Abe fix is Springfield, the state capital. Fans of the 16th president get weak-kneed at the holy trio of sights: **Lincoln's Tomb** *(dnrhistoric.illinois.gov/experience/sites/site.lincoln-tomb.html)*, the **Lincoln Presidential Library & Museum** *(presidentlincoln.illinois.gov)* and the **Lincoln Home** *(nps.gov/liho)*, all in or near downtown.

Oh, and Springfield's Route 66 claim to fame? It's the birthplace of the corn dog (a cornmeal-battered, fried hot dog on a stick).

THE DRIVE: Return to I-55, which supersedes Route 66 here, as in **MOST OF** the state. The **Route 66 Association of Illinois** *(il66assoc.org)* tells you where to veer off for restored gas stations, vintage cafes and giant Lincoln statues. Near Edwardsville get on I-270, on which you'll swoop over the Mississippi River and enter Missouri.

DETOUR

Old Chain of Rocks Bridge

Start: 03 Springfield

Before crossing into Missouri, detour off I-270 at exit 3. Follow Hwy 3 (aka Lewis and Clark Blvd) south, turn right at the first stoplight and drive west to the 1929 Old Chain of Rocks Bridge. Open only to pedestrians and cyclists these days, the mile-long span over the Mississippi River has a 22-degree angled bend (the cause of many a crash – hence the ban on cars). Enjoy the passing barge traffic below, but hide your valuables and lock your car before you go exploring.

04 St Louis

Just over the border is St Louis, a river city that has launched westbound travelers for centuries. To marvel at the city's most iconic attraction, exit I-270 onto Riverview Dr and point your car south toward the 630ft-tall **Gateway Arch** *(gatewayarch.com)*, a graceful reminder of the city's role in westward expansion. For up-close views of the stainless-steel span and the lovely

♥ WHY I LOVE THIS TRIP

RYAN VER BERKMOES, WRITER

The iconic road trip is Route 66. It starts and ends in two of the country's biggest cities, but most of the Mother Road rambles through the nation's heartland on an all-consuming trip through America's past and present. For generations, it was the route to a hoped-for better life in the Golden State of California; now it epitomizes the timeless lure of the open road.

riverfront parkland surrounding it, turn left onto Washington Ave from Tucker Blvd.

THE DRIVE: From St Louis, I-44 closely tracks – and often covers – chunks of original Mother Road. Take the interstate southwest to Stanton, then follow the signs to Meramec Caverns.

05 Meramec Caverns

Admit it: you're curious. Kitschy billboards have been touting **Meramec Caverns** *(americascave.com)* for miles. The family-mobbed attraction and campground has lured road-trippers with its offbeat ads since 1933. From gold panning to riverboat rides, you'll find a day's worth of distractions, but don't miss the historically and geologically engaging cave tour.

THE DRIVE: Continue on I-44; Lebanon makes a good pit stop. Ditch the interstate west of Springfield, taking Hwy 96 to Civil War–era Carthage with its historic town square and **66 Drive-In Theatre**. From Joplin, follow Hwy 66 to Old Route 66 and hold tight: Kansas is on the horizon.

06 Kansas

The sunflower state holds a mere 13 miles of Mother Road (less than 1% of the total) but there's still a lot to see. First you'll pass through mine-scarred Galena, which had a turbulent labor history during the Depression. It's also where a rusty old tow truck inspired Pixar animators to create the character Mater in *Cars*. Four miles west, stop at the redbrick **Nelson's Old Riverton Store** *(oldrivertonstore.com)* and stock up on top-notch sandwiches and Route 66 memorabilia. The 1925 property looks much like it did when it was first built – note the pressed-tin ceiling and the outhouse. Cross Hwy 400 and continue on Hwy 69/Old Route 66 to the 1923 Marsh Arch Bridge, from where it's 3 miles south to Baxter Springs, site of a Civil War massacre and numerous bank robberies.

THE DRIVE: Enter Oklahoma. From Afton, Route 66 parallels I-44 (now a tollway) through Vinita, home to **Clanton's**, a famed chicken-fried-steak cafe. Tulsa to Oklahoma City offers one of the longest (and almost continuous) stretches of Mother Road (110 miles). From here it joins Business I-40 for 20 miles to El Reno and its distinctive onion burgers, and then parallels I-40 to Clinton.

07 Oklahoma Route 66 Museum

Flags from all eight Mother Road states fly high beside the memorabilia-filled **Oklahoma Route 66 Museum** *(okhistory.org/sites/route66)*. This fun-loving treasure trove, run by the Oklahoma Historical Society, isn't your typical mishmash of photos, clippings and knickknacks (though there is an artifact-filled Cabinet of Curios). Instead, it uses music and videos to dramatize six decades of Route 66 history. The bookstore is excellent.

THE DRIVE: Continue west 70 miles to the Texas border. From here Old Route 66 runs immediately south of I-40 through barely changed towns such as Shamrock, with its restored 1930s buildings, including the Tower Station and U-Drop Inn, and minuscule McLean.

08 Devil's Rope Museum

The sprawling grasslands of Texas and other western cattle states were once open range, where steers and cowboys could wander where they darn well pleased. That all changed in the 1880s when the devil's rope – more commonly known as barbed wire – began dividing the land into private parcels. This museum *(barbwiremuseum.com)* in the battered town of McLean has vast barbed-wire displays and a small but homey and idiosyncratic room devoted to Route 66. The detailed map of the road in Texas is a must.

THE DRIVE: I-40 west of McLean glides over low-rolling hills. The landscape flattens at Groom, home of the tilting water tower and a 19-story cross at exit 112. Take exit 96 for Conway to snap a photo of the forlorn VW Beetle Ranch, aka the Slug Bug Ranch, on the south side of I-40. For the Big Texan, take exit 74.

66 Drive-In Theatre, Carthage, Missouri

LOGAN BUSH/SHUTTERSTOCK

ADMISSION PRICES
AGE 13 & OLDER $8.00
AGE 6-12 4.00
AGE 5 & UNDER FREE
TAXES INCLUDED
NO SAVING PARKING SPACES

09 Amarillo

This cowboy town holds a plethora of Route 66 sites: the **Big Texan Steak Ranch**, the historic livestock auction and the **Sixth St Historic District**, which still has original Route 66 businesses.

As for the **Big Texan**, its attention-grabbing gimmick is the 'free 72oz steak' offer – you have to eat this enormous portion plus a multitude of sides in under one hour, or you pay for the entire meal. Fewer than 10% pass the challenge. Crazy gimmicks aside, the ranch is a fine place to eat and makes a good chicken-fried steak.

Ten miles west of Amarillo on the southern side of I-40, between exits 60 and 62, is an iconic Route 66 superstar: the **Cadillac Ranch.** The shells of 10 big-finned 1950s Cadillacs are planted in the deserted ground. Come prepared: the accepted practice is to leave your own mark by spray-painting on the cars.

THE DRIVE: Follow I-40 west 68 miles from the Cadillacs to the New Mexico border. The **Midpoint Cafe** in Adrian makes a fine pit stop en route to the state line. Tucumcari – and its abundance of motel rooms – is 42 miles further.

10 Tucumcari

A ranching and farming town sandwiched between the mesas and the plains, Tucumcari is home to one of the best-preserved sections of Route 66. It's a great place to drive through at night, when dozens of neon signs along Tucumcari Blvd – relics of the town's Mother Road heyday – cast a crazy rainbow-colored glow. Tucumcari's Route 66 motoring legacy and other regional highlights are recorded on 30-plus murals in downtown and the surrounding area. Pick up a map for the murals at the **Tucumcari Chamber of Commerce & Visitor Center** *(tucumcarinm.com)*.

The engaging **Mesalands Dinosaur Museum** *(mesalands.edu)* showcases real dinosaur bones and has hands-on exhibits for kids. Casts of dinosaur bones are done in bronze, which shows fine detail and as a result makes them works of art.

THE DRIVE: West on I-40, dry and windy plains spread into the distance, the horizon interrupted by flat-topped mesas.

Big Texan Steak Ranch, Amarillo, Texas

HEIDI BESEN/SHUTTERSTOCK

To stretch your legs, take exit 277 from Route 66/I-40 to downtown Santa Rosa and the **Route 66 Auto Museum**, which has upwards of 35 cars from the 1920s through the 1960s, all in beautiful condition.

11 Albuquerque

After 1937, Route 66 was realigned from its original path north through Santa Fe to a direct line west into Albuquerque from Santa Rosa (today's I-40). Central Ave follows the post-1937 route east of I-25. It passes through Nob Hill and the university. West of I-25, Central Ave was Route 66 over the decades of its existence through downtown and Old Town.

On Central Ave downtown, look for the spectacular neon-lit tile-and-wood artistry of the **KiMo Theatre** *(cabq.gov/artsculture/kimo)*, across from the old Indian Trading Post. This 1927 icon of pueblo-deco architecture blends American Indian and art-deco design. For prehistoric designs, take exit 154 off I-40, just west of downtown, and drive 3 miles north to **Petroglyph National Monument** *(nps.gov/petr)*, which has more than 23,000 ancient rock etchings.

THE DRIVE: Route 66 dips from I-40 into Gallup, becoming the main drag, lined with beautifully renovated buildings, including the 1928 Spanish Colonial **El Morro Theatre**, and scores of murals. From Gallup, it's 21 miles to Arizona. Once in Arizona, take exit 311 for Petrified Forest National Park. It's 211 miles all up.

DETOUR

Santa Fe

Start: 11 Albuquerque

New Mexico's capital city is an oasis of art and culture lifted 7000ft above sea level, against the backdrop of the Sangre de Cristo Mountains. It was on Route 66 until 1937, when a realignment left it by the wayside. It's well worth the detour to see the **Georgia O'Keeffe Museum**, to fork into super spicy green chile dishes in the superb restaurants, and to stroll past the town's churches and galleries. Route 66 follows the Old Pecos Trail (NM466) into town.

12 Petrified Forest National Park

The 'trees' of the **Petrified Forest** *(nps.gov/pefo)* are fragmented, fossilized 225-million-year-old logs scattered over a vast area of arid grassland. Many are huge – up to 6ft in diameter – and at least one spans a ravine to form a natural bridge. The trees arrived via major floods, only to be buried beneath silica-rich volcanic ash before they could decompose. Groundwater dissolved the silica, carried it through the logs and crystallized it into solid, sparkly quartz mashed up with minerals. Uplift and erosion eventually exposed the logs.

The park, which straddles I-40, has an entrance at exit 311 in the north and another off Hwy 180 in the south. A 28-mile paved scenic road, Park Rd, links the two. To avoid backtracking, westbound travelers should start in the north, eastbound travelers in the south.

THE DRIVE: Take I-40 west 25 miles to Holbrook, a former Wild West town now home to the photo-ready **Wigwam Motel**. Motor on through lonesome Winslow, which has an elegant hotel, and college-y Flagstaff. At Seligman grab a burger before the Mother Road arcs northwest away from I-40 through scrub-covered desert, then rejoins the interstate at quiet Kingman. From here you corkscrew through the Black Mountains and Sitgreaves Pass to Oatman.

13 Oatman

Since the veins of ore ran dry in 1942, crusty Oatman has reinvented itself as a movie set and Wild West tourist trap, complete with staged gunfights and gift stores named **Fast Fanny's Place** and the **Classy Ass**.

Speaking of asses, there are plenty of them (the four-legged kind, that is) roaming the streets. Placid and endearing, they're the descendants of pack animals left by the early miners. These burros may beg for food, but do not feed them your lunch leftovers; instead, buy healthier hay cubes from nearby stores. Squeezed among the shops is the 1902 **Oatman Hotel Restaurant & Saloon**, a surprisingly modest shack (no longer renting rooms) where Clark Gable and Carole Lombard spent their wedding night in 1939. On July 4 the town holds a sidewalk egg-frying contest. It gets quite warm here in summer.

From here, Historic Route 66/Hwy 10 twists down to Topock and I-40.

THE DRIVE: Soon you'll enter California at Needles. About 40 miles later, the road dips south and joins with the National Old Trails Rd. This is some of the coolest stretch of road, with huge skies and vintage signs rusting in the sun.

14 Amboy

In the near-ghost town of Amboy, **Roy's Motel & Cafe** *(visit amboy.com)* has been a popular pit stop since 1938. If you believe the lore, Roy once cooked his famous

NAVIGATING ROUTE 66

Because Route 66 is no longer an official road, it doesn't appear on many maps, although AAA state maps show portions. Consult these sources for additional info:

Historic Route 66 *(historic66.com)* Offers turn-by-turn directions.

National Historic Route 66 Federation *(national66.org)* Links to attractions and resources.

EZ66 Guide for Travelers Jerry McClanahan's intricately detailed book is a must.

Route 66 double cheeseburger on the hood of a '63 Mercury. There's no food or lodging today, but at least Roy's iconic neon sign kicked back into glimmering glory in 2019.

Two miles west, **Amboy Crater** *(blm.gov/visit/amboy-crater-national-natural-landmark)* is a 250ft-high, almost perfectly symmetrical volcanic cinder cone. It's a 3-mile round-trip hike to the top for great views over the lava fields where NASA engineers field-tested the Mars Rover (avoid in summer).

THE DRIVE: Stay on the National Old Trails Rd to Ludlow. Turn right onto Crucero Rd and pass under I-40, then take the north frontage road west and turn left at Lavic Rd. Keep heading west on the National Old Trails Rd through windswept Daggett. Join I-40 at Nebo St. Drive for about 15 minutes before taking the exit for Barstow Rd.

15 Barstow

Exit the interstate onto Main St, which runs through workaday Barstow, a railroad settlement and historic crossroads, where murals adorn empty buildings downtown. Follow 1st St north across the Mojave River over a trestle bridge to the 1911 Harvey House, nicknamed Casa del Desierto, designed by Western architect Mary Jane Colter. Inside is the **Route 66 Mother Road Museum** *(motherroadmuseum.com)*, displaying B&W historical photographs and odds and ends of everyday life in the early 20th century. Next door is the small **Western America Railroad Museum**, which celebrates Barstow's role as a vital junction for rail lines spanning America.

THE DRIVE: Rejoin the National Old Trails Rd. At Victorville take I-15 out of town, heading south to San Bernardino, home to an iconic Route 66 motor court. From there follow Foothill Blvd/Route 66 west through retro-suburban Pasadena and check out the **Fair Oaks Pharmacy** diner. Finally, for your Hollywood ending, take Arroyo Seco Pkwy to LA, where Sunset Blvd connects to Santa Monica Blvd.

16 Santa Monica

This is the end of the line: Route 66 reaches its finish, over 2400 miles from its starting point in Chicago, on an ocean bluff in Palisades Park, where a Will Rogers Hwy memorial plaque marks the official end of the Mother Road. Celebrate on **Santa Monica Pier** *(santamonicapier.org)*, where you can ride a 1920s carousel featured in *The Sting* (1973) and enjoy other attractions and carnival rides. With the glittering Pacific as a backdrop, take a selfie with the 'Santa Monica 66 End of Trail' sign. Then hit the beach.

Route 66 sign, Santa Monica Pier, California

JOHN NILSSON/SHUTTERSTOCK

SANTA MONICA
66
End of the Trail
SAVE
THE
PIER
SPEED
LIMIT
5
RESTROOMS
Emergency
BAR
MONICA POLICE
The joy
of early
holiday
eals.
SANTA MONICA PIER

02

EPIC TRIP: PACIFIC COAST

From the temperate rainforests of Washington and Oregon to the sun-drenched shorelines of Southern California, the Pacific Coast is a wonderland for anyone who appreciates the raw majesty of our natural world. This route leads from pristine woodlands, where centuries-old trees tower high above wave-worn headlands, all the way down to sunny beaches, where you can watch surfers catch some waves while feeling the warm sand beneath your toes. And though the natural beauty of this awe-inspiring region might have you gasping and grinning at every turn, you'll also find historic sites, adorable towns and even a few roadside oddities to add some extra pizazz to your journey.

BY MARGOT BIGG

Cannon Beach (p389), Oregon
GORDON MONTGOMERY/SHUTTERSTOCK

EPIC TRIP

DURATION: 10–14 DAYS

DISTANCE: 1778 MILES / 2681KM

GREAT FOR: NATURE, SLOW TRAVEL

BEST TIME TO GO: SEPTEMBER OFFERS WARM WEATHER, WITH FEWER CROWDS THAN JULY AND AUGUST.

01 Seattle

Seattle is known for its rain and its coffee, and while you'll certainly find plenty of both in the city, it has so much more to offer. Its position as the northernmost major city on the West Coast makes it a perfect place to start a Pacific Coast adventure. Just make sure to give yourself time to check out its top attractions, including the famous **Space Needle** *(spaceneedle.com)* and the **Museum of Pop Culture** *(mopop.org)*, both located at the **Seattle Center** *(seattlecenter.com)* in the heart of the city. If you want to go beyond the big sights, I'd suggest checking out some of the neighborhoods outside the city center. If you can only visit one,

LINK YOUR TRIP

46 Napa Valley
Head inland from Bodega Bay to Napa for an immersive introduction to California's most lauded wine region.

47 Cascade Drive
From Seattle, take I-5 north to Everett to begin this tour into the mountains.

FRANCISCO BLANCO/SHUTTERSTOCK

Hall of Mosses Trail, Olympic National Park, Washington

make it Ballard, which is famous for both its microbreweries and Nordic heritage. Once you've had your fill of city life, head to the Olympic National Park.

THE DRIVE: The quickest way to get from Seattle to the Olympic Peninsula is to take a car ferry to Bainbridge Island and follow the network of state highways that eventually merge onto Hwy 101. However, I generally prefer to take I-5 south to WA-16, which eventually becomes WA-3 near the town of Gorst before connecting to Hwy 101. That way, I don't have to worry about sold-out boats or late departures. Hwy 101 continues to the Olympic Peninsula, past Port Angeles and into Olympic National Park.

02 Olympic National Park

I find **Olympic National Park** *(nps.gov/olym)* to be one of the most magical spots in the Pacific Northwest, and its relative remoteness and vastness mean that it never feels as crowded as better-known national parks. While there are endless trails to hike throughout the park, my favorite spot is the Hoh Rainforest, said to be the wettest – and possibly quietest – spot in the contiguous United States. Best of all, it's easy to visit, even if you're just passing through. Just take a hike down the **Hall of Mosses Trail**, a 0.8-mile loop that starts at the **Hoh Rainforest Visitor Center**, weaving through ancient, moss-strewn trees that wouldn't be out of place in Tolkien's Middle-earth.

THE DRIVE: Backtrack on Upper Hoh Rd to Hwy 101, then continue south along the coast. Consider stopping at Ruby Beach, named for its garnet-hued sand, or Kalaloch Beach to check out the Tree of Life (p41). Continue south on 101 until you reach Aberdeen.

03 Aberdeen

I was a huge Nirvana fan as a kid, so I always get a bit of a nostalgic thrill when I stop in Aberdeen. This rough-around-the-edges (but safe) town was once a thriving Pacific Northwest lumber port, owing to its position at the confluence of two rivers that spill into an ocean bay, and its proximity to millions of acres of coniferous forest. It's best known as the birthplace of Nirvana front man Kurt Cobain, and you

EPIC TRIP

Mission Trail

Its common for travelers to see the US dichotomously, viewing the eastern seaboard as the place for history and architecture, and the Pacific Coast as the land where natural beauty prevails. While there is an element of truth to these assumptions, the Pacific Coast certainly isn't lacking in architectural history.

The best example of this may be the California Missions, which are among the most beautiful – and beautifully preserved – heritage buildings on the West Coast.

The missions began in 1769, when what we now know as the state of California was under Spanish colonial rule as part of a larger territory called Alta California.- Under the auspices of the Spanish crown, priests and auxiliary laypeople began a journey north. The goal was to create a series of missions that were situated close enough to each other to be easily reached on horseback in just one day. For the clergy, the main goal was to spread Catholicism by converting Indigenous Americans. For Spanish leaders, the objective was to seize Native American land. Spain was set on expanding its territory north – and quickly – in response to the growing presence of English, French and Russian traders and fur trappers in the region.

Over the five decades that followed, priests backed by the Spanish Empire established a total of 21 missions near Indigenous settlements, spreading not only the teachings of Catholicism, but also fatal diseases such as measles and tuberculosis. Large numbers of Native Americans died, while others resisted conversion attempts. Some joined the church and even became monks or priests. By the time the final and northernmost mission, Mission San Francisco Solano, was established in 1823, Mexico – including Alta California – had already gained independence from Spain. In 1833, secularization legislation removed mission ownership from the Franciscan order, transferring it to Californios, the descendants of earlier Spanish settlers. In 1850, when the US gained control of Alta California through the Mexican–American War, the missions were slowly returned to the Catholic Church.

All but a few of the missions have active churches to this day, but you don't need to be religious to enjoy them. Many visitors come to simply view the Spanish architecture and wander the grounds of these historic structures. Some of the most famous include the **Mission San Juan Capistrano** *(missionsjc.com)*, which features a beautiful garden and a museum stuffed to the gills with ephemera, and the **Old Mission Santa Barbara** *(santabarbaramission.org)*, a beautiful hilltop mission with a church and spacious museum. The **Carmel Mission** *(carmelmission.org)* is another hit, partially because it houses the first library in California, while the **Mission Basilica San Buenaventura** *(sanbuenaventuramission.org)* stands out for its beautiful blue-and-white tilework. One way to see them all is by following the **California Missions Trail** *(californiamissionstrail.org)*, much of which runs along the Pacific Coast Highway.

Carmel Mission, Carmel-by-the-Sea (p42), California

TMP-AN INSTANT OF TIME/SHUTTERSTOCK

can stop to see his childhood home and head down to the river to pay your respects at the **Kurt Cobain Under the Bridge Memorial**. If you're not a Nirvana fan, Aberdeen is still a good place to fill your tank before continuing south to Oregon. There's also a fun **Mermaid Museum** *(mermaidmuseum.org)* just south of town that focuses on both mer-mythology and ocean ecology.

THE DRIVE: Head south on Hwy 101 toward the Columbia River, which marks the border between Washington and Oregon. Cross into Oregon via the Astoria–Megler Bridge, which, at 4.1 miles, is the longest truss bridge in North America.

04 Astoria

I sometimes forget that Astoria is a coastal town. While this historic spot certainly has a maritime vibe, its position on the bank of the Columbia River, slightly inland from where the river meets the ocean, gives it a feel all its own. While many towns and cities on Oregon's coast feature a mix of contemporary homes and cute beach houses covered with weathered cedar-shake siding, Astoria's architecture is far grander, with stately Victorian residences around seemingly every corner. I adore the **Flavel House Museum** *(astoriamuseums.org)*, a turreted Queen Anne home that's as beautiful on the inside as the outside. Film fans typically come to Astoria to check out the **Goonies House** *(gooniesHome.com)*, the main home featured in *The Goonies*, a 1985 cult classic. As much as I love Astoria's architecture, some of my favorite spots are just outside of the city, including the Wreck of the Peter Iredale, a 1906 shipwreck that sits right on the beach about a 20-minute detour from town, and Fort Clatsop, where the Lewis and Clark Expedition spent its final winter before returning east.

THE DRIVE: Continue your drive along Oregon's coast, giving yourself plenty of time to stop at scenic lookouts and cute towns along the way. Just south of Astoria, Seaside is popular with families and has a carnivalesque appeal, complete with arcades and a carousel. The next town south, Cannon Beach, feels a bit more refined and is a good place to stroll or browse art galleries. Further down the coast, Tillamook is famous for its massive creamery – sample cheese curds and ice cream here on your way to Lincoln City.

05 Lincoln City

When you first drive into Lincoln City, you'd be forgiven for thinking that it looks like a typical Oregon beach city, split into two by a slightly unappealing stretch of Hwy 101 that's flanked by hotels, supermarkets and the odd Thai restaurant or tie-dye shop. But don't let first impressions fool you: Lincoln City is pretty magical. Not only does it have an impressive 7 miles of sandy beachfront, but it also gets some great winds, earning it the title of Oregon's kite-flying capital. It's also the state's glass-art hub, with plenty of artisans displaying their colorful, handblown wares at galleries across town. My favorite is the **Lincoln City Glass Center** *(lincolncityglasscenter.com)*, where you can buy all sorts of glass artworks and baubles, or take a lesson and learn the art yourself. I always make sure to spend a bit of time scouring the beach for glass floats, too – the city's tourism board hides around 3000 of these treasures along the coastline every year for visitors to take home as part of its Finders Keepers program.

THE DRIVE: Hwy 101 skirts the coast for almost the entire stretch between Lincoln City and Coos Bay, with plenty of popular stops along the way. Stop by Newport to check out its famous **Oregon Aquarium** *(aquarium.org)*, or pull off the road at Thor's Well, just south of Yachats, to see a giant basalt hole that creates the illusion of 'swallowing' the ocean waves when the tide is high. If you've got kids with you, don't miss the **Sea Lion Caves** *(sealion caves.com)*, where Stellar sea lions love to congregate, or the **Darlingtonia State Natural Site** (p41), a protected bog full of carnivorous plants.

06 Coos Bay

Coos Bay may be the largest city on Oregon's coast, but it still feels fairly small; while there are some great restaurants and breweries, there's not a ton to do. It's a good place to break up a long drive with a meal or an overnight, but I'd suggest spending less time in town and more time exploring the surrounding area. I love the Oregon Dunes National Recreation Area, an otherworldly expanse of oceanfront dunes that inspired Frank Herbert's bestselling eco sci-fi novel, *Dune*. While many people come here to zoom around on the sand on all-terrain vehicles (ATVs), I prefer to explore on foot, even if it inevitably leads to sore hamstrings and sand in my shoes. My favorite spot in Coos Bay is **Shore Acres State Park** *(shoreacres.net)*, which sits atop an oceanfront bluff that's pummeled by massive waves during

high tide. The park also has a pretty English garden with flowers in bloom from March through October.

THE DRIVE: Drive south along the Oregon Coast Hwy until you reach the Samuel H. Boardman State Scenic Corridor, a famously gorgeous 12-mile stretch that starts just south of Brookings. Slow down and give yourself plenty of time to pull over and take in the views of the offshore sea arches; I'm partial to Arch Rock. Cross into California and head to the checkpoint of the state agriculture department to declare any fruit or vegetables in your car (this helps prevent the spread of pests) and continue through the town of Crescent City. Before you know it, you'll be surrounded by gargantuan redwood trees.

07 Redwood National & State Parks

Redwood National & State Parks *(nps.gov/redw)* is a tad confusing, as it's actually a collection of different groves and protected areas rather than one contiguous park. There are lots of great ways to experience it though, from strolling through the easy 1.5-mile Lady Bird Johnson Grove Trail to descending into the emerald-hued Fern Canyon (waterproof shoes are a boon here). My favorite Redwood hike is the 4.5-mile trail through the Tall Trees Grove, where some of the largest redwoods are found. Permits are required, but you can reserve your spot online *(nps.gov/redw/planyourvisit/talltreespermits.htm)* up to six months in advance.

THE DRIVE: Continue south along 101 to Eureka, perhaps making a pit stop along the way at **Sue-meg State Park** *(parks.ca.gov/sue-meg)* to check out the reconstruction of a traditional Yurok village, or stretch your legs with a 2-mile hike along the Rim Trail, which offers great ocean views. Continue through Arcata, potentially breaking for a hearty meal at my personal favorite, **Wildflower Cafe & Bakery** *(wildflowercafebakery.com)*, just before you reach Eureka.

Sequoias, Redwood National Park
ARTHUR CALEB ROBERTSON/SHUTTERSTOCK

08 Eureka

If you love art and Victorian architecture as much as I do, then you'll love Eureka, a pretty seaside city with great galleries and elegant Victorian homes. I'm particularly fond of the **Old Town Art Gallery** *(oldtownartgalleryeureka.com)*, a local cooperative full of paintings, photography and jewelry by local artists. It's just a couple of blocks from another spot I love: the Romano **Gabriel Wooden Sculpture Garden** *(romanogabriel.com)*, an outdoor display of wooden artworks created by Italian-born Eureka artist Romano Gabriel. Don't leave town before visiting the **Da Gou Rou Louwi' Cultural Center** *(wiyot.us)*, which features changing exhibits on the area's Wiyot Tribe.

THE DRIVE: From Eureka, follow Hwy 101 south for about an hour until you reach the Avenue of the Giants (Hwy 254) exit.

09 Avenue of the Giants

Even if I'm in a hurry, I always make the point of eschewing Hwy 101 in favor of this 31.6-mile redwood-flanked scenic route. While the trees are the big draw, it's also full of places to stop, from stores selling cheesy T-shirts to redwood carvings. There are also plenty of huge old trees with creative backstories. My favorite is the Eternal Tree House, a hollowed redwood stump that I visited as a child when it was still a gift shop. There's also a drive-through tree (though the one further down the coast in Legget is better) and a so-called Immortal Tree that's alleged

♥ WHY I LOVE THIS TRIP

MARGOT BIGG, WRITER

One of my favorite childhood memories is of a Pacific Coast road trip. I was seven years old and traveling through the Redwoods when we stopped at a tiny gift shop that was carved from the trunk of a hollowed-out tree. I fell in love with the place and for years after, I dreamt of living inside my own little tree home, just like Winnie the Pooh.

While I never ended up moving into a tree, I did get the chance to camp in a hollowed-out redwood stump. This was just one of many magical experiences I've had throughout my years of driving different sections of this coastline. I've wandered through mossy rainforests, soaked sore muscles in mineral-rich hot springs, taken in coastal views that have nearly brought me to tears, and – most importantly – met all sorts of fascinating people who call the Pacific Coast their home.

to have survived pretty much every disaster you can imagine, from fires and floods to loggers' axes.

THE DRIVE: The Avenue of the Giants reconnects with Hwy 101 near Garberville. Head south and consider a stop at **Confusion Hill** *(confusionhill.com)* along the way, known for its Gravity House optical illusion that makes everything feel a wee bit crooked. Then continue for a few more miles to Leggett, where it's worth making a pit stop to drive through the **Chandelier Tree** before heading southwest on Hwy 1. After about 22 miles of driving through a forest filled with hairpin turns, you'll reach the Pacific. Drive for 22 more miles to reach Fort Bragg.

10 Fort Bragg

Although it's one of the larger towns on this part of the coast, Fort Bragg is still fairly walkable and fun to explore on foot. It's famous for its glass beaches, which feature colorful morsels of sea glass that have merged with the sand, and though many have been picked through by visitors and collectors, you're supposed to leave them where they are. While you can see great specimens in the **International Sea Glass Museum** *(internationalseaglassmuseum.com),* I think the prettiest glass in town is in the stained-glass windows of the **Guest House Museum** *(fortbragghistory.org)* around the corner. This gorgeous 1892 home, crafted almost entirely in heart redwood, was built by the Union Lumber Company to showcase the versatility of redwood lumber.

THE DRIVE: Continue along the Pacific Coast Hwy, potentially making a quick stop in Mendocino, just south of Fort Bragg, to visit the **Temple of Kwan Tai** *(kwantaitemple.org),* one of California's oldest Chinese temples. You'll eventually pass through Sea Ranch, a 1960s-era planned community with its own distinct architectural style that's best exemplified by the nondenominational **Sea Ranch Chapel** *(searanchchapel.org).* You can't miss its giant shingled roof, which I think resembles a gnome hat. A few more miles down the coast leads to the remains of an 1812 Russian

Cypress Tree Tunnel, San Francisco Bay Area, California

SPONDYLOLITHESIS/GETTY IMAGES

settlement now preserved as **Fort Ross Historical Park** *(parks.ca.gov/fortross)*. A 45-minute drive from the fort leads to Bodega Bay, a good spot to stop for a meal and see some of the filming locations used in Alfred Hitchcock's *The Birds* (1963). From here, you can take a detour to the **Napa Valley** (p364) for some wine tasting, or continue to Point Reyes National Seashore.

11 Point Reyes National Seashore

Protecting around 110 miles of beaches, forests and marsh, **Point Reyes National Seashore** *(nps.gov/pore)* is a great place to quickly stretch your legs or embark on a longer hike. The San Andreas Fault passes right through the park, and I find the 0.6-mile Earthquake Trail (next to the Bear Valley Visitor Center) well worth the visit for its interpretive panels alone. From here, it's roughly 11 miles to the **Cypress Tree Tunnel**, a stretch of road flanked with cypress trees that form a tunnel. You'll have to pull over on the side of the road and walk through the tunnel, as there's a barricade that stops cars from driving through it.

THE DRIVE: Get back on the road and continue south; before you know it, the larger-than-life arches of the Golden Gate Bridge will appear before your eyes. Cross over (you'll get a bill for the toll or a charge from your rental car company later) and head into San Francisco.

12 San Francisco

San Francisco was the first place I ever visited on a road trip, and it's a city that keeps calling me back. I love how each neighborhood has its own distinct feel, something you'll surely notice whether chowing down on tasty burritos in the Mission District or record shopping at **Amoeba Music** *(amoeba.com)* in Haight-Ashbury, the birthplace of the hippie movement. Even the city's many parks have their own unique vibe. Dolores Park is the place to go for picnicking and people watching, whereas **Golden Gate Park** *(sfrecpark.org)* feels like a world of its own, with museums, gardens and even a bison paddock. Just a word to the wise: finding street parking in San Francisco can be a nightmare, so save yourself the time and trouble, and splurge for a spot in a parking lot.

THE DRIVE: Follow Hwy 1 along the Pacific Coast, stopping in the cute coastal town of Half Moon Bay for a cup of coffee or heading straight to Santa Cruz for a longer en-route break. The **Santa Cruz Beach Boardwalk** *(beachboardwalk.com)* amusement park is a great place to break up your journey if you have kids, though many of the rides require them to be at least 4ft tall. From here, it's about a 45-minute drive along the coast to Monterey.

NATURE'S ROADSIDE ATTRACTIONS

Some of the most interesting roadside attractions along the Pacific Coast aren't human-made oddities but natural wonders that sprout from the earth.

Kalaloch Tree of Life, Washington On the coast of Olympic National Park, this beautiful Sitka spruce straddles two adjacent bluffs, with its root system almost entirely exposed due to years of erosion. While shifting tides and increased saltwater exposure mean that this famous tree might not last much longer, its beautiful branches and roots continue to be one of Kalaloch Beach's main draws.

Darlingtonia State Natural Site On Oregon's Central Coast, the compact **Darlingtonia** *(stateparks.oregon.gov)* is dedicated entirely to the preservation of the *Darlingtonia californica*, a carnivorous pitcher plant that's sometimes referred to as the cobra lily. A wooden walkway traverses a bog that's full of the bug-eating plants, making it easy to see the protected plants up close without worrying about trampling them.

Chandelier Tree The most famous drive-thru tree in the Redwood National & State Parks, the **Chandelier Tree** *(drivethrutree.com)* is a 325ft giant that's believed to date back around 2400 years. A giant hole was cut from its trunk in the 1930s, transforming it into a roadside attraction that continues to draw in drivers to this day.

Pygmy Forest While California may have some of the world's tallest trees, it also has some of its smallest, as you'll quickly see if you visit the Pygmy Forest in **Van Damme State Park** *(parks.ca.gov)* near Fort Bragg. This grove is full of mature pines and cypresses that measure between 6in and 8ft in height. Their stunted growth is due to a lack of minerals in the soil.

13 Monterey & Carmel-by-the-Sea

Monterey and its southern neighbor, Carmel-by-the-Sea, are often visited in tandem, but each has its own charm. I usually stay in Monterey, partially because the hotels are more affordable and partially because there are a few more spots to eat in. It's also home to the **Monterey Bay Aquarium** *(montereybayaquarium.org)*, which draws in big crowds with its resident sea otters. I highly recommend making the stop.

From here, it's an easy drive south to Carmel-by-the-Sea, with its adorable storybook homes and lovely little boutiques. Make sure to drop by **Pilgrim's Way Community Bookstore** *(pilgrimsway.com)*, which features a large selection of books and a pretty back garden filled with windchimes, crystals and home decor.

THE DRIVE: While it's only about a half-hour drive from Carmel to the northernmost reaches of Big Sur, the shift feels dramatic. The soft beaches of Carmel Bay give way to rugged, towering cliffs as soon as you cross Point Lobos Natural Reserve.

14 Big Sur Coast

The Big Sur coast is an area to be savored, not rushed. It's a favorite among road trippers for its pinch-me-I'm-dreaming views and is also a great place for hiking and camping (though getting a reservation at state-park-run campgrounds involves some serious luck and planning). For most people, simply coming here to soak in the scenery is enough. The most famous view is that of Bixby Bridge, and many pull over in hopes of getting great shots of the landmark structure – some of the best views are from Castle Rock Viewpoint. As a big hot-springs lover, I adore the **Esalen Institute** *(esalen.org)*, where philosopher Alan Watts and Jungian mythologist Joseph Campbell were regular lecturers. If the new age aspect puts you off, or you want a more remote place to soak, make the 10-mile hike to Sykes Hot Springs instead.

THE DRIVE: Leaving the Big Sur coast at Ragged Point, continue south along Hwy 1. You'll immediately notice the rugged cliffs and dense forests giving way to flatter coastal prairies that offer expansive views. Just after the tiny town of San Simeon, hang a left on Hearst Castle Rd. The Hearst Castle Visitor Center, where you'll leave your car, is less than a mile away.

15 Hearst Castle

Straddling a towering hill overlooking the Pacific, **Hearst Castle** *(hearstcastle.org)* was once

GOOD TO KNOW

North or South?

Because the US is a right-hand-drive country, driving from north to south puts you on the ocean side of the road, which is more practical for pulling over to take in the views. However, there's no right or wrong way to make the drive, and heading from sunny Southern California into the towering coastal forests of the Pacific Northwest certainly has dramatic appeal.

Cellular Service

While you can expect good mobile coverage throughout much of your drive, signal can get patchy, particularly in more remote stretches of the Northern and Central California coast. Download offline maps before you set out.

The Enticing I-5

At different parts of the drive, your GPS may try to divert you to major freeways, notably I-5, the major north–south freeway that runs from the Canadian border clear down to the border with Mexico via Seattle, Portland, San Francisco and Los Angeles. While this route is the fastest, it's also the least scenic.

Electric Vehicles

It's easy to drive the entire length of the coast in an electric vehicle thanks to the **West Coast Electric Highway** *(westcoastgreenhighway.com)* initiative, a network of direct current (DC) fast chargers that extends from British Columbia clear down to Southern California. You'll find DC fast chargers roughly every 30 miles on the Oregon and California coasts. While the rugged Washington coast is not covered by the network, there are plenty of charging stations in the region, including in Olympic National Park and in most larger towns. The **PlugShare** *(plugshare.com)* app is great for finding chargers in unexpected places.

McWay Falls (p320), Big Sur, California
KYLEPOSTPHOTOGRAPHY/SHUTTERSTOCK

Old Mission Santa Barbara, California
ZHONGYUGAN/SHUTTERSTOCK

the private estate of newspaper tycoon William Randolph Hearst, who commissioned the construction of the castle over a number of decades with the help of pioneering architect Julia Morgan. Today, the castle – which blends influences from across Europe – is managed by the state park department, and while booking in advance is wise, it's not required. Tours take you up to the hilltop castle, where a docent shows off the grounds and some of the interiors. My favorite rooms include the massive tapestry-adorned great hall fit for a medieval king and the indoor 'Roman pool' mosaicked with vibrant tiles in hues of blue and yellow.

THE DRIVE: The drive from Hearst Castle to Santa Barbara weaves through pretty beach towns with plenty of surf and sand, but without the crowds that await you further down the coast. Consider a pit stop in Pismo Beach, a chilled-out town with a massive sandy coastline that's popular with swimmers and surfers. From here, you can continue along the coast to reach Santa Barbara, but I'd suggest a detour along Hwy 101 to Solvang, which was founded by Danish immigrants over a century ago (with the timber-framed architecture to prove it).

16 Santa Barbara

I always thought **Santa Barbara** was a playground for the rich and famous. Then I visited and realized that things are a bit more nuanced. While there are certainly plenty of high-end experiences to be had, from gourmet, cuisine and white-tablecloth service to wine tasting at local vineyards, the city is surprisingly accessible to visitors of all stripes. The **Old Mission Santa Barbara** (p334) is among California's most beautiful, and hiking opportunities abound in the Santa Ynez Mountains just beyond the town.

THE DRIVE: Much of the drive down Hwy 1 from Santa Barbara skirts the coast, detouring inland in the uninspired city of Oxnard before dipping back down along the coast. This final

♥ WHY I LOVE THIS TRIP

MARGOT BIGG, WRITER

The Pacific is where I took my first solo road trip, driving from Portland to LA. It was during this trip that I truly fell in love with Pacific California, from the blissfully peaceful sands of the quiet northern coastline to the wow-worthy landscapes of Big Sur. I explored the Santa Barbara Mission with an octogenarian friend, went jogging along Venice Beach canals with a German Shepherd named Bella and hiked up to countless viewpoints to take in the beauty of it all. And while I fell in love with the salty ocean air and the magnificent scenery, it was the people and animals I met along the way who made me truly appreciate this special road-trip route.

stretch is undeniably pretty, and you may be tempted to stop for a bit of rock climbing on the crags at Point Dume, or a beach stroll among the stars in Malibu. From here, you're mere miles from Santa Monica and the adjacent Los Angelino neighborhood of Venice.

17 Santa Monica & Venice

Santa Monica and neighboring Venice Beach have always felt like peas in a pod, but each has its own feel. The lively amusement park at Santa Monica Pier is where I go to take in sunset views from the Ferris wheel or snap my photo with the 'End of Route 66' sign before heading a few blocks inland to grab a bite at a chain restaurant or do a bit of shopping. The boardwalk at Venice Beach, on the other hand, is better for people-watching and draws in a more eclectic crowd. Venice is also where I go if I'm in the mood for a healthy lunch or green smoothie. **Café Gratitude** *(cafegratitude.com)* is one of my top choices.

THE DRIVE: This last stretch may be a long one – not because it's particularly lengthy in terms of distance, but because Los Angeles–area traffic can make the nearly 150-mile drive go a tad slowly. You may be able to forego some of the traffic if you trade in stretches of Hwy 1 for the quicker I-405, but it's worth at least sticking to the coastal road once you reach posh Newport Beach – not a bad place to stop for a quick swim.

18 San Diego

By the time you reach sunny San Diego, Seattle's hipster coffee shops and oversized raindrops will feel worlds away. If you're short on time, I'd advise sticking to the Balboa Park area, where many of the city's top attractions, including the highly acclaimed **Museum of Us** *(museumofus.org),* which focuses on anthropology, and the 12-acre **Japanese Friendship Garden** *(niwa.org)* are situated. With a bit more time, check out the adobe homes in Old Town or go for a swim at La Jolla Cove – just note that you may end up sharing the waters with sea lions. For an extra adventure, consider heading just south of the city and over the border to Tijuana. If you want to visit Mexico for the day or evening, leave your car at San Ysidro on the US side and cross the border on foot.

Sea Lions, La Jolla Cove, San Diego, California
SCENIC CORNER/SHUTTERSTOCK

03

EPIC TRIP: FOUR CORNERS CRUISE

From a distance, the rugged buttes and mesas of Monument Valley resemble the remains of a prehistoric fortress, red-gold ramparts protecting ancient secrets. Yes, they're recognizable from multitudes of Westerns, but the big screen doesn't capture the changing light patterns, imposing height or sense of fathomless antiquity. It's a captivating spell – but by no means the only one cast along this Four Corners Cruise.

BY CHRISTOPHER PITTS

Monument Valley Navajo Tribal Park (p52), Arizona,
ZACK FRANK/SHUTTERSTOCK

EPIC TRIP

★ BEST FOR:

OUTDOORS

Angels Landing Trail in Zion National Park.

DURATION: 10 DAYS

DISTANCE: 1593 MILES / 2564KM

GREAT FOR: FAMILIES, NATURE

BEST TIME TO GO: SPRING AND FALL FOR THINNER CROWDS AND PLEASANT TEMPERATURES.

Angels Landing, Zion National Park, Utah

LINK YOUR TRIP

33 Grand Canyon Voyage
For red rocks and mining history, swing south from Flagstaff on I-17 to Hwy 89A.

36 High & Low Roads to Taos
Take the High or the Low Road between Santa Fe and Taos, with fine craftwork, historic churches and mountain scenery.

01 Las Vegas

Take in Sin City's synthetic charms on a morning walk past the iconic casinos and hotels of the Strip, then spend the afternoon downtown at the **Mob Museum** *(themobmuseum.org)*, a three-storey collection examining organized crime in the USA and its connection to Las Vegas. One block south, zipline over Fremont St from the 11th-story launchpad of **SlotZilla** *(vegasexperience.com/slotzilla-zip-line)*, then end the night with an illuminated stroll at the **Neon Museum** *(neonmuseum.org)*.

The giant pink stiletto in the lobby of the **Cosmopolitan** *(cosmopolitanlasvegas.mgmresorts.com)* is an eye-catcher. Designed by Roark Gourley, the 9ft-tall shoe was supposed to be treated with the reverence due a piece of art, but its protective ropes were soon pushed aside by partygoers seeking 'unique' selfies. In response, the Cosmopolitan removed the ropes and in 16 months the outsize footwear got so much love it needed to be sent out for repairs.

THE DRIVE: Follow I-15 north for 34 miles and take exit 75. From here, the Valley of Fire Hwy travels 18 miles to the state park.

02 Valley of Fire State Park

Before losing yourself in the sandstone sculpture gardens of Utah, swing through this masterwork of desert scenery to prime yourself for what's ahead. It's an easy detour, with the Valley of Fire Hwy running through the park *(parks.nv.gov/parks/valley-of-fire)* and passing close to the psychedelically shaped red rock formations. From the visitor center, take the winding, scenic side road out to **White Domes**, an 11-mile round trip. En route you'll pass **Rainbow Vista**, followed by the turnoff to **Fire Canyon** and **Silica Dome** (where Captain Kirk perished in *Star Trek: Generations*).

TROY TRAN/SHUTTERSTOCK

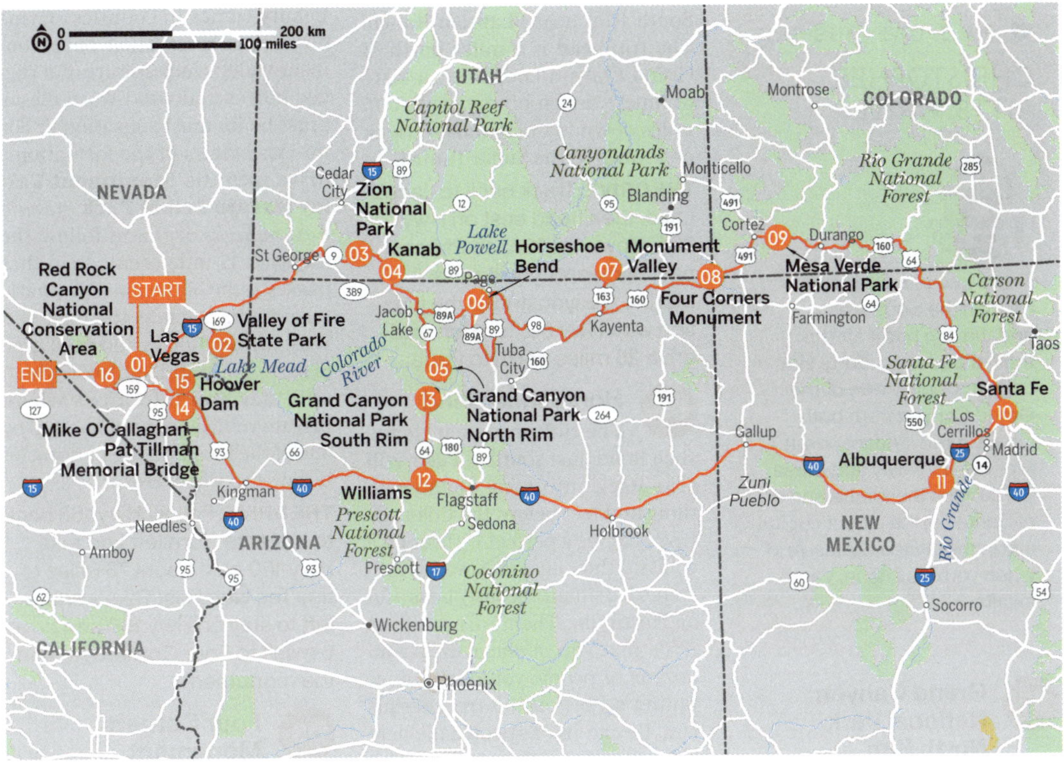

Spring and fall are the best times to visit; avoid summer when temperatures typically exceed 100°F (37°C).

THE DRIVE: Return to I-15 north, cruising through Arizona and into Utah. Leave the highway at exit 16 and follow Hwy 9 east for 32 miles.

03 Zion National Park

The climb up **Angels Landing** in **Zion National Park** *(nps.gov/zion)* may be the best day hike in North America. From Grotto Trailhead, the 5.4-mile roundtrip crosses the Virgin River, hugs a towering cliffside, squeezes through a narrow canyon, snakes up Walters Wiggles, then traverses a razor-thin ridge where steel chains and the encouraging words of strangers are your only safety net. Your reward after the final scramble to the 5790ft summit? A bird's-eye view of Zion Canyon. The hike reflects what's best about the park: beauty, adventure and the shared community of people who love the outdoors.

THE DRIVE: Twist out of the park on Hwy 9 east, driving almost 25 miles to Hwy 89. Follow Hwy 89 south to the vast open-air movie set that is Kanab.

04 Kanab

Sitting between Zion, **Grand Staircase–Escalante National Monument** *(blm.gov)* and the **Grand Canyon North Rim**, Kanab is a good spot for a base camp. Hundreds of Western movies were filmed here – and other gun-slingin' celebs really put the town on the map. Today, animal lovers know that the town is home to the **Best Friends Animal Sanctuary** *(bestfriends.org/sanctuary)*, the country's largest no-kill animal shelter. Tours of the facility – home to dogs, cats, pigs, birds and more – are free, but call ahead to confirm times and to make a reservation. The sanctuary is located in Angel Canyon, also called Kanab Canyon by locals.

THE DRIVE: Continue into Arizona – now on Hwy 89A – and climb the Kaibab Plateau. Turn south onto Hwy 67 at Jacob Lake and drive 44 miles to Grand Canyon Lodge.

♥ WHY I LOVE THIS TRIP

CHRISTOPHER PITTS, WRITER

There's no place I'd rather be than the Southwest, and this trip has it all: the thrill of exploring Zion's slot canyons, epic views of the Grand Canyon from both rims, sacred landscapes in Monument Valley and Mesa Verde, plus the adobe and art of Santa Fe, the oldest capital city in the United States. And when you're all done, Vegas awaits.

05 Grand Canyon National Park North Rim

While driving through the ponderosa forest that opens onto rolling meadows in Kaibab National Forest, keep an eye out for mule deer as you approach the entrance to the park *(nps.gov/grca)*. Stop by the **North Rim Visitor Center**, beside **Grand Canyon Lodge** *(grandcanyonforever.com)*, for information and to join ranger-led nature walks and nighttime programs. If it's five o'clock somewhere, enjoy a cocktail from the lodge terrace of the Rough Rider Saloon while soaking up the view.

For an easy but scenic half-day hike, follow the 4-mile round-trip Cape Final Trail through ponderosa pine forests with great canyon views. The steep and difficult 14-mile North Kaibab Trail is the only maintained rim-to-river trail and connects with trails to the South Rim near Phantom Ranch. The trailhead is 2 miles north of Grand Canyon Lodge. For a taste of inner-canyon hiking, walk 0.75 miles down to Coconino Overlook or 2 miles to the Supai Tunnel.

THE DRIVE: Track back to Jacob Lake, then head east on Hwy 89A, down the Kaibab Plateau, past blink-and-you'll-miss-it Marble Canyon and to the junction with Hwy 89. Turn left and drive 26 miles north to Page.

06 Horseshoe Bend

The clifftop view at Horseshoe Bend, just south of Page, will sear itself into your memory. A thousand feet below, the Colorado River carves a perfect U through a colossal thickness of Navajo sandstone. It's simultaneously beautiful and terrifying. There are no railings – it's just you, a sheer drop and dozens of people you don't know, taking selfies on the treacherous rim. Be careful, as people die here every year. From the parking lot it's a 0.6-mile one-way hike to the rim. There's a moderate hill along the way, and the trail is unshaded, so the walk can be a little strenuous in summer – but it's worth it. The parking lot is on Hwy 89, south of Page near mile marker 545.

THE DRIVE: Rejoin Hwy 89 and drive north a short distance to Hwy 98. Turn right and follow 98 southeast to Hwy 160. Turn left and drive 34 miles north, passing the entrance to Navajo National Monument. In Kayenta, turn left onto Hwy 163 north and drive almost 22 miles to Monument Valley, on the Arizona–Utah border.

07 Monument Valley

'May I walk in beauty' is the final line of a famous Navajo prayer. Beauty comes in countless forms on this vast reservation, but Monument Valley's majestic array of rugged buttes and wind-worn mesas must be its most sensational. For up-close views of the formations, drive into the **Monument Valley Navajo Tribal Park** *(navajonationparks.org)* and follow the unpaved 17-mile scenic loop that passes some of the most dramatic formations, such as the East and West Mitten Buttes and the Three Sisters. For a guided tour, which will take you into areas where private vehicles cannot go, stop by one of the kiosks in the parking lot beside the **View Hotel**.

THE DRIVE: Follow Hwy 163 back to Kayenta. Turn left and take Hwy 160 east about 73 miles to tiny Tee Noc Pos. Take a sharp left to stay on Hwy 160 and drive 6 miles to Four Corners Rd and the monument.

08 Four Corners Monument

It's seriously remote, but you can't skip the **Four Corners Monument** *(navajonationparks.org)* on a road trip through the epicenter of the Southwest. Once you arrive, don't be shy: put a foot into Arizona and plant the other in New Mexico. Slap a hand in Utah and place the other in Colorado. Then smile for the camera. It makes a good photo, even if it's not 100% accurate – government surveyors have admitted that the marker is almost 2000ft east of where it should be (although it remains a legally recognized border point). Half the fun here is watching the contortions performed by happy-snappers determined to straddle all four states.

Horseshoe Bend, Arizona
VAGAMUNDOS/SHUTTERSTOCK

THE DRIVE: Return to Hwy 160 and turn left. It's a 50-mile drive across the northwestern tip of New Mexico and through Colorado to Mesa Verde. Hwy 160 becomes Hwy 491 for around 20 miles of this journey.

09 Mesa Verde National Park

Ancestral Puebloan sites are found throughout the canyons and mesas of **Mesa Verde** *(nps.gov/meve)*, perched on a high plateau south of Cortez and Mancos. According to the experts, the Ancestral Puebloans didn't 'disappear' 700 years ago: they simply migrated south, developing into the American Indian tribes that live in the Southwest to this day. If you only have time for a short visit, check out the **Chapin Mesa Museum** and the nearby views of **Spruce Tree House**.

> PHOTO OPPORTUNITY
>
> The glory of the Grand Canyon from Mather Point on the South Rim.

Mesa Verde rewards travelers who set aside a day or more to take the ranger-led tours of **Cliff Palace** and **Balcony House**, explore **Wetherill Mesa** (the quieter side of the canyon), linger around the museum or participate in one of the campfire programs at **Morefield Campground** *(visitmesaverde.com)*. The park also provides plenty of hiking, cross-country skiing, snowshoeing and mountain-biking options. Visitors can camp out or stay in luxury at the lodge.

THE DRIVE: Hop back onto Hwy 160, following it 36 miles east to Durango and then another 61 miles to join Hwy 84 south for the 151-mile run to Santa Fe. You'll pass through Abiquiú, home of artist Georgia O'Keeffe from 1949 until her death in 1986. Continue toward Santa Fe, exiting onto N Guadalupe St to head toward the Plaza.

10 Santa Fe

This 400-year-old city is pretty darn inviting. You've got the juxtaposition of art and landscape, with cow skulls hanging from sky-blue walls and slender crosses topping centuries-old missions. And then there's the comfortable mingling of American Indian, Hispanic and Anglo cultures, with ancient pueblos, 300-year-old haciendas and

Mesa Verde, Mesa Verde National Park, Colorado

WWW.INFINITAHIGHWAY.COM.BR/GETTY IMAGES

stylish modern buildings standing in easy proximity.

The beauty of the region was captured by New Mexico's most famous artist, Georgia O'Keeffe. Possessing the world's largest collection of her work, the **Georgia O'Keeffe Museum** *(okeeffemuseum.org)* showcases the thick brushwork and luminous colors that don't always come through on the ubiquitous posters. Take your time to relish them here firsthand. The museum is housed in a former Spanish Baptist church with adobe walls that has been renovated to form 10 skylit galleries.

The city is anchored by the Plaza, which was the end of the Santa Fe Trail between 1822 and 1880.

THE DRIVE: The historic route to Albuquerque is the Turquoise Trail, which follows Hwy 14 south for 50 miles through Los Cerrillos and Madrid. If you're in a hurry, take I-25 south.

11 Albuquerque

Most of Albuquerque's top sights are concentrated in Old Town, which is a straight shot west on Central Ave from Nob Hill and the University of New Mexico.

The most extravagant route to the top of 10,378ft Sandia Crest is via the **Sandia Peak Tramway** *(sandiapeak.com)*. The 2.7-mile tram ride starts in the desert realm of cholla cactus and soars to the pine-topped summit. For exercise, take the beautiful 8-mile (one-way) **La Luz Trail** *(laluztrail.com)* back down, connecting with the 2-mile **Tramway Trail** to return to your car. The La Luz Trail passes a small waterfall, pine forests and spectacular views. It gets hot, so start early. Take Tramway Blvd east from I-25 to get to the tramway.

THE DRIVE: From Albuquerque to Williams, in Arizona, I-40 overlaps or parallels Route 66. It's 359 miles to Williams.

12 Williams

Train buffs, Route 66 enthusiasts and Grand Canyon–bound vacationers all cross paths in Williams, an inviting small town with all the charm and authenticity of 'Main Street America.' If you only have time for a day visit to the park, the **Grand Canyon Railway** *(thetrain.com)* is a fun and hassle-free way to get there and back. After a Wild West show beside the tracks, the train departs for its 2½-hour ride to the South Rim, where you can explore by foot or shuttle. From late March through October, passengers can ride in reconditioned open-air Pullman cabooses.

On Route 66 the divey **World Famous Sultana Bar**, which once housed a speakeasy, is a great place to sink some suds beneath a menagerie of stuffed wildlife.

13 Grand Canyon National Park South Rim

A walk along the **Rim Trail** *(nps.gov/grca)* in Grand Canyon Village brings stunning views of the iconic canyon, as well as historic buildings, American Indian crafts and geological displays.

Starting from the plaza at **Bright Angel Trail**, walk east on the Rim Trail to **Kolb Studio** *(nps.gov/grca)*, which holds a small bookstore and an art gallery. Next door is **Lookout Studio** *(nps.gov/grca)*, designed by noted architect Mary Jane Colter to resemble the stone dwellings of the Southwest's Ancestral Puebloans.

Step into the 1905 **El Tovar Hotel** *(grandcanyonlodges.com)* to see its replica Remington bronzes, stained glass, stuffed mounts and exposed beams, or to admire the canyon views from its porches.

Next door, the **Hopi House** *(nps.gov/grca)*, another Colter-designed structure, has sold high-quality American Indian jewelry and other crafts since 1904. Just east, the **Trail of Time** interpretative display traces the history of the canyon's formation. End with the intriguing exhibits and gorgeous views of the **Yavapai Geology Museum** *(nps.gov/grca/planyourvisit/yavapai-geo.htm)*.

THE DRIVE: Having returned to Williams on the train, take I-40 113 miles west to Kingman, then join Hwy 93 north. Head north for 75 miles, crossing into Nevada, where exit 2 leads on to Hwy 172 and the Hoover Dam.

> ☑ TAKE A BREAK
>
> **NO BOTTLED WATER**
>
> As a conservation measure, Grand Canyon National Park no longer sells bottled water. Instead, top up your thermos at water-filling stations along the rim or at the **Visitor Center Complex** *(nps.gov/grca)*. Water bottles had previously constituted 20% of the waste generated in the park.

14 Mike O'Callaghan–Pat Tillman Memorial Bridge

This graceful span, dedicated in 2010, was named for Mike O'Callaghan, governor of Nevada from 1971 to 1979, and for NFL star Pat Tillman, who was a safety for the Arizona Cardinals when he enlisted as a US Army Ranger after September 11. Tillman was killed by friendly fire during a battle in Afghanistan in 2004.

Open to pedestrians along a walkway separated from traffic on Hwy

93, the bridge sits 900ft above the Colorado River. It's the second-highest bridge in the US, and provides a bird's-eye view of Hoover Dam and Lake Mead behind it.

THE DRIVE: Turn right onto the access road and drive a short distance down to the Hoover Dam.

15 Hoover Dam

A statue of bronze winged figures stands atop **Hoover Dam** *(usbr.gov/lc/hooverdam)*, memorializing the workers who built the massive 726ft concrete structure, one of the world's tallest dams. This New Deal public-works project, completed ahead of schedule and under budget in 1936, was the first major dam on the Colorado River. Thousands of men and their families, eager for work in the height of the Depression, came to Black Canyon and worked in excruciating conditions – dangling hundreds of feet above the canyon in desert heat of up to 120°F (49°C). Over 100 lost their lives.

Today, guided tours begin at the visitor center, where a video screening features original footage of the construction. After the movie, take an elevator ride 50 stories below to view the dam's massive power generators, each of which alone could power a city of 100,000 people.

THE DRIVE: Return to Hwy 93, following it west and then north as it joins I-515. Take exit 61 for I-215 north. After 11 miles, I-215 becomes Clark County 215. Follow it just over 13 miles to Charleston Blvd/Hwy 159 at Exit 26 and follow it west.

16 Red Rock Canyon National Conservation Area

The awesome natural forces in evidence in this national conservation area *(redrockcanyonlv.org)* can't be exaggerated. Created about 65 million years ago, the canyon is more like a valley, with a steep, rugged red rock escarpment rising 3000ft on its western edge, the dramatic result of tectonic-plate collisions.

The 13-mile, one-way scenic drive passes some of the canyon's most striking features, where you can access hiking trails and rock-climbing routes. The 2.5-mile round-trip hike to **Calico Tanks** climbs through the sandstone and ends atop rocks offering a grand view of the desert and mountains, with Vegas thrown in for sizzle. National Park passes are accepted for admission.

Grand Canyon National Park (p55), Arizona

FOTOGRO/SHUTTERSTOCK

CANADA
USA
Lake Ontario
0 100 km
0 50 miles
Watertown
Adirondack Park
NEW YORK
Oneida Lake
Rome
Rochester
Niagara Falls
Welland
Buffalo
Seneca Falls
Syracuse
Utica
Saratoga Springs
Schenectady
Albany
Troy
Geneva
Auburn
Penn Yan
Dansville
Cortland
04
Ithaca
Bath
Oneonta
MASSACHUSETTS
Jamestown
Salamanca
Catskill
Hudson
Corning
Elmira
Binghamton
Corry
Bradford
CONNECTICUT
Warren
Mansfield
Towanda
Monticello
Poughkeepsie
Allegheny National Forest
PENNSYLVANIA
Carbondale
St Marys
Scranton
Newburgh
DuBois
Williamsport
Wilkes-Barre
Bridgeport
Punxsutawney
Clearfield
Milton
Stroudsburg
Stamford
Paterson
State College
Sunbury
Tyrone
Bronx
New York City
Indiana
Lewistown
Allentown
Brooklyn
Altoona
06
New Brunswick
Long Branch
Harrisburg
Hershey
Trenton
Asbury Park
Somerset
Bedford
Lancaster
Point Pleasant
York
Philadelphia
05
Hancock
Hagerstown
Cumberland
07
Newark
NEW JERSEY
Martinsburg
Frederick
MARYLAND
Long Beach
Romney
Millville
Atlantic City
Winchester
Baltimore
Ocean City
Dover
Rockville
Front Royal
WASHINGTON, DC
Annapolis
Cape May
Wildwood
Franklin
Luray
Warrenton
DELAWARE
Harrisonburg
Culpeper
Cambridge
Ocean City
ATLANTIC OCEAN
Salisbury
Staunton
Fredericksburg
08
Waynesboro
Charlottesville
Tappahannock
Crisfield
Assateague Island National Seashore
VIRGINIA
Chincoteague Island
Richmond
Saluda

ZACK FRANK/SHUTTERSTOCK

Finger Lakes, New York

NEW YORK & THE MID-ATLANTIC

EXPLORE

NEW YORK & THE MID-ATLANTIC

Along the East Coast, between picturesque New England hamlets and the gracious plantations of the South, you'll find the Northeast Corridor. Stretching from Washington, DC, to Boston, this scenic strip includes America's most dynamic, cosmopolitan metropolis: New York City. But there's so much more to be discovered in this beautifully diverse area.

After 48 unforgettable hours in Manhattan, seek out the Jersey Shore or Pennsylvania's back roads. Further south, Appalachian landscapes await on Virginia's Skyline Drive, while waterfalls and vineyards provide food for the soul around the Finger Lakes. Wherever you find yourself, you're guaranteed to discover something unexpected and delightful.

Ithaca

You could base yourself anywhere out west in New York State (Buffalo, for example, or lakeside Rochester), or even New York City itself. But Ithaca has charm. For a start, it's an artsy university town, filled with museums, art-house cinemas and leafy gardens. In the town, there are vibrant restaurant, cafe and bar scenes, while on its doorstep there are nature reserves and state parks. Excellent transport links make it the ideal gateway for the Finger Lakes.

Atlantic City

Like a slightly tacky belle or beau living on questionable past glories, Atlantic City never quite lived up to its epithet of 'Vegas on the East Coast'. But there is a faded, slightly over-the-top feel to Atlantic City these days and therein lies its special character. If you forget all of that, Atlantic City has a lovely beach that's rarely crowded and its hotels are much better value than many other places along the Jersey Shore. It also has some fine places to eat, not to mention a beach resort called the Tropicana.

Lancaster

It may be a relatively small town, but Lancaster can feel like a busy metropolis when compared to the rest of the county that surrounds it. It's the necessary counterpoint (not to mention starting point...) for journeys into the bucolic, low-tech

WHEN TO GO

The best weather for these drives is in summer. It's also when everything is open. But high-season crowds can turn some routes into processions, and accommodations, restaurants and hiking trails can be similarly oversubscribed. April–June or September/October offer the best of both worlds. Spring and fall are great for wildflowers, especially in Shenandoah.

farmlands of Amish Country, and it eases the introduction with some excellent museums dedicated to its much-misunderstood neighbors, as well as some good restaurants and hotels. In fact, Lancaster is just the right size – any bigger and brasher and the transition between 20th-century city and old-world rural world would be just too much of a culture shock.

Baltimore

Baltimore is America. At once a working-class port city and a master of reinventing itself with genuine entrepreneurial zeal, the city is a fascinating place to explore and take the pulse of the nation. Increasingly, it's becoming known for its boutique hotels, edgy exhibits at world-class museums, and once-forgotten neighborhoods now bustling with farm-to-table restaurants, cosmopolitan restaurants and a thriving brewpub scene. In fact, Baltimore (that's 'Bawlmer' or 'B'more' to locals) belongs among the elite when it comes to the craft-beer scene. And from April through September, don't miss the chance to see the Baltimore Orioles play at what is arguably the best ballpark in America.

TRANSPORTATION

You're never far from an airport in these parts, whether you fly into Baltimore, Buffalo, Ithaca or Atlantic City. Then again, you'll have more choice if you fly to New York, Philadelphia or Washington, DC, and drive out from there. Elsewhere, Amtrak trains get you to Lancaster or Richmond, and buses serve Ithaca.

Richmond

Virginia's capital is an intriguing place, where Southern roots meet the new America. It may be home to a slew of outstanding museums and stirring architecture that dates back to complicated Civil War days, but it doesn't just look to the past, thanks to its exciting multicultural culinary and nightlife scenes, a happening arts precinct, and a location that puts you in the perfect position for setting out toward Shenandoah and the Skyline Drive.

WHERE TO STAY

There's good accommodations to be had across the five regions, from high-altitude campgrounds along Shenandoah's Skyline Drive to historic beach resorts along the sea-level Jersey Shore. All across the regions covered in this chapter, towns and cities have charming and well-preserved historical architecture and the best places to stay fit that profile by telling a unique historical local story. There are many such places from which to choose, from the converted tobacco warehouse of **Lancaster Arts Hotel** *(lancasterartshotel.com)* in Pennsylvania to **Frederick's Hollerstown Hill B&B** *(hollerstownhill.com)* or **Pendry Baltimore** *(pendry.com/baltimore)* in Maryland.

RESOURCES

- **The Shore Blog**
  Excellent resource for information on the Jersey Shore. *theshoreblog.com*
- **Visit Baltimore**
  Everything you need for a deep dive into the city. *baltimore.org*
- **Shenandoah National Park**
  Lots of information on the park, especially its attractions and activities. *nps.gov/shen*

WHAT'S ON

- **Night Sky Festival**
  It's all about the stars at this four-day festival in Shenandoah National Park in August.
- **Preakness Stakes**
  Held on the third Saturday in May at Baltimore's Pimlico; it's one of the country's most prestigious thoroughbred horse races.
- **First Saturday**
  Maryland's Frederick is a great place to be on the first Saturday of every month with live music, late-night shopping and a real buzz in the restaurants.

04

NEW YORK & THE MID-ATLANTIC

FINGER LAKES LOOP

★ BEST FOR

WINE

With more than 120 vineyards, a designated driver is needed.

Vineyard, Cayuga Lake, New York

DURATION: 3 DAYS

DISTANCE: 144 MILES/231KM

GREAT FOR: WINE, NATURE

BEST TIME TO GO: MAY TO OCTOBER FOR FARMERS MARKETS AND GLORIOUS SUNNY VISTAS.

A bird's-eye view of this region of rolling hills and 11 long narrow lakes – the eponymous fingers – reveals an outdoor paradise stretching all the way from Albany to far-western New York. Of course there's boating, fishing, cycling, hiking and cross-country skiing, but this is also the state's premier wine-growing region, with enough variety for the most discerning oenophile and palate-cleansing whites and reds available just about every few miles.

LINK YOUR TRIP

06 Pennsylvania Dutch Country
Journey south through Scranton and Allentown to southern PA to reach these tranquil country roads.

10 Fall Foliage Tour
Make your way east from Ithaca through Albany to the Berkshires to experience legendary New England colors.

01 Ithaca

Ithaca, perched above Cayuga Lake, is an idyllic home for college students and older generations of hippies who cherish elements of the traditional collegiate lifestyle – laid-back vibes, art-house cinemas, green quads and good eats.

Founded in 1865, **Cornell University** boasts a lovely campus, mixing traditional and contemporary architecture, and sits high on a hill overlooking the picturesque town below. The modern **Herbert F Johnson Museum of Art** *(museum.cornell.edu)*, in a brutalist building designed by IM Pei, has a major Asian collection, plus pre-Columbian, American and European exhibits. Just east of the center of the campus is **Cornell Botanic Gardens** *(cornellbotanic*

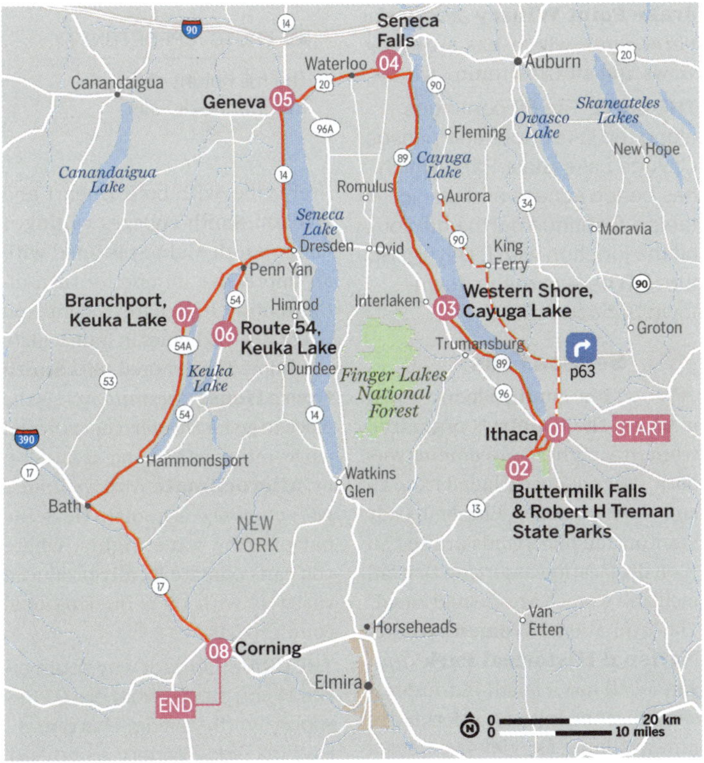

gardens.org), an expertly curated herb and flower garden and arboretum. Kids can go interactive-wild at the extremely hands-on **Sciencenter** *(sciencenter.org).*

The area around Ithaca is known for its waterfalls, gorges and gorgeous parks.

THE DRIVE: It's only 2 miles south on Rte 13 to Buttermilk Falls State Park.

DETOUR

Aurora

Start: 01 Ithaca

Around 28 miles north of Ithaca on the east side of Cayuga Lake is the picturesque village of Aurora. Established in 1795, the village has over 50 buildings on the National Register of Historic Places, including parts of the campus of **Wells College**, founded in 1868 for the higher education of women (it's now co-ed). The **Inns of Aurora** *(innsofaurora.com),* which comprises five grand properties – the Aurora Inn (1833), EB Morgan House (1858), Rowland House (1903), Zabriskie House (1904) and Wallcourt Hall (1909) – is a wonderful place to stay. Alternatively stop by the Aurora Inn's lovely dining room for a meal with lakeside views and pick up a copy of the self-guided walking tour of the village.

02 Buttermilk Falls & Robert H Treman State Parks

A sprawling swath of wilderness, **Buttermilk Falls State Park** *(parks.ny.gov)* has something for everyone – a beach, cabins, fishing, hiking, recreational fields and camping. The big draw, however, is the waterfalls. There are more than 10, with some sending water tumbling as far as 500ft below into clear pools. Hikers like the raggedy **Gorge Trail** that brings them up to all the best cliffs. It parallels Buttermilk Creek, winding up about 500ft. On the other side of the falls is the equally popular **Rim Trail**, a loop of about 1.5 miles. Both feed into Bear Trail, which will take you to neighboring **Treman Falls**.

It's a trek of about 3 miles to Treman, or you can pop back in the car after exploring Buttermilk and drive the 3 miles south to **Robert H Treman State Park** *(parks.ny.gov/parks/roberttreman),* still on bucolic Rte 13. Also renowned for cascading falls, Treman's gorge trail passes a stunning 12 waterfalls in under 3 miles. The two biggies you don't want to miss are **Devil's Kitchen** and **Lucifer Falls**, a multi-tiered wonder that spills Enfield Creek over rocks for about 100ft. At the bottom of yet another watery gorge – Lower Falls – there's a natural swimming hole.

THE DRIVE: Take Rte 13 back into Ithaca to connect with Rte 89 that hugs Cayuga Lake shore for 10 miles. The entrance to Taughannock Falls State Park is just after crossing the river gorge.

03 Western Shore, Cayuga Lake

Trumansburg, a one-street town about 15 miles north of Ithaca, is the gateway to **Taughannock Falls State Park** *(parks.ny.gov/parks/taughannock)*. At 215ft, the falls of the same name are 30ft higher than Niagara Falls and the highest cascade east of the Rockies. There are 5 miles of hiking trails, most of which wind their way around the slippery parts to bring you safely to the lookout spots at the top. One trail follows the stream bed to the falls.

A little further along on Rte 89, near the village of Interlaken, is **Lucas Vineyards** *(lucasvineyards.com)*, one of the pioneers of Cayuga wineries. A little further north again, down by the lake shore and a small community of modest but charming summer homes, is **Sheldrake Point Winery** *(sheldrakepoint.com)*, which has stunning views and award-winning whites.

THE DRIVE: Rte 89 continues along the lake shore and passes Cayuga Lake State Park, which has beach access and picnic tables. Continue north until you hit the junction with E Bayard St; turn left here to reach downtown Seneca Falls.

♥ WHY I LOVE THIS TRIP

SIMON RICHMOND, WRITER

Where you find good wine – and the Finger Lakes region produces some of the country's best bottles – it's a sure bet you'll also find great food. Relax, as gourmet isn't stuffy and white-tablecloth here, but friendly and communal, such as at Geneva's FLX Table. Also not to be missed is Hazelnut Kitchen near Ithaca, where you'll also find a stellar farmers market.

04 Seneca Falls

This small, sleepy town is where the country's organized women's rights movement was born. After being excluded from an anti-slavery meeting, Elizabeth Cady Stanton and her friends drafted an 1848 declaration asserting that 'all men and women are created equal.' The inspirational **Women's Rights National Historical Park** *(nps.gov/wori)* has a small but impressive museum, with an informative film available for viewing, plus a visitor center offering tours of Cady Stanton's house. The tiny **National Women's Hall of Fame** *(womenofthehall.org)* honors inspiring American women. Learn about some of the 302 inductees, including first lady Abigail Adams and civil-rights activist Rosa Parks.

THE DRIVE: The 10 miles on I-20 west to Geneva passes through strip-mall-lined Waterloo; Mac's Drive In, a classic 1961-vintage burger joint, is worth a stop. As you drive into town you pass Seneca Lake State Park, which is a good spot for a picnic.

05 Geneva

Geneva, one of the larger towns on this route, has interesting, historic architecture and a

PHOTO OPPORTUNITY

The full height of Taughannock Falls.

lively vibe, with both Hobart and William Smith colleges calling it home. South Main St is lined with an impressive number of turn-of-the-century Italianate, Federal and Greek Revival homes in immaculate condition. The restored 1894 **Smith Opera House** *(thesmith.org)* is the place to go for theater, concerts and performing arts in the area. Stop by **Microclimate** *(microclimategeneva.com)*, a cool little wine bar offering wine flights, where you can compare locally produced varietals with their international counterparts.

THE DRIVE: On your way south on Rte 14 you pass – what else? – a winery worth visiting. This one is Red Tail Ridge Winery, a certified gold Leadership in Energy & Environmental Design (LEED) little place on Seneca Lake. Then turn right on Rte 54 to Penn Yan.

06 Route 54, Keuka Lake

Y-shaped Keuka is about 20 miles long and in some parts up to 2 miles wide, its lush vegetation uninterrupted except for neat patches of vineyards. If you have a trail bike you could get a workout on the **Keuka Lake Outlet Trail**, a 7.5-mile route following the old Crooked Lake Canal between Penn Yan and Dresden on Seneca Lake.

Just south of Penn Yan, the largest village on Keuka Lake's shores, you come to **Keuka Spring Vineyards** *(keukaspringwinery.com)* and then

Rooster Hill Vineyards *(rooster hill.com)* – two local favorites that offer tastings and tours. Keuka Spring has won many awards for its oaky cabernet franc and Rooster Hill's fine whites spark a buzz among wine aficionados. A few miles further south along Rte 54 brings you to **Barrington Cellars** *(barrington cellars.com)*, 500ft off the lake and flush with labrusca and vinifera wines made from local grapes.

On Saturdays in summer everyone flocks to the **Windmill Farm & Craft Market** *(thewindmill.com)*, just outside Penn Yan. Check out Amish and Mennonite goods, ranging from carved wooden rockers to homegrown veggies and flowers.

THE DRIVE: After about 5.5 miles on Rte 54A take a detour south onto Skyline Drive, which runs down the middle of 800ft Bluff Point for outstanding views. Backtrack to Rte 54A and Branchport is only a few miles further along.

07 Branchport, Keuka Lake

As you pass through the tiny village of Branchport at the tip of Keuka's left fork in its Y, keep an eye out for **Hunt Country Vineyards** *(huntwines.com)* and **Stever Hill Vineyards** *(steverhillvineyards.com)*, the latter of which has its tasting room in a restored old barn.

Taughannock Falls State Park, New York

FELIX LIPOV/SHUTTERSTOCK

Both wineries are family run and edging into their sixth generation. On top of tastings there are tours of the grape-growing facilities and snacks from the vineyards' own kitchens.

THE DRIVE: Rte 54A along the west branch of Keuka passes by several other wineries as well as the Taylor Wine Museum just north of Hammondsport, a quaint town with a charming square. Carry on through to Bath, where you connect with I-86 east/Rte 17 east for another 19 miles to Corning.

08 Corning

The huge **Corning Museum of Glass** *(cmog.org)* complex is home to fascinating exhibits on glassmaking arts. It's possibly the world's finest collection, both in terms of its historic breadth – which spans 35 centuries of artisanship – as well as its sculptural pieces. Next stop by **Vitrix Hot Glass Studio** *(vitrixhotglass.com)* in the charming Market Street district to see fine glass pieces ranging from functional bowls to organic-shaped sculptures.

Housed in the former City Hall, a Romanesque revival building c 1893, the **Rockwell Museum** *(rockwell museum.org)* has a wide-ranging collection of art of the American West, including great works by Albert Bierstadt, Charles M Russell and Frederic Remington, plus Native American art.

05

NEW YORK & THE MID-ATLANTIC

THE JERSEY SHORE

DURATION: 3–7 DAYS

DISTANCE: 129 MILES/208KM

GREAT FOR: WINE, FAMILIES, NATURE

BEST TIME TO GO: JUNE – CROWDS ARE SMALLER. END OF SEPTEMBER – INDIAN SUMMER TEMPS.

The New Jersey coastline is studded with resort towns from classy to tacky that fulfill the Platonic ideal of how a long summer day should be spent. Supersized raucous boardwalks where singles more than mingle are a short drive from old-fashioned intergenerational family retreats. When the temperature rises, the entire state tips eastward and rushes to the beach to create memories that they'll view later with nostalgia and perhaps some regret.

LINK YOUR TRIP

06 Pennsylvania Dutch Country
From Atlantic City, head northwest through Philadelphia and make your way west to US 30 for the rural byways of Amish country.

07 Maryland's National Historic Road
Take the Atlantic City Expwy north toward Camden and connect with I-95 south to Baltimore to take in the diversity of this bay-to-mountains trip.

01 Asbury Park

Let's start with the town that Bruce Springsteen, the most famous of a group of musicians who developed the Asbury Sound in the 1970s, immortalized in song. Several of these musicians – such as Steve Van Zandt, Garry Tallent, and the late Danny Federici and Clarence Clemons – formed Springsteen's supporting E Street Band. The main venues to check out are the still-grungy, seen-it-all clubs **Stone Pony** *(stoneponyonline.com)* and **Wonder Bar** *(wonderbarasburypark.com)*; the latter is across the street from the majestic redbrick **Paramount Theatre** *(apboardwalk.com/the-paramount-theater)* where big acts perform and free movies are shown.

Led by wealthy gay men from NYC who snapped up blocks of forgotten Victorian homes and storefronts to refurbish, the downtown area (probably the hippest on the shore)

★ BEST TWO DAYS

Polar opposites, Wildwood and Cape May: both classics.

ANDREW F. KAZMIERSKI/SHUTTERSTOCK

Beach, Asbury Park, New Jersey

includes several blocks of Cookman and Bangs Aves, lined with charming shops, bars, cafes, restaurants and a restored art-house cinema.

The boardwalk itself is short and unspectacular by Jersey standards: at one end is the gorgeous but empty shell of a 1920s-era carousel and casino building, the Paramount Theatre is near the other end, and there's an attractive, well-cared-for stretch of sand in front. Asbury Park's amusements tend to be more for adults than children: its clubs and bars rock late into the night, it has decent surf, and it has the shore's liveliest gay scene.

THE DRIVE: There's no beachfront road to Ocean Grove – the two towns are separated by narrow Wesley Lake. Take the generically commercial Main St/Rte 71 and turn left on Ocean Grove's own Main Ave. It might be worthwhile, however, to first head north on Rte 71 for a few miles to take a gander at the impressively grand homes in the community of Deal.

02 Ocean Grove

Next to Asbury Park is Ocean Grove, one of the cutest Victorian seaside towns anywhere, with a boardwalk boasting not a single business to disturb the peace and quiet. Known as 'God's Square Mile at the Jersey Shore,' Ocean Grove is perfectly coifed, sober, conservative and quaint – it used to shut down entirely on Sundays. Founded by Methodists in the 19th century, the place retains what's left of a post–Civil War Tent City revival camp – now a historic site with 114 cottage-like canvas tents clustered together that are used for summer homes.

Towering over the tents, the 1894 mustard-yellow **Great Auditorium** *(oceangrove.org)* shouldn't be missed: its vaulted interior, amazing acoustics and historical organ recall Utah's Mormon Tabernacle. Make sure to catch a concert or recital (Thursday during the summer) or one of the open-air services held in the boardwalk pavilion (May to September).

THE DRIVE: Follow Rte 71 south through a string of relatively sleepy towns (Bradley Beach, Belmar) for just over 5 miles to reach Spring Lake.

03 Spring Lake

The quiet streets of this prosperous community, once known as the 'Irish Riviera,' are lined with grand oceanfront Victorian houses set in meticulously manicured lawns.

PARTY TIME

Yes, in summer, every day is a party at the Jersey Shore and here are some events not to miss:

- **Jersey Pride**
  Asbury Park, early June *(jerseypride.org)*
- **New Jersey Sandcastle Contest**
  Belmar, July *(beachnj.com)*
- **New Jersey State Barbecue Championship**
  Wildwood, mid-July *(njbbq.com)*
- **Ocean City Baby Parade**
  Ocean City, July *(ocnj.us/babyparade)*
- **Asbury Park Oysterfest**
  Mass munching of mollusks every September *(asburyparkchamber.com)*
- **Asbury Park Zombie Walk**
  Brings gaggles of ghouls to the Shore every October for over a decade *(asburypark zombiewalk.com)*

As a result of Hurricane Sandy, the gorgeous beach is extremely narrow at high tide. If you're interested in a low-key quiet base, a stay here is about as far from the typical shore boardwalk experience as you can get.

Only 5 miles inland from Spring Lake is the quirky **Historic Village at Allaire** *(allairevillage.org)*, the remains of what was a thriving 19th-century village called Howell Works. You can still visit various 'shops' in this living history museum, all run by folks in period costume. It has miles of easy hiking paths, too.

THE DRIVE: For a slow but pleasant drive, take Ocean Ave south – at Wreck Pond you turn inland before heading south again. At Crescent Park in the town of Sea Girt, Washington Ave connects back to Union Ave/Rte 71, which leads into Rte 35 and over the Manasquan Inlet. The first exit for Broadway takes you past several marina-side restaurants.

04 Point Pleasant

Point Pleasant is the first of five quintessential bumper-car-and-Skee-Ball boardwalks. On a July weekend, Point Pleasant's long beach is jam-packed: squint, cover up all that nearly naked flesh with striped unitards, and it could be the 1920s, with umbrellas shading every inch of sand and the surf clogged with bodies and bobbing heads.

Families with young kids love Point Pleasant, as the boardwalk is big but not overwhelming, and the squeaky-clean amusement rides, fun house and small aquarium – all run by **Jenkinson's** *(jenkinsons.com)* – are geared to the height and delight of the 10-and-under set. That's not to say Point Pleasant is only for little ones. Martell's **Tiki Bar** *(tikibar.com)*, a place margarita pitchers go to die, makes sure of that: look for the neon-orange palm trees and listen for the live bands.

THE DRIVE: Head south on Rte 35 past several residential communities laid out on a long barrier island only a block or two wide in parts – Seaside Heights is where it's at its widest on this 11-mile trip.

05 Seaside Heights

Coming from the north, Seaside Heights has the first of the truly overwhelming boardwalks: a sky ride and two rollicking amusement piers with double corridors of arcade games and adult-size, adrenalin-pumping rides, roller coasters and various iterations of the vomit-inducing 10-story drop. During the day, it's as family-friendly as Point Pleasant, but once darkness falls Seaside Heights becomes a scene of such hedonistic mating rituals that an evangelical church has felt the need for a permanent booth on the pier. Packs of young men – caps askew, tatts gleaming – mingle with packs of young women in shimmering spaghetti-strap micro-dresses as everyone rotates among the string of loud bars, with live bands growling out Eagles tunes. It's pure Jersey.

Detour south on Rte 35 to the 10-mile-long **Island Beach State Park** *(islandbeachnj.org)*, a completely undeveloped barrier island backed by dunes and tall grasses separating the bay from the ocean.

THE DRIVE: To reach the mainland, take Rte 37 from Seaside Heights; you cross a long bridge over Barnegat Bay before

JORGE MORO/GETTY IMAGES

Island Beach State Park, New Jersey

reaching the strip-mall-filled sprawl of Toms River. Hop on the Garden State Pkwy south, then Rte 72 and the bridge over Manahawkin Bay.

06 Long Beach Island

Only a very narrow inlet separates this long sliver of an island, with its beautiful beaches and impressive summer homes, from the very southern tip of Island Beach State Park and the northern shore towns. Within throwing distance of the park is the landmark **Barnegat Lighthouse** *(dep.nj.gov)*, which offers panoramic views from the top. Fishers cast off from a jetty extending 2000ft along the Atlantic Ocean, and a short nature trail begins just in front of a visitor center with small history and photography displays.

Nearly every morning practically half the island is jogging, walking, blading or biking on **Beach Ave**, the 7.5-mile stretch of asphalt that stretches from Ship Bottom to Beach Haven (south of the bridge); it's a great time to exercise, enjoy the sun and people-watch. Tucked down a residential street is **Hudson House**, a nearly locals-only dive bar about as worn and comfortable as an old pair of flip-flops. Don't be intimidated by the fact that it looks like a crumbling biker bar – it is.

THE DRIVE: Head back over the bridge, then take the Garden State Pkwy south past the marshy pinelands area and Atlantic City. Take exit 30 for Somers Point; Laurel Dr turns into MacArthur Blvd/Rte 52 and then a long causeway crosses Great Egg Harbor Bay. All up, this is a 48-mile drive. When you cross the causeway, turn left for peace and quiet, right for the action.

07 Ocean City

An almost heavenly amalgam of Ocean Grove and Point Pleasant, Ocean City is a dry town with a roomy boardwalk packed with genuine family fun and facing an exceedingly pretty beach. There's a small water park, and **Gillian's Wonderland** has a heart-thumpingly tall Ferris wheel, a beautifully restored merry-go-round, and kiddie rides galore – and no microphoned

PHOTO OPPORTUNITY

Cape May at sunset.

teens hawking carnie games. The mood is light and friendly (a lack of alcohol will do that).

Mini-golf aficionados: dingding-dingding! You hit the jackpot. Pint-size duffers can play through on a three-masted schooner, around great white sharks and giant octopuses, under reggae monkeys piloting a helicopter and even in black light. If you haven't yet, beat the heat with a delicious Kohr's soft-serve frozen custard, plain or dipped. While salt-water taffy is offered in many places, **Shriver's Taffy** *(shrivers.com)* is, in our humble opinion, the best: watch machines stretch and wrap it, and then fill a bag with two dozen or more flavors.

THE DRIVE: If time isn't a factor, cruise down local streets and over several small bridges ($2.50 toll on two of the four in each direction; coins only) through the beachfront communities of Strathmere, Sea Isle City, Avalon and Stone Harbor. Otherwise, head back to the Garden State Pkwy and get off at one of two exits for the Wildwoods on a 30-mile drive.

08 Wildwoods

A party town popular with teens, twenty-somethings and the young, primarily Eastern Europeans who staff the restaurants and shops, Wildwood is the main social focus here (North Wildwood and Wildwood Crest are to the north and south respectively). Access to all three beaches is free, and the width of the beach – more than 1000ft in parts, making it the widest in New Jersey – means there's never a lack of space. Several massive piers are host to water parks and amusement parks – easily the rival of any Six Flags Great Adventure – with roller coasters and rides best suited to aspiring astronauts anchoring the 2-mile-long Grand Daddy of Jersey Shore boardwalks. Glow-in-the-dark 3D mini-golf is a good example of the Wildwood boardwalk ethos – take it far, then one step further. Maybe the best ride of all, and one that doesn't induce nausea, is the tram running the length of the boardwalk from Wildwood Crest to North Wildwood. There's always a line for a table at Jersey Shore staple pizzeria **Mack's Pizza** on the boardwalk (it also has other shore boardwalk locations). **Maui Dog House** *(mauisdoghouse.com)* is a must-stop, too.

Wildwood Crest is an archaeological find, a kitschy slice of 1950s Americana – whitewashed motels with flashing neon signs, turquoise curtains and pink doors. Check out eye-catching motel signs like the Lollipop at 23rd and Atlantic Aves.

THE DRIVE: Take local roads: south on Pacific Ave to Ocean Dr, which passes over a toll bridge over an estuary area separating Jarvis Sound from Cape May Harbor. Then left on Rte 109 over the Cape May harbor itself. You can turn left anywhere from here, depending on whether you want to head to town or the beach.

☑ TOP TIP

PLAN AHEAD

We love the shore but let's be honest, in summer months, the traffic is a nightmare, parking is impossible and the beaches are overflowing. Pack the car the night before, leave at dawn and, if at all possible, come midweek. And if you want something besides a run-down, sun-bleached, three-blocks-from-the-water flea box to stay in, make reservations six months to a year in advance.

09 Cape May

Founded in 1620, Cape May – the only place in the state where the sun both rises and sets over the water – is on the state's southern tip and is the country's oldest seashore resort. Its sweeping beaches get crowded in summer, but the stunning Victorian architecture is attractive year-round.

In addition to 600 gingerbread-style houses, the city boasts antique shops and places for dolphin-, whale- (May to December) and bird-watching, and is just outside the **Cape May Point State Park** and its 157ft **Cape May Lighthouse** *(capemaymac.org)*, with 199 steps to the observation deck at the top; there's an excellent visitor center and museum with exhibits on wildlife in the area, as well as trails to ponds, dunes and marshes. A mile-long loop of the nearby **Cape May Bird Observatory** *(njaudubon.org)* is a pleasant stroll through preserved wetlands. The wide sandy beach at the park (free) or the one in town is the main attraction in summer months. **Aqua Trails** *(aquatrails.com)* offers kayak tours of the coastal wetlands.

Cape May Llighthouse, New Jersey
PKUJIAHE/GETTY IMAGES

06

NEW YORK & THE MID-ATLANTIC

PENNSYLVANIA DUTCH COUNTRY

★ BEST FOR

FOODIES

Almost everything here comes in a buffet.

Seed drilling, Dutch Country, Pennsylvania

DURATION: 3–4 DAYS

DISTANCE: 102 MILES/164KM

GREAT FOR: FAMILY, WINE, HISTORY

BEST TIME TO GO: LESS CROWDED IN EARLY SPRING OR SEPTEMBER.

The Amish really do drive buggies and plow their fields by hand. In Dutch Country, the pace is slower, and it's no costumed reenactment. For the most evocative Dutch Country experience, go driving along the winding, narrow lanes between the thruways – past rolling green fields of alfalfa, asparagus and corn, past pungent working barnyards and manicured lawns, waving to Amish families in buggies and straw-hatted teens on scooters.

LINK YOUR TRIP

05 The Jersey Shore
Head east to Philadelphia, where you can connect to a number of routes that will transport you to the boardwalks of Jersey Shore towns.

07 Maryland's National Historic Road
Continue on US 30 west to York and then head south to Baltimore for a journey through this state's defining small towns.

01 Lancaster

A good place to start is the walkable, redbrick historic district of Lancaster (LANK-uh-stir), just off Penn Sq. The Romanesque-revival-style **Central Market** *(centralmarketlancaster.com)*, which is like a smaller version of Philadelphia's Reading Terminal Market, has all the regional gastronomic delicacies – fresh horseradish, whoopie pies, soft pretzels and sub sandwiches stuffed with cured meats and dripping with oil. You'll find surprises too, such as Spanish and Middle Eastern food. Plus, of course, the market is crowded with handicraft booths staffed by plain-dressed, bonneted Amish women.

In the 18th century, German immigrants flooded southeastern Pennsylvania, and only some were Amish. Most lived like the costumed docents at the **Landis Valley Village & Farm Museum** *(landisvalleymuseum.org)*, a re-creation

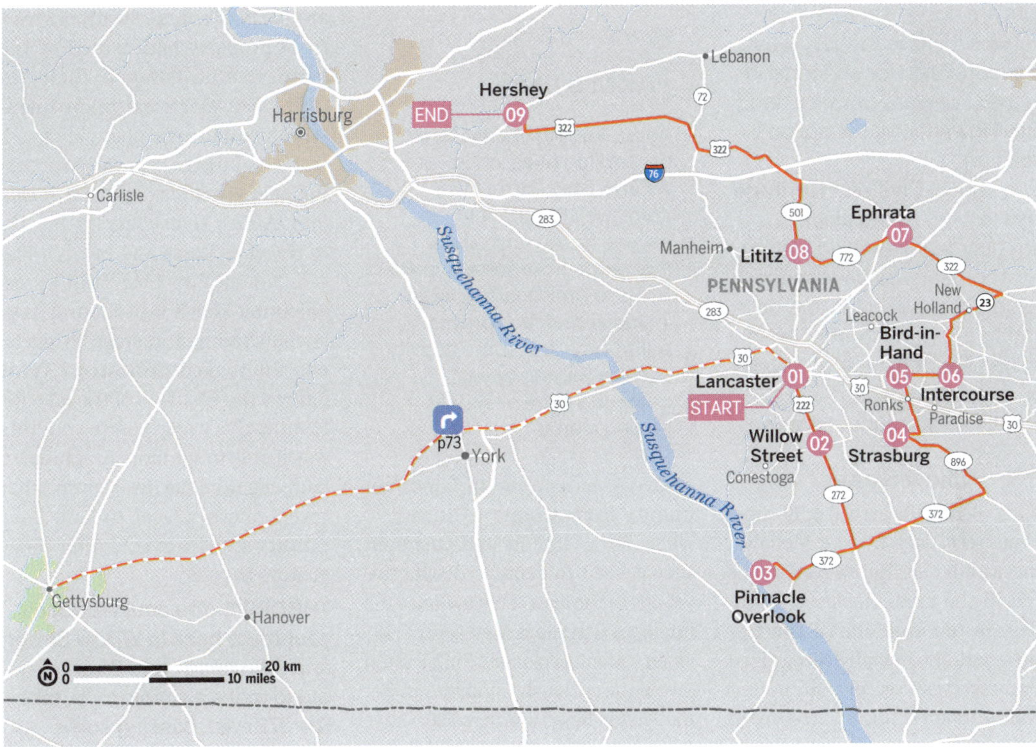

HUTCH PHOTOGRAPHY/SHUTTERSTOCK

of Pennsylvania German village life that includes a working smithy, weavers, stables and more. It's only a few miles north of Lancaster off Rte 272/Oregon Pike.

THE DRIVE: From downtown Lancaster head south on Prince St, which turns into Rte 222 and then Rte 272 all the way to Willow Street.

DETOUR

Gettysburg

Start: 01 Lancaster

Take US 30 west (also referred to as Lincoln Hwy) for 55 miles right into downtown Gettysburg. This tranquil, compact and memorial-laden town saw one of the Civil War's most decisive and bloody battles for three days in July 1863. It's also where, four months later, Lincoln delivered his Gettysburg Address consecrating, eulogizing and declaring the mission unfinished. At only 200-plus words, surely it's one of the most defining and effective rhetorical examples in US history. Much of the ground where Robert E Lee's Army of Northern Virginia and Major General Joseph Hooker's Union Army of the Potomac skirmished and fought can be explored – either on your own, on a bus tour or on a two-hour guide-led tour in your own car. The latter is most recommended, but if you're short on time it's still worth driving the narrow lanes past fields with dozens of monuments marking significant sites and moments in the battle.

Don't miss the massive Gettysburg National Military Park Museum & Visitor Center *(nps.gov/gett)* several miles south of town, which houses a fairly incredible museum filled with artifacts and displays exploring every nuance of the battle; a film explaining Gettysburg's context and why it's considered a turning point in the war; and Paul Philippoteaux' 377ft cyclorama painting of Pickett's Charge. The aforementioned bus tours and ranger-led tours are booked here. While overwhelming, in the very least, it's a foundation for understanding the Civil War's primacy and lingering impact in the nation's evolution.

The annual **Civil War Heritage Days** festival, taking place in early July, features living history encampments, battle reenactments, a lecture series and book fair that draws war reenactment aficionados from near and wide. You can find reenactments at other times throughout the year.

02 Willow Street

Before the arrival of European émigrés, Coney, Lenape, Mohawk, Seneca and other Native Americans lived in the area. However, Pennsylvania remains one of the few states with no officially recognized tribal reserves – or, for that matter, tribes. In something of a gesture to rectify their erasure from history, a replica longhouse now stands on the property of the 1719 **Hans Herr House** *(mennonitelife.org)*, generally regarded as the oldest original Mennonite meeting house in the western hemisphere. Today, Hans Herr House displays colonial-era artifacts in period furnished rooms; there's also a blacksmith shop and a barn. 'Living history interpreters' provide an idea of how life was lived in the 18th century.

The interior of the longhouse, a typical narrow, single-room multi-family home built only from natural materials, is divided into pre- and post-European contact sides and decorated and furnished with artifacts typical of each era. The primary mission, which is done quite well, is to teach visitors about the history of Native American life in Lancaster County from around 1570 to 1770 when, for all intents and purposes, they ceased to exist as distinctive groups in the area. This includes the infamous Conestoga Massacre of 1763 when vigilante colonists from Paxton (given the curiously anodyne epithet the 'Paxton Boys') murdered 20 Native American men, women and children from the settlement of Conestoga.

> ☑ TOP TIP
>
> ### FARM STAYS
>
> If you like your vacations to be working ones, check out **A Farm Stay** *(farmstayus.com)*, which represents several dozen farm stays that range from stereotypical B&Bs to Amish farms. Most include breakfast, private bathrooms and some activity such as milking cows, gathering eggs or simply petting a goat.

THE DRIVE: The simplest route is Rte 272 south to Rte 372 west. If you have time, however, head west on W Penn Grant Rd and then left on New Danville Pike, which turns into Main St in Conestoga. From there, follow Main St to a T-junction and turn left on River Rd, passing Tucquan Glen Nature Preserve on the way.

03 Pinnacle Overlook

High over Lake Aldred, a wide portion of the Susquehanna River just up from a large dam, is this overlook with beautiful views and eagles and other raptors soaring overhead. This and the adjoining Holtwood Environmental Preserve are parts of a large swath of riverfront property maintained by the Pennsylvania Power & Light Co (PPL). But electrical plant infrastructure and accompanying truck traffic is largely kept at bay, making this a popular spot for locals (non-Amish that is, as it's too far to travel by horse and buggy). The 4-mile-long Fire Line Trail to the adjoining Kelly's Run Natural Area is challenging and steep in parts, and the rugged **Conestoga Trail** follows the east side of the lake for 15 miles. It's worth coming out this way if only to see more rough-hewn landscape and the rural byways that reveal another facet to Lancaster County's character, which most visitors bypass.

THE DRIVE: You could retrace your route back to Willow Street and then head on to Strasburg, but to make a scenic loop, take Rte 372 east, passing some agrarian scenes as well as suburban housing to the small hamlet of Georgetown. Make a left onto Rte 896 – vistas open up on either side of the road.

04 Strasburg

The main attraction in Strasburg is trains – the old-fashioned, steam-driven kind. Since 1832, the **Strasburg Rail Road** *(strasburgrailroad.com)* has run the same route (and speed) to Paradise and back that it does today, and wooden train cars are gorgeously restored with stained glass, shiny brass lamps and plush burgundy seats. Several classes of seats are offered including the private President's Car.

Strasburg Rail Road, Strasburg, Pennsylvania
CEW/SHUTTERSTOCK

89
CANADIAN
89
NATIONAL

The **Railroad Museum of Pennsylvania** *(rrmuseumpa.org)* has 100 gigantic mechanical marvels to climb around and admire, but even more delightful is the HO-scale **National Toy Train Museum** *(tcatrains.org/museum)*. The push-button interactive dioramas are so up-to-date and clever (such as a 'drive-in movie' that's a live video of kids working the trains), and the walls are packed with so many gleaming railcars, that you can't help but feel a bit of that childlike Christmas-morning wonder. Stop at the Red Caboose Motel next to the museum - you can climb the silo in the back for wonderful views, and kids can enjoy a small petting zoo.

THE DRIVE: Continue north on S Ronks Rd past Ronks' bucolic farmland scenery, cross busy Rte 30 – Miller's Smorgasbord restaurant is at this intersection – and carry on for another 2 miles to Bird-in-Hand.

PHOTO OPPORTUNITY

A windmill or grain silo with a horse-drawn plow in the foreground.

05 Bird-in-Hand

The primary reason to make your way to this delightfully named Amish town is the **Bird-in-Hand Farmers Market** *(birdinhandfarmersmarket.com)*, which is pretty much a one-stop shop of Dutch Country highlights. There's fudge, quilts and crafts, and you can buy scrapple (pork scraps mixed with cornmeal and wheat flour, shaped into a loaf and fried), homemade jam and shoofly pie (a pie made of molasses or brown sugar sprinkled with a crumbly mix of brown sugar, flour and butter). Two lunch counters sell cheap sandwiches, homemade pretzels and healthy juices and smoothies. It's worth bringing a cooler to stock up for the onward drive.

THE DRIVE: It's less than 4 miles east on Old Philadelphia Pike/Rte 340 to Intercourse, but traffic can back up, in part because it's a popular route for tourist horse-and-buggy rides.

Amish family on a horse-drawn buggy Intercourse, Pennsylvania

GEORGE SHELDON/SHUTTERSTOCK

06 Intercourse

Named for the crossroads, not the act, Intercourse is a little more amenable to walking than Bird-in-Hand. The horse-drawn buggy rides *(amishbuggyrides.com)* on offer can also be fun. How much fun depends largely on your driver: some Amish are strict, some liberal, and Mennonites are different again. All drivers strive to present Amish culture to the 'English' (the Amish term for non-Amish, whether English or not), but some are more openly personal than others.

Kitchen Kettle Village, essentially an open-air mall for tourists with stores selling smoked meats, jams, pretzels, gifts and tchotchkes, feels like a Disneyfied version of the Bird-in-Hand Farmers Market. It's a one-stop shop for the commercialized 'PA Dutch Country experience,' which means your perception of it will depend on your attitude toward a parking lot jammed with tour buses.

THE DRIVE: Head north on Rte 772 and make your first right onto Centerville Rd, which becomes S Shirk Rd, a country lane that takes you to Rte 23. Turn right here and it's a few miles to Blue Ball (try not to giggle that you're so close to Intercourse) – and then left on the busier Rte 322 all the way to Ephrata.

07 Ephrata

One of the country's earliest religious communities was founded in 1732 by Conrad Beissel, an émigré escaping religious persecution in his native Germany. Beissel, like others throughout human history dissatisfied with worldly ways and distractions (difficult to imagine what these were in his pre-pre-pre-digital age), sought a mystical, personal relationship with God. At its peak there were close to 300 members, including two celibate orders of brothers and sisters, known collectively as 'the Solitary,' who patterned their dress after Roman Catholic monks (the last of these passed away in 1813), as well as married 'households' who were less all-in, if you will.

ZACK FRANK/SHUTTERSTOCK

Ephrata Cloister, Lancaster County, Pennsylvania

Today, the collection of austere, almost medieval-style buildings of the **Ephrata Cloister** *(ephratacloister.org)* have been preserved and are open to visitors; guided tours are offered or take an audio cellphone tour on your own. There's a small museum and a short film in the visitor center that very earnestly and efficiently tells the story of Ephrata's founding and demise – if the narrator's tone and rather somber mise-en-scène are any indication, not to mention the extremely spartan sleeping quarters, it was a demanding existence. No doubt Beissel would disapprove of today's Ephrata, the commercial Main St of which is anchored by a Walmart.

If you're around on a Friday, be sure to check out the **Green Dragon Farmers Market** *(greendragonmarket.com)*.

THE DRIVE: This is a simple 8.5-mile drive; for the most part, Rte 772/Rothsville Rd between Ephrata and Lititz is an ordinary commercial strip.

08 Lititz

Like other towns in Pennsylvania Dutch Country, Lititz was founded by a religious community from Europe, in this case Moravians who settled here in the 1740s.

HP
STROLLER PARKING
GIANT

However, unlike Ephrata, Lititz was more outward looking and integrated with the world beyond its historic center. Many of its original handsome stone-and-wood buildings still line its streets today. Take a stroll down E Main St from the **Julius Sturgis Pretzel Bakery** *(juliussturgis.com)*, the first pretzel factory in the country – you can try your hand at rolling and twisting the dough. Across the street is the **Moravian Church** (c 1787); then head to the intersection with S Broad St. Rather than feeling sealed in amber, the small shops, which do seem to relish their small-town quality, are nonetheless the type that sophisticated urbanites cherish. There's an unusual effortlessness to this vibe, from the **Bulls Head Public House** *(lititzspringsinn.com/bulls-head-public-house)*, a traditional English-style pub with an expertly curated beer menu, to **Greco's Italian Ices**, a little ground-floor hole-in-the-wall where local teenagers and families head on weekend nights for delicious homemade ice-cream.

THE DRIVE: It's an easy 27 miles on Rte 501 to Hwy 322 and on to Hershey. Both roads pass through a combination of farmland and suburban areas, though the latter is generally a fast-moving highway.

THE AMISH

The Amish (ah-mish), Mennonite and Brethren religious communities are collectively known as the 'Plain People.' All are Anabaptist sects (only those who choose the faith are baptized) who were persecuted in their native Switzerland, and from the early 1700s settled in tolerant Pennsylvania. Speaking German dialects, they became known as 'Dutch' (from 'Deutsch'). Most Pennsylvania Dutch live on farms and their beliefs vary from sect to sect. Many do not use electricity, and most opt for horse-drawn buggies – a delightful sight, and sound, in the area. The strictest believers, the Old Order Amish who make up the majority of Lancaster County's Amish, wear dark, plain clothing (no zippers, only buttons, snaps and safety pins), and live a simple, Bible-centered life – but have, ironically, become a major tourist attraction, thus bringing busloads of gawkers and the requisite strip malls, chain restaurants and hotels that lend this entire area an oxymoronic quality, to say the least. Because there is so much commercial development – fast-food restaurants, mini-malls, big-box chain stores, tract housing – continually encroaching on multigenerational family farms, it takes some doing to appreciate the unique nature of the area.

09 Hershey

Hershey is home to a collection of attractions that detail, hype and, of course, hawk the many trappings of Milton Hershey's chocolate empire. The pièce de résistance is **Hersheypark** *(hersheypark.com)*, an amusement park with more than 60 thrill rides, a zoo and a water park, plus various performances and frequent fireworks displays. Don a hairnet and apron and punch in a few choices on a computer screen and then voilà, watch your very own chocolate bar roll down a conveyor belt at the Create Your Own Candy Bar attraction, part of Hershey's Chocolate World, a mock factory and massive candy store with overstimulating features such as singing characters and free chocolate galore. For a more low-key informative visit, try the Hershey Story, The Museum on Chocolate Avenue, which explores the life and fascinating legacy of Mr Hershey through interactive history exhibits; try molding your own candy in the hands-on Chocolate Lab.

Hersheypark, Hershey, Pennsylvania
BIG BLINK CREATIVE/SHUTTERSTOCK

07

NEW YORK & THE MID-ATLANTIC

MARYLAND'S NATIONAL HISTORIC ROAD

★ BEST FOR

OUTDOORS

Hiking along the bottom of the Patapsco Valley.

Inner Harbor Baltimore, Maryland

DURATION: 2 DAYS

DISTANCE: 92 MILES/148KM

GREAT FOR: HISTORY, FAMILIES

BEST TIME TO GO: APRIL TO JUNE TO SOAK UP LATE SPRING'S SUNNINESS AND WARMTH.

For such a small state, Maryland has a staggering array of landscapes and citizens, and this trip engages both of these elements of the Old Line State. Move from Chesapeake Bay and Baltimore, a port that mixes bohemians with blue-collar workers, through the picturesque small towns of the Maryland hill country, into the stately cities that mark the lower slopes of the looming Catoctin Mountains.

LINK YOUR TRIP

06 Pennsylvania Dutch Country
Take I-95 north from Baltimore and then MD-222 toward Lancaster to begin exploring this patch of bucolic farmland.

08 Skyline Drive
From Gathland State Park head 55 miles southwest to Front Royal, VA, to this trip along one of the nation's most scenic roadways.

01 Baltimore

Maryland's largest city is one of the most important ports in the country, a center for the arts and culture and an entrepôt of immigrants from Greece, El Salvador, East Africa, the Caribbean and elsewhere. These streams combine into an idiosyncratic culture that, in many ways, encapsulates Maryland's depth of history and prominent diversity – not just of race, but creed and socioeconomic status.

Baltimore was a notable holdout against the British military during the War of 1812, even after Washington, DC, fell. The morning after an intense shelling, staring 'through the rockets' red glare,' local lawyer Francis Scott Key saw that 'our flag was still there' and wrote 'The Star-Spangled Banner.' The history of that battle and the

F11PHOTO/SHUTTERSTOCK

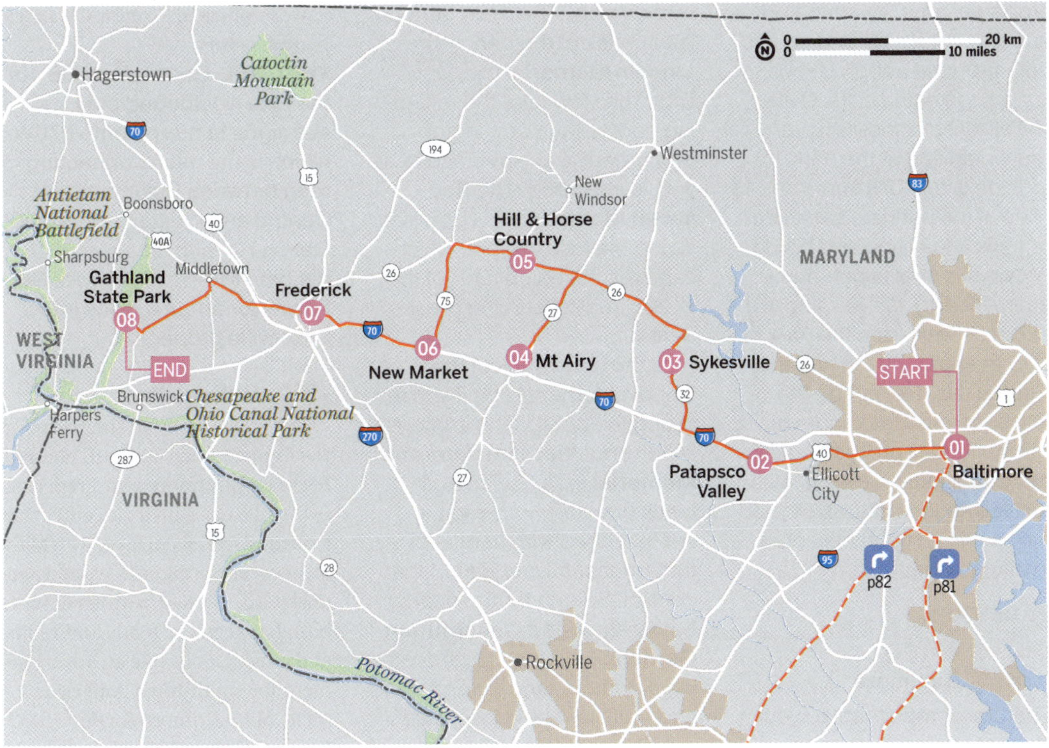

national anthem are explored at **Fort McHenry** *(nps.gov/fomc)*, located in South Baltimore.

Have a wander through nearby Federal Hill Park, a 70-acre hill that rises above the city, and admire the view out over the harbor.

THE DRIVE: Get on US 40 (Baltimore National Pike – and the basis of the National Historic Road this trip is named for) westbound in Baltimore. The easiest place to access it is at Charles and Franklin St. Franklin becomes US 40/the Pike as you head west out of downtown Baltimore, into the woods that mark the edges of the Patapsco Valley. The whole drive takes about 30 minutes in traffic.

DETOUR

Calvert Cliffs

Start: 01 Baltimore

In Southern Maryland, 75 miles south of Baltimore via US 301 and MD-4, skinny Calvert County scratches at the Chesapeake Bay and the Patuxent River. This is a gentle landscape ('user-friendly' as a local ranger puts it) of low-lying forests, estuarine marshes and placid waters, but there is one rugged feature: the Calvert Cliffs. These burnt umber pillars stretch along the coast for some 24 miles, and form the seminal landscape feature of **Calvert Cliffs State Park** *(dnr.maryland.gov/publiclands)*, where they front the water and a pebbly, honey-sand beach scattered with driftwood and drying beds of kelp.

Back in the day (10 to 20 million years ago), this area sat submerged under a warm sea. Eventually, that sea receded and left the fossilized remains of thousands of prehistoric creatures embedded in the cliffs. Fast-forward to the 21st century, and one of the favorite activities of Southern Maryland families is coming to this park, strolling across the sand and plucking out fossils and sharks' teeth from the pebbly debris at the base of the cliffs. Over 600 species of fossils have been identified at the park. In addition, a full 1079 acres and 13 miles of the park are set aside for trails and hiking and biking.

While this spot is pet- and family-friendly, fair warning: it's a 1.8-mile walk from the parking lot to the open beach and the cliffs, so this may not be the best spot to go fossil hunting with very small children unless they can handle the walk. Also: don't climb the cliffs, as erosion makes this an unstable and unsafe prospect.

DETOUR

Washington, DC

Start: 01 Baltimore

A natural complement to your historical tour is the nation's capital, just 40 miles south of Baltimore on the BWI Pkwy. The National Mall is the site of some of the nation's most iconic protests, from Martin Luther King's March on Washington to recent rallies for women's rights and Black Lives Matter.

The east end of the mall is filled with the (free!) museums of the Smithsonian Institution. All are worth your time. We could easily get lost amid the silk screens, Japanese prints and sculpture of the often-bypassed **National Museum of Asian Art** *(asia.si.edu)*.

On the other side of the mall is a cluster of memorials and monuments. The most famous is the back of the penny: the **Lincoln Memorial** *(nps.gov/linc)*. The view over the reflecting pool to the Washington Monument is as spectacular as you've imagined. The **Roosevelt Memorial** *(nps.gov/frde)* is notable for its layout, which explores the entire term of the USA's longest-serving president.

On the north flank of the Lincoln Memorial (left if you're facing the pool) is the immensely powerful **Vietnam Veterans Memorial** *(nps.gov/vive)*, a black granite 'V' cut into the soil inscribed with names of the American war dead of that conflict. Search for the nearby but rarely visited **Constitution Gardens** *(nps.gov/coga)*, featuring a tranquil, landscaped pond and artificial island inscribed with the names of the signers of the Constitution.

02 Patapsco Valley

The Patapsco River and river valley are the defining geographic features of the region, running through Central Maryland to the Chesapeake Bay. To explore the area, head to **Patapsco Valley State Park** *(dnr.maryland.gov/publiclands)*, an enormous protected area – one of the oldest in the state – that runs for 32 miles along a whopping 170 miles of trails. The main visitor center provides insight into the settled history of the area, from Native Americans to the present, and is housed in a 19th-century stone cottage that looks as though it were plucked from a CS Lewis bedtime story.

THE DRIVE: Get back on US 40/the Pike westbound until you see signs to merge onto I-70W, which is the main connecting road between Baltimore and Central and Western Maryland. Get on 70, then take exit 80 to get onto MD-32 (Sykesville Rd). Follow for about 5 miles into Sykesville proper.

03 Sykesville

Like many of the towns in the Central Maryland hill country between Baltimore and Frederick, Sykesville has a historic center that looks and feels picture perfect. Main St, between Springfield Ave and Sandosky Rd, is filled with structures built between the 1850s and 1930s, and almost looks like an advertisement for small-town America.

The old Baltimore & Ohio (B&O) train station at 7618 Main St, now the **Sykesville Station** restaurant, was built in 1883 in the Queen Anne style. The station was the brainchild of E Francis Baldwin, a Baltimore architect who designed many B&O stations, giving that rail line a satisfying aesthetic uniformity along its extent.

Fun fact: Sykesville was founded on land James Sykes bought from George Patterson. Patterson was the son of Elizabeth Patterson and Jerome Bonaparte, brother of Napoleon. The French emperor insisted his brother marry royalty and never let his sister-in-law (the daughter of a merchant) into France; her family estate (which formed the original parcel of land that the town grew

Vietnam Veterans Memorial and Washington Monument, Washington, DC
DANITA DELIMONT/SHUTTERSTOCK

PHOTO OPPORTUNITY

The solemnity of the Vietnam Veterans Memorial at night.

from) is the grounds of Sykesville proper.

THE DRIVE: Although this trip is largely based on US 40 – the actual National Historic Road – detour up to Liberty Rd (MD-26) and take that west 8 miles to Ridge Rd (MD-27). Take Ridge Rd/MD-27 south for 5.5 miles to reach Mt Airy.

04 Mt Airy

Mt Airy is the next major (take that term with a grain of salt) town along the B&O railroad and US 40/National Historic Road. Like Sykesville, it's a handsome town, with a stately center that benefited from the commerce the railway brought westward from Baltimore. When the railway was replaced by the highway, Mt Airy, unlike other towns, still retained much of its prosperity thanks to the proximity of jobs in cities like DC and Baltimore.

Today the town centers on a historic district of 19th- and early-20th-century buildings, many of which can be found around Main St. The upmarket historical homes near 'downtown' Mt Airy were built in the Second Empire, Queen Anne and Colonial revival styles, while most 'regular' homes are two-story, center-gable 'I-houses,' once one of the most common housing styles in rural America in the 19th century, but now largely displaced in this region by modern split-levels.

THE DRIVE: Take Ridge Rd/MD-27 back to Liberty Rd/MD-26. Turn left and proceed for 10 miles to reach Elk Run.

05 Hill & Horse Country

Much of Frederick, Carroll, Baltimore and Hartford Counties consist of trimmed, rolling grassy hills intersected by copses of pine and broadleaf woods and tangled hedgerows; it's the sort of landscape that could put you in mind of the bocage country of northern France or rural England. A mix of working farmers and wealthy city folks live out here, and horse breeding and raising is a big industry.

It can be pretty enchanting just driving around and getting lost on some of the local back roads, but if you want a solid destination, it's tough to go wrong with **Elk Run**

American Visionary Art Museum Baltimore, Maryland

STONIKO/SHUTTERSTOCK

Vineyards *(elkrun.com)*, almost exactly halfway between Mt Airy and New Market. Free tours are offered at 1pm and 3pm on weekends, and tastings include the star cabernet franc.

THE DRIVE: Continue west on Liberty Rd/MD-26 for 6 miles, then turn left (southbound) onto MD-75/Green Valley Rd. After about 7 miles, take a right onto Old New Market Rd to reach New Market's Main St.

06 New Market

Pretty New Market is the smallest and best preserved of the historical towns that sit between Baltimore and Frederick. Main St, full of antique shops, is lined with Federal and Greek Revival houses. More than 90% of the structures are of brick or frame construction, as opposed to modern vinyl, sheet rock and/or dry wall; the National Register of Historical Places deems central New Market 'in appearance, the quintessence of the circa 1800 small town in western central Maryland.'

THE DRIVE: Frederick is about 7 miles west of New Market via I-70. Take exit 56 for MD-144 to reach the city center.

07 Frederick

Frederick boasts a historically preserved center, but unlike the previous listed small towns, this is a mid-sized city, an important commuter base for thousands of federal government employees and a biotechnology hub in its own right.

Central Frederick is, well, perfect. For a city of its size (around 65,000), what more could you want? A historic, pedestrian-friendly center of redbrick row houses with a large, diverse array of restaurants usually found in a larger town; an engaged, cultured arts community anchored by the excellent events calendar at the **Weinberg Center for the Arts** *(weinbergcenter.org)*; and meandering Carroll Creek running through the center of it all. Walking around downtown is immensely enjoyable.

The creek is crossed by a lovely bit of community art: the mural on **Frederick Bridge**, at S Carroll St between E Patrick and E All Saints. The trompe l'oeil–style art essentially transforms a drab concrete span into an old, ivy-covered stone bridge from Tuscany.

THE DRIVE: Head west on old National Pike (US 40A) and then, after about 6.5 miles, get on MD-17 southbound/Burkittsville Rd. Turn right on Gapland Rd after 6 miles and follow it for 1.5 miles to Gathland.

08 Gathland State Park

This tiny park *(dnr.maryland.gov/publiclands)* is a fascinating tribute to a profession that doesn't lend itself to many memorials: war correspondents. Civil War correspondent and man of letters George Alfred Townsend fell in love with these mountains and built an impressive arch decorated with classical Greek mythological features and quotes that emphasize the needed qualities of a good war correspondent.

MORE OF BALTIMORE'S BEST

Everyone knows DC is full of museums, but the capital's scruffier, cooler neighbor to the northeast gives Washington a run for its money in the museum department.

Out by the Baltimore waterfront is a strange building, seemingly half enormous warehouse, half explosion of intense artsy angles, multicolored windmills and rainbow-reflecting murals, like someone had bent the illustrations of a Dr Seuss book through a funky mirror. This is quite possibly the coolest art museum in the country: the **American Visionary Art Museum** *(avam.org)*. It's a showcase for self-taught (or 'outsider' art), which is to say, art made by people who aren't formally trained artists. It's a celebration of unbridled creativity utterly free of arts-scene pretension. Some of the work comes from asylums, others are created by self-inspired visionaries, but it's all rather captivating and well worth a long afternoon.

The Baltimore & Ohio railway was (arguably) the first passenger train in America, and the **B&O Railroad Museum** *(borail.org)* is a loving testament to both that line and American railroading in general. Train spotters will be in heaven among more than 150 different locomotives. Train rides cost an extra $6; call for the schedule.

If you're traveling with a family, or if you just love science and science education, come by the **Maryland Science Center** *(mdsci.org)*. This awesome center features a three-story atrium, tons of interactive exhibits on dinosaurs, outer space and the human body, and the requisite IMAX theater.

STAY AWHILE

WASHINGTON, DC

BY MARGOT BIGG

Washington, DC, has long been where everyone from US policy-makers to corporate lobbyists has congregated to shape the nation's political and economic landscape. This makes it a great place to spend a day or two taking a deep dive into American history and thought, even if you aren't crazy about politics.

The city's most popular attractions are situated just south of downtown. These include the **White House** *(whitehouse.gov)* and the **US Capitol** *(visitthecapitol.gov),* where both bodies of Congress meet to create and reform legislation. While these sights are certainly worth checking out for their political and architectural value, what I love most about DC is its museums.

The bulk of DC's museums are run by the Smithsonian Institution. Almost all offer free admission, and most are along or near the **National Mall** *(nps.gov/nama),* DC's main cultural drag. The oldest museum, **Smithsonian Castle** *(si.edu/castle),* is undergoing extensive renovations but is still worth checking out for its glorious Romanesque-revival exterior. The **National Museum of African American History & Culture** *(nmaahc.si.edu)* does an exceptional job of centering the history and stories of African Americans, while the **National Museum of Natur-al History** *(naturalhistory.si.edu)* wows visitors with its incredible specimens. You can't miss its star, Henry, a taxidermied African bush elephant and the museum's de facto mascot.

While DC's culinary scene is eclectic and global, the city is renowned for its Ethiopian fare. I always make a point of getting a meal in Little Ethiopia, near 9th and U St Northwest; **Eatopia Eatery** *(eatopiaeatery.com)* is one of my favorites.

LINK YOUR TRIP

Washington, DC, is about 31 miles south of 07 **Maryland's National Historic Road** (p80).

Left: National Museum of African American History and Culture, Washington, DC;
Right: US Capitol, Washington, DC

LEFT TO RIGHT: NIGEL JARVIS/SHUTTERSTOCK, ORHAN CAM/SHUTTERSTOCK

PLACE TO STAY...

- **Generator Washington, DC**
  You'll find some of the cheapest digs at this central hostel, which features a mix of traditional dorms and rooms with en-suite bathrooms. *staygenerator.com*

- **Hay Adams**
  Directly across from the White House, this swanky, pet-friendly hotel has been a hotspot for dignitaries and well-heeled visitors since the 1920s. *hayadams.com*

- **Hotel Lombardy**
  This historic spot in Foggy Bottom has classic, vaguely European-inspired rooms and a refined bistro that's great for brunch. *hotellombardy.com*

- **Tabard Inn**
  Dating to 1922, this cozy inn is the oldest operating inn and restaurant in town – an achievement reflected in its colorful, individually decorated townhouse rooms. *tabardinn.com*

08

NEW YORK & THE MID-ATLANTIC

SKYLINE DRIVE

★ BEST FOR

CULTURE

Byrd Visitor Center offers an illuminating peek into Appalachian folkways.

DURATION: 3 DAYS

DISTANCE: 150 MILES/240KM

GREAT FOR: NATURE

BEST TIME TO GO: FROM MAY TO NOVEMBER FOR GREAT WEATHER, OPEN FACILITIES AND CLEAR VIEWS.

Skyline Drive, Shenandoah National Park, Virginia

The centerpiece of the ribbon-thin Shenandoah National Park is the jaw-dropping beauty of Skyline Drive, which runs for just over 100 miles atop the Blue Ridge Mountains. Unlike the massive acreage of western parks like Yellowstone or Yosemite, Shenandoah is at times only a mile wide. That may seem to narrow the park's scope, yet it makes it a perfect space for traversing and road-tripping goodness.

LINK YOUR TRIP

06 Pennsylvania Dutch Country
From wherever you are on Skyline Drive, hop on I-81 for the journey northeast to Lancaster and its Amish communities.

07 Maryland's National Historic Road
US-340 takes you north from Front Royal to historic Frederick, the gateway to a region of quintessential stately small towns.

01 Front Royal

Straddling the northern entrance to the park is the tiny city of Front Royal. Although it's not among Virginia's fanciest ports of call, this lush riverside town offers all the urban amenities you might need before a camping or hiking trip up in the mountains.

If you need to gather your bearings, an obvious place to start is the **Front Royal Visitor Center** *(discoverfront-royal.com)*. Friendly staff are on hand to overwhelm you with information about what to do in the area.

THE DRIVE: Dinosaur Land is 10 miles north of Front Royal, toward Winchester, via US 340 (Stonewall Jackson Hwy).

DETOUR

Museum of the Shenandoah Valley

Start: 01 Front Royal

Of all the places where you can begin your journey into She-

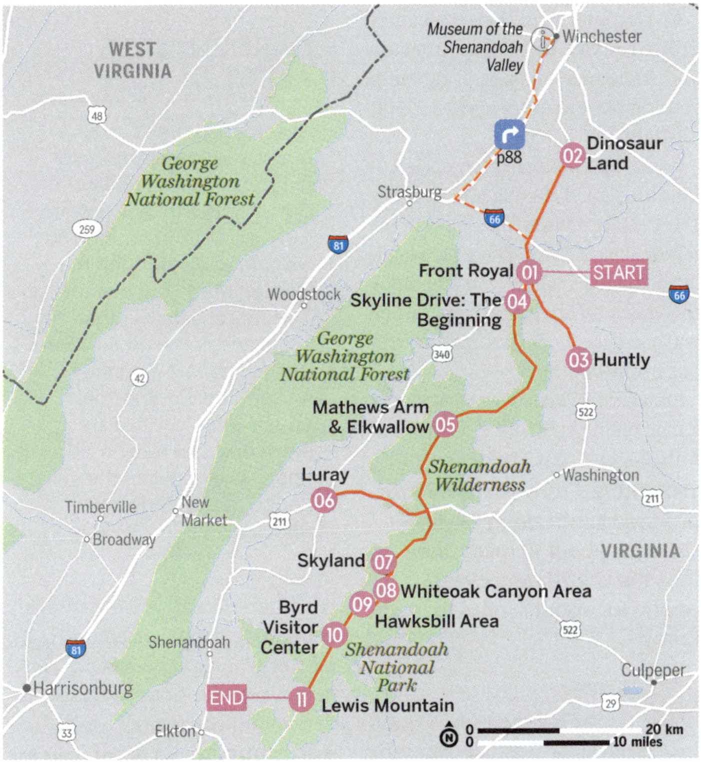

nandoah National Park, none seem to make quite as much sense as the **Museum of the Shenandoah Valley** *(themsv.org)*, an institution dedicated to its namesake. Located in the town of Winchester, some 25 miles north of Front Royal, the museum is an exhaustive repository of information on the valley, Appalachian culture and its associated folkways, some of the most unique in the USA. Exhibits are divided into four galleries, accompanied by the restored Glen Burnie historical home and 6 acres of gardens.

To get here, take I-66 west from Front Royal to I-81 and head north for 25 miles. In Winchester, follow signs to the museum, which is on the outskirts of town.

02 Dinosaur Land

Before you head into the national park and its stunning natural beauty, visit **Dinosaur Land** *(dinosaurland.com)* for some fantastic human-made tackiness. This spectacularly low-brow shrine to concrete sculpture is not to be missed. Although it's an 'educational prehistoric forest,' with more than 50 life-size dinosaurs (and a King Kong for good measure), you'd probably learn more about the tenants by fast-forwarding through Jurassic Park 3. But that's not why you've stopped here, so grab your camera and sidle up to the triceratops for memories that will last a millennium.

THE DRIVE: Head back to Front Royal, then go south on US 522 (Remount Rd) for about 9 miles to reach Huntly.

03 Huntly

Huntly is a small-ish town nestled in the green foothills of the Shenandoahs, lying just in the southern shadows of Front Royal. It's a good spot to refuel on some cosmopolitan culture and foodie deliciousness in the form of **Rappahannock Cellars** *(rappahannockcellars.com)*, one of the nicer wineries of north-central Virginia, where vineyard-covered hills shadow the horizon, like some slice of northern Italian pastoral prettiness that got lost somewhere in the upcountry of the Old Dominion. Give the port a whirl (well, maybe not if you're driving).

THE DRIVE: Head back to Front Royal, as you'll enter Skyline Drive from there. From the beginning of Skyline Drive, it's 5.5 miles to Dickey Ridge.

04 Skyline Drive: The Beginning

Skyline Drive is the scenic drive to end all scenic drives. The 75 overlooks, with views into the Shenandoah Valley and the Piedmont, are all breathtaking. In spring and summer, endless variations on the color green are sure to enchant, just as the vibrant reds and yellows will amaze you in autumn. This might be your chance to finally hike a section of the Appalachian Trail, which crosses Skyline Drive in 32 places.

The logical first stop on an exploration of Skyline Drive and Shenandoah National Park is the **Dickey Ridge Visitor Center** *(nps.gov/shen)*. It's not just an informative leaping-off point; it's a building with a fascinating history all of its own. This spot originally operated as a 'wild' dining hall in 1908 (back then that simply meant it had a terrace for dancing). However, it closed during WWII and didn't reopen until 1958, when it became a visitor center. Now it's one of the park's two main information centers and contains a little bit of everything you'll need to get started on your trip along Skyline Drive.

THE DRIVE: It's a twisty 19 more miles along Skyline Drive to Mathews Arm.

05 Mathews Arm & Elkwallow

Mathews Arm is the first major section of Shenandoah National Park you encounter after leaving Dickey Ridge. Before you get there, you can stop at a pullover at Mile 19.4 and embark on a 4.8-mile loop hike to **Little Devils Stairs**. Getting through this narrow gorge is as tough as the name suggests; expect hand-over-hand climbing for some portions.

> ☑ TOP TIP
>
> ### STONE MILEPOSTS
>
> Handy stone mileposts (MP) are still the best means of figuring out just where you are on Skyline Drive. They begin at Mile 0 near Front Royal, and end at Mile 105 at the park's southern entrance near Rockfish Gap.

At Mathews Arm there's a campground as well as an amphitheater, and some nice breezes; early on in your drive, you're already at a 2750ft altitude.

From the amphitheater, it's a 6.5-mile moderately taxing hike to lovely **Overall Run Falls**, the tallest in the national park (93ft). There are plenty of rock ledges where you can enjoy the view and snap a picture, but be warned that the falls sometime dry out in the summer.

Elkwallow Wayside, which includes a nice picnic area and lookout, is at Mile 24, just past Mathews Arm.

THE DRIVE: From Mathews Arm, proceed south along Skyline Drive for about 10 miles, then take the US 211 ramp westbound for about 7 miles to reach Luray.

06 Luray

Luray is a good spot to grab some grub and potentially rest your head if you're not into camping. It's also where you'll find the wonderful **Luray Caverns** *(luraycaverns.com)*, one of the most extensive cavern systems on the East Coast.

Here you can take a one-hour, roughly 1-mile guided tour of the caves, opened to the public more than 100 years ago. The rock formations throughout are quite stunning, and Luray boasts what is surely a one-of-a-kind attraction – the **Stalacpipe Organ** – in the pit of its belly. This crazy contraption has been banging out melodies on the rock formations for decades. As the guide says, the caves are 400 million years old 'if you believe in geological dating' (if the subtext is lost on you, understand this is a conservative part of the country where Creationism is widely accepted, if hotly debated). No matter what you believe in, you'll be impressed by the fantastic underground expanses.

> ### GARDEN MAZE ALERT
>
> Next to the Luray Caverns is an excellent opportunity to let your inner Shelley Duvall or Scatman Crothers run wild. Go screaming *The Shining*–style through the Garden Maze, but beware! This maze is harder than it looks and some could spend longer inside it than they anticipated. Paranormal and psychic abilities are permitted, but frowned upon, when solving the hedge maze. Redrum! Redrum!

THE DRIVE: Take US 211 east for 10 miles to get back on Skyline Drive. Then proceed 10 miles south along Skyline Drive to get to Skyland. Along the way you'll drive over the highest point of Skyline Drive (3680ft). At Mile 40.5, just before reaching Skyland, you can enjoy amazing views from the parking overlook at Thorofare Mountain (3595ft).

07 Skyland

Horse-fanciers will want to book a trail ride through Shenandoah at **Skyland Stables** *(goshenandoah.com)*. Rides last up to 2½ hours and are a great way to see the wildlife and epic vistas. Pony rides are also

Luray Caverns, Virginia
KATRINA HOFFMAN/SHUTTERSTOCK

available for the wee members of your party. This is a good spot to break up your trip if you're into hiking (and if you're on this trip, we're assuming you are).

You've got great access to local trailheads around here, and the sunsets are fabulous. The accommodations are a little rustic, but in a charming way (the Trout Cabin was built in 1911 and it feels like it, but we mean this in the most complimentary way possible). The place positively oozes nostalgia, but if you're into amenities, you may find it a little dilapidated.

THE DRIVE: It's only 1.5 miles south on Skyline Drive to get to the Whiteoak parking area.

PHOTO OPPORTUNITY

The fabulous 360-degree horizon at the top of Bearfence Mountain.

08 Whiteoak Canyon Area

At Mile 42.6, Whiteoak Canyon is another area of Skyline Drive that offers unmatched hiking and exploration opportunities. There are several parking areas that all provide different entry points to the various trails that snake through this ridge- and stream-scape.

Most hikers are attracted to Whiteoak Canyon for its waterfalls – there are six in total, with the tallest topping out at 86ft high. At the Whiteoak parking area, you can make a 4.6-mile round-trip hike to these cascades, but beware – it's a steep climb up and back to your car. To reach the next set of waterfalls, you'll have to add 2.7 miles to the round trip and prepare yourself for a steep (1100ft) elevation shift.

The **Limberlost Trail** and parking area is just south of Whiteoak Canyon. This is a moderately difficult 1.3-mile trek into spruce upcountry thick with hawks, owls and other birds; the boggy ground is home to many salamanders.

THE DRIVE: It's about 3 miles south of Whiteoak Canyon to the Hawksbill Area via Skyline Drive.

Whiteoak Canyon, Shenandoah National Park, Virginia

PHOTO SPIRIT/SHUTTERSTOCK

09 Hawksbill Area

Once you reach Mile 45.6, you've reached Hawksbill, the name of both this part of Skyline Drive and the tallest peak in Shenandoah National Park. Numerous trails in this area skirt the summits of the mountain.

Pull into the parking area at Hawksbill Gap (Mile 45.6). You've got a few hiking options to pick from. The **Lower Hawksbill Trail** is a steep 1.7-mile round trip that circles Hawksbill's lower slopes. The huff-inducing ascent yields a pretty great view over the park. Another great lookout lies at the end of the **Upper Hawksbill Trail**, a moderately difficult 2.1-mile trip. You can link up with the Appalachian Trail here via a spur called the Salamander Trail.

If you continue south for about 5 miles you'll reach Fishers Gap Overlook. The attraction here is the **Rose River Loop**, a 4-mile, moderately strenuous trail that is positively Edenic. Along the way you'll pass by waterfalls, under thick forest canopy and over swift-running streams.

THE DRIVE: From Fishers Gap, head about a mile south to the Byrd Visitor Center, technically located at Mile 51.

10 Byrd Visitor Center

The **Harry F Byrd Visitor Center** *(nps.gov/shen)* is the central visitor center of Shenandoah National Park, marking (roughly) a halfway point between the two ends of Skyline Drive. It's devoted to explaining the settlement and development of the Shenandoah Valley via a series of small but well-curated exhibitions; as such, it's a good place to stop and learn about the surrounding culture (and pick up backcountry camping permits). There are camping and ranger activities in the **Big Meadows** area, located across the road from the visitor center.

The **Story of the Forest** trail is an easy, paved, 1.8-mile loop that's quite pretty; the trailhead connects to the visitor center. You can also explore two nearby waterfalls. **Dark Hollow Falls**, which sounds (and looks) like something out of a Tolkien novel, is a 70ft-high cascade located at the end of a quite steep 1.4-mile trail. **Lewis Falls**, accessed via Big Meadows, is on a moderately difficult 3.3-mile trail that intersects the Appalachian Trail; at one point you'll be scrabbling up a rocky slope.

THE DRIVE: The Lewis Mountain area is about 5 miles south of the Byrd Visitor Center via Skyline Drive. Stop for good overlooks at Milam Gap and Naked Creek (both clearly signposted from the road).

JON BILOUS/SHUTTERSTOCK

Hawksbill Trail, Virginia

11 Lewis Mountain

Lewis Mountain is both the name of one of the major camping areas of Shenandoah National Park and a nearby 3570ft mountain. The trail to the mountain is only about a mile long with a small elevation gain, and leads to a nice overlook. But the best view here is at the **Bearfence Rock Scramble**. That name is no joke; this 1.2-mile hike gets steep and rocky, and you don't want to attempt it during or after rainfall. The reward is one of the best panoramas of the Shenandoahs. After you leave, remember there's still about 50 miles of Skyline Drive between you and the park exit at Rockfish Gap.

QUÉBEC
CANADA
USA
MAINE
Millinocket
Moosehead Lake
Lincoln
Flagstaff Lake
Mooselookmeguntic Lake
Pittsfield
Bangor
Waterville
Belfast
Bar Harbor
Augusta
Camden
Acadia National Park
Brunswick
Portland
St Albans
VERMONT
Lake Champlain
Burlington
Montpelier
Berlin
Littleton
Mt Washington
North Conway
White Mountain National Forest
Middlebury
Breadloaf Wilderness
Hanover
Rutland
Lake Winnipesaukee
NEW HAMPSHIRE
Concord
Manchester
Kittery
Hampton
ATLANTIC OCEAN
Bennington
Wilmington
Brattleboro
Gloucester
Marblehead
Pittsfield
October Mountain
MASSACHUSETTS
Boston
Springfield
Plymouth
Provincetown
RHODE ISLAND
Providence
Hartford
Sandwich
Cape Cod National Seashore
Waterbury
Hyannis
New Bedford
CONNECTICUT
New Haven
New London
Newport
Nantucket
09
10
11
12
13
14
15
0 100 km
0 50 miles

JOSEPH SOHM/SHUTTERSTOCK

Acadia National Park (p132), Maine

NEW ENGLAND

EXPLORE

NEW ENGLAND

New England is synonymous with a memorable medley of sights, smells and sounds. Craggy coastlines dotted with lonely lighthouses. Fresh lobsters served on weathered picnic tables. The shimmering colors of the autumnal flag flanking a quiet country road. Old, ivy-clad colleges, the hallowed halls of which are filled with hot-blooded scholars.

This collection of trips covers the best of New England. Perhaps you'll be moved to pick up a paintbrush, dust off your typewriter, maybe even get a PhD. Somehow, the country's northeast nook has that effect on folks.

Gloucester

On eastern Massachusetts' North Shore, Gloucester is one of New England's oldest towns (1623). It's a refreshingly authentic fishing town with museums, art galleries, beaches and even whale-watching tours out into the sheltered Stellwagen Bank. Lots of hotels and restaurants (the seafood couldn't, of course, be any fresher) make this a good base. And like any port town, there's a lively pub and live-music scene.

Burlington

With barely 50,000 souls, Vermont's largest city is also its most cosmopolitan. Burlington has a large student population, one of New England's more ethnically diverse populations, and a leafy ambience that makes it one of the country's greenest and most liveable cities. Selling points include museums, a buzzing arts scene, and a winery; Burlington's teddybear factory is something every town should have. B&Bs and inns, coupled with fabulously diverse restaurants, also take care of the necessaries. Close by, there's the magnificent Shelburne Farm and Shelburne Museum, and the Green Mountains loom just beyond the 'city' limits.

Newport

What's not to like about Newport, RI? The compact city is brimful of architecture that tells a fascinating historical story, from immaculately preserved 18th-century relics to ornate mansions overlooking the sea.

WHEN TO GO

Wherever you go, New England's world-renowned leafy fall hues are glorious (and roads can be crowded) from mid-September to late October. Ivy League campuses are full September through November, and the sun shines and everything is open (and busy) May through August. Vermont's high country can be snow-bound in winter.

There's a full calendar of festivals and activities, most of them inspired by Newport's prime seaside position, and the town's museums are excellent. Fine accommodations, from boutique belles to friendly B&Bs in suitably old-world structures, fine seafood-centric restaurants, and busy pubs mean you could easily spend a few days here before heading out for a drive.

Hanover

If you're setting out on a tour of New England's Ivy League towns, Hanover is almost guaranteed to put you in the right mood. Home to Dartmouth College, New Hampshire's Hanover is a New England university town par excellence. Leafy grounds and town commons, rivers animated by rowing crews, historic ivy-covered buildings: they're all here in abundance. Cafes, restaurants and bookshops line Main St, and there's a cluster of good places to stay in the town center as well.

Boston

Blessed by a history that places it at the center of the American story, Boston is so much more than one of the oldest cities in America. This has always been one of the most forward-looking cities in the country. Whether in the arts, the city's sporting endeavors or the seafood-meets-fusion-food-lab culinary scene, this is one metropolis that knows how to live. What else would you expect from a city that came of age during a revolution?

TRANSPORTATION

Airports abound in New England, with Boston far and away the main hub. Other state capitals (Providence, Hartford, Augusta, Concord and Montpelier) and other towns have airports but far fewer connections. Amtrak services along the New York–Boston–Montreal triangle stop in many New England towns, with buses serving the rest.

WHERE TO STAY

Rural guesthouses and B&Bs with bucketloads of charm coexist with historic hotels and Boston chic. Because New England is so compact, you're never far from any of these. Look for lavish boutique hotels in historic towns like New Haven, Little Compton and the myriad other small towns along the New England byways; try for a lake or water view in Rhode Island or Lake Champlain. Boston takes care of all budgets, from contemporary to timeless refits, while the **Blackwoods Campsite** in Acadia is the antithesis of the big city noise (and facilities).

RESOURCES

Fall Foliage Tracker
New Hampshire's up-to-the-minute guide to fall leaves. *visitnh.gov/seasonal-trips/fall/foliage-tracker*

Acadia National Park
Definitive guide to this beautiful park. *nps.gov/acad/index.htm*

Vermont
Among the best online resources for one of New England's prettiest corners. *vermontvacation.com*

Boston Magazine
An online resource full of great local tips on dining and the arts in Boston. *bostonmagazine.com*

WHAT'S ON

Fall Festivals
From Maine to Vermont, small fall festivals bring fall weekends to life.

Celebration of Lupine
This June festival showcases the incredible wildflowers of New Hampshire's Franconia region.

Boston Marathon
One of the world's best and most famous marathons.

Patriots' Day
Commemorates the 1775 Battle of Lexington and the American Revolution; it'll be 250 years in 2025 .

09

★ BEST FOR

HISTORY

The first 35 miles (stops one to four) showcase coastal New England, past and present.

NEW ENGLAND

COASTAL NEW ENGLAND

Boston Harbor Lighthouse, Boston (p100), Massachusetts

DURATION: 6–8 DAYS

DISTANCE: 240 MILES / 386KM

GREAT FOR: FAMILIES, HISTORY, NATURE

BEST TIME TO GO: SITES ARE OPEN AND WEATHER IS FINE FROM MAY TO SEPTEMBER.

From a pirate's perspective, there was no better base in Colonial America than Newport, given the easy access to trade routes and friendly local merchants. Until 1723, that is, when the new governor ceremoniously hanged 26 sea bandits at Gravelly Point. This classic trip highlights the region's intrinsic connection to the sea, from upstart pirates to upper-crust merchants, from Gloucester fisherfolk to New Bedford whalers, from clipper ships to submarines.

LINK YOUR TRIP

11 Rhode Island: East Bay
Join at Newport, or head north on I-95 and south on RI 77 to start at Little Compton.

14 Ivy League Tour
Start in New Haven and do the Ivy League Tour in reverse.

01 Gloucester

Founded in 1623 by English fisherfolk, Gloucester is among New England's oldest towns. This port on Cape Ann has made its living from fishing for almost 400 years, and has inspired works like Rudyard Kipling's Captains Courageous and Sebastian Junger's The Perfect Storm. Visit the **Maritime Gloucester** *(maritimegloucester.org)* museum to see the working waterfront in action. There is plenty of hands-on educational fun, including an outdoor aquarium and exhibits. **Cape Ann Whale Watch** *(seethewhales.com)* boats depart from nearby for the excellent **Stellwagen Bank National Marine Sanctuary** *(stellwagen.noaa.gov)* offshore.

THE DRIVE: Head out of town on Western Ave (MA 127), cruising past *The Gloucester Fisherman* memorial and Stage Fort Park. This road follows the coastline

SHORETIE/SHUTTERSTOCK

south through swanky seaside towns like Manchester-by-the-Sea and Beverly Farms, with glimpses of the bay. After about 14 miles, cross Essex Bridge and continue south into Salem. For a quicker trip, take MA 128 S to MA 114.

02 Salem

Salem's glory dates to the 18th century, when it was a center for clipper-ship trade with the Far East, thanks to the enterprising efforts of merchant Elias Hasket Derby. His namesake Derby Wharf is now the center of the **Salem Maritime National Historic Site** *(nps.gov/sama),* which includes the 1871 lighthouse, the tall ship *Friendship* and the state custom house.

Many Salem vessels followed Derby's ship *Grand Turk* around the Cape of Good Hope, and soon the owners founded the East India Marine Society to provide warehousing services for their ships' logs and charts. The new company's charter required the establishment of 'a museum in which to house the natural and artificial curiosities' brought back by members' ships. The collection was the basis for what is now the world-class **Peabody Essex Museum** *(pem.org).* Still today, the museum contains an amazing collection of Asian art, among other treasures.

A stroll around town reveals some impressive architecture – grand houses that were once sea captains' homes.

THE DRIVE: Take Lafayette St (MA 114) south out of Salem center, driving past the campus of Salem State College. After crossing an inlet, the road bends east and becomes Pleasant St as it enters Marblehead center.

03 Marblehead

First settled in 1629, Marblehead is a maritime village with winding streets, brightly painted houses, and sailing yachts bobbing at moorings in the harbor. This is the Boston area's premier yachting port and one of New England's most prestigious addresses. Clustered around the harbor, Marblehead center is dotted with historic houses, art galleries and waterside parks.

LUA CARLOS MARTINS/SHUTTERSTOCK

Boston Harbor Islands, Massachusetts

THE DRIVE: Drive south on MA 129, exiting Marblehead and continuing through the seaside town of Swampscott. At the traffic circle, take the first exit onto MA 1A, which continues south through Lynn and Revere. Take the VFW Pkwy (MA 1A) to the Revere Beach Pkwy (MA 16) to the Northeast Expwy (US 1), which goes over Tobin Bridge and into Boston.

04 Boston

Boston's seaside location has influenced every aspect of its history, but it's only in recent years that the waterfront has become an attractive and accessible destination for visitors. Now you can stroll along the **Rose Kennedy Greenway** *(rosekennedy greenway.org)*, with the sea on one side and the city on the other. The focal point of the waterfront is the excellent **New England Aquarium** *(neaq.org)*, home to seals, penguins, turtles and oodles of fish.

From Long Wharf, you can catch a ferry out to the **Boston Harbor Islands** *(bostonharborislands.org)* for berry picking, beachcombing and sunbathing. Harbor cruises and trolley tours also depart from these docks. If you prefer to keep your feet on dry land, take a walk to explore Boston's flower-filled parks and shop-lined streets.

THE DRIVE: Drive south out of Boston on I-93. You'll recognize the urban 'hood of Dorchester by pretty Savin Hill Cove and the landmark Rainbow Swash painted on the gas tank. At exit 4, take MA 24 S toward Brockton, then MA 140 S toward New Bedford. Take I-195 E for 2 miles, exiting onto MA 18 for New Bedford.

05 New Bedford

During its heyday as a whaling port (1765–1860), New Bedford commanded some 400 whaling ships – a vast fleet that brought in hundreds of thousands of barrels of whale oil for lighting lamps. Novelist Herman Melville worked on one of these ships for four years, and thus set his celebrated novel *Moby-Dick* in New Bedford.

The excellent, hands-on **New Bedford Whaling Museum** *(whaling museum.org)* commemorates this history. A 66ft skeleton of a blue whale welcomes you at the entrance. Inside, you can tramp the decks of the Lagoda, a fully rigged, half-size replica of an actual whaling bark.

> PHOTO OPPORTUNITY
>
> Pose for a snap alongside *The Gloucester Fisherman.*

THE DRIVE: Take I-195 W for about 10 miles. In Fall River, head south on MA 24, which becomes RI 24 as you cross into Rhode Island. Cross the bridge, with views of Mt Hope Bay to the north and Sakonnet River to the south, then merge onto RI 114, heading south into Newport.

06 Newport

Blessed with a deepwater harbor, Newport has been a shipbuilding base since 1646. Bowen's and Bannister's Wharves, once working wharves, now typify Newport's transformation from a working city-by-the-sea to a resort town. Take a narrated cruise with **Classic Cruises of Newport** *(cruisenewport.com)* on *Rum Runner II*, a Prohibition-era bootlegging vessel, or *Madeleine*, a 72ft schooner.

Newport's harbor remains one of the most active yachting centers in the country, while its waterfront boasts a standout lineup of other attractions. Make sure to tour at least one of the city's magnificent mansions, such as the **Breakers** or **Rosecliff** *(newportmansions.org)*, then stop in for a visit at **Fort Adams** *(fortadams.org)*, one of the largest seacoast fortifications in the US. In summer it's the venue for the **Newport Jazz Festival** *(newport jazz.org)* and the **Newport Folk Festival** *(newportfolk.org)*.

THE DRIVE: Head west out of Newport on RI 138, swooping over Newport Bridge onto Conanicut Island and then over Jamestown Bridge to pick up US 1 for the drive into Mystic. The views of the bay from both bridges are a highlight.

07 Mystic

Many of Mystic's clipper ships launched from George Greenman & Co Shipyard, now the site of the **Mystic Seaport Museum** *(mysticseaport.org)*. Today the museum covers 17 acres and includes more than 60 historic buildings, four tall ships and almost 500 smaller vessels. Interpreters staffing all the buildings are glad to discuss their crafts and trades. The museum's exhibits also include a replica of the 77ft slave ship *Amistad*.

If the call of the sea beckons, set sail on the **Argia** *(argiamystic.com)*, a replica of a 19th-century schooner, which cruises down the Mystic River to Fishers' Island Sound.

THE DRIVE: The 7-mile drive from Mystic to Groton along US 1 S is through built-up suburbs and light industrial areas. To hop across the Thames River to New London, head north along North St to pick up I-95 S.

08 Groton & New London

Groton is home to the US Naval Submarine Base, the first and the largest in the country. It is off-limits to the public, but you can visit the **Historic Ship Nautilus & Submarine Force Museum** *(ussnautilus.org)*, which is home to Nautilus, the world's first nuclear-powered submarine and the first sub to transit the North Pole.

☑ TOP TIP

PARKING IN BOSTON

Parking in downtown Boston is prohibitively expensive. For more affordable rates, cross the Fort Point Channel and park in the Seaport District. There are some (relatively) reasonable deals to be found in the lots on Northern Ave (near the Institute of Contemporary Art); alternatively, head for the Necco Street Garage (further south, off A St), which charges only $14 per day on weekends and $14 for overnight parking on weekdays.

Salem Maritime National Historic Site (p99), Salem, Massachusetts

WANGKUN JIA/SHUTTERSTOCK

♥ WHY I LOVE THIS TRIP

ISABEL ALBISTON, WRITER

Pretty seaside towns and worthwhile museums are two highlights of this trip, but another is the drive itself. It's hard to beat the exhilaration of driving with the window down, hair whipping in the wind, with the Atlantic at your side and the open road ahead, grabbing glimpses of grand mansions that allow you to slip, for a moment, into a different life.

Across the river, New London has a similarly illustrious seafaring history, although these days it's built a reputation for itself as a budding creative center. Each summer it hosts **Sailfest** *(sailfest.org)*, a three-day festival with free entertainment, topped off by the second-largest fireworks display in the Northeast. There's also a Summer Concert Series, organized by **Hygienic Art** *(hygienic.org)*.

THE DRIVE: It's a 52-mile drive from Groton or New London to New Haven along I-95 S. The initial stages of the drive plow through the suburbs, but after that the interstate runs through old coastal towns such as Old Lyme, Old Saybrook and Guilford.

09 New Haven

Although most famous for its Ivy League university, Yale, New Haven also played an important role in the burgeoning antislavery movement when, in 1839, the trial of mutineering Mendi tribesmen was held in New Haven's District Court.

Following their illegal capture by Spanish slave traders, the tribesmen, led by Joseph Cinqué, seized the schooner *Amistad* and sailed to New Haven seeking refuge. Pending the successful outcome of the trial, the men were held in a jailhouse on the green, where a 14ft-high bronze memorial now stands. It was the first civil-rights case held in the country.

For a unique take on the New Haven shoreline, take the 3-mile round trip on the **Shore Line Trolley** *(shorelinetrolley.org)*, which takes you from East Haven to Short Beach in Branford. A wealth of art and architecture is packed into the streets of downtown New Haven.

Rosecliff (p100), Newport, Massachusetts

FELIX LIPOV/SHUTTERSTOCK

WANGKUN JIA/SHUTTERSTOCK

Revere Beach, Massachusetts

REVERE BEACH

Cruising through Revere, MA 1A parallels the wide, sandy stretch of Revere Beach, which proudly proclaims itself America's first public beach, established in 1896. Scenic but soulless, the condo-fronted beach belies the history of this place, which was a raucous boardwalk and amusement park for most of the 20th century. Famous for roller coasters, dance halls and the Wonderland dog track, Revere Beach attracted hundreds of thousands of sunbathers and fun-seekers during summer months.

The area deteriorated in the 1970s due to crime and pollution. In 1978 a historic blizzard wiped out many of the remaining buildings and businesses, and the 'Coney Island of New England' was relegated to the annals of history.

Revere Beach benefited from a cleanup effort in the 1980s; nowadays, the beach itself is lovely to look at and a safe place to swim. Unfortunately, dominated by high-end condominium complexes, the area retains nothing of its former charm. Only one vestige of 'old' Revere Beach remains: the world-famous **Kelly's Roast Beef** *(kellysroastbeef.com)*, which has been around since 1951 and still serves up the best roast-beef sandwiches and clam chowder in town. There's no indoor seating, so pull up some sand and enjoy the view. Beware of the seagulls: they're crazy for roast beef.

STAY AWHILE

BOSTON

BY MARGOT BIGG

As New England's academic, economic and cultural hub, Boston feels like a city that's simultaneously anchored in tradition and history, and poised for the future. It's one of the oldest cities in the US, with four centuries of architecture to show for it. Boston also played a pivotal role in the American Revolution and the founding of the United States, drawing in history buffs from across the nation as a result.

I love that Boston has the big-city vibe of an American metropolis without the endless sprawl. The city is compact and walkable, making it easy to stroll between key attractions such as the **Museum of Fine Arts** *(mfa.org)* and the **Boston Public Library** *(bpl.org)* without having to hail a cab. If you love walking as much as you enjoy history, I recommend taking the Freedom Trail (thefreedomtrail.org), a 2.5-mile path connecting 16 of the city's top historic sites.

Of course, the fabric of Boston stretches beyond its public institutions and downtown core. To get a feel for daily life, I'd suggest spending some time in the South End, aka 'Southie,' a hip neighborhood with beautiful Victorian brownstones and lots of places to eat (especially along Tremont St). If you visit between May and October, hit up the neighborhood's **SoWa Open Market** *(sowaboston.com)*, a massive Sunday bazaar packed with artisan stalls and food trucks. For an even more local feel, head further south to the Jamaica Plain ('JP') neighborhood, where you'll find great shopping and dining along Centre St, one of the neighborhood's main drags.

LINK YOUR TRIP

Boston is a great place to stop while on the **09 Coastal New England** (p98) road trip.

Left: Boston Public Library, Boston, Massachusetts; Right: Old State House, Boston, Massachusetts

LEFT TO RIGHT: KIMBERLY MAROON/LONELY PLANET, SEAN PAVONE/SHUTTERSTOCK

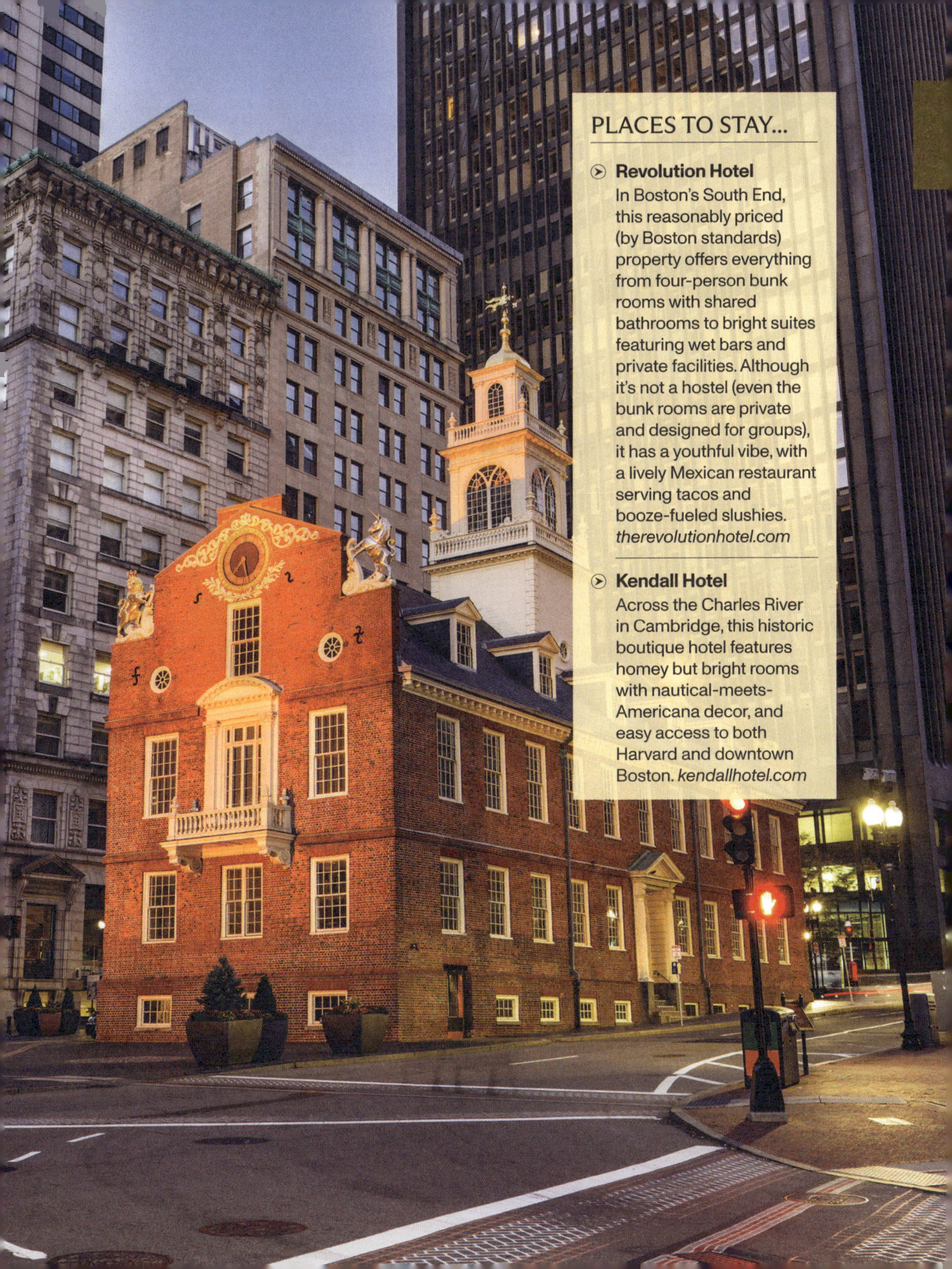

PLACES TO STAY...

Revolution Hotel
In Boston's South End, this reasonably priced (by Boston standards) property offers everything from four-person bunk rooms with shared bathrooms to bright suites featuring wet bars and private facilities. Although it's not a hostel (even the bunk rooms are private and designed for groups), it has a youthful vibe, with a lively Mexican restaurant serving tacos and booze-fueled slushies. *therevolutionhotel.com*

Kendall Hotel
Across the Charles River in Cambridge, this historic boutique hotel features homey but bright rooms with nautical-meets-Americana decor, and easy access to both Harvard and downtown Boston. *kendallhotel.com*

10

★ BEST FOR

OUTDOORS

Ziplining through the tree canopy in Bretton Woods.

NEW ENGLAND

FALL FOLIAGE TOUR

DURATION: 5–7 DAYS

DISTANCE: 424 MILES / 682KM

GREAT FOR: NATURE, FAMILIES

BEST TIME TO GO: MID-SEPTEMBER TO LATE OCTOBER FOR THE HARVEST AND AUTUMN LEAVES.

Housatonic River, Connecticut

The brilliance of fall in New England is legendary. Scarlet and sugar maples, ash, birch, beech, dogwood, tulip tree, oak and sassafras all contribute to the carnival of autumn color. But this trip is about much more than just flora and fauna: the harvest spirit makes for family outings to seasonal fairs, leisurely walks along dappled trails, and tables groaning beneath delicious seasonal produce.

LINK YOUR TRIP

09 Coastal New England
From North Conway, take NH 16 south to I-95, then head east on MA 128 to Gloucester.

14 Ivy League Tour
Follow NH 16 and I-93 northwest into Vermont. Then follow I-91 south all the way to Hanover, NH.

01 Candlewood Lake

With a surface area of 8.4 sq miles, Candlewood is the largest lake in Connecticut. On the western shore, the **Squantz Pond State Park** *(ct.gov)* is popular with leaf-peepers, who come to amble along the pretty shoreline. In Brookfield and Sherman, quiet vineyards with acres of gnarled grapevines line the hillsides. Visitors can tour the intimate **White Silo Farm** *(whitesilowinery.com),* where the focus is on specialty wines made from farm-grown fruit.

On the lake's further shore, Lover's **Leap State Park** *(ctparks.gov)* allows a short walk over a classic iron bridge to a divine view of the Housatonic River, framed by foliage.

THE DRIVE: From Danbury, at the southern tip of the lake, you have a choice of heading 28 miles north via US 7, taking in Brookfield and New Milford (or trailing the scenic eastern

SHANSHAN0312/SHUTTERSTOCK

shoreline along Candlewood Lake Rd S); or heading 26 miles north along CT 37 and CT 39 via New Fairfield, Squantz Pond and Sherman, before reconnecting with US 7 to Kent.

02 Kent

Kent has previously been voted the spot in all of New England (yes, even beating Vermont) for fall foliage viewing. Situated prettily in the Litchfield Hills on the banks of the Housatonic River, it is surrounded by dense woodlands. For a sweeping view of them, hike up **Cobble Mountain in Macedonia Brook State Park** *(ctparks.gov)*, a wooded oasis 2 miles north of town. The steep climb to the rocky ridge affords panoramic views of the foliage against a backdrop of the Taconic and Catskill mountain ranges.

Don't miss the 250ft waterfall at **Kent Falls State Park**, which though spectacular is not too challenging a climb, with plenty of viewing platforms along the way.

The 2175-mile Georgia-to-Maine **Appalachian National Scenic Trail** *(appalachiantrail.com)* also runs through Kent and up to Salisbury on the Massachusetts border. Unlike much of the trail, the Kent section offers a mostly flat 5-mile river walk alongside the Housatonic. The trailhead is accessed on River Rd, off CT 341.

THE DRIVE: The 15-mile drive from Kent to Housatonic Meadows State Park along US 7 is one of the most scenic drives in Connecticut. The single-lane road dips and weaves between thick stands of forest, past Kent Falls State Park with its tumbling waterfall (visible from the road), and through West Cornwall's picturesque covered bridge, which spans the Housatonic River.

03 Housatonic Meadows State Park

During the spring thaw, the churning waters of the Housatonic challenge kayakers and canoeists. By summer the scenic waterway transforms into a lazy, flat river, perfect for fly-fishing. In **Housatonic Meadows State Park** *(ctparks.gov)*, campers vie for a spot on the banks of the river while hikers take to the hills on the Appalachian Trail. **Housatonic River Outfitters** *(dryflies.com)* runs guided fishing trips with gourmet picnics.

Popular with artists and photographers, one of the most photographed fall scenes is the **Cornwall Bridge**, an antique covered bridge that stretches across the broad river, framed by vibrantly colored foliage.

THE DRIVE: Continue north along US 7 toward the Massachusetts border and Great Barrington, 27 miles away. After a few miles you leave the forested slopes of the park behind and enter expansive rolling countryside dotted with large, red-and-white barns. Look out for hand-painted signs advertising farm produce and consider stopping overnight in Falls Village, which has an excellent B&B.

04 Berkshires

Blanketing the westernmost part of Massachusetts, the rounded mountains of the Berkshires turn crimson and gold as early as mid-September. The effective capital of the Berkshires is Great Barrington, a formerly industrial town whose streets are now lined with art galleries and upscale restaurants. It's the perfect place to pack your picnic or rest your legs before or after a hike in nearby **Beartown State Forest** *(mass.gov/dcr)*.

Crisscrossing some 12,000 acres, hiking trails yield spectacular views of wooded hillsides and pretty Benedict Pond.

Further north, October Mountain State Forest (mass.gov/dcr) is the state's largest tract of green space (16,127 acres), also interwoven with hiking trails. The name – attributed to Herman Melville – gives a good indication of when this park is at its loveliest.

THE DRIVE: Drive north on US 7, the spine of the Berkshires, cruising 11 miles through Great Barrington and Stockbridge. In Lee, the highway merges with scenic US 20, from where you can access October Mountain. Continue 16 miles north through Lenox and Pittsfield to Lanesborough. Turn right on N Main St and follow the signs to the Mt Greylock State Reservation entrance.

LOCAL KNOWLEDGE

KENT FALLS

Kent is a great place to base yourself in the fall, with lots of accessible spots for viewing the leaves and good amenities in the pretty town center. The best hiking trail in season is the section that connects with the Appalachian Trail at Caleb's Peak, affording fantastic views. If you're less able to hike, the easiest way to get a beautiful vista is to head 5 miles south out of town on US 7 to **Kent Falls State Park** *(ctparks.gov)*, which is unmissable on your right. The falls' wonderfully lazy cascade is right before you and there are lots of easy trails into the forest.

05 Mt Greylock State Reservation

At 3491ft, Massachusetts' highest peak is perhaps not very high, but a climb up the 92ft **War Veterans Memorial Tower** rewards you with a panorama stretching up to 100 verdant miles, across the Taconic, Housatonic and Catskill ranges, and over five states. Even if the weather seems drab from the foot, driving up to the summit may well lift you above the gray blanket. Note parking at the summit costs $20.

Mt Greylock State Reservation *(mass.gov/locations/mount-greylock-state-reservation)* has some 45 miles of hiking trails, including a portion of the Appalachian Trail. Pull-offs on the road up – including some that lead to waterfalls – make it easy to get at least a little hike in before reaching the top of Mt Greylock.

THE DRIVE: Return to US 7 and continue north through the quintessential college town of Williamstown. Cross the Vermont border and continue north through the historic village of Bennington. Just north of Bennington, turn left on VT 7A and continue north to Manchester (51 miles total).

06 Manchester

Stylish Manchester is known for its magnificent New England architecture. For fall foliage views, head south of the center and take the **Mt Equinox Skyline Drive** *(equinoxmountain.com)* to the summit of 3848ft Mt Equinox, the highest mountain accessible by car in the Taconic Range. Wind up the 5.2 miles, seemingly to the top of the world, where the 360-degree panorama offers views of the Adirondacks, the lush Battenkill Valley and Montreal's Mt Royal.

If early snow makes Mt Equinox inaccessible, visit 412-acre **Hildene** *(hildene.org)*, a Georgian Revival mansion that was once home to the Lincoln family. It's filled with presidential memorabilia and sits nestled at the edge of the Green Mountains, with access to 8 miles of wooded walking trails.

THE DRIVE: Take VT 7 north, following the western slopes of the Green Mountains through Rutland and Middlebury to reach Burlington (100 miles) on the shores of Lake Champlain.

07 Lake Champlain

With a surface area of 490 sq miles straddling New York, Vermont and Quebec, Lake Champlain is the largest freshwater lake in the US after the Great Lakes.

On its eastern side, Burlington is a gorgeous base for enjoying the lake. Explore it on foot, then scoot down to the wooden promenade, take a swing on the four-person rocking benches and consider a bike ride along the 7.5-mile lakeside bike path.

For the best offshore foliage views, we love the *Friend Ship* sailboat at **Whistling Man Schooner Company** *(whistlingman.com)*, a 43ft sloop that accommodates just 17 passengers. Next door, **ECHO, Leahy Center for Lake Champlain**

Echo Lake, Franconia Notch State Park (p111), New Hampshire
HAVESEEN/SHUTTERSTOCK

WHY I LOVE THIS TRIP

BRIAN KLUEPFEL, WRITER

Imagine you are a painter. Or a hiker. Or a writer (oh, that's me). As the hills of New England turn from the color of old broccoli to an autumnal range of browns, yellows, oranges and reds, you can't help but be inspired: to paint, hike, write or just gawk at this wonder as it frames waterfalls, christens the hummocks and hills, and is brilliantly reflected in awaiting lakes.

LOCAL KNOWLEDGE

NORTHERN BERKSHIRE FALL FOLIAGE PARADE

If your timing is right, you can stop in North Adams for the **Northern Berkshire Fall Foliage Parade** *(berkshire.com)* – and festival – held in late September or early October. Held for over 70 years, the event follows a changing theme, but it always features music, food and fun – and, of course, foliage.

(echovermont.org) explores the history and ecosystem of the lake, including a famous snapshot of 'Champ,' Lake Champlain's mythical sea creature.

THE DRIVE: Take I-89 S to Montpelier, savoring gorgeous views of Vermont's iconic Mt Mansfield and Camel's Hump, then continue northeast on US 2 to St Johnsbury, where you can pick up I-93 S across the New Hampshire line to Littleton. Take the eastbound US 302 exit and continue toward Crawford Notch State Park and Bretton Woods. The drive is 115 miles.

08 Bretton Woods

Unbuckle your seat belts and step away from the car. You're not just peeping at leaves today, you're swooping past them on ziplines that drop 1000ft at 30mph. The four-season **Bretton Woods Canopy Tour** *(brettonwoods.com)* includes a hike through the woods, a stroll over sky bridges and a swoosh down 10 cables to tree platforms.

If this leaves you craving even higher views, cross US 302 and drive 6 miles on Base Rd to the coal-burning, steam-powered **Mount Washington Cog Railway** *(thecog.com)* at the western base of Mt Washington, the highest peak in New England. This railway has been hauling sightseers to the summit since 1869.

THE DRIVE: Cross through Crawford Notch and continue 20 miles southeast on US 302, a gorgeous route through the White Mountains that parallels

Bretton Woods, New Hampshire

RUDY MAREEL/SHUTTERSTOCK

the Saco River and the Conway Scenic Railroad. At the junction of NH 16 and US 302, continue 5 miles on US 302 into North Conway.

09 North Conway

Many of the best restaurants, pubs and inns in North Conway come with expansive views of the nearby mountains. If you're traveling with kids or you skipped the cog railway ride up Mt Washington, consider an excursion on the antique steam-powered Valley Train with the **Conway Scenic Railroad** *(conwayscenic.com);* it's a short but sweet round-trip ride through the Mt Washington Valley from North Conway to Conway, 11 miles south, with the Moat Mountains and the Saco River as your scenic backdrop.

DETOUR

Kancamagus Scenic Byway
Start: 09 North Conway

Just south of North Conway, the 34.5-mile Kancamagus Scenic Byway, otherwise known as NH 112, passes through the White Mountains from Conway to Lincoln, NH. You'll drive alongside the Saco River and enjoy sweeping views of the Presidential Range from Kancamagus Pass. Inviting trailheads and pull-offs line the road. From Lincoln at the highway's western end, a short drive north on I-93 leads to **Franconia Notch State Park** *(nhstateparks.org),* where the foliage in September and October is simply spectacular.

RITU MANOJ JETHANI/SHUTTERSTOCK

PHOTO OPPORTUNITY

Kent Falls set against a backdrop of autumnal colors.

Kent Falls, Kent Falls State Park (p107), Connecticut

11

NEW ENGLAND

RHODE ISLAND: EAST BAY

DURATION: 3–4 DAYS

DISTANCE: 65 MILES / 106KM

GREAT FOR: HISTORY, FAMILIES, NATURE

BEST TIME TO GO: MAY TO OCTOBER FOR GOOD WEATHER AND FARM FOOD.

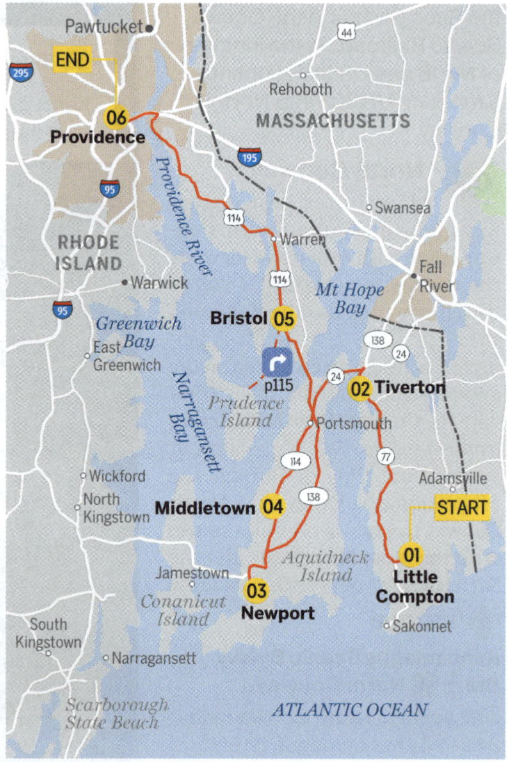

Rhode Island's jagged East Bay tells the American story in microcosm. Start in Little Compton with the grave of Elizabeth Pabodie (1623–1717), the first European settler born in New England. Then meander through historic Tiverton and Bristol, where enslavers and merchants grew rich. Prosperous as they were, their modest homes barely hold a candle to the mansions, museums and libraries of Newport's capitalist kings and Providence's intelligentsia.

LINK YOUR TRIP

05 The Jersey Shore
Drive south on I-95 and take the Garden State Pkwy to Asbury Park.

10 Fall Foliage Tour
Take I-95 south from Providence to CT 9 heading northwest across the state. Take I-84 west to the border. CT 37 and CT 39 lead to Sherman.

01 Little Compton

No doubt tiring of the big-city bustle of 17th-century Portsmouth, early settler Samuel Wilbor crossed the Sakonnet River to Little Compton. His plain family home, **Wilbor House** *(littlecompton.org)*, built in 1690, still stands on a manicured lawn behind a traditional five-bar gate and tells the story of eight generations of Wilbors who lived here.

The rest of Little Compton, from the hand-hewn clapboard houses to the white-steepled **United Congregational Church**, overlooking the Old Commons Burial Ground, is one of the oldest and quaintest villages in all of New England. Elizabeth Pabodie, daughter of *Mayflower* pilgrims Priscilla and John Alden and the first settler born in New England, is buried here.

Lovely, ocean-facing **Goosewing Beach** is the only good public beach. Parking costs $20 ($25 on weekends and public holidays) at **South Shore Beach**, from where you can walk across a small tidal inlet.

NAGEL PHOTOGRAPHY/SHUTTERSTOCK

★ BEST FOR

HISTORY

Find modern America's beginnings in Little Compton.

Rhode Island State House (p115), Providence, Rhode Island

THE DRIVE: Head north along RI 77 at a leisurely pace, enjoying the peaceful country scenery of rambling stone walls and clapboard farmhouses. As you approach Tiverton, look out to your left and you'll occasionally get glimpses out to the water, which is particularly pretty in the late afternoon.

02 Tiverton

En route to Tiverton's Four Corners historic quarter, stop in at Carolyn's **Sakonnet Vineyard** *(sakonnet wine.com)* for a glass of rosé or sparkling wine. This will set you up nicely for the gourmet treats that await in Tiverton, such as **Gray's Ice Cream** *(graysicecream.com)*, where over 20 flavors are made on-site daily, and waterfront dining at the fabulous **Boat House** *(boathousetiverton.com)*. Tiverton also has a clutch of local artists as well as chic boutiques hawking classy, original wares.

THE DRIVE: Head north up Main St, leaving Tiverton and its green fields behind you, and merge onto the westbound RI 138/RI 24 S, which leads you directly into Newport.

03 Newport

Established by religious moderates fleeing persecution from Massachusetts Puritans, the 'new port' flourished to become the fourth-richest city in the newly independent colony. Downtown, the Colonial-era architecture is well-preserved along with notable landmarks, such as Washington Sq's **Colony House**.

Just off the square, the gaslights of the **White Horse Tavern**, America's oldest tavern, still burn, and on Touro St, America's first synagogue, **Touro Synagogue** *(tourosynagogue.org)*, still stands. Tour the past on a guided **Newport Historical Society Walking Tour** *(newporthistorytours.org)*.

Fascinating as Newport's early history is, it struggles to compete with the town's latter-day success, when wealthy industrialists made Newport their playground and built summer houses along lantern-lined Bellevue Ave. Modeled on Italianate palazzos, French chateaux and Elizabethan manor houses, the stately

FAINA GUREVICH/SHUTTERSTOCK

Blithewold Mansion, Bristol, Rhode Island

LOCAL KNOWLEDGE

POLO IN PORTSMOUTH

Drab though the urban environs of Portsmouth may seem, in-the-know locals rate Portsmouth as a family-friendly destination. Not least because the polo matches hosted at **Glen Farm** make for a great family day out. Home to the **Newport Polo Club** *(newportpolo.com)*, the 700-acre 'farm' was assembled by New York businessman Henry Taylor, who sought to create a gentleman's country seat in the grand English tradition. In summer, the farm is host to the club's polo matches (check the website for dates), which are a perfect way to enjoy the property and get an authentic taste of Newport high life.

homes are now collectively referred to as the **Newport Mansions**. Tour the most outstanding with the **Preservation Society of Newport County** *(newportmansions.org)*, or view them from the **Cliff Walk** *(cliffwalk.com)*, a narrow footpath that snakes along the ocean's edge and offers stunning views.

THE DRIVE: Leave Newport by way of 10-mile Ocean Dr, which starts just south of Fort Adams and curls around the southern shore, past the grand mansions, and up Bellevue Ave before intersecting with Memorial Blvd. Turn right here for a straight shot into Middletown.

04 Middletown

Flo's *(flosclamshacks.com)* jaunty red-and-white clam shack and her competition, **Anthony's Seafood** *(anthonysseafood.net)*, would be enough reason to visit Middletown, which now merges seamlessly with Newport. But the best fried clams in town taste better after a day on **Second Beach**, the largest and most beautiful beach on Aquidneck Island. Curving around Sachuest Bay, it is backed by the 450-acre **Norman Bird Sanctuary** *(normanbirdsanctuary.org)*, which teems with migrating birds. All this driving might inspire you to check out the stunning collection of antique, luxury, hot-rod and muscle cars at the **Newport Car Museum** *(newportcarmuseum.org)*, located just north of Middletown, in Portsmouth.

THE DRIVE: Leave Aquidneck Island via East Main Rd, which takes you north through the suburbs of Middletown and Portsmouth. After 6.5 miles, pick up RI 114 and cross the bay via the scenic Mt Hope suspension bridge. From here it's a short 3-mile drive into Bristol.

05 Bristol

One-fifth of all enslaved people transported to America were brought in Bristol ships and by the 18th century the town was one of the country's major commercial ports. The world-class **Herreshoff Marine Museum** *(herreshoff.org)* showcases some of America's finest yachts.

Local resident Augustus Van Wickle bought a 72ft Herreshoff yacht for his wife Bessie in 1895, but having nowhere suitable to moor it, he then had to build **Blithewold Mansion** *(blithewold.org)*. The arts-and-crafts mansion sits in a peerless position on Narragansett Bay and is particularly lovely in spring.

Bristol's **Colt State Park** *(riparks.ri.gov/parks/colt-state-park)* is Rhode Island's most scenic park, with its entire western border front-

YINGNA CAI/SHUTTERSTOCK

Cliff Walk, Newport (p113), Rhode Island

ing Narragansett Bay, fringed by 4 miles of cycling trails.

THE DRIVE: From Bristol it's a straight drive north along RI 114, through the suburbs of Warren and Barrington, to Providence. After 17 miles, merge onto I-195 W, which takes you the remaining 18 miles into the center of town.

DETOUR

Prudence Island
Start: 05 Bristol

Idyllic Prudence Island sits in the middle of Narragansett Bay, an easy 25-minute ferry ride from Bristol *(prudencebayislands transport.com)*. Originally used for farming and later as a summer vacation spot for families from Providence and New York, who traveled here on the Fall River Line steamer, the island now has only 88 inhabitants. There are some fine Victorian and beaux-arts houses near **Stone Wharf**, a lighthouse and a small store, but otherwise it's wild and unspoiled. Perfect for mountain biking (BYO bike), barbecues, fishing and paddling.

06 Providence

A stroll along Benefit St or, better still, a **Rhode Island Historical Society** *(rihs.org)* walking tour, reveals the city's rich architectural legacy. Here alone are scores of Colonial, Federal and Revival houses. Amid them you'll find William Strickland's 1838 **Providence Athenaeum** *(providenceathenaeum.org)*, with a book collection that dates to 1753.

Atop the hill sits **Brown University**, with its Gothic and beaux-arts buildings. Nearby is the **John Brown House Museum** *(rihs.org/locations/the-john-brown-house-museum)*, a must-see for American history buffs.

End the tour with a nod toward the bronze statue of Independent Man, which graces the pearly white dome of the impressive **Rhode Island State House** *(ristatehouse.org)*.

12

NEW ENGLAND

LAKE CHAMPLAIN BYWAY

DURATION: 1–2 DAYS

DISTANCE: 53 MILES / 85KM

GREAT FOR: WINE, NATURE

BEST TIME TO GO: JUNE TO OCTOBER FOR LONG, SUMMERY DAYS AND ABUNDANT LEAF-PEEPING OPPORTUNITIES.

Tucked between the Green Mountains and the Adirondacks, beautiful Lake Champlain is the defining feature of northwest Vermont's landscape. Survey the lake from the stellar museum in Shelburne and the waterfront in Burlington, then explore the Champlain Islands, a 27-mile ribbon of isles where simpler pleasures prevail: swimming, boating, apple-picking, wine-tasting, or rambling along sleepy farm roads and inter-island causeways.

LINK YOUR TRIP

10 Fall Foliage Tour
Intersect with The Fall Foliage tour in Burlington.

13 Vermont's Spine: Route 100
Drive south on I-89 to hook up with VT 100 at Waterbury.

01 Shelburne

Feast your eyes on the impressive array of 17th- to 20th-century American artifacts – folk art, textiles, toys, tools, carriages and furniture – spread over the 45-acre grounds and gardens at **Shelburne Museum** *(shelburnemuseum.org)*. This remarkable place is set up as a mock village, with 150,000 objects housed in 39 buildings. Highlights include a full-size covered bridge, a classic round barn, an 1871 lighthouse, a one-room schoolhouse, a railway station with a locomotive and a working blacksmith's forge.

The collection's sheer size lets you tailor your visit. Families are drawn to the carousel, the Owl Cottage children's center and the *Ticonderoga* steamship, while aficionados of quilts or, say, duck decoys can spend hours investigating their personal passion. Indeed, the buildings themselves are exhibits. Many were moved here from other parts of New England in order to ensure their preservation.

JULIE DESHAIES/SHUTTERSTOCK

★ BEST FOR

FOODIES

Indulge in Burlington's vibrant restaurant scene and local cider houses.

Church Street Marketplace, Burlington, Vermont

THE DRIVE: Head north on US 7 for 8 miles until you reach Burlington.

02 Burlington

Perched above glistening Lake Champlain, Vermont's largest city would be small in most other states. Yet Burlington's diminutive size is one of its charms, with an easily walkable downtown and a gorgeous, accessible lakefront. With the University of Vermont swelling the city (by 13,000 students) and a vibrant cultural and social life, Burlington has a spirited, youthful character. And when it comes to nightlife, this is Vermont's epicenter.

Just before you reach the city center, a chocolate stop is in order. The aroma of rich melted cocoa is intoxicating as you enter the gift shop next to the glass wall overlooking the small factory at **Lake Champlain Chocolates** *(lakechamplainchocolates.com)*. Take the tour to get the history of the chocolatier and ample samples to taste-test the gooey goodness. Oh, and this shop is the only one with factory-seconds shelves containing stacks of chocolate at a discount. It tastes the same as the pretty stuff but for cosmetic reasons can't be sold at regular prices. The cafe serves coffee drinks and its own luscious ice-cream.

THE DRIVE: From downtown Burlington, follow N Willard St until it curves right to join Riverside Ave, then look for the Intervale signs on your left.

03 Intervale

One of Vermont's most idyllic green spaces is less than 2 miles from downtown Burlington. Tucked among the lazy curves of the Winooski River, the **Intervale Center** *(intervale.org)* encompasses half a dozen organic farms and a delightful trail network, open 365 days a year for hiking, biking, skiing, bird-watching, paddling and more. On Thursday evenings in July and August, stop for local food tastings, live music and kids' events.

THE DRIVE: Cast off for the Champlain Islands, cruising 8 miles north of Intervale on I-89 to exit 17, then west on US 2 for 9 miles. After Sand Bar State Park, a great picnic and swimming spot, cross the causeway and look for the photo-perfect parking island halfway across.

04 South Hero Island

Settle into the slower pace of island life at **Allenholm Farm**, just outside the town of South Hero; grab a creemee (that's Vermont-speak for soft-serve ice-cream) or pick a few apples for the road ahead. About 3 miles west is **Snow Farm Vineyard** *(snowfarm.com)*, Vermont's first vineyard, which boasts a sweet tasting room tucked away down a dirt road (look for the signs off US 2). Sample its award-winning whites or have a sip of ice wine in the rustic barn (three tastes are free), or drop by on Thursday summer evenings at 6.30pm for the concert series on the lawn next to the vines – you can expect anything from jazz to folk to rock.

THE DRIVE: Continue north on US 2 for 8 miles.

> **PHOTO OPPORTUNITY**
>
> Water's edge on Isle La Motte.

05 Grand Isle

The **Hyde Log Cabin**, the oldest (1783) log cabin in Vermont and one of the oldest in the US, is worth a short stop to see how settlers lived in the 18th century and to examine traditional household artifacts from Vermont.

THE DRIVE: Continue north on US 2 for another 8 miles.

06 North Hero Island

Boaters for miles around cast anchor at popular general store **Hero's Welcome General Store** *(heroswelcome.com)*. The store's amusing wall display of 'World Time Zones' – four clocks showing identical hours for Lake Champlain's North Hero, South Hero, Grand Isle and Isle La Motte – reflects the prevailing island-centric attitude. Buy a souvenir, grab a sandwich or coffee and snap some pics on the outdoor terrace overlooking the boat landing.

THE DRIVE: From US 2, head west 4 miles on VT 129 to historic Isle La Motte.

DETOUR

Burton Island

Start: 06 North Hero Island

For a deeper immersion in Lake Champlain's natural beauty, spend a night or two camping at **Burton Island State Park** *(vtstateparks.com/burton.html)*, in the middle of the lake. Between Memorial Day and Labor Day, the Island Runner ferry (10 minutes) shuttles campers and their gear across a narrow channel from the mainland near St Albans to this pristine, traffic-free island with more than two dozen lakefront

Shelburne (p116), Vermont

VERMONTALM/SHUTTERSTOCK

lean-tos and campsites. Park facilities include boat rentals, a nature center with daily kids' activities and a store selling breakfast, lunch and groceries; the sign outside ('No shoes, no shirt, no problem!') epitomizes the island's laid-back vibe.

It's an easy 45-minute loop around the lake from North Hero to the ferry dock at Kill Kare State Park. Head 10 miles north on US 2 and then 10 miles east on VT 78 to get to Swanton; from there drive 10 miles south on VT 36 and turn right onto Hathaway Point Rd for the final 2.5 miles.

MEAGAN MARCHANT/SHUTTERSTOCK

07 Isle La Motte

Pristine Isle La Motte is one of the most historic of the Champlain Islands. Signs along its western shore signal its traditional importance as a crossroads for Native Americans and commemorate French colonizer and explorer Samuel de Champlain's landing here in 1609.

Tool around the loop road hugging the coast, stopping at **St Anne's Shrine** *(saintannesshrine.org)* on the site of Fort St Anne, Vermont's oldest settlement. (Though it is welcoming to all, this is a religious place, so be respectful of those who come to pray.) The site features a striking granite statue of Samuel de Champlain, and its waterfront has spectacular views and a large picnic area.

Isle La Motte is also home to the 20-acre **Fisk Quarry Preserve** *(ilmpt.org)*, the world's largest fossil reef, 4 miles south of St Anne's Shrine. Half a million years old, the reef once provided limestone for Radio City Music Hall and Washington's National Gallery. Interpretive trails explain the history of the quarry.

Lake Champlain, Vermont

LOVABLE LAKE MONSTER

Dinosaur relic or ice age proto-whale? Tree trunk? Really really big fish? Lake Champlain's legendary lake monster – nicknamed 'Champ' – has long fascinated local residents. Known to the Abenaki as Tatoskok, Champ was even sighted by French explorer Samuel de Champlain back in the early 17th century. Indulge your curiosity at the Champ display in Burlington's **ECHO, Leahy Center for Lake Champlain**. For a more dependable sighting, attend a Vermont Lake Monsters baseball game, where a lovable green-costumed Champ mascot dances on the dugout roof between innings.

13

NEW ENGLAND

VERMONT'S SPINE: ROUTE 100

DURATION: 3–4 DAYS

DISTANCE: 153 MILES / 246KM

GREAT FOR: WINE, HISTORY, FAMILIES

BEST TIME TO GO: MAY TO OCTOBER FOR SNOW-FREE ROADS AND SUN-FILLED DAYS.

Spanning the state from bottom to top, Vermont's revered Rte 100 winds past the Northeast's most legendary ski resorts and through some of New England's prettiest scenery, with the verdant Green Mountains always close at hand. This drive takes you on a slow meander through the state, though you might speed up in anticipation of the Ben & Jerry's Factory tour beckoning on the final stretch of road.

LINK YOUR TRIP

04 Finger Lakes Loop
From Wilmington, drive west across the border into New York, then pick up I-88 to Ithaca.

10 Fall Foliage Tour
Drive west from Rte 100 to pick up the Fall Foliage Tour at Manchester or Lake Champlain.

01 Wilmington

Chartered in 1751, Wilmington is the winter and summer gateway to **Mt Snow**, one of New England's best ski resorts and an excellent summertime mountain-biking and golfing spot. There are no main sights per se, but the **Historic District** on W Main St is a prime example of 18th- and 19th-century architecture and is chock-full of restaurants and boutiques; the bulk of the village is on the National Register of Historic Places. This is an excellent base where you can stay overnight and grab a bite before your journey up north.

THE DRIVE: Ski country (look for Mt Snow on your left) gives way to sleepy hamlets as you drive 26 miles north on VT 100 to the village of Jamaica.

02 Jamaica

A prime dose of rural Vermont, with a country store and several antique shops, this artsy community tucked into the ever-

★ BEST FOR

FAMILIES

Poking around the Weston country store and taking a Ben & Jerry's Factory tour.

BRIAN LOGAN PHOTOGRAPHY/SHUTTERSTOCK

Vermont Country Store, Weston, Vermont

green forest is also home to **Jamaica State Park** *(vtstateparks.com/jamaica.html)*, the best place in Vermont for riverside camping. The annual **Whitewater Weekend** held here in late September draws kayaking enthusiasts from all over New England to pit their skills against the rampaging West River. There's good swimming right in the heart of the campground, and walkers can also head 3 miles upstream along a 19th-century railway bed to **Hamilton Falls**, a 50ft ribbon of water cascading into a natural swimming hole.

THE DRIVE: Continue north 17 miles on VT 100 to Weston.

03 Weston

Picturesque Weston is home to the **Vermont Country Store** *(vermontcountry store.com)*, founded in 1946 and still going strong under the Orton family's ownership, four generations later. It's a time warp to a simpler era, when goods were made to last and quirky products with appeal had a home. The eclectic mix filling the shelves today ranges from the genuinely useful (cozy old-fashioned flannel nighties) to the nostalgic (vintage tiddlywinks and the classic 1960s boardgame *Mystery Date*) to the downright weird (electronic yodeling pickles, anyone?). For a midtrip pick-me-up, prowl through the vast array of traditional penny-candy jars and enjoy free tastes of Vermont cheeses, cookies and other delicacies.

THE DRIVE: Continue north on VT 100. At Plymouth Union, veer off to the right onto VT 100A for about a mile until you reach Plymouth Center. The total drive is 22 miles.

04 Plymouth

Gazing across the high pastures of Plymouth, you feel a bit like Rip Van Winkle – only it's the past you've woken up to. President Calvin Coolidge's boyhood home looks much as it did a century ago, with houses, barns, a church, a one-room schoolhouse and a general store gracefully arrayed among old maples on a bucolic hillside. At Plymouth's heart is the preserved

President Calvin Coolidge State Historic Site *(historicsites.vermont.gov)*. The village's streets are sleepy today, but the museum tells a tale of an earlier America filled with elbow grease and perseverance. Tools for blacksmithing, woodworking, butter making and hand laundering are indicative of the hard work and grit it took to wrest a living from Vermont's stony pastures. As a boy, Calvin hayed with his grandfather and kept the woodbox filled.

Originally cofounded by Coolidge's father, **Plymouth Artisan Cheese** *(plymouthartisancheese.com)* still produces a classic farmhouse cheddar known as granular curd cheese. Its distinctively sharp tang and grainy texture are reminiscent of the wheel cheese traditionally found at general stores throughout Vermont. Panels downstairs tell the history of local cheese-making, while a museum upstairs displays cheese-making equipment from another era.

> PHOTO OPPORTUNITY
>
> The 360-degree views from the K1 Gondola above Killington.

THE DRIVE: Drive back along VT 100A and turn right to return to VT 100 N. The drive is 13 miles.

05 Killington

The largest ski resort in the east, Killington spans seven mountains, highlighted by 4241ft Killington Peak, the second highest in Vermont. It operates the largest snow-making system in North America and its numerous outdoor activities – from skiing and snowboarding in winter to mountain biking and hiking in summer – are all centrally located on the mountain. **Killington Resort** *(killington.com)*, the East Coast's answer to Vail, runs the efficient K1-Express Gondola, which in winter transports up to 3000 skiers per hour in heated cars along a 2.5-mile cable – it's the highest lift in Vermont. In summer and fall it whisks you to impeccable vantage points above the mountains: leaf-peeping atop the cascading rainbow of copper, red and gold in foliage season is truly magical.

THE DRIVE: Enter the idyllic valley of the White River as you drive 24 miles north on VT 100

Killington, Vermont

ALEC HARRIGAN/SHUTTERSTOCK

to Rochester.

06 Rochester

This unassuming blink-and-you'll-miss-it town, with a vast village green lined with well-maintained, historic New England homes, is worth a stop to experience rural Vermont life minus the masses of tourists in other towns along VT 100.

Stop in at **Sandy's Books & Bakery** *(sandysbooksandbakery.com)*, a cafe, bookstore and popular local hangout. With homemade everything – granola, bagels, whole-wheat bread – Sandy's serves up mean dishes such as spinach-and-egg-filled biscuits, spanakopita, salads and soups. Tables are scattered between bookshelves, so it's a great spot for a java break and a browse of the new and used books (or the locally made Vermont soap). We dare you to resist the cookies.

THE DRIVE: Continue north on VT 100. Roughly 10 miles past Rochester, a pullout on the left provides views to Moss Glen Falls. A mile or so later, the small ponds of Granville Gulf comprise one of the state's most accessible moose-watching spots. About 5 miles further north, turn right onto Covered Bridge Rd and cross the bridge into Warren village.

DETOUR

Middlebury & Lincoln Gaps
Start: 06 Rochester

The 'gap roads' that run east–west over the Green Mountains offer some of the most picturesque views in Vermont. Ready to explore? Four miles north of Rochester, in Hancock, scenic VT 125 splits west off VT 100 and climbs over Middlebury Gap. Stops to look out for as you make the 15-mile crossing from Hancock to East Middlebury include beautiful **Texas Falls** (3 miles from Hancock), **Middlebury Gap** (6 miles) and the **Robert Frost Interpretive Trail**, an easygoing loop trail enlivened by plaques featuring Frost's poetry (10 miles).

For a scenic loop back to the main route, continue west on VT 125 to East Middlebury, then take VT 116 north. Soon after crossing through the pretty village of Bristol, turn right on Lincoln Gap Rd and follow it 14 miles east to rejoin the main route at Warren.

The return trip also offers some nice stops. As you turn onto Lincoln Gap Rd, look for the parked cars at **Bartlett Falls**, where the New Haven River's raging waters cascade into one of Vermont's most pristine swimming holes. Later, after a crazy-steep climb (partly unpaved) to **Lincoln Gap**, stop at the 2428ft summit for lovely views and some nice trails, including the 5-mile round trip to the 4000ft summit of **Mt Abraham**.

> ♥ DON'T MISS
>
> ### COVERED BRIDGES OF MONTGOMERY
>
> A 38-mile drive north from Stowe via VT 100 and VT 118 takes you to the covered-bridge capital of Vermont. In an idyllic valley at the confluence of multiple watersheds, the twin villages of Montgomery and Montgomery Center share seven spans crisscrossing the local rivers. Especially beautiful – though challenging to find – is remote Creamery Bridge just off Hill West Rd, which straddles a waterfall with a swimming hole at its base.

07 Warren

This sweet village is the southern gateway into Vermont's picturesque Mad River Valley. The river is popular with swimmers and kayakers, while the surrounding mountains are a mecca for skiers, who flock to the slopes at nearby **Sugarbush** *(sugarbush.com)* and **Mad River Glen** *(madriverglen.com)*.

Stop in at the **Warren Store** *(warrenstore.com)* in the village center, an animated community hangout with wavy 19th-century wood floors, a deli serving gourmet sandwiches and pastries, and a front porch ideal for sipping coffee while poring over the New York Times. The store upstairs sells an eclectic mix of jewelry, toys, Vermont casual clothing and knickknacks, while the sundeck below overlooks a pretty swimming hole framed by sculpted granite rocks.

THE DRIVE: Continue north 20 miles on VT 100 through pretty farm country to Waterbury, then follow signs for Stowe, crossing the overpass over I-89 to reach Ben & Jerry's.

DETOUR

Vermont Icelandic Horse Farm
Start: 07 Warren

Icelandic horses are one of the oldest, and some say most versatile, breeds in the world. They're also friendly and unbelievably affectionate creatures, and are fairly easy to ride even for novices – they tend to stop and think (rather than panic) if something frightens them. The **Vermont Icelandic Horse Farm** *(icelandichorses.com)*, 3 miles west of

VT 100 (where the tarmac ends and becomes a dirt road), takes folks on one- to three-hour or full-day jaunts year-round; it also offers two- to five-day inn-to-inn treks (some riding experience required). The farm also runs **Mad River Inn** *(madriverinn.com)*, a pleasant place a short trot away.

Head 9 miles north of Warren on VT 100 and follow the signs to the horse farm.

08 Ben & Jerry's

No trip to Vermont would be complete without a visit to **Ben & Jerry's Factory** *(benjerry.com/about-us/factory-tours)*, the biggest production center for America's most famous ice-cream. Sure, the manufacturing process is interesting, but a visit here also explains how school pals Ben and Jerry went from a $5 ice-cream-making correspondence course to a global enterprise, and offers a glimpse of the fun, in-your-face culture that made these frozen-dessert pioneers so successful. You're treated to a (very) small free taste at the end – for larger doses head to the on-site scoop shop.

Quaintly perched on a knoll overlooking the parking lot, the Ben & Jerry's Flavor Graveyard's neat rows of headstones pay silent tribute to flavors that flopped, like Makin' Whoopie Pie and Dastardly Mash. Each memorial is lovingly inscribed with the flavor's brief life span on the grocery store of this earth and a tribute poem. Rest in Peace, Holy Cannoli (1997–98)! Adieu, Miss Jelena's Sweet Potato Pie (1992–93)!

THE DRIVE: Wipe that ice-cream smile off your face and replace it with an ear-to-ear grin as you continue 9 miles up VT 100 to the legendary ski village of Stowe.

09 Stowe

In a cozy valley where the West Branch River flows into the Little River and mountains rise to the sky in all directions, the quintessential Vermont village of Stowe (founded in 1794) bustles quietly. Nestled in the Green Mountain National Forest, the highest point in Vermont, Mt Mansfield (4393ft) towers in the background, juxtaposed against the pencil-thin steeple of Stowe's **Community Church**, creating the classic Vermont picture-postcard scene.

With more than 200 miles of cross-country ski trails, some of the finest mountain biking and downhill skiing in the east and world-class hiking, this is a natural hub for adrenalin junkies and active families. If shopping and cafe-hopping are more your style, the village center also makes a delightful spot for a leisurely stroll. In addition to winter snow sports, **Stowe Mountain Resort** *(stowe.com)* opens from spring through to fall with gondola sky rides, an alpine slide and a scenic auto toll road that zigzags to the top of Mt Mansfield.

If *The Sound of Music* is one of your favorite things, the hilltop **Trapp Family Lodge** boasts sprawling views and oodles of activities, such as hiking, horse-drawn sleigh and carriage rides, lodge tours detailing the family history (often led by a member of the Trapp family), summer concerts on their meadow and some frothy goodness at the nearby **Von Trapp Bierhall** *(vontrapp brewing.com/bierhall.htm)*.

Stowe, Vermont
SONGQUAN DENG/SHUTTERSTOCK

14

NEW ENGLAND

IVY LEAGUE TOUR

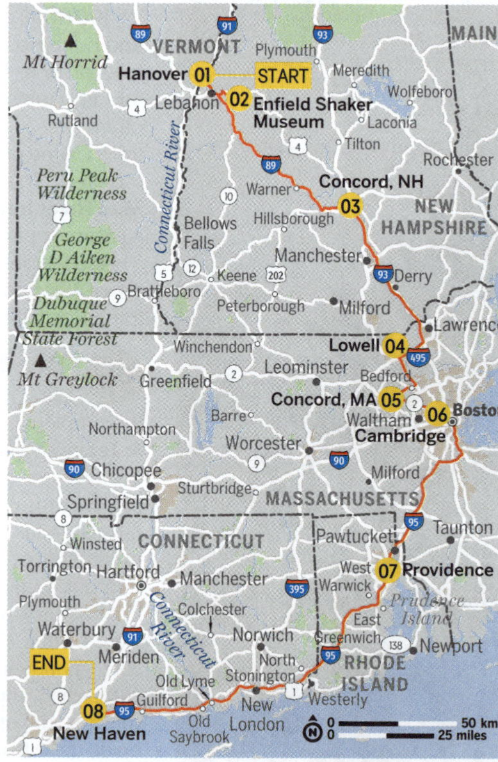

DURATION: 5 DAYS

DISTANCE: 315 MILES / 501 KM

GREAT FOR: HISTORY, FAMILIES

BEST TIME TO GO: CATCH STUDENT-FILLED CAMPUSES FROM SEPTEMBER TO NOVEMBER.

What's most surprising about a tour of the Ivy League? The distinct personalities of the different campuses, which are symbiotically fused with their surrounding landscapes. Compare fresh-faced Dartmouth, with its breezy embrace of New Hampshire's outdoors, to enclaved Yale, its Gothic buildings fortressed against the urban wilds of New Haven. But the schools all share one trait – vibrant, diverse and engaged students who dispel any notions that they're out-of-touch elites.

LINK YOUR TRIP

11 Rhode Island: East Bay
Take a detour from Providence for a drive around the East Bay.

13 Vermont's Spine: Route 100
South of Hanover, take US 4 west to hook up with Rte 100 near Killington.

01 Hanover, New Hampshire

When the first big snowfall hits **Dartmouth College** *(dartmouth.edu)*, an email blasts across campus, calling everyone to the central Green for a midnight snowball fight. The Green is also the site of elaborate ice sculptures during Dartmouth's **Winter Carnival**, a week-long celebration that's been held annually for more than 100 years.

North of the Green is **Baker Berry Library**, which holds an impressive mural called the Epic of American Civilization. Painted by Jose Clemente Orozco, it traces the course of civilization in the Americas from the Aztec era to modern times. At 4pm, stop by the adjacent **Sanborn Library**, where tea is served during the academic year for 10¢. This tradition honors a 19th-century English professor who invited students for chats and afternoon tea. For a free student-led walking tour of the campus, stop by the admissions office on the 2nd

MARCIO JOSE BASTOS SILVA/SHUTTERSTOCK

★ BEST FOR

HISTORY

Learn about the USA's oldest university during a Harvard tour.

Harvard University (p128), Cambridge, Massachusetts

floor of **McNutt Hall** on the west side of the Green. Call or check online to confirm departure times.

Dartmouth's **Hood Museum of Art** *(hoodmuseum.dartmouth.edu)* includes nearly 70,000 items. The collection is particularly strong in American pieces, including Native American art. A highlight is a set of Assyrian reliefs dating to the 9th century BCE.

From the museum, turn left onto E Wheelock St and walk toward the **Hanover Inn**. You'll soon cross the Appalachian Trail, which runs through downtown. From here, it's 431 miles to Mt Katahdin in Maine.

THE DRIVE: From Hanover, follow NH 120 E to I-89 S. Take exit 117 to NH 4 E, following it to NH 4A. Turn right and follow NH 4A 3.5 miles to the museum.

02 Enfield Shaker Museum

The Enfield Shaker site sits in stark contrast to today's college campuses. In fact, the two couldn't be more different – except for the required communal housing with a bunch of nonrelatives. But a trip here is illuminating. Set in a valley overlooking Mascoma Lake, the Enfield Shaker site dates to the late 18th century. At its peak, the Enfield community numbered 300. Farmers and craftspeople, they built impressive wood and brick buildings and took in converts, orphans and children of the poor – essential for the Shaker future since sex was not allowed in the pacifist, rule-abiding community. By the early 1900s the community had gone into decline and the last family left in 1917.

The **museum** *(shakermuseum.org)* centers on the Great Stone Dwelling, the largest Shaker dwelling house ever built. You can also explore the gardens and grounds. The guide might even let you ring the rooftop bell. Spend the night on the 3rd and 4th floor of the building; **accommodations** *(shakermuseum.org/stay)* feature traditional Shaker furniture, but not phones or TVs, although there is wi-fi.

THE DRIVE: Return to I-89 S. After 54 miles, take I-93 N 3 miles to exit 15E for I-393 E. From there, take exit 1 and follow the signs.

03 Concord, New Hampshire

New Hampshire's capital is a trim and tidy city with a wide Main St dominated by the striking **State House** *(gencourt.state.nh.us)*, a granite-hewed 19th-century edifice topped with a glittering dome.

Nearby, the New Hampshire schoolteacher Christa McAuliffe, chosen to be America's first teacher-astronaut, is honored at the **McAuliffe-Shepard Discovery Center** *(starhop.com)*. She died in the *Challenger* explosion on January 28, 1986. The museum also honors New Hampshire native Alan B Shepard, a member of NASA's elite Mercury corps who became America's first astronaut in 1961. Some exhibits feel a bit tired, but you can view a life-size replica of a NASA rocket and the Mercury capsule that transported Shepard to space. For hands-on adventure, you can try to land a *Discovery* space shuttle from inside a mock cockpit and learn about space travel to Mars and the power of the sun. There's also a planetarium.

THE DRIVE: Return to I-93 S, passing through Manchester before entering Massachusetts. Follow I-495 S toward Lowell.

04 Lowell, Massachusetts

In the early 19th century, textile mills in Lowell churned out cloth by the mile, driven by the abundant waterpower of Pawtucket Falls. Today, the historic buildings in the city center – connected by the trolley and canal boats – comprise the **Lowell National Historical Park**, which gives a fascinating peek at the workings of a 19th-century industrial town. Stop first at the **Visitors Center** *(nps.gov/lowe)* to pick up a map and check out the general exhibits. Five blocks northeast along the river, the **Boott Cotton Mills Museum** has exhibits that chronicle the rise and fall of the industrial revolution in Lowell, including technological changes, labor movements and immigration. The highlight is a working weave room, with 88 power looms. A special exhibit on *Mill Girls & Immigrants* examines the lives of working people, while seasonal exhibits are sometimes on display in other historic buildings around town.

PHOTO OPPORTUNITY

Stand beside the statue of John Harvard, the man who didn't found Harvard.

THE DRIVE: Take the Lowell Connector to US 3 heading south. In Billerica, exit to Concord Rd. Continue south on Concord Rd (MA 62) through Bedford. This road becomes Monument St and terminates at Monument Sq in Concord center. Walden Pond is about 3 miles south of Monument Sq, along Walden St (MA 126) south of MA 2.

05 Concord, Massachusetts

Tall, white church steeples rise above ancient oaks in Colonial Concord, giving the town a stateliness that belies the American Revolution drama that occurred centuries ago. It is easy to see how so many writers found their inspiration here in the 1800s.

Ralph Waldo Emerson was the paterfamilias of literary Concord and the founder of the transcendentalist movement (and, incidentally, a graduate of Harvard College). His home of nearly 50 years, the **Ralph Waldo Emerson Memorial House** *(rwema.org/visit-the-emerson-house)*, often hosted his renowned circle of friends.

One of them was Henry David Thoreau (another Harvard grad), who put transcendentalist beliefs into practice when he spent two years in a rustic cabin on the shores of **Walden Pond** *(mass.gov/dcr)*. The glacial pond is now a state park, surrounded by acres of forest. A footpath circles the pond, leading to the site of Thoreau's cabin on the northeast side.

THE DRIVE: Take MA 2 east to its terminus in Cambridge. Go left on the Alewife Brook Pkwy (MA 16), then right on Massachusetts Ave and into Harvard Sq. Parking spaces are in short supply, but you can usually find one on the streets around the Cambridge Common.

06 Cambridge, Massachusetts

Founded in 1636 to educate men for the ministry, **Harvard** *(harvard.edu)* is America's oldest college. The geographic heart of the university – where redbrick buildings and leaf-covered paths exude academia – is Harvard Yard. For maximum visual impact, enter the yard through the wrought-iron Johnston Gate, which is flanked by the two oldest buildings on campus, Harvard Hall and Massachusetts Hall.

The focal point of the yard is the John Harvard statue, by Daniel Chester French. Inscribed 'John Harvard, Founder of Harvard College, 1638,' it is commonly known as the 'statue of three lies': John Harvard was not the college's founder,

New Hampshire State House, Concord, New Hampshire
ZACK FRANK/SHUTTERSTOCK

DANIEL
WEBSTER

but its first benefactor; Harvard was actually founded in 1636; and finally, the man depicted isn't even Mr Harvard himself! This symbol hardly lives up to the university's motto, Veritas (truth).

Most Harvard hopefuls rub the statue's shiny foot for good luck; little do they know that campus pranksters regularly use the foot like dogs use a fire hydrant.

The revamped **Smith Campus Center** *(commonspaces.harvard.edu/smith-campus-center/about)* across from the yard is also worth a look. Hosting lectures, movies and several cafes, it's sure to be a campus hub. It's also home to 12,000 plants!

Overflowing with coffeehouses and pubs, bookstores and record stores, street musicians and sidewalk artists, panhandlers and professors, nearby **Harvard Square** exudes energy, creativity and nonconformity – and it's all packed into a handful of streets between the university and the river. Spend an afternoon browsing bookstores, riffling through records and trying on vintage clothing, then camp out in a local cafe.

> ☑ TOP TIP
>
> ### ALL ABOUT HAHVAHD
>
> Want to know more? Get the inside scoop from savvy students on the unofficial **Hahvahd Tour** *(trademarktours.com)*.

THE DRIVE: Hop on Memorial Dr and drive east along the Charles River. At Western Ave, cross the river and follow the signs to I-90 E (toll road). Cruise through the tunnel (product of the notorious Big Dig) and merge with I-93 S. Follow I-93 S to I-95 S. Take I-95 S to Providence.

07 Providence, Rhode Island

College Hill rises east of the Providence River, and atop it sits **Brown University** *(brown.edu)*, the rambunctious younger child of an uptight New England household. Big brothers Harvard and Yale carefully manicure their public image, while the little black sheep of the family prides itself on staunch liberalism. Founded in 1764, Brown was the first American college to accept

Harvard Book Sore, Harvard Square, Cambridge, Massachusetts

M_SOVINSKII/SHUTTERSTOCK

students regardless of religious affiliation, and the first to appoint an African American woman, Ruth Simmons, as president in 2001. Of its small 700-strong faculty, five Brown professors and two alumni have been honored as Nobel laureates.

The campus, consisting of 235 buildings, is divided into the Main Green and Lincoln Field. Enter through the wrought-iron Van Wickle Gates on College St. The oldest building on the campus is University Hall, a 1770 brick edifice, which was used as a barracks during the Revolutionary War. Free tours of the campus begin from the **Galen V. Henderson Admission Welcome Center** *(brown.edu/about/visit)* most weekdays.

THE DRIVE: Take Memorial Blvd out of Providence and merge with I-95 S. The generally pleasant tree-lined interstate will take you around the periphery of Groton, Old Lyme, Guilford and Madison, where you may want to stop for a coffee or snack. Exit at junction 47 for downtown New Haven.

GETTY IMAGES

Harkness Tower, Yale University, New Haven, Connecticut

08 New Haven, Connecticut

Gorgeous, Gothic Yale University is America's third-oldest university. Head to the **Yale University Visitor Center** *(visitor center.yale.edu)* to pick up a free map or take a free one-hour tour.

The tour does a good job of fusing historical and academic facts and passes by several standout monuments, including Yale's tallest building, **Harkness Tower**. Guides refrain, however, from mentioning the tombs scattered around the campus. No, these aren't filled with corpses; they're secret hangouts for senior students. The most notorious Tomb (64 High St) is the HQ for the Skull & Bones Club, founded in 1832. Its list of members reads like a who's who of high-powered politicos and financiers over the last two centuries.

New Haven's spacious green has been the spiritual center of the city since its Puritan fathers designed it in 1638 as the prospective site for Christ's second coming. Since then it has held the municipal burial grounds – graves were later moved to Grove St Cemetery – several statehouses and an array of churches, three of which still stand. A short walk along the green also passes numerous spots for appreciating art and architecture.

15

NEW ENGLAND

ACADIA NATIONAL PARK

★ BEST FOR

OUTDOORS

Hike a 'ladder trail' up a challenging cliff.

Bass Harbor Head Lighthouse (p136), Tremont, Maine

DURATION: 3 DAYS

DISTANCE: 112 MILES / 180KM

GREAT FOR: FAMILIES, FOOD & DRINK, NATURE

BEST TIME TO GO: MAY THROUGH OCTOBER FOR GOOD WEATHER AND OPEN FACILITIES.

Drivers and hikers can thank John D Rockefeller Jr and other wealthy landowners for the aesthetically pleasing bridges, overlooks and stone steps that give Acadia National Park its artistic oomph. Rockefeller worked diligently with architects and masons to ensure that the infrastructure complemented the surrounding landscape. Today, you tour the wonderful Park Loop Rd by car, but be sure to explore on foot and by bike wherever you can.

LINK YOUR TRIP

09 Coastal New England
For more scenes from coastal New England, head south on I-95 to Gloucester.

14 Ivy League Tour
Take I-95 south to Augusta, then head west into New Hampshire. Take I-93 north and I-91 south to Hanover.

01 Hulls Cove Visitor Center

Whoa, whoa, whoa. Before zooming into Bar Harbor on ME 3, stop at the park visitor center *(nps.gov/acad)* to get the lay of the land and pay the admission fee. Inside, head directly to the large diorama, which provides a helpful overview of Mount Desert Island (MDI). As you'll see, the island is shared with several nonpark communities, which are tucked here and there beside Acadia's borders.

From the visitor center, the best initiation to the park is to drive the 27-mile Park Loop Rd, which links the park's highlights in the eastern section of MDI. It's one way (traveling clockwise) for most of its length.

THE DRIVE: From the visitor center, turn right onto the Park Loop Rd, not ME 3 (which leads into Bar Harbor). Take in a nice view of Frenchman Bay on your left before passing the spur

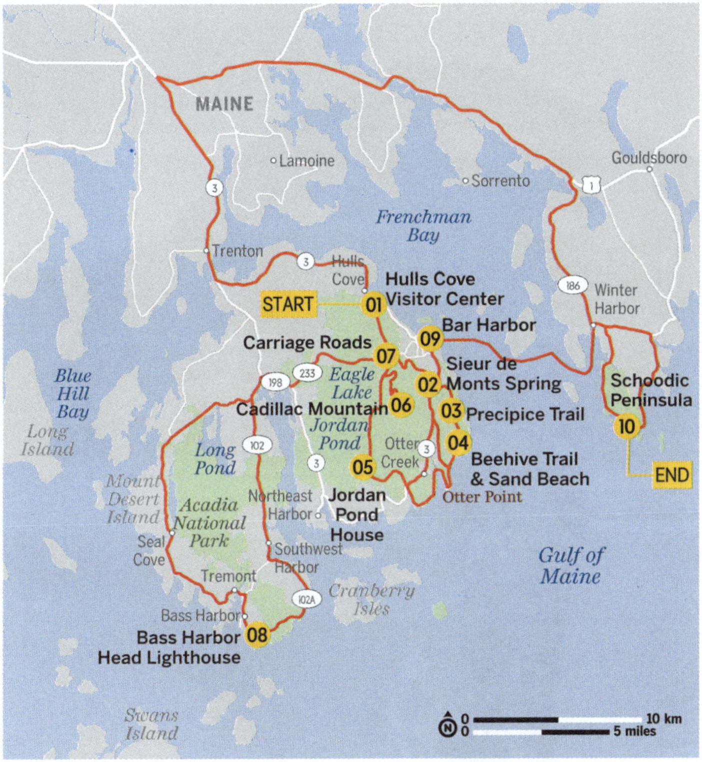

CONNY POKORNY/SHUTTERSTOCK

to ME 233. A short distance ahead, turn left to begin the one-way loop on the Park Loop Rd.

02 Sieur de Monts Spring

Nature lovers and history buffs will enjoy a stop at the **Sieur de Monts Spring** area at the intersection of ME 3 and the Park Loop Rd. Here you'll find a nature center and the summer-only branch of the **Abbe Museum** *(abbemuseum.org)*, which sits in a lush, nature-like setting. Twelve of Acadia's biospheres are displayed in miniature at the **Wild Gardens of Acadia**, from bog to coniferous woods to meadow. Botany enthusiasts will appreciate the plant labels. There are also some amazing stone-step trails here, appearing out of the talus as if by magic.

THE DRIVE: If you wish to avoid driving the full park loop, you can follow ME 3 from here into Bar Harbor. Push on for the full experience – you won't regret it.

03 Precipice Trail

What's the most exciting way to get a bird's-eye view of the park? By climbing up to where the birds are. Two 'ladder trails' cling to the sides of exposed cliffs on the northeastern section of the Park Loop Rd, dubbed Ocean Dr. If you're fit and the season's right, tackle the first of the ladder trails, the steep, challenging 1.6-mile **Precipice Trail**, which climbs the east face of Champlain Mountain on

ISLAND VISIT PLANNER

ACADIA NATIONAL PARK

Camping
There are two great rustic campgrounds on Mount Desert Island, with nearly 500 sites between them. Both are densely wooded and near the coast; reservations *(recreation.gov)* are essential. Seawall is 4 miles south of Southwest Harbor on the 'Quiet Side' of Mount Desert Island, while Blackwoods is closer to Bar Harbor (5 miles south, on ME 3).

Bar Harbor & Mount Desert Island
Before your trip, check lodging availability at the **Bar Harbor Chamber of Commerce** *(visitbarharbor.com)*. Staff can mail you a copy of the visitor guide. Otherwise, stop by the welcome center itself for lodging brochures, maps and local information. It's located north of the bridge onto Mount Desert Island. There is a second visitor center in Bar Harbor itself.

iron rungs and ladders. (Note that the trail is typically closed late spring to mid-August because it's a nesting area for peregrine falcons. If it is closed, you might catch volunteers and staff monitoring the birds through scopes from the trailhead parking lot.) Skip the trail on rainy days.

THE DRIVE: Continue south on Park Loop Rd. The Beehive Trail starts 100ft north of the Sand Beach parking area.

04 Beehive Trail & Sand Beach

Another good ladder trail is the **Beehive Trail**. The 0.8-mile climb includes ladders, rungs, narrow wooden bridges and scrambling – with steep drop-offs. As with the Precipice Trail, it's recommended that you descend via a nearby walking route, rather than climbing down.

Don't let the crowds keep you away from **Sand Beach**. It's home to one of the few sandy shorelines in the park, and it's a don't-miss spot. But you don't have to visit in the middle of the day to appreciate its charms. Beat the crowds early in the morning, or visit at night, especially for the **Stars over Sand Beach** program. During these free one-hour talks, lie on the beach, look up at the sky and listen to rangers share stories and science about the stars. Even if you miss the talk, the eastern coastline along Ocean Dr is worth checking out at night, when you can watch the Milky Way slip right into the ocean.

THE DRIVE: Swoop south past the crashing waves of Thunder Hole. If you want to exit the loop road, turn right onto Otter Cliff Rd, which hooks up to ME 3 north into Bar Harbor. Otherwise, pass Otter Point then follow the road inland past Wildwood Stables.

05 Jordan Pond House

Share hiking stories with other nature lovers at the lodge-like **Jordan Pond House** *(jordanpondhouse.com)*, where afternoon tea has been a tradition since the late 1800s. Steaming pots of Earl Grey come with hot popovers (hollow rolls made with egg batter) and strawberry jam. Eat on the broad lawn overlooking the lake. On clear days the glassy waters of 176-acre **Jordan Pond** reflect the image of Mt Penobscot like a mirror. Take the 3.2-mile nature trail around the pond after finishing your tea.

Mt Penobscot and Jordan Pond, Acadia National Park, Maine

MICHAEL CARNI/SHUTTERSTOCK

THE DRIVE: Look up for the rock precariously perched atop South Bubble from the pull-off almost 2 miles north. Continue north to access Cadillac Mountain Rd.

06 Cadillac Mountain

Don't leave the park without driving – or hiking – to the 1530ft summit of **Cadillac Mountain**. For panoramic views of Frenchman Bay, walk the paved 0.5-mile **Cadillac Mountain Summit loop**. The summit is a popular place in the early morning because it's long been touted as the first spot in the US to see the sunrise. The truth? It is, but only between October 7 and March 6. The crown is passed to northern coastal towns the rest of the year because of the tilt of the earth. But, hey, the sunset is always a good bet.

THE DRIVE: Drunk on the views, you can complete the loop road and exit the park, heading for your accommodations or next destination. But consider finding a parking lot and tackling walking trails, or heading to Bar Harbor to hire bikes.

> TOP TIP
>
> ### PARK SHUTTLES
>
> With millions of visitors coming to the park each summer, traffic and parking can be a hassle. On arrival, drive Park Loop Rd straight through for the views and the driving experience. Then leave the driving to others by using the **Island Explorer** *(exploreacadia.com)*, free with park admission. Shuttles run along 10 routes that connect visitors to trails, carriage roads, beaches, campgrounds and in-town destinations. They can even carry mountain bikes.

07 Carriage Roads

John D Rockefeller Jr, a lover of old-fashioned horse carriages, gifted Acadia some 45 miles of crisscrossing carriage roads. Made from crushed stone, the roads are free from cars and are popular with cyclists, hikers and equestrians. Several of them fan out from **Jordan Pond House**, but if the lot is too crowded, continue north to the parking area at Eagle Lake on US 233 to link to the carriage-road network. If you're planning to explore by bike, the **Bicycle Express Shuttle** runs to Eagle Lake from the Bar Harbor Village Green from late June through September. Pick up a Carriage Road User's Map at the visitor center.

THE DRIVE: Still in the mood for cruising? Before you head for the bright lights of Bar Harbor, take a detour: drive ME 233 toward the western part of MDI, connecting to ME 198 west, then drop south on ME 102 toward Southwest Harbor. Pass Echo Lake Beach and Southwest Harbor, then bear left onto ME 102A for a dramatic rise up and back into the park near the seawall.

08 Bass Harbor Head Lighthouse

There is only one lighthouse on MDI, and it sits in the somnolent village of Bass Harbor in the far southwest corner of the park. Built in 1858, the 36ft lighthouse still has a Fresnel lens from 1902. It's in a beautiful location that's a photographers' favorite. The lighthouse is a coast guard residence, so you can't go inside, but you can take photos. You can also walk to the coast on two easy trails near the property: the **Ship Harbor Trail**, a 1.2-mile loop, and the **Wonderland Trail**, a 1.4-mile round trip. These trails are spectacular ways to get through the forest and to the coast, which looks different to the coast on Ocean Dr.

THE DRIVE: For a lollipop loop, return on ME 102A to ME 102 through the village of Bass Harbor. Follow ME 102 then ME 233 all the way to Bar Harbor.

09 Bar Harbor

Tucked on the rugged coast in the shadows of Acadia's mountains, Bar Harbor is a busy gateway town with a J Crew joie de vivre. Restaurants, taverns and boutiques are scattered along Main St, Mt Desert St and Cottage St. Shops sell everything from books to camping gear to handicrafts and art. For a fascinating collection of natural artifacts related to Maine's Native American heritage, visit the **Abbe Museum** *(abbemuseum.org)*. The collection holds more than 50,000 objects, such as pottery, tools, combs and fishing instruments spanning the last 2000 years, including contemporary pieces. (There's a smaller summer-only branch in Sieur de Monts Spring.)

Done browsing? Spend the rest of the afternoon, or early evening, exploring the area by water. Sign up in Bar Harbor for a half-day or sunset sea-kayaking trip. Both **National Park Sea Kayak Tours** *(mainestatekayak.com)* and **Coastal Kayaking Tours** *(acadiafun.com)* offer guided trips along the jagged coast.

THE DRIVE: There's another part of the park you haven't yet explored. Reaching it involves a 44-mile drive (north on Rte 3 to US 1, following it about 17 miles to ME 186 S). ME 186 passes through Winter Harbor and then links to Schoodic Point Loop Rd. It's about an hour's drive one way. Alternatively, hop on a Downeast Windjammer ferry from the pier beside the Bar Harbor Inn.

10 Schoodic Peninsula

The Schoodic Peninsula is the only section of Acadia National Park that's part of the mainland. It's also home to the Park Loop Rd, a rugged, woodsy drive with splendid views of MDI and Cadillac Mountain. You're more likely to see a moose here than on MDI – what moose wants to cross a bridge?

Much of the drive is one way. There's an excellent campground *(recreation.gov)* near the entrance, then a picnic area at **Frazer Point**. Further along the loop, turn right for a short ride to Schoodic Point, a 440ft-high promontory with ocean views.

The full loop from Winter Harbor is 11.5 miles. If you're planning to come by ferry, you could rent a bike beforehand at **Bar Harbor Bicycle Shop** *(barharborbike.com)* – the Park Loop Rd's smooth surface and easy hills make it ideal for cycling.

In July and August, the **Island Explorer Schoodic** shuttle bus runs from Winter Harbor to the peninsula ferry terminal and around the Park Loop Rd. It does not link to Bar Harbor.

Cadillac Mountain (p135), Acadia National Park, Maine

SANDRA FOYT/SHUTTERSTOCK

PHOTO OPPORTUNITY

Capture that sea-and-sunrise panorama from atop Cadillac Mountain.

MISSOURI
St Louis
OHIO
WEST VIRGINIA
Charleston
George Washington National Forest
Louisville
Lexington
KENTUCKY
Henderson
Paducah
Bowling Green
Roanoke
Johnson City
Greensboro
Nashville
Dale Hollow Lake
Knoxville
Jonesboro
Jackson
TENNESSEE
Bryson City
NORTH CAROLINA
Little Rock
Memphis
Charlotte
Chattahoochee River National Recreation Area
Greenville
ARKANSAS
Mississippi River
Decatur
Florence
Tupelo
Columbia
Atlanta
Birmingham
SOUTH CAROLINA
ALABAMA
Augusta
Greenville
Cheaha Mountain
MISSISSIPPI
Macon
LOUISIANA
Charleston
Vicksburg
Montgomery
Columbus
Jackson
Meridian
Savannah
Natchez
Hattiesburg
GEORGIA
Cumberland Island National Seashore
DeSoto National Forest
Baton Rouge
Mobile
Valdosta
Bristol
Tallahassee
Jacksonville
Pensacola
St Augustine
New Orleans
Lake Borgne
Gulf Islands National Seashore
Gainesville
FLORIDA
Canaveral National Seashore
Orlando
Tampa
Gulfport
St Petersburg
Gulf of Mexico
Tampa Bay
Lake Okeechobee
Fort Lauderdale
Miami
Everglades National Park
Florida Keys
Key West
16
17
18
19
20
21
0 300 km
0 150 miles

MARIAKRAY/SHUTTERSTOCK

Fort Lauderdale (p148), Florida

FLORIDA & THE SOUTH

EXPLORE

FLORIDA & THE SOUTH

Between the Carolinas and the Gulf of Mexico, a different America awaits, warmed by sultry winds that blow up from the Caribbean. From the mighty Mississippi River to the Florida Keys, from the Blues Highway to Cajun Country and from the Smoky Mountains to the art-deco glam of Miami, you'll find that life moves to its own rhythm in the South.

On these trips, we'll show you the jazz club of your dreams, country calm and city chic. We'll also show you sun-kissed beaches and a highway floating above a perfect blue ocean.

St Augustine

If you weren't just passing through, you'd make St Augustine a destination in its own right. The oldest continuously occupied European settlement in the US, it has fascinating old-world buildings (including its very own fort) and museums to go with its excellent array of historic hotels, B&Bs and luxury hotels. Just as good are its cafes and restaurants serving up a representative sample of regional American and international cooking.

Lafayette

Music and fine Cajun cooking run deep in Lafayette, which makes sense as a brilliant base for exploring Louisiana as you drive around the state. The 'city' is rich in all versions of the arts, including museums and live music. They also love a good brunch down Lafayette way, with diners, Cajun stalwarts and down-home Southern cooking making sure all other meals are taken care of as well.

Memphis

Memphis is holy ground to music lovers and is beloved by Americans who consider its blues to be something of a national soundtrack. It's the classic riverside town of the Mississippi, a touchstone of the American South, and a city on the up all at once – stay a while before driving further into the South. Memphis has fine accommodations, a varied cuisine with some real Southern specials, and, as you'd expect, some of America's best music museums and live music.

WHEN TO GO

As a general rule, avoid high summer to miss the big crowds and oppressive heat of the South. Florida is best from November to April when the weather's warm but bearable. Spring has festivals from Louisiana to Tennessee in March through June, while fall promises lovely weather and colorful leaves from September to November.

Nashville

America's country music capital is a toe-tapping city with vibrant neighborhoods, graceful old mansions, a genuinely artsy soul and lots of leafy green parks. Great accommodations, incredibly varied food and lots of nightlife help cement its role as both a waystation on a longer journey and simply a great place to spend a few days.

Charlotte

Charlotte is a window on the American South, from the NASCAR Hall of Fame and elegant plantation-era mansions to trendy inner-city neighborhoods with cutting-edge art galleries where brunch can seem like an occupation. Great food, stylish boutique hotels, lots of microbreweries and brewpubs, and even the US National Whitewater Center round out a really cool city. It's handy for both the Blue Ridge Parkway and the Great Smokies.

Gatlinburg

A study in American kitsch, Gatlinburg is the gateway to the Great Smoky Mountains. What it lacks in class and sophistication, it makes up for with great pancakes and steakhouses, amusement parks and cable cars, and more motels than you'll ever need. It won't be to everyone's taste, but it's a quintessentially American experience and we love it all the more for (and perhaps only because) of that fact.

TRANSPORTATION

You could join the sunbirds and drive to Florida from just about anywhere in the US, but it's easier to fly into Miami, Memphis, Charlotte or Nashville and drive from there. Smaller towns like Lafayette are served by bus or Amtrak, while other smaller gateway towns like Gatlinburg or Natchez have limited bus services.

WHERE TO STAY

The big cities – Miami, Memphis, Nashville, Jacksonville and more – have something to suit every taste and budget, from hostels to five-star boutique gems. But it's often the smaller, more out-of-the-way places where you'll find the charm – try St Augustine or Amelia Island in Florida, or one of the campsites sprinkled around the Great Smoky Mountains. The latter's campgrounds are often overrun in summer; try **Big Creek**, a smaller walk-in option right by the rapids, more remote **Abrams Creek Campground**, or the cabins of **LeConte Lodge**.

RESOURCES

- **National Park Service**
  Detailed info on camping, activities, permits and reservations for the Great Smoky Mountains, Natchez Trace Pkwy and more. *nps.gov*
- **Blue Ridge Parkway**
  Comprehensive guide to this popular drive, with good seasonal info. *blueridgeparkway.org*
- **Visit Music City**
  Nashville attractions, restaurants, accommodations, neighborhoods and, yes, music. *visitmusiccity.com*

WHAT'S ON

- **Festival International de Louisiane**
  Fantastic five-day free festival of Francophone music and culture in Lafayette in April.
- **Beale Street Music Festival**
  One of America's best but least-known music festivals; it's devoted to old-school blues and more in Memphis in May.
- **Elvis Week**
  One of America's quirkiest festivals devoted to all things The King in Memphis in August.
- **Tennessee State Fair**
  Wonderfully old-fashioned celebration of community life in Lebanon in August.

16

FLORIDA & THE SOUTH

HIGHWAY 1

DURATION: 6 DAYS

DISTANCE: 475 MILES / 764KM

GREAT FOR: FOOD, OUTDOORS, HISTORY & CULTURE

BEST TIME TO GO: NOVEMBER TO APRIL, WHEN IT'S WARM BUT NOT TOO HOT.

Drive the length of Florida all the way down the coast and you'll get a sampling of all the highlights of the Sunshine State. You'll find the oldest permanent settlement in the US, family-friendly attractions, the Latin flavor of Miami and – oh, yeah – miles and miles of beaches right beside you, inviting you to stop as often as you want.

LINK YOUR TRIP

17 Cajun Country
Follow I-10 west, then head south from Baton Rouge to Thibodaux to start your Cajun Country trip.

20 Blue Ridge Parkway
Take I-95 north along the coast and head inland on I-26 through Columbia. From there take Hwy 321 all the way to Boone.

01 Amelia Island

Start your drive just 13 miles south of the Georgia state line on Amelia Island, a glorious barrier island with the moss-draped charm of the Deep South. Vacationers have been flocking here since the 1890s, when Henry Flagler's railroad converted the area into a playground for the rich. That legacy is visible today in Amelia's central town of **Fernandina Beach**, with 50 blocks of historic buildings, and restaurants housed in converted fishing cottages.

THE DRIVE: Meander down Hwy 1A for about half an hour, passing both Big and Little Talbot Island State Parks. After you enter Fort George Island take the right fork in the road to get to the Ribault Club.

02 Fort George Island

History runs deep at **Fort George Island Cultural State Park** *(floridastateparks.org/parks-and-trails/fort-george-island-cultural-state-park)*. Enormous

VIAVAL TOURS/SHUTTERSTOCK

★ BEST FOR

HISTORY

St Augustine is the oldest permanent settlement in the US.

Lightner Museum (p144), St Augustine, Florida

shell middens date the island's habitation by Native Americans to over 5000 years ago. In 1736 British General James Oglethorpe erected a fort in the area, though it's long since vanished and its exact location is uncertain. In the 1920s flappers flocked to the ritzy **Ribault Club** *(theribaultclub.com)* for Gatsby-esque bashes with lawn bowling and yachting. Today it houses the island's visitor center, which can provide you with a self-guided audio tour of the area.

Perhaps most fascinating – and certainly most sobering – is **Kingsley Plantation** *(nps.gov/timu)*, Florida's oldest plantation house, built in 1798. Due to its remote location it's not a grand Southern mansion, but it does provide a fairly unflinching look at slavery through exhibits and the former cabins of enslaved people.

THE DRIVE: Follow Hwy 105 inland 15 miles to I-95 then shoot straight south into downtown Jacksonville, a distance of about 24 miles.

03 Jacksonville

With its high-rises, freeways and chain hotels, Jacksonville is a bit of a departure from our coastal theme, but it offers lots of dining options and its restored historic districts are worth a wander. Check out **Five Points** and **San Marco**; both are charming, walkable areas lined with bistros, boutiques and bars.

Jacksonville is also a good chance to work in a little culture at the **Cummer Museum of Art** *(cummermuseum.org)*, which has a genuinely excellent collection of American and European paintings, Asian decorative art and antiquities; or the **Museum of Modern Art Jacksonville** *(mocajacksonville.unf.edu)*, which houses contemporary paintings, sculptures, prints, photography and film.

THE DRIVE: Take US 1 southwest for an hour straight into St Augustine, where it becomes Ponce de Leon Blvd.

04 St Augustine

Founded by the Spanish in 1565, St Augustine is the oldest permanent settlement in the US. Tourists flock here to stroll the ancient streets, and horse-drawn carriages clip-clop past townsfolk dressed in period costume. It's touristy and authentic in equal measure, with tons of museums, tours and attractions vying for your attention. Start with the **Colonial Quarter** *(colonialquarter.com)*, a re-creation of 18th-century St Augustine complete with craftspeople demonstrating blacksmithing, leather working and other trades.

While you're here, don't miss the **Lightner Museum** *(lightnermuseum.org)* located in the former Hotel Alcazar. We love the endless displays of everything from Gilded Age furnishings to collections of marbles and cigar-box labels.

Stop by the **Visitor Information Center** *(visitstaugustine.com)* to find out about your other options, including ghost tours, the **Pirate and Treasure Museum**, **Castillo de San Marcos National Monument** and the **Fountain of Youth**, a goofy tourist attraction disguised as an archaeological park that is purportedly the very spot where Ponce de Leon landed.

THE DRIVE: Take the Bridge of Lions toward the beach then follow Hwy 1A south for 13 miles to Fort Matanzas. To catch the 35-person ferry, go through the visitor center and out to the pier. The ride lasts about five minutes and launches hourly from 9:30am to 4:30pm, weather permitting.

05 Fort Matanzas National Monument

By now you've seen firsthand that the Florida coast isn't all about fun in the sun; it also has a rich history that goes back hundreds of years. History buffs will enjoy a visit to this tiny Spanish **fort** *(nps.gov/foma)* built in 1742. Its purpose? To guard Matanzas Inlet – a waterway leading straight up to St Augustine – from British invasion.

On the lovely (and free) boat ride over, park rangers narrate the fort's history and explain the gruesome origins of the name. ('Matanzas' means 'slaughters' in Spanish; let's just say things went badly for a couple of hundred French Huguenot soldiers back in 1565.)

THE DRIVE: Hopping over to I-95 will only shave a little bit off the hour-long trip; you might as well enjoy puttering along Hwy 1A to Daytona Beach, 40 miles south.

06 Daytona Beach

With typical Floridian hype, Daytona Beach bills itself as 'The World's Most Famous Beach.' But its fame is less about quality – there are better beaches in Florida's north – than the size of the parties this expansive beach has witnessed during spring break, Speedweeks, and motorcycle events when half a million bikers roar into town. One Daytona title no one disputes is 'Birthplace of NASCAR,' which started here in 1947. Its origins go back as far as 1902 to drag races held on the beach's hard-packed sands.

☑ TOP TIP

THE ROAD LESS TAKEN

Despite its National Scenic Byway designation, oceanfront Hwy A1A often lacks ocean views, with wind-blocking vegetation growing on both sides of the road. Unless you're just moseying up or down the coast, Hwy 1 or I-95 are often better – or rather, faster – choices for driving long distances.

♥ WHY I LOVE THIS TRIP

VESNA MARIC, WRITER

If you've ever wanted to have the perfect beachside road trip – where you hop out of your car and dip – this is it. The beaches are stunning, the seafood fresh and there's loads of sunshine year-round. This brilliant drive culminates in the out-of-this-world city of Miami, with diversions along the way that include decent art exhibits, peaceful nature preserves and some of the USA's oldest historical sites.

NASCAR is the main event here, with the **Daytona 500** a classic. Catch a race at the **Daytona International Speedway** *(daytonainternationalspeedway.com)*. When there's no race, take a tram tour of the track, pit area, stands and Hall of Fame. Race-car fanatics can indulge in the **Richard Petty Driving Experience** *(nascarracingexperience.com)* and feel the thrill of riding shotgun or even taking the wheel themselves.

THE DRIVE: Take South Atlantic Ave 10 miles south along the coast to get to Ponce Inlet.

07 Ponce de Leon Inlet

About 6 miles south of Daytona Beach is the **Ponce de Leon Inlet Lighthouse & Museum** *(ponceinlet.org)*.

Daytona Beach, Florida

RUDENKOSTUDIO/SHUTTERSTOCK

Stop by for a photo op with the handsome 1887 red brick tower, then climb the 203 steps to the top for great views. A handful of historic buildings comprise the museum portion of your tour, including the lightkeeper's house and the Lens House, with a collection of Fresnel lenses.

THE DRIVE: Backtrack up Atlantic, then cut over to US 1/FL 5 and head south for 20 minutes. Pre-planning pays here, because your route depends on where you're heading. One road goes 6 miles south from New Smyrna Beach, and another 6 miles north from the wildlife refuge. Both dead-end, leaving 16 miles of beach between them.

08 Canaveral National Seashore

These 24 miles of pristine, wind-swept beaches comprise the longest stretch of undeveloped beach on Florida's east coast. On the north end is family-friendly **Apollo Beach**, with gentle surf and miles of solitude. On the south end, **Playalinda Beach** is surfer central.

Just west of (and including) the beach, the 140,000-acre **Merritt Island National Wildlife Refuge** *(fws.gov/merrittisland)* is an unspoiled oasis for birds and wildlife. More endangered and threatened species of wildlife inhabit the swamps, marshes and hardwood hammocks here than at any other site in the continental US.

THE DRIVE: Although Kennedy Space Center is just south of the Merritt Island Refuge, you have to go back into Titusville, travel south 5 miles on US 1/Hwy 5, then take the NASA Causeway back over to get there.

09 Space Coast

The Space Coast's main claim to fame (other than being the setting for the iconic 1960s TV series *I Dream of Jeannie*) is being the real-life home to the **Kennedy Space Center** *(kennedyspacecenter.com)* and its massive visitor complex. Once a working space-flight facility, Kennedy Space Center has shifted from a living museum to a historical one since the end of NASA's space shuttle program in 2011.

THE DRIVE: Hop back onto the freeway (I-95) for the 2½-hour drive south to Palm Beach.

PHOTO OPPORTUNITY

Rows of colorful art-deco hotels along Ocean Ave at Miami Beach.

DETOUR

Space Coast Wildlife

Start: 09 Space Coast

Located off the A1A, the **Pelican Island National Wildlife Refuge** *(fws.gov/pelicanisland)* was established in 1903 as a refuge for the endangered brown pelican. Pelican Island was America's first federal bird reservation, the forerunner of today's national wildlife-refuge system. The preserve now encompasses 500 acres along the Indian River Lagoon as well as the 2.2-acre Pelican Island, which can be seen from the observation tower at the end of the **Centennial Trail**. Two trails loop 2.5 miles along the shore and are perfect for bike rides and long hikes. Pelican Island itself can also be viewed by boat and there are several public boat ramps to access the refuge waters.

Very close by and stretching along a narrow strip of the barrier island is **Sebastian Inlet State Park** *(floridastateparks.org/sebastian-inlet),* popular with fishers, surfers, boaters and families. It is divided into two sections by the inlet bridge. On the north side swimming is safe for children in the calm-water lagoon.

10 Palm Beach

History and nature give way to money and glitz as you reach the southern part of the coast, and Palm Beach is basically the playground for the filthy rich. You can stroll along the beach – kept pleasantly seaweed-free by the town – and ogle the massive gated compounds on A1A or window-shop in uber-ritzy Worth Ave, if that rocks your boat.

The best reason to stop here is the **Flagler Museum** *(flaglermuseum.us),* housed in the spectacular, beaux-art Whitehall Mansion built by railroad mogul Henry Flagler in 1902.

3, 2, 1...BLASTOFF!

Along the Space Coast even phone calls get a countdown, thanks to the local area code: 321. It's no coincidence: in 1999 residents led by Robert Osband petitioned to get the digits in honor of the rocket launches that took place at Cape Canaveral.

Art deco buildings, Ocean Drive (p148), Miami Beach, Florida

LUNAMARINA/SHUTTERSTOCK

THE DRIVE: As you head back inland, West Palm Beach is just a causeway away.

11 West Palm Beach

West Palm Beach has the largest art museum in Florida, the **Norton Museum of Art** *(norton.org)*. The Nessel Wing features a colorful crowd-pleaser: a ceiling made from nearly 700 pieces of handblown glass by Dale Chihuly. Across the street, the **Ann Norton Sculpture Garden** *(ansg.org)* is a real West Palm gem.

Come evening head to **CityPlace** *(cityplace.com)*, a massive outdoor shopping and entertainment center.

THE DRIVE: Fort Lauderdale is a straight shot down I-95, 45 miles south of Palm Beach.

12 Fort Lauderdale

Fort Lauderdale's promenade is a magnet for runners, in-line skaters, walkers and cyclists. The white-sand beach, meanwhile, is one of the nation's cleanest and best. Few visitors venture far inland except maybe to dine and shop along Las Olas Blvd.

The best way to see Fort Lauderdale is from the water. Hop on board the **Carrie B** *(carriebcruises.com)* for a 1½-hour riverboat tour along the Intracoastal and New River. Or, for the best unofficial tour of the city, hop on the **Water Taxi** *(watertaxi.com)*, whose drivers offer lively narration of the passing scenery.

THE DRIVE: Miami is just half an hour south of Fort Lauderdale down I-95.

13 Miami

Miami is all pastel-hued, subtropical beauty set amid the diversity of Latin America. On Calle Ocho (8th St) you'll find Little Havana, the most prominent Cuban American community in the US. Visit on the last Friday of the month for **Viernes Culturales** *(viernesculturales.org)*, a street fair showcasing Latinx artists and musicians. Or catch the vibe at **Máximo Gómez Park**, where old-timers gather to play dominoes and talk trash.

Wynwood and the Design District are Miami's official arts neighborhoods; don't miss the murals at **Wynwood Walls** *(thewynwoodwalls.com)*.

THE DRIVE: We've saved the best for last. Cross over the Julia Tuttle Causeway or the MacArthur Causeway to find yourself in art-deco-filled Miami Beach.

14 Miami Beach

Miami Beach has some of the best beaches in the country, with white sand and warm, blue-green water, and it's world-famous for its people-watching. It also has the largest concentration of art deco structures anywhere in the world, with approximately 1200 buildings around Ocean Dr and Collins Ave. Arrange a tour at the **Art Deco Welcome Center** *(mdpl.org)* or pick up a walking tour map in the gift shop.

Running alongside the beach, **Ocean Ave** is lined with cafes that spill out onto the sidewalk; stroll along until you find one that suits your cravings. Another highly strollable area is **Lincoln Road Mall**, a pedestrian promenade lined with stores, restaurants and bars.

DETOUR

Biscayne National Park

Start: 14 Miami Beach

About an hour's drive south of Miami Beach, **Biscayne National Park** *(nps.gov/bisc)* is a protected marine sanctuary harboring amazing tropical coral reef systems, most within sight of Miami's skyline. It's only accessible by water: you can take a glass-bottomed-boat tour, snorkel or scuba dive, or rent a canoe or kayak to lose yourself in this 300-sq-mile system of islands, underwater shipwrecks and mangrove forests.

Lincoln Road, Miami Beach, Florida

FOKKE BAARSSEN/SHUTTERSTOCK

COMPASS
LINCOLN THEATRE
H&M
H&M

17

FLORIDA & THE SOUTH

CAJUN COUNTRY

★ BEST FOR

CULTURE

The unique folkways of Cajun Country, aka Acadiana, permeate south Louisiana.

Crawfish

DURATION: 4 DAYS

DISTANCE: 230 MILES / 370KM

GREAT FOR: FOOD & DRINK, HISTORY & CULTURE

BEST TIME TO GO: MARCH TO JUNE IS FESTIVAL SEASON HERE; WARM WEATHER AND LOTS OF PARTIES.

Cross into south Louisiana, and you venture into a land that's intensely, immediately unique. You will drive past dinosaur-laced wetlands where standing water is uphill from the floodplain, through villages where French is still the language of celebration and, sometimes, the home, and towns that love to fiddle, dance, two-step and, most of all, eat well. Bienvenue en Louisiane: this is Cajun Country, a waterlogged, toe-tapping nation unto itself.

LINK YOUR TRIP

16 Highway 1
From Thibodaux make your way to Baton Rouge then head east on I-12 and I-10 all the way to the start of your Florida coast cruise.

18 The Blues Highway
From Thibodaux head north to Baton Rouge then east on I-12. At Hammond, head north on I-55 to Memphis.

01 Thibodaux

Thibodaux (tib-ah-doe), huddled against the banks of Bayou Lafourche, is the traditional gateway to Cajun Country for those traveling from New Orleans. Thanks to a city center lined with historic homes, it's a fair bit more attractive than nearby Houma, which is often also cited as a major Cajun Country destination but is in reality more of a charmless oil town.

The main attraction in Thibodaux is the **Wetlands Acadian Cultural Center** *(nps.gov/jela)*, part of the Jean Lafitte National Park system. NPS rangers lead boat tours from here that chug into the bayou to the **ED White Plantation** home on Wednesday, Thursday and Friday. The center also hosts an excellent on-site museum and helpful staff provide free walking tours of Thibodaux town. If you're lucky, you'll land here on a Monday evening, when Cajun musicians jam out.

THE DRIVE: Get on Hwy 90 and drive to Breaux Bridge. It's

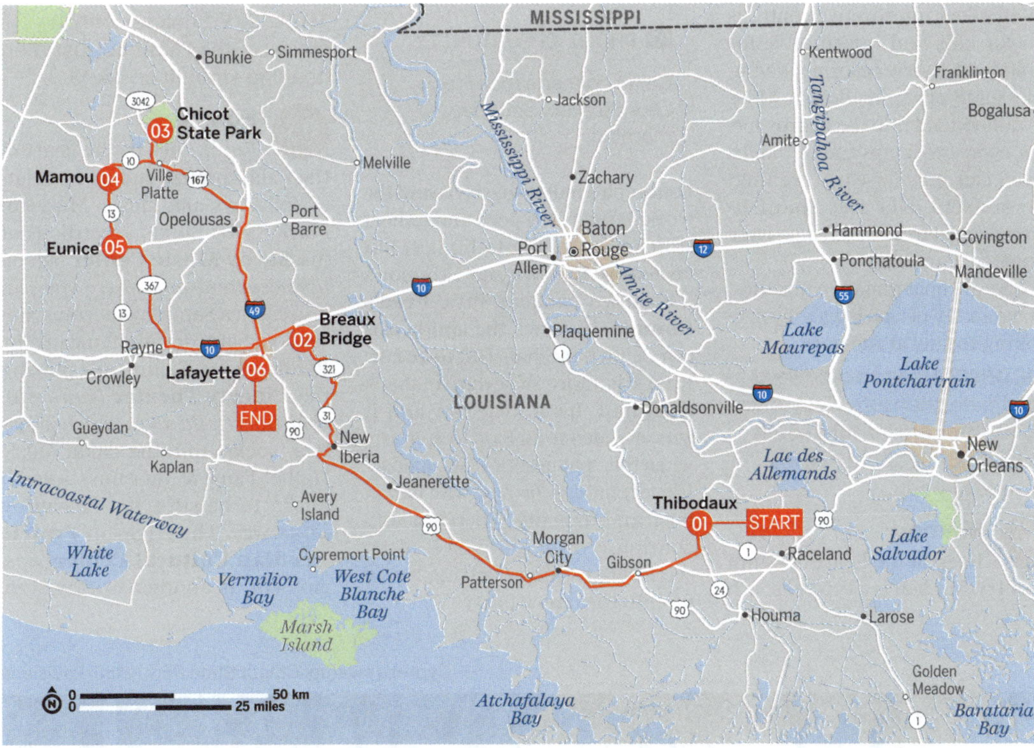

about two hours nonstop, but don't be afraid to occasionally peel off and check out some side roads.

02 Breaux Bridge

Little Breaux Bridge boasts a pretty 'downtown' of smallish side streets, Cajun hospitality and a silly amount of good food. Your main objective is to eat at **Buck & Johnny's** *(buckandjohnnys.com)*, where sinfully good Cajun fare is often served alongside live local music. On Saturday mornings, make sure to pop in for the toe-tapping zydeco brunch. If you're feeling dance-y, head to **La Poussiere** *(lapoussiere.com)*, an old-school Cajun dancehall that's like a throwback to another century. Beyond these two, there's not a lot to do in Breaux Bridge but stroll around the handsome town center and, if you're here during the first weekend in May, check out the **Breaux Bridge Crawfish Festival**.

Three miles south of Breaux Bridge is **Lake Martin**, a bird sanctuary that hosts thousands of great and cattle egrets, blue herons and more than a few gators. A small walkway extends over the algae-carpeted black water and loops through a pretty cypress swamp, while birds huddle in nearby trees.

Stop by Henderson, 8 miles northeast of Breaux Bridge. Nearby **Pat's** *(patsfishermanswharf.com)* serves decent seafood of the fried variety, and dancing of the two-step and Cajun genre.

THE DRIVE: From Breaux Bridge you can take Hwy 49 north for about 24 miles, then US 167 north to Ville Platte, then LA-3042 to Chicot State Park, a total trip time of about 80 minutes.

03 Chicot State Park

Cajun Country isn't just a cultural space – it's a physical landscape as well, a land of shadowy, moss-draped pine forest and slow-water bayous and lakes. Sometimes it can be tough seeing all this from the roadways, as roads have understandably been built away from floodable bottomlands.

Chicot State Park *(lastateparks.com)* is a wonderful place to access the natural beauty of Cajun Country.

An excellent interpretive center is fun for kids and informative for adults, and deserves enormous accolades for its open, airy design. Miles of trails extend into the nearby forests, cypress swamps and wetlands. If you can, stay for early evening; the sunsets over the Spanish-moss-draped trees that fringe Lake Chicot are superb.

There are boat rentals, campsites, cabins and 14-person lodges if you're looking to stay at the park.

THE DRIVE: Head back toward Ville Platte, then turn west onto LA-10. After 7 miles turn south onto LA-13; it's about 4 miles more to Mamou.

04 Mamou

Deep in the heart of Cajun Country, Mamou is a typical south Louisiana small town six days of the week; it's worth a peek and a short stop before rolling to Eunice. But on Saturday mornings, Mamou's hometown hangout, little **Fred's Lounge**, becomes the apotheosis of a Cajun dancehall. OK, to be fair: Fred's is more of a dance shack than hall. It's a little bar and it gets crowded from 8am to 2pm-ish, when this spot hosts a Francophone-friendly music morning, with bands, beer and dancing. There's a welcoming crowd, and you'll often see foreign visitors getting swept up into the dance party.

> PHOTO OPPORTUNITY
>
> Cajun concerts rock Fred's Lounge every Saturday morning.

THE DRIVE: Eunice is only 11 miles south of Mamou; just keep heading straight on LA-13.

05 Eunice

Eunice lies in the heart of the Cajun prairie and its associated folkways and music. Musician Mark Savoy builds accordions at his **Savoy Music Center** *(savoy musiccenter.com)*, where you can also catch a Saturday-morning jam session. Saturday night means the Rendez-Vous Cajuns are playing the **Liberty Theater** *(eunice-la.com/liberty-theater)*, which is just two blocks from the Cajun Music Hall of Fame & Museum – a small affair, to be sure, but charming in its way. The NPS-run **Prairie Acadian Cultural Center** *(nps.gov/jela)* is another worthy stop,

Cypress swamp, Chicot State Park (p151), Louisiana

JAYL/SHUTTERSTOCK

and often hosts music nights and educational lectures.

THE DRIVE: Head east on US 190 (Laurel Ave) and turn right onto LA-367. Follow LA-367 for around 19 miles (it becomes LA-98 for a bit), then merge onto I-10 eastbound. Follow I-10 for around 14 miles, then take exit 101 onto LA-182/N University Ave; follow it into downtown Lafayette.

06 Lafayette

Lafayette, capital of Cajun Country and fourth-largest city in Louisiana, has a wonderful concentration of good eats and culture. On most nights you can catch zydeco, country, blues, funk, swamp rock and even punk blasting out of the excellent **Blue Moon Saloon** *(bluemoonpresents.com)*; the crowd here is young, hip and often tattooed, but they'll get down to a fiddle as easily as drum-and-bass. During the last weekend in April, Lafayette hosts **Festival International de Louisiane** *(festivalinternational.org)*, the largest Francophone musical event in the western hemisphere.

Vermilionville *(bayouvermilion district.org)*, a restored/re-created 19th-century Cajun village, wends its way along the bayou near the airport. Costumed docents explain Cajun, Creole and Native American history, local bands perform on Sundays and boat tours of the bayou are offered. The not-as-polished **Acadian Village** *(acadianvillage.org)* offers a similar experience, minus the boat tours. Next to Vermilionville, the NPS runs the **Acadian Cultural Center** *(nps.gov/jela)*, containing exhibits on Cajun life.

NINA ALIZADA/SHUTTERSTOCK

Acadian Village, Lafayette, Louisiana

CAJUNS & CREOLES

A lot of tourists in Louisiana use the terms 'Cajun' and 'Creole' interchangeably, but the two cultures are different and distinct. 'Creole' refers to descendants of the original European settlers of Louisiana, a blended mix of mainly French and Spanish ancestry. The Creoles tend to have urban connections to New Orleans and consider their own culture refined and civilized. Many (but not all) were descended from aristocrats, merchants and skilled people.

The Cajuns can trace their lineage to the Acadians, colonists from rural France who settled Nova Scotia. After the British conquered Canada, the proud Acadians refused to kneel to the new crown, and were exiled in the mid-18th century – an act known as the Grand Dérangement. Many exiles settled in south Louisiana; they knew the area was French, but the Acadians ('Cajun' is an English bastardization of the word) were often treated as country bumpkins by the Creoles. The Acadians-cum-Cajuns settled in the bayous and prairies, and to this day self-conceptualize as a more rural, frontier-style culture.

Adding confusion to this is the practice, standard in many postcolonial French societies, of referring to mixed-race individuals as 'Creoles.' This happens in Louisiana, but there is a cultural difference between Franco-Spanish Creoles and mixed-race Creoles, even though these two communities very likely share actual blood ancestry.

18

FLORIDA & THE SOUTH

THE BLUES HIGHWAY

DURATION: 3 DAYS

DISTANCE: 310 MILES / 499KM

GREAT FOR: HISTORY & CULTURE

BEST TIME TO GO: BLUES FESTIVALS IN APRIL AND JUNE, AND OCTOBER IS A PLEASANT MONTH.

In the alluvial plains of the Mississippi Delta, along Hwy 61, American music took root. It arrived from Africa in the souls of enslaved people, morphed into field songs and wormed into the brain of a sharecropping troubadour waiting for a train. In Clarksdale, Robert Johnson reputedly made a deal with the devil and became America's first guitar hero. But to fully grasp the influence of the blues, start in Memphis.

LINK YOUR TRIP

17 Cajun Country
From Cleveland drive south to Indianola, get on Hwy 49 to Jackson, and then I-55 south until Hammond. From there head west to Baton Rouge and then south to Thibodaux and Cajun Country.

19 Natchez Trace Parkway
From Memphis head east on I-40 to Nashville where the Natchez Trace trail begins.

01 Memphis

The Mississippi Delta and Memphis have always been inextricably linked. Memphis, the region's biggest city, was a beacon for the Delta bluesmen, offering certain freedoms, African American-owned businesses, and the bright lights and foot-stomping crowds of Beale St – which is still rocking. **Rum Boogie** *(rumboogie.co)* is a Cajun-themed blues bar with a terrific house band. The original **BB King's** *(bbkingclubs.com)* is a living monument to the Mississippi genius who made good here. And it was Memphis where WC Handy was first credited with putting the blues to paper when he wrote 'Beale Street Blues' in 1916. You can visit the **house** *(wchandymemphis.org)* where Handy lived. The Mississippi Delta legacy bubbles up at **Sun Studio** *(sunstudio.com)*, where you can tour the studios that launched Elvis – whose interpretation of the blues birthed rock and roll. And it's running through the veins of the

★ BEST FOR

MUSIC

Strolling on Beale St with live music everywhere.

BRUCE YUANYUE BI/GETTY IMAGES

Beale Street, Memphis, Tennessee

wonderful **Stax Museum of American Soul Music** *(staxmuseum.com)*. Those connections are explained perfectly at the **Memphis Rock 'n' Soul Museum** *(memphisrocknsoul.org)*.

THE DRIVE: US 61 begins in Memphis, where it is a wide avenue snaking through the city's rough seam. Eventually the urban landscape gives way to flat farmland, and the highway becomes rural as you enter Mississippi. It's about 25 miles to Tunica.

02 Tunica

A collection of casinos rests near the riverbanks in Tunica, Hwy 61's most prosperous and least authentic town. Nevertheless, it is the gateway to the blues and home to a juke-joint mock-up of a **visitor center** *(tunicatravel.com/blues)*, where a cool interactive digital guide comes packed with information on famed blues artists and the **Mississippi Blues Trail** itself. The attached museum is a good place to learn about Delta bluesmen, get inspired about what you are about to experience, and do some plotting and planning. Unless you're here to gamble, however, Tunica is not otherwise noteworthy.

THE DRIVE: Continue on the arrow-straight road for 19 miles, then veer west on US 49 and drive 10 miles over the Mississippi River into Helena.

03 Helena

Helena, a depressed mill town 32 miles north and across the Mississippi River from Clarksdale, was once the home of blues legend Sonny Boy Williamson II. He was both a host of and performer on *King Biscuit Time,* America's original blues radio show. It still broadcasts out of the **Delta Cultural Center** *(deltaculturalcenter.com)*, a worthwhile blues museum. The **King Biscuit Blues Festival** is held over three days each October.

THE DRIVE: From Helena, take US 49 until it converges with US 61 in Mississippi. From there it's 30 miles south to the Crossroads. Peeking out above the trees on the northeast corner of US 61 and US 49, where the roads diverge once again, is the landmark weather vane of three interlocking guitars. You have arrived in Clarksdale, the Delta's beating heart.

04 Clarksdale

Clarksdale is the Delta's most useful base – with more comfortable hotel rooms and modern kitchens than the rest of the Delta combined. It's also within a couple of hours of the blues sights. If you want to know who's playing where, come see Roger Stolle at **Cat Head** *(cathead.biz)*. He also sells a good range of blues souvenirs, and is the main engine behind the annual **Juke Joint Festival**. Wednesday through Saturday, live music sweeps through Clarksdale like a summer storm. Morgan Freeman's **Ground Zero** *(groundzerobluesclub.com)* has the most professional bandstand and sound system, but it will never compare to **Red's**, a funky, red-lit, juke joint run with in-your-face charm by Red himself. He'll fire up his enormous grill outside on occasion. The **Delta Blues Museum** *(deltabluesmuseum.org)*, in the city's old train depot, has a fine collection of blues memorabilia, including Muddy Waters' reconstructed Mississippi cabin. The creative, multimedia exhibits also honor BB King, John Lee Hooker, Big Mama Thornton and WC Handy.

THE DRIVE: From Clarksdale, take US 49 south from the Crossroads for 15 miles to the tiny town of Tutwiler.

KING BISCUIT TIME

Sonny Boy Williamson II was the host of *King Biscuit Time* when BB King was a young man. King recalls listening to the lunch-hour program, and dreaming of possibilities. When he moved to Memphis as a teenager and began playing Beale St gigs, Williamson invited King to play on his radio show, and a star was born. Williamson remained an important mentor for King as his career took off. The radio show (AM 1360; *kffa.com*), which begins weekdays at 12:15pm, is still running. It was hosted by Sunshine Sonny Payne from 1951 until his death in 2018.

BB King Museum & Delta Interpretive Center, Indianola, Mississippi

NINA ALIZADA/SHUTTERSTOCK

05 Tutwiler

Sleepy Tutwiler is where WC Handy heard a man playing slide guitar with a knife at a train station in 1903. Handy, known as the 'father of the blues,' was inspired to (literally) write the original blues song, in 12 bars with a three-chord progression and AAB verse pattern, in 1912, though he wasn't widely recognized as an originator until 'Beale Street Blues' became a hit in 1916. That way-back divine encounter, which birthed blues and jazz, is honored along the **Tutwiler Tracks** *(msbluestrail.org)*, where the train station used to be. The murals there also reveal the directions to the grave of Sonny Boy Williamson II. He's buried amid a broken-down jumble of gravestones and his headstone is set back in the trees. Rusted harmonicas, candles and half-empty whiskey bottles have been left here as marks of respect.

THE DRIVE: Continue south on US 49 through more farmland for 42 miles, across the Yazoo River and into the city of Greenwood.

DETOUR

Water Valley

Start: 05 Tutwiler

From Tutwiler, take MS 32 east for about 55 miles to reach **Water Valley**, a town that's about as pretty as its name implies. This was once a depressed railroad hub until young professionals and artists from nearby Oxford came here attracted by its glut of gorgeous, if crumbling, historical homes. Veritable mansions were bought and restored for the cost of less than a year's rent in New York, yielding a small-town civic revival that's a joy to soak up. Wander along Main St and pop into galleries and restaurants, or marvel at the architecture of restored homes on Leland and Panola Sts.

06 Greenwood

This bustling small city is home to the headquarters of the Viking Range corporation, which builds its magnificent ranges here and whose wares you can buy in upscale showrooms. The company also owns the wonderful **Alluvian Hotel** *(thealluvian.com)*, which anchors downtown. Cruise past the oak-fronted mansions on Grand Ave then drive north 4 miles to the **Little Zion Missionary Baptist Church** and **Robert Johnson's grave** – one of three alleged burial spots for the legendary bluesman. Scenes from the 2011 movie *The Help* were shot in and around the city. On a somber note, Greenwood is forever attached to Byron De La Beckwith, a member of the local White Citizens' Council, who murdered Civil Rights activist Medgar Evers in 1963.

THE DRIVE: From Greenwood, take US 82 west for 30 miles, over the Yazoo River, through leafy horse country and an ugly commercial bloom of big chain stores, into Indianola.

07 Indianola

You have reached the hometown of arguably the Delta's biggest star. When BB King was still a child, Indianola was home to **Club Ebony** *(facebook.com/bbkingsclubebony)*, a fixture on the so-called 'chitlin' circuit.' Ebony gave BB his first steady work, and hosted legends like Howlin' Wolf, Muddy Waters, Count Basie and James Brown. The corner of Church and 2nd is where BB used to strum his guitar for passersby. Nearby, the fantastic **BB King Museum & Delta Interpretive Center** *(bbkingmuseum.org)* is set in a complex around the old Indianola cotton gin. The experience starts with a 12-minute film covering King's work. Afterward you are free to roam halls packed with interactive exhibits, tracing King's history and his musical

BB KING'S BLUES

BB King grew up in the cotton fields on the outskirts of Indianola, a leafy middle-class town, and it didn't take long before he learned what it meant to have the blues. His parents divorced when he was four, and his mother died when he was nine. His grandmother passed away when he was 14. All alone, he was forced to leave Indianola – the only town he ever knew – and live with his father in Lexington, MS. He quickly became homesick, and made his way back, riding his bicycle for two days to return to Indianola. As a young musician he was convinced he would become a cotton farmer. There weren't many other possibilities to consider. Or so he thought. When he went to Memphis for the first time in the 1940s, his world opened. From there he drifted into West Memphis, AR, where he met Sonny Boy Williamson, who put the young upstart on the radio for the first time, launching his career. When King died in 2015, it felt as if the entire Delta took a few days to mourn the loss of a legend.

FAVORITE BLUES FESTS

To make the most of your music-loving dollar, hit the Delta during one of its many blues festivals. Rooms can be scarce. Book well in advance.

Juke Joint Festival *(jukejointfestival.com)* Clarksdale
King Biscuit Blues Festival *(kingbiscuitfestival.com)* Helena
Bentonia Blues Festival *(facebook.com/BentoniaBluesFestival)* Bentonia
Sunflower River Blues & Gospel Festival *(sunflowerfest.org)* Clarksdale

influences – African, gospel and country. Other interactive exhibits demonstrate his influence on the next generation of artists, including Jimi Hendrix and the Allman Brothers.

THE DRIVE: From Indianola, go west through 15 miles of fast-food jumble along US 82 into Leland.

08 Leland

Leland is a small, down-on-its-luck town, but one with a terrific museum. The **Highway 61 Blues Museum** *(highway61blues.com)* offers details on local folks like Ruby Edwards and David 'Honeyboy' Edwards.

Luminary Jim Henson, the creator of the Muppets, is also from Leland, and his life and work are celebrated at the **Jim Henson Exhibit** on the bank of Deer Creek.

THE DRIVE: Head west on US 82 for 10 miles until it ends near the river.

09 Greenville

The Mississippi River town of Greenville was a fixture on the riverboat route and has long been a gambling resort area. For years it supported blues and jazz musicians who played the resorts. Although it's scruffy around the edges, Greenville can be pleasant along the river. But the real reason to visit is to try the steaks, tamales and chili at **Doe's Eat Place** *(doeseatplace.com)* – a classic hole-in-the-wall joint you may never forget.

THE DRIVE: Return to Leland on US 82 then pick up US 61N, following it for about 25 miles to Cleveland. To track the Mississippi River instead, take MS 1N to MS 446E.

10 Cleveland

The **Grammy Museum Mississippi** *(grammymuseumms.org)*, which opened in 2016 on the campus of Delta State University in Cleveland, is a modern-day music incubator. This glossy outpost of the Grammy Museum – the other is in Los Angeles – encourages visitors to write their own songs and try their hand at various instruments. Other exhibits trace the history of recorded music, with a focus on its cultural context and on Mississippi's rich musical heritage.

WC Handy may have 'discovered' the blues at the Tutwiler Depot, but practically speaking, the genre truly emerged at the cotton plantations scattered across the Delta. Frequented by early blues musician Charley Patton, **Dockery Farms** *(dockeryfarms.org)*, around 7 miles east of Cleveland, was one of the best-known gathering spots for musicians. On the grounds of the farm today, you'll find an interpretive marker, a cotton gin, a view of the Sunflower River and the very occasional live performance.

For another evocative blues sight, drive 6 miles north of Cleveland on Hwy 61 to Merigold. Here you'll find the slouching remains of **Po' Monkey's Lounge** *(msbluestrail.org/blues-trail-markers/po-monkeys)*. Perched between cotton fields and a bayou, this legendary juke joint, famous for its Thursday night parties, closed in 2016 after the death of proprietor Willie 'Po' Monkey' Seaberry.

Intersection sign Hwys 49 & 61, Clarksdale (p156), Mississippi
HEIDI BESEN/SHUTTERSTOCK

61
49
The CROSSROADS

19

FLORIDA & THE SOUTH

NATCHEZ TRACE PARKWAY

DURATION: 3 DAYS

DISTANCE: 444 MILES / 715KM

GREAT FOR: HISTORY & CULTURE

BEST TIME TO GO: THE CLIMATE IS LOVELY IN SPRING (APRIL TO JUNE) AND FALL (SEPTEMBER TO NOVEMBER).

The USA grew from infancy to adolescence in the late 18th and 19th centuries. That's when it explored and expanded, traded and clashed with Native Americans, and eventually confronted its own shadow during the Civil War. Evidence of this drama borders the Natchez Trace, an ancient footpath transformed into a parkway by the Civilian Conservation Corps in the 1930s. Before you begin, hit Nashville's honky-tonks for rollicking country music.

LINK YOUR TRIP

17 Cajun Country
Head south on Hwy 61 from Natchez to Cajun Country's launching point in Thibodaux.

18 The Blues Highway
At Tupelo head northwest on I-78 to Memphis to link up with the Blues Highway.

01 Nashville

Although this leafy, sprawling Southern city – with its thriving economy and hospitable locals – has no scarcity of charms, it really is all about the music. Boot-stomping honky-tonks lure aspiring stars from across the country, all of them hoping to ascend into the royalty on display at the **Country Music Hall of Fame** *(countrymusichalloffame.org)*. Don't miss **Bluebird Cafe** *(bluebirdcafe.com)*, tucked into a suburban strip mall. No chitchat in this singer-songwriter haven, or you'll get bounced. Enjoy a less-controlled musical environment at **Tootsie's Orchid Lounge** *(tootsies.net)*, a glorious dive smothered with old photographs and handbills from the Nashville Sound's glory days. Bluegrass fans will adore **Station Inn** *(stationinn.com)*, where you'll sit at a small cocktail table, swill beer (only) and marvel at the lightning fingers of fine bluegrass players. Before hopping onto the Natchez

JOSEPH D WASHBURN/SHUTTERSTOCK

★ BEST FOR

HISTORY

Touring the Civil War–era Carter House in Franklin.

Carter House, Franklin, Tennessee

Trace, fuel up with country ham and red-eye gravy at the **Loveless Cafe** *(lovelesscafe.com),* beside the start of the parkway. It's been serving Southern fare to travelers for more than 65 years.

THE DRIVE: Heading south, you will traverse the Double-Arch Bridge, 155ft above the valley, before settling in for a pleasant country drive on the parkway. You'll notice dense woods encroaching and arching elegantly over the baby-bottom-smooth highway for the next 444 miles. It's about 10 miles from Nashville to Franklin.

02 Franklin

Before you embark on the Trace, swing a side trip to Franklin, just 10 miles outside Nashville. The Victorian-era downtown of this tiny historic hamlet is charming, and the nearby artsy enclave of Leiper's Fork is fun and eclectic. But you're in the area to check out one of the Civil War's bloodiest battlefields. On November 30, 1864, 37,000 men (20,000 Confederates and 17,000 Union soldiers) fought over a 2-mile stretch of Franklin's outskirts. Nashville's sprawl has turned much of that battlefield into suburbs, but you can see a preserved 8-acre chunk at the **Carter House** *(boft.org),* still riddled with 1000-plus bullet holes.

THE DRIVE: The parkway carves a path through dense woodland as you swerve past another historic district at Leiper's Fork, before coming to the first of several Old Trace turnouts after about 40 miles.

03 Old Trace

At Mile 403.7 (don't mind the 'backward' mile markers as we think a north–south route works best) you'll find the first of several sections of the **Old Trace**. In the early 19th century, Kaintucks (boatmen from Ohio and Pennsylvania) floated coal, livestock and agricultural goods down the Ohio and Mississippi Rivers aboard flat-bottom boats. Often their boats were emptied in Natchez, where they disembarked and began the long walk home up the Old Trace to Nashville, where they could access established roads further north.

This path intersected Choctaw and Chickasaw country, which meant it was hazardous. In fact, Indigenous travelers were the first to beat this earth. You can walk a 2000ft section of that original trail at this turnout.

THE DRIVE: There follows a beautiful 20-mile stretch of road, as the parkway flows past Baker Bluff (Mile 405.1), a pull-off with views over Duck River. Just south, a parking lot for Jackson Falls (Mile 404.7) can be reached by a short, steep trail (900ft one way). You can also hike to the falls from Baker Bluff; it just takes a little longer.

04 Meriwether Lewis Site

At Mile 385.9, you'll come to the **Meriwether Lewis Site**, where the famed explorer and first governor of the Louisiana Territory died mysteriously at Grinders Inn. His fateful journey began in September 1809, and his plan was to travel to Washington, DC, to defend his spending of government funds (think of it as an early-days subpoena before a Congressional committee). At Fort Pickering, a remote wilderness outpost near modern-day Memphis, he met up with a Chickasaw agent named James Neely, who was to escort the Lewis party safely through Chickasaw land. They traveled north, through the bush, and along the Old Trace to Grinder's Stand, and checked into the inn run by the pioneering Grinder family. Mrs Grinder made up a room for Lewis and fed him, and after he retired, two shots rang out. The legendary explorer was shot in the head and chest and died at 35. Lewis' good friend, Thomas Jefferson, was convinced it was suicide. His family disagreed. His grave marker is in the pioneer cemetery at the back of the adjacent loop road. The inn no longer stands, but a small cabin at the site, staffed by docents, has a few exhibits.

THE DRIVE: It's about 77 miles to your next stop. You'll cross into Alabama at Mile 341.8. In Alabama, music buffs can detour to Muscle Shoals, where producers and local studios worked with Bob Dylan, the Rolling Stones, Otis Redding, Aretha Franklin, Wilson Pickett and other artists. You'll cross into Mississippi at Mile 308.

05 Bear Creek Mound

Just across the Alabama state line in Mississippi, at Mile 308.8, you'll find **Bear Creek**

Rope bridge, Tishomingo State Park, Mississippi

RHONDA HICKOX/SHUTTERSTOCK

Mound, an ancient Indigenous ceremonial site. There are seven groups of Native American mounds found along the parkway, all of them in Mississippi. Varying in shape from Maya-like pyramids to domes to small rises, they were used for worship and burying the dead; a number were seen as power spots for local chiefs who sometimes lived on top of them. That was arguably the case at Bear Creek, which was built between 1100 and 1300 CE. Archaeologists are convinced that there was a temple and/or a chief's dwelling at the top of the rise.

THE DRIVE: The highway bisects Tishomingo State Park at Mile 304.5.

06 Tishomingo State Park

Named for the Chickasaw Chief Tishomingo, this lovely **park** *(mdwfp.com/parks-destinations/park/tishomingo-state-park)* is an inviting place to camp and explore. It's home to evocative, moss-covered sandstone cliffs and rock formations, fern gullies, waterfalls in Bear Creek canyon and a photogenic suspension bridge built by the Civilian Conservation Corps in the 1930s. Hiking trails abound, and you can paddle Bear Creek in a rented canoe. Wildflowers bloom in spring. It's a special oasis, and one that was utilized by the Chickasaw and their Paleo-Indian antecedents. Evidence of their civilization in the park dates back to 7000 BCE.

THE DRIVE: Just under 20 miles of more wooded beauty leads from Tishomingo State Park to the next stop, a series of Native American mounds at Mile 286.7.

07 Pharr Mounds

This is a 2000-year-old, 90-acre complex of eight **Indigenous burial sites**. Four were excavated in 1966 and found to have fireplaces and low platforms where the dead were cremated. Ceremonial artifacts were also found, along with copper vessels, which raised some eyebrows. Copper is not indigenous to Mississippi, and its presence here indicates an extensive trade network with other nations and peoples.

THE DRIVE: About 17 miles on, at Mile 269.4, you'll come across a turnout that links up to another section of the Old Trace and offers a bit more recent history.

08 Confederate Gravesites

Just north of Tupelo, on a small rise overlooking the Old Trace, lies a row of 13 **graves** of unknown Confederate soldiers. What led to their fate has been lost in time. Some believe they died during the Confederate retreat from Corinth, MS, following the legendary Battle of Shiloh; others think they were wounded in the nearby Battle of Brice's Crossroads, and buried by their brothers here.

THE DRIVE: Less than 10 miles later you will loop into the comparatively large hamlet of Tupelo, at Mile 266, where you can gather road supplies for the southward push.

09 Tupelo

Here, the **Natchez Trace Parkway Visitor Center** *(nps.gov/natr)* is a fantastic resource with good natural- and American-history displays, and detailed parkway maps. Tupelo is world famous for its favorite son, and **Elvis Presley's Birthplace** *(elvispresleybirthplace.com)* is a pilgrimage site for those who kneel before the King. The original structure has a new roof and furniture, but no matter the decor – it was within these humble walls that Elvis was born on January 8, 1935, learned to play the guitar and began to dream big. His family's church, where he was first bitten by the music bug, has been transported and restored here, too. Downtown's Tupelo Hardware Co is where Elvis bought his first guitar. It closed in 2025, but you can still visit from the outside – rumor has it that the city might purchase the historic building.

THE DRIVE: Barely out of Tupelo, at Mile 261.8, is Chickasaw Village. The Bynum Mounds are nearly another 30 miles south. You'll see the turnoff just after leaving the Tombigbee National Forest.

DETOUR

Oxford

Start: 09 Tupelo

If you plan on driving the entire Natchez Trace from Nashville to Natchez, you should make the 50-mile detour along Hwy 6 to Oxford, a town rich in culture and history. This is Faulkner country, and Oxford is a thriving university town with terrific restaurants and bars. Don't miss the catfish dinner at **Taylor Grocery** *(taylorgrocery.com)*, 15 minutes south of Oxford, via County Rd 303.

10 Chickasaw Village & Bynum Mounds

South from Tupelo, the Trace winds past the **Chickasaw Village site**, where displays document how the Chickasaw lived and traveled during the fur-trade heyday of the early 19th century. It was 1541 when Hernando de Soto entered Mississippi under the Spanish flag. They fought a bitter battle, and though de Soto survived, the Chickasaw held strong. By the 1600s the English had engaged the Chickasaw in what became a lucrative fur trade. Meanwhile, the French held sway just west in the massive Louisiana Territory. As allies to England, the Chickasaw found themselves up against not only the French, but also their Choctaw allies.

Further down the road is the site of six 2100-year-old **Bynum Mounds**. Five were excavated just after WWII, and copper tools and cremated remains were found. Two of the mounds have been restored for public viewing.

THE DRIVE: It's about 39 miles from the Bynum Mounds to Jeff Busby Park at Mile 193.1.

11 Jeff Busby Park

Don't miss this hilltop park with picnic tables and a fabulous overlook taking in low-lying, forested hills that extend for miles. Exhibits at the top include facts and figures about local flora and fauna, as well as a primer on indigenous tools. **Little Mountain Trail**, a half-mile loop that takes 30 minutes to complete, descends from the parking lot into a shady hollow. Another half-mile spur trail branches from that loop to the campground below.

THE DRIVE: Thirteen miles down the road, near Mile 180, the forest clears and an agrarian plateau emerges, jade-hued and perfect, as if this land has been cultivated for centuries.

12 French Camp

In the hamlet of French Camp, the site of a former French pioneer settlement, you can walk around an plantation-era home, built by Revolutionary War veteran Colonel James Drane. Nearby it's possible to check out the ornate stagecoach of Greenwood LeFlore, which carried the last chief of the Choctaw Nation east of the Mississippi on his two trips to Washington to negotiate with President Andrew Jackson. For locally made crafts, step into the **Log Cabin Gift Shop**. Sandwiches, soup and desserts are served at the attached **Council House Cafe**. The gift shop and cafe are run by French Camp Academy, a Christian boarding school nearby.

THE DRIVE: As you head south, the forest clears for snapshot scenes of horses on the prairie, before the trees encroach again and again. The next stop is about 55 miles down the Trace. You'll pass Kosciusko, the birthplace and childhood hometown of media star Oprah Winfrey, at Mile 150.

13 Tupelo-Baldcypress Swamp

At Mile 122, you can examine some of these trees up close as you tour the stunning **Tupelo-Baldcypress Swamp**. The 20-minute trail snakes through an abandoned channel and continues on a boardwalk over the milky green swamp shaded by water tupelo and bald cypresses. Look for turtles on the rocks and gators in the murk.

THE DRIVE: The swamp empties into the Ross R Barnett Reservoir, visible to the east as you roll toward the state capital of Jackson. Exit the parkway at Old Canton Rd for arts and crafts at the Mississippi Craft Center. Beyond Jackson, there is the photogenic Sunken Trace at Mile 41.5.

DETOUR

Jackson

Start: 13 Tupelo-Baldcypress Swamp

Twenty-two miles south of the swamp, and just a bit further along the interstate, is Mississippi's capital. With its fine downtown museums, and artsy-funky Fondren District, Jackson offers a blast of 'Now!' The city's two best museums stand side by side: the **Museum of Mississippi History** *(mmh.mdah.ms.gov)* and the **Mississippi Civil Rights Museum** *(mcrm.mdah.ms.gov)*. Literature fans should tour the **Eudora Welty House** *(welty.mdah.ms.gov)*. This is where the literary giant, and Pulitzer Prize winner, crafted all her books. Do not leave town without enjoying lunch or dinner at **Walker's Drive-In** *(walkersdrivein.com)*.

EWY MEDIA/SHUTTERSTOCK

Greek Revival Melrose, Natchez, Mississippi

14 Emerald Mound

Near Mile 10.3, accessible by a graded road leading west from the parkway, the eye-catching **Emerald Mound** *(nps.gov/natr)* is by far the best of the Indigenous mound sites. Using stone tools, pre-Columbian ancestors to the Natchez people graded this 8-acre mountain into a flat-topped pyramid. It is now the second-largest mound in America. There are shady, creekside picnic spots, and if you climb to the top, you'll find a vast lawn along with a diagram of what the temple may have looked like. It would have been perched on the secondary and highest of the mounds. It's a perfect diversion on an easy spring afternoon just before the sun smolders, when birdsong rings from the trees and mingles with the call of a distant train.

THE DRIVE: Drive on for about 13 more miles. As you approach Natchez, the mossy arms of southern oaks spread over the roadway, and the air gets just a touch warmer and more moist. You can almost smell the river from here.

15 Natchez

When the woods part, revealing historic plantation-era mansions, you have reached Natchez. In the 1840s, Natchez had more millionaires per capita than any city in the world (because the plantation owners didn't pay their workers). Opulent and undeniably beautiful, these homes were built on the back of the labor of enslaved people. The mansions open for tours in the spring and fall 'pilgrimage seasons,' and some are open year-round. Tours of the **Greek Revival Melrose** *(nps.gov/natc)* house take a multi-perspective look at life on the city estate of an enslaver and cotton magnate.

Natchez has dirt under its fingernails, too. When Mark Twain came through (which he did on numerous occasions), he crashed in a room above the local watering hole. **Under the Hill Saloon**, across the street from the mighty Mississippi River, remains the best bar in town, with terrific live music on weekends.

STAY AWHILE

NASHVILLE

BY MARGOT BIGG

The first time I visited Nashville, I didn't know what to expect. While I love discovering new music, I was worried that the city might be too country and western for my tastes. How wrong I was. While country is certainly the dominant genre in Music City, spend a couple of days here and any preconceived notions about it being all about fishing, pickup trucks and rusty spurs will quickly vanish. Head to some open mics or check out a performance at church-turned-venue **Ryman Auditorium** *(ryman.com)*, or the historic **Grand Ole Opry** *(opry.com)*, and you'll see just how acoustically and lyrically versatile the all-American genre really is.

LINK YOUR TRIP

Nashville lies at the northern end of the **19 Natchez Trace Parkway** (p160).

For a deep dive into Nashville's country-fueled party scene, join the masses of bachelorette parties and revelers for a night out at Lower Broadway, aka the Honky Tonk Highway. While you won't see many locals partying it up at the neon-signed, multistory bars that make up this rowdy strip, you will hear plenty of local musicians bashing out danceable country tunes. Most venues don't charge entry fees, so bring cash tips for performers.

If you're up for a meal, Lower Broadway has branches of two of the most popular stops to pick up Nashville's famous hot chicken: **Prince's Hot Chicken** *(princeshotchicken.com)* and **Hattie B's Hot Chicken** *(hattieb.com)*. For a plant-based version of this much-loved dish, make a beeline to my favorite place to eat in Nashville, **Vegelicious** *(vegeliciousllc.com)*, a 15-minute walk north of the honky-tonk action.

Left: Grand Ole Opry, Nashville Tennessee; Right: Lower Broadway, Nashville, Tennessee

LEFT TO RIGHT: GRINDSTONE MEDIA GROUP/SHUTTERSTOCK, PHOTO SPIRIT/SHUTTERSTOCK

PLACES TO STAY...

Bobby Nashville
One of Nashville's newest upscale properties, this sleek downtown spot makes a convenient base for checking out the lively honky-tonk scene on Lower Broadway, a mere three blocks away. *opalcollection.com/nashville*

Gallatin Hotel
Check yourself in at this 'concierge-less' hotel before retiring to one of the brightly hued rooms and suites (most of which, admittedly, resemble children's playrooms). The hotel donates all of its profits to charity. *thegallatinhotel.com*

Urban Cowboy
Housed in an East Nashville Victorian mansion, this inn leans into the masculine whiskey-and-leather aesthetic, with dark, moody-dude decor and regular live music. Guests must be 21 or older to stay. *urbancowboy.com*

20

FLORIDA & THE SOUTH

BLUE RIDGE PARKWAY

★ BEST FOR

FAMILIES

Enjoy a steam-train ride, gem mining, easy hiking and old-fashioned candy.

DURATION: 5 DAYS

DISTANCE: 210 MILES / 338KM

GREAT FOR: NATURE, FAMILIES

BEST TIME TO GO: MAY TO OCTOBER FOR LEAFY TREES AND SEASONAL ATTRACTIONS.

Linn Cove Viaduct, Blue Ridge Parkway (p170), North Carolina

The Blue Ridge Parkway winds for 469 sumptuous miles, from Virginia's Shenandoah National Park to the Great Smoky Mountains. As it carves through a rugged landscape of craggy peaks, crashing waterfalls and thick forests, each languid curve unveils another panorama of multihued trees and mist-shrouded mountains, with tantalizing viewpoints encouraging frequent stops. No billboards spoil the views, and there's seldom even a sign of human presence.

LINK YOUR TRIP

08 Skyline Drive
Head north from Asheville on I-26 till you reach I-81. Follow that northeast for 300 miles to Strasburg, where you'll take I-66 east to Front Royal.

21 The Great Smokies
From Waterrock Knob Visitor Center, head north until you reach Hwy 19. Follow this west through Cherokee to the start of the Great Smokies at Nantahala Outdoor Center.

01 Valle Crucis

How do you start a road trip through the mountains? With a good night's sleep and all the right gear, of course. You'll find both in Valle Crucis, a bucolic village 8 miles west of Boone. After slumbering beneath sumptuous linens at the 200-year-old **Mast Farm Inn**, ease into the day sipping coffee in a rocking chair on the former farmhouse's front porch.

Down the road lies the **Original Mast General Store** *(mastgeneral store.com)*. The first of the many Mast general stores that dot the High Country, this rambling clapboard building still sells many of the same products that it did back in 1883. As well as bacon, axes and hard candy, though, you'll now find hiking shoes, lava lamps and French country hand towels.

The store's annex, just south along Hwy 194, sells outdoor apparel and hiking gear.

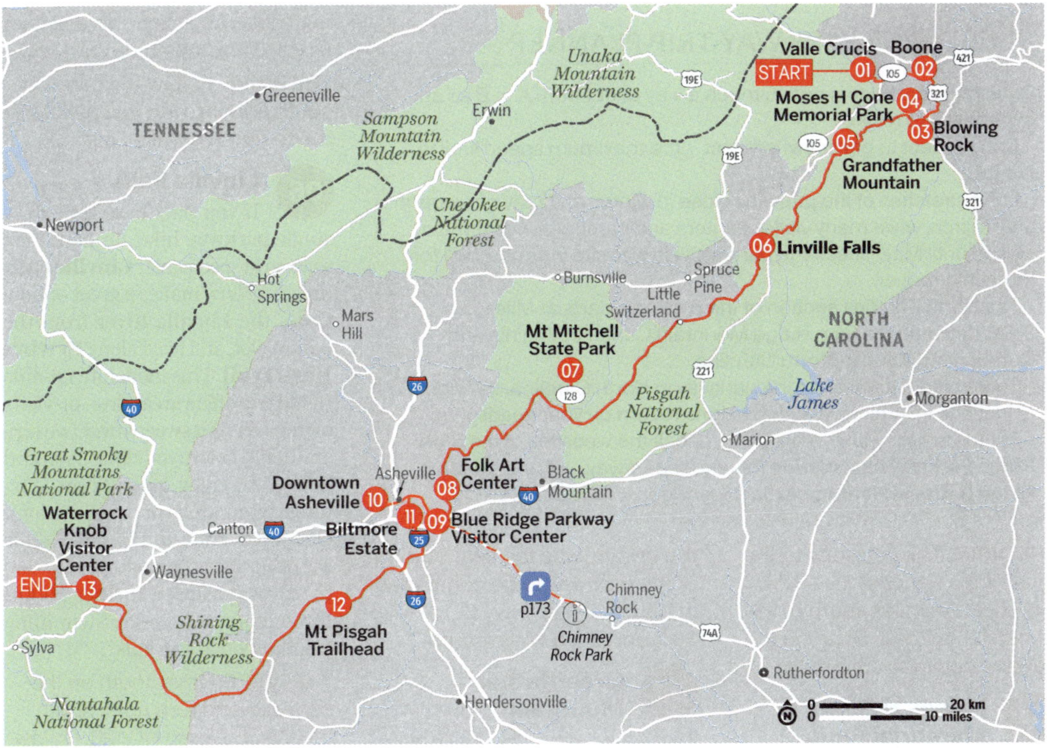

BILANOL/SHUTTERSTOCK

THE DRIVE: Drive southeast on Hwy 194, also known as Broadstone Rd, through 3 miles of rural splendor, then turn left at Hwy 105.

02 Boone

If you're traveling with kids or are a wannabe prospector yourself, stop at **Foggy Mountain Gem Mine** *(foggymountaingems.com)* to pan for semiprecious stones. Several gem-mining spots are located in these parts, but the graduate gemologists here take their craft a bit more seriously. Rough stones are sold by the bucketload, which you sift in a flume line. For additional fees, they'll cut and mount your favorite finds.

In downtown Boone, the bustling home of Appalachian State, you'll find quirky shopping and dining along King St, where **Melanie's Food Fantasy** is a good option for a hearty breakfast or tasty lunch. Keep an eye out for the bronze statue of bluegrass legend Doc Watson, born nearby in 1923 and depicted strumming a Gallagher guitar on a street corner.

THE DRIVE: From King St, turn onto Hwy 321 just past the Dan'l Boone Inn restaurant. Drive 4 miles then turn right at the theme park.

03 Blowing Rock

The parkway runs just above the village of Blowing Rock, which sits at an elevation of 4000ft. On a cloudy morning, drive south on Hwy 321 to the top of the mountain to check out the cloud-capped views of surrounding peaks. The eastern Continental Divide runs through the bar at the **Green Park Inn**, a grand white-clapboard hotel that opened in 1891. Author Margaret Mitchell stayed here while writing *Gone with the Wind*. For a memorable meal stop by **Bistro Roca**.

Riding the **Tweetsie Railroad** *(tweetsie.com)*, a 1917 coal-fired steam locomotive that chugs on a 3-mile loop, is a rite of passage for every North Carolina child. It's the centerpiece of a theme park where Appalachian culture meets the Wild West, with midway rides, fudge shops and family-friendly shows to round out the fun.

BLUE RIDGE PARKWAY TRIP PLANNER

Driving the parkway is not so much a way to get from A to B as an experience to relish.

Don't expect to get anywhere fast – the maximum speed limit is 45mph.

Long stretches of the parkway close in winter, and may not reopen until March, while many visitor centers and campgrounds remain closed until May. Check the park-service website *(nps.gov/blri)* for more information.

The North Carolina section of the parkway starts at Mile 216.9, between the Blue Ridge Mountain Center in Virginia and Cumberland Knob in North Carolina.

There are 26 tunnels on the parkway in North Carolina, as opposed to just one in Virginia. Watch for signs to turn on your headlights.

For more help with trip planning, check the websites of the **Blue Ridge Parkway Association** *(blueridgeparkway.org)* and the **Blue Ridge National Heritage Area** *(blueridgeheritage.com)*.

THE DRIVE: The entrance to the Blue Ridge Parkway is in Blowing Rock, 2.3 miles south of the Tweetsie Railroad. Once on the parkway, drive south 2 miles.

04 Moses H Cone Memorial Park

Hikers and equestrians share 25 miles of carriage roads on the former estate of Moses H Cone, a philanthropist and conservationist who made his fortune in denim. Moses built a Colonial Revival mansion, **Flat Top Manor**, in 1901, which was given, along with the grounds, to the National Park Service in the 1950s. Directly accessible from the parkway at Mile 294, it now holds both a museum and the **Parkway Craft Center** *(southernhighlandguild.org)*, where the Southern Highland Craft Guild sells superb Appalachian crafts at reasonable prices.

THE DRIVE: Head south on the parkway, passing split rail fences, stone walls, streams and meadows. Just south of Mile 304, the parkway curves across the Linn Cove Viaduct, which, because of the fragility of the terrain, was the final section of the parkway to be completed, in 1987. Exit onto Hwy 221 at Mile 305, and drive 1 mile south.

05 Grandfather Mountain

The highest of the Blue Ridge Mountains, **Grandfather Mountain** *(grandfather.com)* looms north of the parkway 20 miles southwest of Blowing Rock. As a visitor destination, it's famous as the location of the Mile High Swinging Bridge, the focus of a privately owned attraction that also includes hiking trails plus a small museum and wildlife reserve. Don't let a fear of heights scare you away. Though the bridge is a mile above sea level, and on gusty days you can hear its steel girders 'sing,' it spans a less fearsome chasm that's just 80ft deep.

Much of Grandfather Mountain – including its loftiest summit, Calloway Peak (5946ft), a strenuous 2.4-mile hike from the swinging bridge – is a UNESCO Biosphere Reserve belonging to **Grandfather Mountain State Park** *(ncparks.gov)*. Its 12 miles of wilderness hiking trails can also be accessed for free at Mile 300 on the parkway.

THE DRIVE: Follow the parkway south and turn left just past Mile 316 to reach Linville Falls.

06 Linville Falls

If you only have time for a single parkway hike, an hour-long sojourn at spectacular **Linville Falls** *(nps.gov/blri)* makes a great option. Cross the Linville River from the parking lot, and head along **Erwin's View Trail**. This moderate 1.6-mile round trip offers great close-up views of the river as it sweeps over two separate falls, before you climb a wooded hillside to enjoy magnificent long-range panoramas in two directions. One looks back to the falls, while the other faces downstream, where the river crashes a further 2000ft through a rocky gorge. Swimming is forbidden at the falls.

THE DRIVE: Drive south on the parkway and turn right, south of Mile 355, onto NC 128. Follow NC 128 into the park.

07 Mt Mitchell State Park

Be warned: a major decision awaits visitors to North Carolina's first-ever **state park** *(ncparks.gov)*. Will you drive up Mt Mitchell, at 6684ft the highest peak east of the Mississippi, or will you hike to the top? Make your mind up at the park office, which sits beside a steep 2.2-mile summit trail that typically takes around 1½ hours one way.

Once up there, you'll see the grave of University of North Carolina professor Elisha Mitchell. He came here in 1857 to prove his previous estimate of the mountain's height, only to fall from a waterfall and die.

Mile High Swinging Bridge,, Grandfather Mountain, North Carolina
ANTHONY GEORGE VISUALS/SHUTTERSTOCK

PHOTO OPPORTUNITY

The mile-high suspension bridge at Grandfather Mountain.

A circular ramp leads to dramatic views over and beyond the surrounding Black Mountains.

THE DRIVE: Return to the parkway and drive south to Mile 382. Look out for blooming rhododendrons during the last two weeks of June.

08 Folk Art Center

Part gallery, part store, and wholly dedicated to Southern artisanship, the superb **Folk Art Center** *(southernhighlandguild.org)* is 6 miles east of downtown Asheville. The handcrafted Appalachian chairs that hang above its lobby make an impressive appetizer for the permanent collection of the Southern Highland Craft Guild, a treasury of pottery, baskets, quilts and woodcarvings that's displayed on the 2nd floor. There are daily demonstrations by experts, and the **Allanstand Craft Shop** on the 1st floor sells high-quality traditional crafts.

THE DRIVE: Turn right onto the parkway and drive south. Cross the Swannanoa River and I-40, then continue to Mile 384.

09 Blue Ridge Parkway Visitor Center

At the Blue Ridge Parkway's helpful Asheville-area **visitor center** *(nps.gov/blri)*, you can sit back and let the scenery come to you, courtesy of a big-screen movie that captures the beauty and wonder of 'America's favorite journey.' Park rangers at the front desk gladly advise on parkway hiking trails, and sliding the digital panel across the amazing 'I-Wall' map brings up details of regional sites and activities. A separate desk is stocked with brochures and coupons for Asheville's attractions.

Folk Art Center, Asheville, North Carolina
EWY MEDIA/SHUTTERSTOCK

THE DRIVE: Drive north, backtracking over the interstate and river, and exit at Tunnel Rd, which is Hwy 70. Drive west to Hwy 240, and follow it west to the exits for downtown Asheville.

DETOUR

Chimney Rock Park

Start: 09 Blue Ridge Parkway Visitor Center

The stupendous 315ft monolith known as Chimney Rock towers above the slender, forested valley of the Rocky Broad River, a gorgeous 28-mile drive southeast of Asheville on Hwy 74A. Protruding in naked splendor from soaring granite walls, its flat top bears the fluttering American flag. It's now the focus of a popular **state park** *(chimneyrockpark.com)*. Climb the rock via the 499 steps of the **Outcropping Trail** or simply ride the elevator deep inside the rock.

The leisurely and less-crowded **Hickory Nut Falls Trail** leads in around 15 minutes through lush woods to the foot of a 404ft waterfall, high above the river. If it looks familiar, you may be remembering it from dramatic scenes in The *Last of the Mohicans*, filmed here.

Charming **Chimney Rock village**, immediately below the park, is a pleasant place to spend the night.

10 Downtown Asheville

The undisputed 'capital' of the North Carolina mountains, Asheville is both a major tourist destination and one of the coolest small cities in the South. Home to an invigorating mix of hipsters, hippies and hikers, and offering easy access to outdoor adventures of all kinds, it's also a rare liberal enclave in the conservative countryside.

Strolling between downtown's historic art-deco buildings, you'll encounter literary pilgrims celebrating the city's angsty famous son – and author of *Look Homeward, Angel* – at the **Thomas Wolfe Memorial** *(wolfememorial.com)*; nostalgic gamers flipping the flippers at the **Pinball Museum** *(ashevillepinball.com)*; left-leaning intellectuals browsing at **Malaprop's Bookstore & Cafe** *(malaprops.com)*; and design connoisseurs shopping for crafts in **Horse & Hero** *(@horseandhero)*.

Head down the adjoining South Slope to find specialist microbreweries, such as spooky **Burial** *(burialbeer.com)*, which have earned Asheville the nickname 'Beer City,' or hit the River Arts District to enjoy barbecue emporium **12 Bones**. Budget travelers looking to stay in Asheville should head for downtown's excellent **Sweet Peas Hostel**.

♥ WHY I LOVE THIS TRIP

GREG WARD, WRITER

For any card-carrying member of the road-trip fan club, the iconic Blue Ridge Parkway ranks with the finest of America's fabled four-wheeled journeys. In the fall, the parkway comes alive in a kaleidoscopic cavalcade of intense color, turning this majestic mountain highway into a processional extravaganza of deep ruby-red and burnt-orange foliage, the very stuff from which dreams are woven.

BLUEGRASS & MOUNTAIN MUSIC

For locally grown fiddle-and-banjo music, grab your dance partner and head deep into the hills of the High Country. Regional shows and music jams are listed on the **Blue Ridge Music Trails** *(blueridgemusicnc.com)* and **Blue Ridge National Heritage Area** *(blueridgeheritage.com)* websites.

Here are two to get you started.

Mountain Home Music Concert Series *(mountainhomemusic.com)* Spring through fall, enjoy shows by Appalachian musicians in Boone on scheduled Friday and Saturday nights.

Historic Orchard at Altapass *(altapassorchard.org)* On weekends in May through October, settle in for an afternoon of music at Little Switzerland, Mile 328.

THE DRIVE: Follow Asheland Ave, which becomes McDowell St, south. After crossing the Swannanoa River, the entrance to the Biltmore Estate is on the right.

11 Biltmore Estate

The destination that put Asheville on the map, **Biltmore House** *(biltmore.com)* is the largest privately owned home in the US. Completed in 1895 for shipping and railroad heir George Washington Vanderbilt II, it was modeled after three châteaux that he'd seen in France's Loire Valley, and it still belongs to his descendants. It's extraordinarily expensive to visit, but there's a lot to see; allow several hours to explore the entire 8000-acre estate.

All visits to the grounds include tastings, while house-and-grounds tickets add on a 60-minute audio tour. A 5-mile drive through the manicured estate, which also holds several cafes and two top-end hotels, leads to the winery and dairy farm in Antler Hill Village.

THE DRIVE: Exit the grounds, then turn right onto Hwy 25 and continue for almost 3.5 miles to the parkway, and drive south.

12 Mt Pisgah Trailhead

To enjoy an hour or two of hiking that culminates in a panoramic view, pull into the parking lot beside the **Mt Pisgah trailhead**, just beyond Mile 407. The 1.6-mile trail (one way) climbs to the mountain's 5721ft summit, topped by a lofty TV tower. The going gets steep and rocky in its final stretches, but you'll be rewarded with views of the French Broad River Valley as well as Cold Mountain, made famous by Charles Frazier's eponymous novel. One mile south you'll find a campground, a general store, a restaurant and an inn.

THE DRIVE: The drive south passes the Graveyard Fields Overlook, where short trails lead to scenic waterfalls. From the 6047ft Richland Balsam Overlook at Mile 431.4 – the highest point on the parkway – continue south for another 20 miles.

13 Waterrock Knob Visitor Center

This trip ends at the **Waterrock Knob Visitor Center** (Mile 451.2), which sits at an elevation of nearly 6000ft. With a four-state view, this scenic spot is a great place to see where you've been and to assess what lies ahead.

Biltmore House, Asheville, North Carolina
KONSTANTIN L/SHUTTERSTOCK

21

★ BEST FOR

OUTDOORS

Cycle the Cades Cove Loop on an official 'no-car' morning.

FLORIDA & THE SOUTH

THE GREAT SMOKIES

DURATION: 4–5 DAYS

DISTANCE: 160 MILES / 257KM

GREAT FOR: NATURE, FAMILIES, HISTORY & CULTURE

BEST TIME TO GO: APRIL TO JUNE FOR WATERFALLS, AND SEPTEMBER AND OCTOBER FOR COLORFUL LEAVES.

Cades Cove loop (p178), Great Smoky Mountains, Tennessee

You can observe the beauty of the Great Smokies from your car, but the exhilarating, crash-bang, breathe-it-in wonder of the place can't be fully appreciated until you leave your vehicle. Hold tight as you bounce over Nantahala rapids. Nod to foraging black bears as you cycle Cades Cove. And press your nose against windows in downtown Gatlinburg, where ogling short stacks is the best way to choose the right pancake place.

LINK YOUR TRIP

19 Natchez Trace Parkway
Head northwest on Hwy 321/Rte 73 from Maryville until you reach I-40. Take this west until you hit on musical Nashville.

20 Blue Ridge Parkway
Continue east on Hwy 19 from Cherokee to link up with the Blue Ridge Parkway.

01 Nantahala Outdoor Center

Splash, bang, wheeeeee…there's no easing into this trip, which starts in the mountain-fed rivers and rugged valleys of western North Carolina, a region famed for its fantastic kayaking and white-water rafting.

The **Nantahala Outdoor Center** *(noc.com)* launches trips on the class II and III rapids of the Nantahala River from its sprawling outpost near Bryson City. Ride a group raft or a two-person ducky through the wide, brown river gorge. The company also offers white-water trips on six other Appalachian rivers.

At the Adventure Center, which is part of the NOC campus, sign up to zipline or to climb an alpine tower. Also on-site are an outdoor store, a year-round restaurant, and lodging that includes campsites, cabins, a hostel and a motel. The Appalachian Trail crosses the property, and the Great Smoky Mountains Railroad stops here.

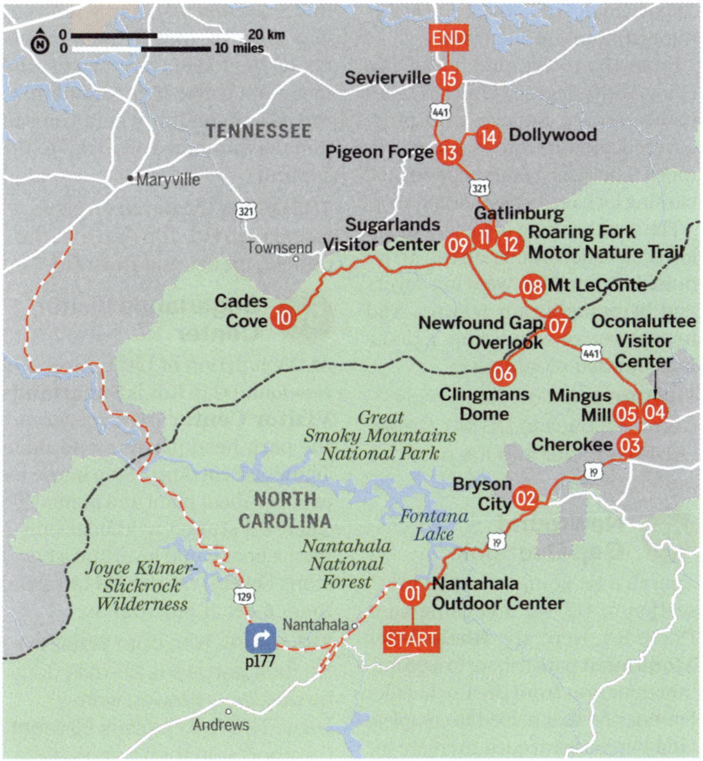

THE DRIVE: Follow US 19 north for about 12.5 miles on a twisty, wooded path that winds past rafting companies and oh-so-many signs for boiled peanuts. Take exit 67 into downtown Bryson City.

DETOUR

Tail of the Dragon

Start: 01 Nantahala Outdoor Center

A dragon lurks in the rugged foothills. This particular monster is an infamous drive that twists through Deals Gap beside the national park. According to legend, the 11-mile route, known as the Tail of the Dragon, has 318 curves. From the Nantahala Outdoor Center, drive south on US 19/74 to US 129. Follow US 129 north. The dragon starts at the North Carolina and Tennessee state line. Godspeed and drive slowly. And may you tame the dragon like a Targaryen.

02 Bryson City

This friendly mountain town is a great base camp for exploring the North Carolina side of the Smokies. The marquee attraction is the historic **Great Smoky Mountains Railroad** *(gsmr.com)*, which departs from downtown and plows through the dramatic Nantahala Gorge and across the Fontana Trestle. The former Murphy Branch Line, built in the late 1800s, brought unheard-of luxuries such as books, factory-spun cloth and oil lamps. Themed trips on the red-and-yellow trains include a Great Pumpkin–themed trip in the fall and the Christmastime Polar Express, which stops at the North Pole to pick up Santa.

THE DRIVE: Continue 11 miles north on US 19.

03 Cherokee

The Cherokee people have lived in this area since the last ice age, though many died on the Trail of Tears. The descendants of those who escaped or returned are known as the Eastern Band of the Cherokee. Make time for the **Museum of the Cherokee Indian** *(mci.org)*. The earth-colored halls trace the history of the tribe, with artifacts such as pots, deerskins, woven skirts and an animated exhibit on Cherokee lore. The tribe's modern story is particularly compelling, with a detailed look at the tragedy and injustice of the Trail of Tears. This mass exodus occurred in the 1830s, when President Andrew Jackson ordered more than 16,000 Native Americans removed from their southeastern homelands and resettled in what's now Oklahoma. The museum also spotlights a fascinating moment in Colonial-era history: the 1760s journey of three Cherokee to England, where they met with George III.

THE DRIVE: Drive 3 miles north on US 441, passing the Blue Ridge Parkway.

04 Oconaluftee Visitor Center

If they're offering samples of regional preserves at the **Oconaluftee Visitor Center** *(nps.gov/grsm)*, say yes. But pull out your money, too, because you'll want to buy a jar to take home. Here you'll also find interactive exhibits about the park's history and ecosystems. Helpful guides about specific attractions are also available. For this trip, the Day Hikes pamphlet and the guides to Cades Cove and the Roaring

Fork Motor Nature Trail are helpful supplements.

Behind the visitor center, the pet-friendly **Oconaluftee River Trail** follows the river for 1.5 miles to the boundary of the Cherokee reservation. Pick up a free backcountry camping permit if you plan to go off-trail. The adjacent **Mountain Farm Museum** *(nps.gov/grsm)* is a 19th-century farmstead assembled from buildings from various locations around the park. The worn, wooden structures, including a barn, a blacksmith shop and a smokehouse, give a glimpse of the hardscrabble existence of Appalachian settlers.

THE DRIVE: Drive half a mile north on US 441. The parking lot is on the left.

05 Mingus Mill

Interested in old buildings and 1800s commerce? Then take the short walk to Mingus Mill. This 1886 gristmill was the largest in the Smokies. If the miller is there, he can explain how the mill grinds corn into cornmeal. Outside, the 200ft-long wooden millrace directs water to the building. There's no waterwheel here because the mill used a cast-iron turbine.

THE DRIVE: Return to US 441 and turn left, continuing toward Gatlinburg. Turn left onto Clingmans Dome Rd and drive for 7 miles.

06 Clingmans Dome

At 6643ft, **Clingmans Dome** is the third-highest mountain east of the Mississippi. You can drive almost all the way to the top, but the final climb to the summit's Jetsons-like observation tower requires a half-mile walk on a paved trail. It's a very steep ascent, but there are resting spots along the way. The trail crosses the 2174-mile Appalachian Trail, which reaches its highest point on the Dome.

From the tower, on a clear day, enjoy a 360-degree view that takes in five states. Spruce- and pine-covered mountaintops sprawl for miles. The visitor station beside the parking lot has a bookstore and shop.

The weather here is cooler than at lower elevations, and rain can arrive quickly. Consider wearing layers and bringing a rain poncho. And in case you're wondering, a dome is a rounded mountain.

THE DRIVE: Follow Clingmans Dome Rd back to US 441. Cross US 441 and pull into the overlook parking area.

07 Newfound Gap Overlook

There's a lot going on at the intersection of US 441 and Clingmans Dome Rd. Here, the **Rockefeller Monument** pays tribute to a $5 million donation from the Rockefeller Foundation that helped to complete land purchases needed to create the park. President Franklin D Roosevelt formally dedicated Great Smoky Mountains National Park in this spot in 1940. The overlook sits at the border of North Carolina and Tennessee, within the 5046ft Newfound Gap. Enjoy expansive mountain views from the parking area or hop on the **Appalachian Trail** for a stroll.

THE DRIVE: From here, follow US 441 north into Tennessee for about 5 miles to the parking lot.

08 Mt LeConte

Climbing 6593ft **Mt LeConte** is probably the park's most popular challenge, and sure to give you serious hamstring burn.

The **Alum Cave Trail**, one of five routes to the peak, starts from the Alum Cave parking area on the main road. Follow a creek, pass under a stone arch and wind your way steadily upward past thickets of rhododendron, myrtle and mountain laurel. It's a 5.5-mile hike to LeConte Lodge, where you can join the Rainbow Falls Trail to the summit.

THE DRIVE: Continue on Newfound Gap Rd. Turn left into the parking lot at Little River Rd.

09 Sugarlands Visitor Center

At the junction of Little River and Newfound Gap Rds is **Sugarlands Visitor Center** *(nps.gov/grsm)*, the park headquarters and main Tennessee entrance. Step inside for exhibits about plant and animal life (there's a stuffed wild boar only a mama boar could love) and a bookstore. Several ranger-led talks and tours meet at Sugarlands.

THE DRIVE: Turn onto Little River Rd for a gorgeous 25-mile drive beside lively flowing waterways. The road passes Elkmont Campground then becomes Laurel Creek Rd. Watch for cars stopping suddenly as drivers pull over to look at wildlife.

10 Cades Cove

This secluded valley contains the remnants of a 19th-century settlement. It's accessed by an 11-mile, one-way loop road that has numerous pull-offs. From these, you can poke around old churches and farmhouses or hike trails through postcard-perfect meadows filled with deer, wild turkeys and the occasional bear. For good wildlife viewing, come in the late afternoon, when the animals romp with abandon.

The narrow loop road has a speed limit of 10mph and can get crowded

Oconaluftee Visitor Center (p177), Cherokee, North Carolina
ZACK FRANK/SHUTTERSTOCK

(and maddeningly slow) in high season. For a more tranquil experience, ride your bike, or walk, on a Wednesday from early May through late September – cars are banned on that day of the week. Rent a bike at the **Cades Cove Campground Store**. Also recommended is the 5-mile round-trip hike to **Abrams Falls**. Trailhead parking is just beyond the Elijah Oliver Place, an old homestead.

Stop by the **Cades Cove Visitor Center** *(nps.gov/grsm)* for ranger talks.

THE DRIVE: Return to Sugarlands Visitor Center, then turn left onto US 441, which is called Parkway between Gatlinburg and Sevierville. Drive 2 miles to Gatlinburg.

11 Gatlinburg

Driving out of the park on the Tennessee side is disconcerting. You pop out of the tranquil green tunnel of trees into a blinking, shrieking welter of cars, motels, pancake houses, moonshine distilleries and Ripley's Believe It or Not! museums. Welcome to Gatlinburg. It's Heidi meets hillbilly in this vaguely Bavarian-themed tourist wonderland, catering to Smokies visitors since the 1930s. Most of the tourist attractions are within the compact, hilly little downtown.

The **Gatlinburg SkyLift** *(gatlinburgskylift.com)*, a repurposed ski-resort chairlift, whisks you high over the Smokies. An observation deck and a 680ft-long suspension bridge, the longest in North America, opened at the top of the lift in spring 2019.

THE DRIVE: From Parkway in downtown Gatlinburg, turn right onto Historic Nature Trail/Airport Rd at the Gatlinburg Convention Center. Follow it into the national park, continuing to the marked entrance for the one-way Roaring Fork Motor Nature Trail.

12 Roaring Fork Motor Nature Trail

Built on the foundations of a 150-year-old wagon road, the 6-mile Roaring Fork loop twists through strikingly lush forest. Sights include burbling cascades, abundant hardwoods, mossy boulders and old cabins once inhabited by farming families. The isolated community of Roaring Fork was settled in the mid-1800s, along a powerful mountain stream. The families that lived here were forced to move when the park was established about 100 years later.

For a waterfall hike, try the 2.6-mile round-trip walk to **Grotto Falls** from the Trillium Gap Trailhead. Further down the road, check out the **Ephraim Bales cabin**, once home to 11 people.

The Roaring Fork Auto Tour Guide, for sale for in the Oconaluftee and Sugarlands visitor centers, provides details about plant life and buildings along the drive. No buses, trailers or RVs are permitted on the motor road.

Grotto Falls, Gatlinburg, Tennessee
GETTY IMAGES/ISTOCKPHOTO

NATIONAL PARK TRIP PLANNER

Established in 1934, **Great Smoky Mountains National Park** *(nps.gov/grsm)* attracts more than 11 million travelers per year, making it the most-visited national park in America.

Newfoundland Gap Rd/US 441 is the only thoroughfare crossing the entire 521,000-acre park, traversing 33 miles of deep oak and pine forest, and wildflower meadows. The park sits in two states: North Carolina and Tennessee. The **Oconaluftee Visitor Center** welcomes visitors arriving on US 441 in North Carolina; **Sugarlands Visitor Center** is its Tennessee counterpart.

Orientation & Fees

Great Smoky charges no admission fee, nor will it ever; this proviso was written into the park's original charter as a stipulation for a $5-million Rockefeller family grant. Stop by a visitor center to pick up a park map and the free **Smokies Guide** newspaper. The park is open all year, although some facilities are only open seasonally, and roads may close due to bad weather. Leashed pets are allowed in campgrounds and on roadsides but not on trails, with the exception of the Gatlinburg and Oconaluftee River trails.

Camping

The park currently operates 10 developed campgrounds. None has showers or hookups. Reservations *(recreation.gov)* are required at Abrams Creek, Balsam Mountain, Big Creek and Cataloochee Campground, and they may be made at Elkmont, Smokemont, Cosby, Deep Creek and Cades Cove.

Traffic

If you're visiting on a summer weekend, particularly on the Tennessee side, accept that there's going to be a lot of traffic. Take a break by following trails into the wilderness.

WATERFALLS OF THE SMOKIES

The Smokies are full of waterfalls, from icy trickles to roaring cascades. Here are a few of the best.

Abrams Falls Gorgeous 20ft-high falls off Cades Cove Loop Rd.

Grotto Falls You can walk behind these 25ft-high falls, off Trillium Gap Trail.

Laurel Falls This popular 80ft fall is located down an easy 2.6-mile paved trail.

Mingo Falls At 120ft, this is one of the highest waterfalls in the Appalachians.

Rainbow Falls On sunny days, the mist here produces a rainbow.

THE DRIVE: At the end of Roaring Fork Rd, turn left onto E Pkwy. Less than 1 mile ahead, turn right at US 321 S/US 441. Drive 7 miles to Pigeon Forge.

13 Pigeon Forge

The town of **Pigeon Forge** is an ode to that big-haired angel of East Tennessee, Dolly Parton – who's known to be a pretty cool lady.

Born in a one-room shack in the nearby hamlet of Locust Ridge, Parton started performing on Knoxville radio at age 11 and moved to Nashville at 18 with all her worldly belongings in a cardboard suitcase. She's made millions singing about her Smoky Mountains roots and continues to be a huge presence in her hometown, donating money to local causes.

Wacky museums and over-the-top dinner shows line Parkway.

THE DRIVE: From Patriot Park, turn right onto Old Mill Ave and follow it to Teaster Lane. Turn right onto Teaster Lane, then turn left at the light onto Veterans Blvd. Follow signs to Dollywood, about 2 miles away. You can also catch the Fun Time Trolley ($2.50 one way) to Dollywood from Patriot Park, where there's free parking.

14 Dollywood

Dolly Parton's theme park **Dollywood** *(dollywood.com)* is a love letter to mountain culture. Families pour in to ride the country-themed thrill rides and see demonstrations of traditional Appalachian crafts. The roller coasters are nationally acclaimed. You can also tour the bald-eagle sanctuary or worship at the altar of Dolly in the **Chasing Rainbows** life-story museum. Geared to younger kids, the 6-acre **Wildwood Grove** has 11 'experiences.' The adjacent Dollywood's **Splash Country** takes these themes and adds water.

THE DRIVE: Return to Parkway and follow it north 4.5 miles into downtown Sevierville. Turn left onto Bruce St and drive one block to Court Ave.

16 Sevierville

On the front lawn of the downtown courthouse you might see a few happy folks getting their pictures taken in front of the **statue** of a young Dolly Parton. Wearing a ponytail, her guitar held loose, it captures something kind of nice. You know where she's from, where her music's going to take her, and how it all ties into this tough, but beautiful, mountain country.

Newfound Gap (p178), Great Smoky Mountains, Tennessee
JERRY WHALEY/SHUTTERSTOCK

PHOTO OPPORTUNITY

Photograph tree-covered mountains from the Newfound Gap Overlook.

Thunder Bay
Grand Portage
Lake Superior
ONTARIO
Bemidji
Chippewa National Forest
Boundary Waters Canoe Area Wilderness
Tofte
24
Superior National Forest
Grand Rapids
MINNESOTA
23
Apostle Islands
Isle Royale Wilderness
Houghton
Duluth
Superior
Ashland
Ironwood
Marquette
MICHIGAN
Chequamegon National Forest
Ottawa National Forest
Hiawatha National Forest
Mille Lacs Lakes
Lake Chippewa
Mackinaw City
Escanaba
St Cloud
Saint Croix National Scenic Riverway
Nicolet National Forest
Petoskey
Sleeping Bear Dunes National Lakeshore
Boyne City
Alpena
Minneapolis
St Paul
Wausau
Menominee
Eau Claire
Mississippi River
WISCONSIN
Green Bay
Traverse City
West Branch
Mankato
Appleton
Manistee
Cadillac
Tawas City
Rochester
Winona
Oshkosh
Manitowoc
Manistee National Forest
Albert Lea
La Crosse
Lake Winnebago
Fond Du Lac
Sheboygan
Midland
Bay City
22
Port Washington
Lake Michigan
MICHIGAN
Saginaw
Muskegon
Grand Rapids
Prairie du Chien
Madison
Milwaukee
Flint
Fort Dodge
Holland
Lansing
Janesville
Dubuque
Kenosha
Detroit
Dearborn
IOWA
Cedar Rapids
Rockford
Benton Harbor
Marshall
Windsor
Kalamazoo
Des Moines
New Buffalo
Chicago
Davenport
Gary
Three Oaks
South Bend
Toledo
Rock River
OHIO
Des Moines River
Wilmington
Galesburg
Kankakee
Fort Wayne
Findlay
Fort Madison
Burlington
Peoria
Lima
Marion
23
Bloomington
Lafayette
Marysville
Quincy
Illinois River
Danville
Muncie
Chillicothe
Hannibal
Champaign
Urbana
Springfield
Decatur
Indianapolis
Richmond
Washington Court House
Dayton
ILLINOIS
Moberly
Terre Haute
INDIANA
Mississippi River
Columbus
Cincinnati
Hillsboro
Litchfield
Columbia
St Louis
MISSOURI
Lexington
Henderson
Owensboro
Carbondale
KENTUCKY
Cape Girardeau
Paducah
0 200 km
0 100 miles

JOE FERRER/SHUTTERSTOCK

Great River Road (p194) Alma, Wisconsin

GREAT LAKES

EXPLORE

GREAT LAKES

The Midwest is much more than a flat, endless field. Intrepid road-trippers find that out as soon as they set wheels on red-cliffed Hwy 61 in northern Minnesota. Or on the dune-backed thoroughfares of western Michigan. Or on the River Road twisting along the Big Muddy.

The Great Lakes are huge, like inland seas. Dairy farms and orchards blanket the region, meaning fresh pie and ice cream await trip-takers. Big cities such as Chicago and Minneapolis provide hefty doses of culture and entertainment.

And when the Midwest does flatten out? There's always the World's Largest Six-Pack to revive imaginations.

Duluth

Duluth has grit to go with its beauty, and it's what gives this fun city its distinctive character. There's lots to do here: visit Bob Dylan's Birthplace, visit the Great Lakes Aquarium, track down a murder mystery at Glensheen Mansion, take a brewery tour and go kayaking (not in that order). Accommodations don't match the food and nightlife scenes, but the latter two are awash in brewpubs (especially west of downtown), cool cafes, barbecue joints, retro diners and ice-cream parlors. Located at the innermost point of Lake Superior, it's the perfect base for exploring the lake and its western hinterland.

St Paul

The quieter of the Twin Cities, St Paul is a fine base for exploring Minnesota and the Great Lakes region. Historic buildings southwest of downtown, the birthplace of F Scott Fitzgerald and a thriving tradition of craft beers and brewpubs give the city an eclectically broad appeal. And the Mississippi flows right past/through the city. Throw in a handful of excellent hotels and a decent culinary scene, and St Paul is the kind of city that really sneaks up on you and sometimes doesn't let go.

WHEN TO GO

June to October is the best time to drive these Great Lakes routes. The weather's at its best, and fall brings autumn colors and Michigan orchard harvests. During the winter months, snowfalls and snow drifts can be a problem along the Great River Road, and temperatures can plummet around the lakes.

Traverse City

The cherry capital of Michigan, Traverse City, on Lake Michigan's Grand Traverse Bay, is one of the state's best-kept secrets. The town has a lovely waterside aspect, with first-rate food and arts scenes. But its location is equally a winner, ideal for everything from kayaking expeditions onto the lake to sampling the delights of U-pick apple orchards and the Mission Peninsula wineries. Best of all, you're just a short drive from the Sleeping Bear Dunes, one of the Great Lakes' true natural treasures.

St Louis

The largest city in the Great Plains, St Louis is best known for its beer (craft), bowling (tenpin) and baseball. The city also has a distinguished musical heritage, one of America's newest national parks (Gateway Arch), A terrific brewpub-centric nightlife, and a cosmopolitan Pan-American culinary culture. It also occupies a fine stretch of the Mississippi River, just for good measure. As handy if you're heading out west as it is if you're traveling to or from the Great Lakes, St Louis is worth at least a few days of your time and is a fine place to mark the transition between two iconic American worlds.

TRANSPORTATION

By far the easiest way to reach the region is to fly into one of the major airports – Minneapolis-St Paul, St Louis, or even Chicago, Madison or Lansing. Greyhound buses ply many routes close to these Great Lakes itineraries, with Amtrak trains between Chicago and Minneapolis-St Paul offering a few convenient entry points to the region.

WHERE TO STAY

As always, look for friendly B&Bs in the rural backcountry of Minnesota, Wisconsin, Illinois and Missouri. Another quiet and relatively off-the-beaten-track option is the campgrounds and cabins of state parks and other protected areas like the Chippewa National Forest or Itasca State Park (where the Mississippi begins its journey). Otherwise, cities like St Paul, Minneapolis or St Louis have lots of boutique hotels, guesthouses and B&Bs to go with the ubiquitous cookie-cutter motels that line every city outskirts. Smaller lakeside towns often have waterfront hotels; ask for a room with a view.

RESOURCES

Pure Michigan
A comprehensive guide to Michigan travel presented by the state tourism board.
michigan.org

Mississippi Valley Traveler Podcast
Stories, history and quirky characters from up and down the Mississippi River.
mississippivalleytraveler.com/podcast

State Parks
Find a state park near the route you're driving. It's sure to be worth a detour.
americasparks.com

WHAT'S ON

St Paul Winter Carnival
In winter, head to St Paul for 10 days of ice sculptures, ice skating and ice fishing.

Big Muddy Blues Festival
Early September blues by the river in St Louis on the Labor Day Weekend.

Apple Harvests
Drink hot apple cider and feast on fresh-baked doughnuts during Michigan's fall harvest season.

National Cherry Festival
Traverse City celebrates the humble cherry in the first week of July.

22

GREAT LAKES

MICHIGAN'S GOLD COAST

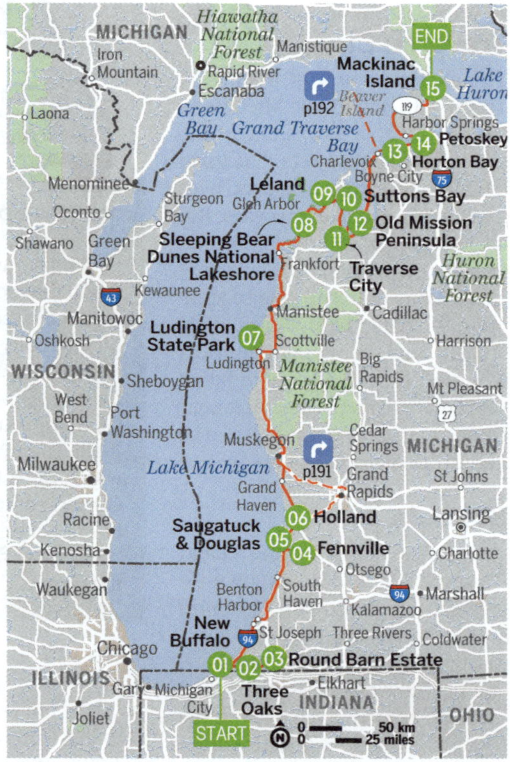

DURATION: 4 DAYS

DISTANCE: 475 MILES / 765KM

GREAT FOR: NATURE, WINE

BEST TIME TO GO: JULY THROUGH OCTOBER FOR PLEASANT WEATHER AND ORCHARD HARVESTS.

While Michigan's shore has been a holiday hot spot for over a century, it still surprises: the Caribbean-blue water, the West Coast surfing vibe, the French-style cider house that pops up by the road. Ernest Hemingway used to spend summers in the northern reaches, and he never forgot it. Even after traveling the world, he once wrote that the best sky is in northern Michigan in the fall.

LINK YOUR TRIP

01 Route 66
The time-warped thoroughfare is America's original road trip, and it kicks off in Chicago, 70 miles west of New Buffalo.

24 Highway 61
Ready to drive? It's 420 miles from Mackinaw City, the final stop in the Gold Coast itinerary, across the wild Northwoods of Michigan and Wisconsin to your starting point in Duluth.

01 New Buffalo

Hit the waves first in **New Buffalo**, a busy little resort town that is home to the Midwest's first surf shop. Yes, you can surf Lake Michigan.

Not a surfer? Not a problem. Lounge on the wide, sandy beach; watch boats glide in and out of the marina; and lick an ice-cream cone or three.

THE DRIVE: Follow Hwy 12 as it curves inland for 6 miles to the wee town of Three Oaks.

02 Three Oaks

Three Oaks is where Green Acres meets Greenwich Village in a bohemian farm-and-arts blend. Rent bikes and cycle lightly used roads past orchards and vineyards. In the evening, catch a provocative play or art-house flick at Three Oaks' theaters.

Or just swing by for an hour or two to putter around the antiques stores and concrete-lawn-ornament shops. Be sure to stop in at **Journeyman Distillery** *(journeymandistillery.*

★ BEST FOR

FOODIES

Traverse City has artisanal food shops selling local wines, ciders and produce.

GARY ENNIS/GETTY IMAGES

Cherries, Traverse City (p192), Michigan

com), located in the old Featherbone Factory that used to make corsets and buggy whips. Today it produces organic whiskies, gins and other booze, and serves them in its rustic bar and restaurant.

THE DRIVE: Head north on Elm St, which becomes Three Oaks Rd. After 2.5 miles turn right onto Warren Woods Rd for six farm-flecked miles. Turn left onto Cleveland Ave for 4 miles, and then right onto Browntown Rd for 2 miles. When it ends at Hills Rd turn left. Soon you'll see Round Barn.

03 Round Barn Estate

By now you've noticed all the wineries signposted off the roads. Around 20 vineyards and tasting rooms cluster between New Buffalo and Saugatuck. The **Lake Michigan Shore Wine Trail** provides a map to several of them.

A good one to start at is **Round Barn Estate** *(roundbarn.com)*. It goes beyond vino with its grapes – it also uses the fruit to make DiVine Vodka. Try it in the tasting room. During the week, you're welcome to picnic on the grounds; a food truck serves snacks on weekends. Events ranging from concerts to trivia nights take place here throughout the year.

THE DRIVE: Take Hills Rd to 1st St in Baroda; turn west on Lemon Creek Rd and go to the Red Arrow Hwy (6.5 miles total). The Red Arrow becomes Lakeshore Dr as it nears St Joseph. After a few blocks as Main St it converges with Hwy 63, and in 10 miles meets the Blue Star Hwy (County Rd A-2). Follow the latter 30 miles north, then take Hwy 89 east to Fennville.

04 Fennville

It may be a teeny farm town with a lone traffic light, but pie fanatics have been swarming here for decades. The draw: **Crane's Pie Pantry, Restaurant & Winery** *(cranespiepantry.com)*. Sure, you can pick your own apples and peaches in the surrounding orchards, but those in need of a quick fix beeline to the tchotchke-filled bakery for a bulging slice of flaky goodness.

Nearby **Virtue Cider** *(virtuecider.com)* lets you sip a pint while sheep bleat, pigs oink and chickens cluck on the farm around you. The taproom is in a barrel-strewn barn, where the crisp, dry Brut is the star of the taps.

THE DRIVE: Return to the Blue Star Hwy. Drive north for 4 miles to Saugatuck.

05 Saugatuck & Douglas

The strong arts community and gay-friendly vibe draw boatloads of vacationers to pretty Saugatuck. Galleries of pottery, paintings and glasswork proliferate downtown along Water and Butler Sts. Climb aboard the clackety **Saugatuck Chain Ferry** *(facebook.com/thesaugatuckchainferry)* and the operator will pull you across the Kalamazoo River. On the other side, walk to the dock's right (north) and you'll come to **Mt Baldhead**, a 764ft-high sand dune. Huff up the stairs to see the grand view, then race down the other side to beautiful **Oval Beach**. Can't get enough sand? **Saugatuck Dune Rides** *(saugatuckduneride.com)* provides 40 minutes of fun zipping over nearby mounds.

Next door to Saugatuck is Douglas, a twin village that extends the artsy, beachy bounty.

THE DRIVE: The Blue Star Hwy makes its slowpoke, two-lane way northeast through farmland. It becomes 58th St, then Washington Ave, then Michigan Ave and River Ave before reaching downtown Holland 12 miles later.

PHOTO OPPORTUNITY

Atop the Dune Climb at Sleeping Bear Dunes.

06 Holland

You don't have to cross the ocean for tulips, windmills and clogs. Michigan's Holland has the whole kitschy package. Take your pick of gardens and wooden-shoe factories, or better yet, seek out the city's famous suds. **New Holland Brewing** *(newhollandbrew.com)* is known for its robust beers, such as Tangerine Space Machine and Dragon's Milk stout, all flowing in the pub.

Beach buffs can swing by **Holland State Park**, whose strands of sand are among the state's most popular thanks to lighthouse views, fiery sunsets and boating action.

Dune Climb, Sleeping Bear Dunes National Lakeshore, Michigan

COLCATKAN/SHUTTERSTOCK

THE DRIVE: At Holland State Park's northeast edge pick up Lakeshore Ave, the back-road alternative to Hwy 31. Ramble 20 miles north to Grand Haven, then filter on to Hwy 31 to speed up for 65 miles. Take exit 166 for Ludington; the park is about 10 miles north of town.

DETOUR

Grand Rapids

Start: 06 Holland

The second-largest city in Michigan, Grand Rapids has gotten its groove on through beer tourism. Some 25 craft breweries operate in the city proper, and about 20 more in nearby towns. The **Ale Trail** takes you there. What makes the scene so popular is the breweries' density – you can walk between many makers – and the relatively low cost of drinking.

If you only have time for one stop, make it **Brewery Vivant** *(breweryvivant.com)*, which specializes in Belgian-style beers. It's set in an old chapel with stained-glass windows, a vaulted ceiling and farmhouse-style communal tables. Beer geeks adore it.

Grand Rapids lies 29 miles inland from Holland via I-196.

FREDERICK MILLETT/SHUTTERSTOCK

Big Sable Point Lighthouse, Ludington State Park, Michigan

07 Ludington State Park

It's time to stretch the legs at Ludington State Park. Once inside, people simply pull over on the roadside and make a break for the beautiful stretches of beach. It also has a top-notch trail system and the renovated **Big Sable Point Lighthouse** to hike to (or live in, as the volunteer lighthouse keeper). Tours of the 112ft beacon cost $8.

THE DRIVE: Return to Hwy 31 and head north to Manistee. A few miles beyond town, hop on Hwy 22 toward Frankfort. The byway takes its time past inland lakes, clapboard towns and historic lighthouses as it winds to the Sleeping Bear Dunes. It's about 85 miles in total.

08 Sleeping Bear Dunes National Lakeshore

Stop at the park's **visitor center** *(nps.gov/slbe)* in Empire for information, trail maps and vehicle entry permits. Then steer north for 4 miles to the **Pierce Stocking Scenic Drive**. The 7-mile, one-lane, picnic-grove-studded loop is one way to absorb the stunning lake vistas. Another is the **Dune Climb**, which entails trudging up a 200ft-high sand pile to a grand view of the azure water. There's also the **Sleeping Bear Heritage Trail**, which paves 22 miles from Empire north past the Dune Climb and through dreamy forested areas. Trailheads with parking lots are located roughly every 3 miles.

THE DRIVE: After the Dune Climb, stay on Hwy 109 until it ends in bustling Glen Arbor. Rejoin Hwy 22 for 18 miles as it continues through the national lakeshore to Leland.

09 Leland

Little Leland couldn't be any cuter. Grab a bite at a waterfront restaurant downtown, and poke around atmospheric Fishtown with its weather-beaten shops. Ferries depart from here to the forest-cloaked **Manitou Islands**. Day trips for hiking and beach-combing are doable from mid-June to early September, though rising lake levels and dock damage have halted some excursions. Check with **Manitou Island Transit** *(manitoutransit.com)*, which also runs a sunset cruise along the shoreline four days per week.

THE DRIVE: Take Hwy 22 north for 4 miles. Zig right on N Eagle Hwy, then zag left on E Kolarik Rd. A mile onward, take the first right you come to, which is Setterbo Rd. You'll spy the cider house 3.5 miles later.

10 Suttons Bay

On the outskirts of Suttons Bay, **Tandem Ciders** *(tandemciders.com)* pours delicious hard ciders made from local apples in its small tasting room on the family farm. In town, **Grand Traverse Bike Tours** *(grandtraversebiketours.com)* offers guided rides to local wineries, as well as self-guided tours for which staff provide route planning and van pickup of your wine purchases.

THE DRIVE: Hwy 22 rides down the coast of Grand Traverse Bay and eventually rolls into Traverse City.

11 Traverse City

Michigan's 'cherry capital' is the largest city in the region. Outdoor adventures abound, and the superb food and arts scenes are comparable to those of a much larger urban area.

Front St is the main drag to wander. Pop in to **Cherry Republic** *(cherryrepublic.com)*. Although touristy, it's a hoot to see all the products: cherry ketchup, cherry-dusted tortillas, cherry butter, cherry wine – you get the point. Filmmaker and local resident Michael Moore renovated the gorgeous, century-old **State Theatre** *(stateandbijou.org)*. It shows first-run movies and art-house flicks, with $1 kids matinee shows. And what's more perfect than a kayak-and-bike tour of local breweries? **Paddle TC** *(paddletc.com)* makes it happen with its half-day KaBrew tour.

THE DRIVE: Take Front St (Hwy 31) east out of downtown. In a half mile, turn left on Garfield Ave (Hwy 37). Follow Hwy 37 north, sallying through the grape- and cherry-planted Old Mission Peninsula.

12 Old Mission Peninsula

Taste-tripping through the peninsula's wineries is a popular pastime. With 10 vineyards in 19 miles, you won't go thirsty. At **Brys Estate Vineyard & Winery** *(brysestate.com)*, cabernet franc and dry riesling are best sipped on the sprawling deck with bay views. **Chateau Chantal** *(chateauchantal.com)* pours crowd-pleasing chardonnay and pinot noir. **Peninsula Cellars** *(peninsulacellars.com)*, in an old schoolhouse, makes fine whites and is often less crowded.

THE DRIVE: Retrace your path back to Hwy 31 in Traverse City and head north. In roughly 50 miles, north of affluent Charlevoix, look for Boyne City Rd. It skirts Lake Charlevoix and eventually arrives at the Horton Bay General Store.

13 Horton Bay General Store

Ernest Hemingway fans will recall the **Horton Bay General Store** *(hortonbaygeneralstore.com)*, with its 'high false front,' from his short story 'Up in Michigan.' As a youth, Hemingway used to hang out here. His family had a cottage on nearby Walloon Lake. The retro shop now sells groceries, souvenirs and snacks, plus wine and tapas in the evening.

THE DRIVE: Backtrack on Boyne City Rd a quarter mile to County Rd C-71 (aka Horton Bay Rd N) and turn right. Take it for 5 miles until it meets Hwy 31 north, which carries you to Petoskey in 6 miles.

DETOUR

Beaver Island

Start: 13 Horton Bay

For an alternative to Mackinac Island, sail to quieter Beaver Island, an Irish-influenced enclave of some 600 people that offers hiking, biking and kayaking, and snorkeling to shipwrecked schooners. The **ferry** *(bibco.com)* departs from downtown Charlevoix. The trip takes two hours.

14 Petoskey

A vintage resort town jammed with yachts, foodie cafes and gastro-pubs, Petoskey also features a couple of Hemingway sights. The **Little Traverse Historical Museum** *(petoskeymuseum.org)* has a collection dedicated to the author, including rare first-edition books that Hemingway autographed for a friend when he visited in 1947. Afterward, toss back a drink at **City Park Grill** *(cityparkgrill.com)*, where Hemingway was a regular. Just north of town you

SHRIRAM PATKI/SHUTTERSTOCK

Arch Rock, Mackinac Island, Michigan

can hunt for famed Petoskey stones (honeycomb-patterned fragments of ancient coral) at **Petoskey State Park**.

THE DRIVE: Time for a choice: take the 'fast' way to Mackinaw City via Hwy 31 (a 45-minute drive) or dawdle on narrow Hwy 119 (a 90-minute drive). The latter curves through thick forest as part of the Tunnel of Trees scenic route. It ends in Cross Village, where Levering Rd takes you east to rejoin Hwy 31.

15 Mackinac Island

Mackinaw City is the jumping-off point to Mackinac Island, a petite charmer speckled with Victorian cottages and 18th-century fortresses. Cars are banned, and all travel is by horse or bicycle, adding to the old-time mood. Highlights include **Fort Mackinac** *(mackinacparks.com)*, built in 1780 and known for its views and costumed interpreters who fire cannons; and **Arch Rock**, which curves 150ft above the lake and provides dramatic photo ops. You can cycle around the island in an hour. Bike rentals ($10 to $15 per hour) are ubiquitous.

Two ferry companies – **Shepler's** *(sheplersferry.com)* and **Star Line** *(mackinacferry.com)* – have docks in Mackinaw City and make frequent trips. The ride takes 20 minutes, so it's easy to do as a day trip.

23

GREAT LAKES

THE GREAT RIVER ROAD

DURATION: 6–7 DAYS

DISTANCE: 1075 MILES / 1730KM

GREAT FOR: NATURE, HISTORY & CULTURE

BEST TIME TO GO: JUNE THROUGH SEPTEMBER FOR SNOW-FREE WEATHER.

It happens time and again. The road curves around a bluff and Old Man River appears, wider than you remember, a swift-moving expanse dotted with woodsy islands and behemoth barges. An eagle swoops overhead, diving to the water and rising with a floppy fish. Every once in a while you reach a city, say Minneapolis or Dubuque, but mostly the road unfurls through forgotten towns where it becomes Main St.

LINK YOUR TRIP

01 Route 66
Join the Mother Road in St Louis and mosey 2100 miles southwest to LA or 300 miles northeast to Chicago.

28 The Mighty Mo
Here's another one to pick up in St Louis, a history-studded trip along the Missouri River heading northwest to the Dakotas.

01 Itasca State Park

Begin where the river begins: in Minnesota's **Itasca State Park** *(dnr.state.mn.us)*. A carved pole denotes the headwaters of 'the Mighty Mississippi' – a good thing, because it's puny enough to mistake for a creek. Wade in the knee-deep flow and hop over a couple of stepping stones, then boast you walked across the Father of Waters. The park also offers canoeing, hiking, biking and camping, plus a rustic lodge and cabins.

THE DRIVE: Drive northeast, zigzagging on various county roads. Take County Rd 2 to 40 to 9, through Becida. Turn left onto 169th Ave, which becomes County Rd 7 and rolls into Bemidji (an overall trip of 30 miles).

02 Bemidji

In this piney Northwoods region of Minnesota, the towns are known for lakes, lumberjacks and fishing. A classic example is Bemidji, where an enormous, mustachioed

★ BEST 2 DAYS

The road between stops 4 and 10 offers bluff-strewn scenery, historic towns and foodie pit stops.

JOSEPH KREISS/SHUTTERSTOCK

Potosi Brewing Company (p197), Ptosi, Wisconsin

Paul Bunyan statue awaits. Standing 18ft and weighing 2.5 tons, he raises his concrete head by the **tourist information center** *(visit bemidji.com)* flanked by Babe, his faithful blue ox. Together they make a mighty photo op. Did we mention they created the Mississippi? As legend has it, Paul and Babe were in the forest to cut trees, and Babe was hauling the water wagon that paved the winter logging roads with ice. The giant tank sprang a leak, which trickled down to New Orleans and formed the Big Muddy.

THE DRIVE: The road drifts east then south, rolling along remote Forest Service lanes, gravel roads and county highways that skirt wee communities chockfull of outdoorsy energy. After 360 miles, it drops into glassy, high-rise Minneapolis.

03 Minneapolis

The Riverfront District at downtown's northern edge makes a fine pause with its parks, museums and cafes. At the foot of Portland Ave is the car-free **Stone Arch Bridge** over the Mississippi, from which you can view the cascading St Anthony Falls. A few blocks east is the cobalt-blue **Guthrie Theater**. Make your way up the escalator to its Endless Bridge, a cantilevered walkway overlooking the river. You don't need a theater ticket – it's intended as a public space.

A stone's throw downstream, some 50,000 students hit the books (and live-music venues) at the University of Minnesota. The university's **Weisman Art Museum** *(wam.umn.edu)* occupies a swooping, silver waterfront structure by architect Frank Gehry. Peek in to see its airy galleries of American art.

THE DRIVE: Cross the Mississippi and get on W River Pkwy heading southeast. In 5 miles Minnehaha Park and its poetic waterfall offer a fine stop. St Paul is 7 miles onward via Hwy 55 (Hiawatha Ave) to Hwy 13 to I-35E to Shepard Rd.

04 St Paul

Smaller and quieter than its twin city Minneapolis, St Paul has retained more of its historic character. The **Mississippi River Visitor Center** *(nps.gov/miss)* occupies an alcove in the science museum's lobby. Stop by to pick up trail maps and see what sort of ranger-guided activities are happening along the waterway.

Two nearby neighborhoods are worth a stroll to gawk at the bonanza of Victorian mansions. On **Cathedral Hill** – named for the hulking church that marks the spot – Summit Ave was the old stomping ground of author F Scott Fitzgerald. He lived in the brownstone at 599 Summit Ave when he published This Side of Paradise. Closer to the river, the **Irvine Park** district is all fountains, gardens and turreted manors. It's next to W 7th St, an eating and drinking hub.

THE DRIVE: Take Hwy 61/Hwy 10 going southeast from St Paul. In 21 miles, near Hastings, the Mississippi River becomes the border between Minnesota and Wisconsin. Stay on the Wisconsin side and veer onto Hwy 35. Forty miles later, after curving past impressive bluffs near Maiden Rock, you'll arrive at Stockholm, where the irresistible pie shop tempts. Six miles beyond is button-cute Pepin.

05 Pepin

Hwy 35 becomes 3rd St in town, convenient for *Little House on the Prairie* fans who want to make a pit stop at the **Laura Ingalls Wilder Museum** *(lauraingallspepin.com)*. This is where she was born and lived in the abode that starred in *Little House in the Big Woods*. There's not a lot in the museum (and the building itself is a replica), but die-hards will appreciate being on the authentic patch of land once homesteaded by Ma and Pa Ingalls. While Wilder's writing remains near and dear to her devotees, it's worth noting that her wider reputation has taken a hit in recent years as many readers view her references to African Americans and Native Americans as racist.

THE DRIVE: Continue 8 miles southeast on Hwy 35 to Nelson.

06 Nelson & Wabasha

These two towns lie across the river from each other. Nelson is on the Wisconsin side and home to the **Nelson Cheese Factory** *(nelsoncheese.com)*. The name is a bit misleading: the refurbished building no longer produces cheese, but the shop carries a big stash of Wisconsin hunks, and the cozy wine bar serves 'em on tasting plates. The queues, though, are for the ice

Paul Bunyan and Babe the Blue Ox (p195), Bemidji, Minnesota

PHOTO OPPORTUNITY

Paul Bunyan and his blue ox Babe in Bemidji.

KEN WOLTER/SHUTTERSTOCK

cream (emphasis on cream, which is used in abundance in the mega-rich treat).

Across the water in Wabasha, MN, is the **National Eagle Center** *(nationaleaglecenter.org)*. A large population of bald eagles flocks to the area each winter, where they nest in waterside trees and feast on the river's fat silvery fish. The center has the lowdown. It also introduces you to Donald, Angel and the other rehabilitated birds who live on-site.

THE DRIVE: From Wabasha, stay on Hwy 61 for 60 miles through a landscape of small farms, big skies and endless green hills. When you reach La Crescent, the orchard-rich 'Apple Capital of Minnesota,' cross the Mississippi via Hwy 61 to its Wisconsin twin La Crosse.

07 La Crosse

Get your camera ready as the road (which becomes 3rd St S on the Wisconsin side) swings by the **World's Largest Six-Pack**. The 'cans' are actually storage tanks for City Brewery and hold enough beer to provide one person with a six-pack a day for 3351 years (or so the sign says).

Honky-tonk bars, breakfast joints, antique shops and lots of mid-century American charm stuff La Crosse's landmark downtown, making it a choice spot for an overnight stay. And don't leave without driving up to **Grandad Bluff** *(explore lacrosse.com)* for a sweeping valley view that spans three states. It's east of town along Main St (which becomes Bliss Rd); follow Bliss Rd up the hill and then turn right on Grandad Bluff Rd.

THE DRIVE: Return to Hwy 35, which clasps the river for 24 miles to the Iowa border, then 35 miles more to the old fur-trading post of Prairie du Chien. Cross the river to Marquette, IA, and take Hwy 76 north for 4 miles to the Effigy Mounds.

08 Effigy Mounds

Effigy Mounds National Monument *(nps.gov/efmo)* consists of more than 200 mysterious Native American burial mounds sitting in the bluffs above the Mississippi River. Most are built in the shape of animals, with bear and bird forms being the most popular. The park offers a quiet, sacred space to explore, prime for listening to songbirds as you hike the lush trails that lead to the mounds. Striking river vistas pop up along the way.

THE DRIVE: Retrace your route to Prairie du Chien and pick up Hwy 35 continuing south for 20 miles. In Bloomington turn right on Hwy 133 for 30 rural miles to Potosi.

09 Potosi

The River Rd becomes Main St as it moseys into town. The **Potosi Brewing Company** *(potosi brewery.com)* is your one-stop shop for food, drink, memorabilia and historical information. The thick-stone building began brewing beer in 1852. Imbibe indoors amid neon-lit beer signs or outdoors in the attractive beer garden. Supplement with a burger and the famous beer cheese soup.

The building also holds the National Brewery Museum, stuffed with old beer bottles and advertising signs, and a transportation museum (free) that shows early beer-hauling equipment. The Great River Road interpretation center likewise is on-site and provides maps and info for onward travel.

THE DRIVE: Go east on Hwy 133 to Hwy 35/61; turn right. Follow it for 8 miles to the junction with Hwy 151. The three roads merge into one for 10 miles to the Iowa border. Stay on Hwy 61/151 to cross the river. Veer off for Dubuque at the 9th St-11th St exit.

10 Dubuque

This historic city charms with its 19th-century Victorian homes lining narrow streets between the river and seven steep limestone hills. The **Fourth Street Elevator** *(fenelonplaceelevator.com)*, a funicular railway built in 1882, climbs one of them from downtown for huge views.

Nearby at the **National Mississippi River Museum & Aquarium** *(rivermuseum.com)*, learn about life (of all sorts) along the length of the Big Muddy. Exhibits span steamboating, aquatic creatures and Indigenous Mississippi River dwellers. Immediately north of downtown past 6th St, the Millwork District houses great restaurants and nightlife in old wood-working factories.

THE DRIVE: Take Hwy 52 south for 45 miles toward Sabula, then follow Hwy 67 to Davenport for 55 miles.

11 Davenport

Davenport is arguably the coolest of the 'Quad Cities,' a foursome that also includes Bettendorf in Iowa and Moline and Rock Island in Illinois. Downtown, the glass-walled **Figge Art Museum** *(figge artmuseum.org)* sparkles above the River Road. The museum's Midwest Regionalist Collection includes many works by Iowa native (and American Gothic painter) Grant Wood; you can also stroll through the world-class Haitian and Mexican Colonial collections.

THE DRIVE: On Davenport's west side catch Hwy 22 west for 25 miles. The route gets tricky after this, following a series of Iowa county roads south along the water for 70 miles. Eventually you'll putter onto Hwy 61 and roll into Fort Madison, crossing the Mississippi on a cool swing bridge. On the Illinois side, take Hwy 96 for 10 miles into Nauvoo.

12 Nauvoo

Little **Nauvoo** *(beautifulnauvoo.com)* has long been a pilgrimage site for Mormons. Joseph Smith, the religion's founder, brought his flock here in 1839 after they were kicked out of Missouri. Nauvoo (Hebrew for 'beautiful place') grew quickly. Almost 12,000 Mormons took up residence, rivaling Chicago's population. By 1846 they were gone. Tensions rose, Smith was killed, and Brigham Young led the group west to Utah. Today the tiny town is a historic district loaded with impressive structures, such as the homes of Smith and Young. The centerpiece is the gleaming white temple, built in 2002 on the site of the Mormons' burned-down original sanctuary.

THE DRIVE: Follow Hwy 96 south for 40 miles. Veer onto Hwy 24 and then Hwy 57 (20 miles total). At the junction with I-172, you could detour 10 miles to Hannibal, MO, the classic river town where writer Mark Twain grew up. Or mosey back to Hwy 96, which leads to Hwy 100. Relax for 36 miles as bucolic farms give way to wind-hewn bluffs en route to Elsah.

RUSH JAGOE/LONELY PLANET

Mississippi River, Hannibal (p233), Missouri

GREAT RIVER ROAD RESOURCES

Turn-by-turn directions for the Great River Road are complex, spanning an incredible number of highways and byways. We've provided some road information here, but for nitty-gritty instructions you'll need additional resources. **Minnesota** *(mnmississippiriver.com)*, **Wisconsin** *(wigrr.com)*, **Illinois** *(greatriverroad-illinois.org)* and **Iowa** *(iowagreatriverroad.com)* each maintain their own River Road website. Or check **America's Byways** *(fhwaapps.fhwa.dot.gov/bywaysp)* for designated sections. The one constant, wherever you are: the paddle-wheel sign that marks the way.

13 Elsah

You can't help but slow down in itty-bitty Elsah, a hidden hamlet of 19th-century stone cottages, wood-buggy shops and farmhouses. Most of the town sits on two parallel streets. Around the bend lies **Principia College**, a small liberal arts school and one of the few for Christian Scientists. Outdoors enthusiasts can zipline and cycle bluff-side trails.

THE DRIVE: Take Hwy 100 to Alton for a super-scenic 12 miles. After that, the River Road gets lost around St Louis. A good place to pick up the trail again is Ellis Grove, IL, 75 miles south of Alton via Hwy 3. From there it's 5 miles more to Fort Kaskaskia.

14 Fort Kaskaskia

Set high on a bluff beside the river, the French built Fort Kaskaskia around 1759 to defend against British attacks. All that remains today are lonely earthworks around the perimeter, a cemetery from the late 1800s and

PHOTO SPIRIT/SHUTTERSTOCK

World's Largest Six-Pack (p197), La Crosse, Wisconsin

a view-tastic overlook. It's a great spot for a picnic, with tables and grills. If you're into French colonial architecture, take the footpath down to ogle the **Pierre Menard Home**, built in 1802 for the gent who eventually became Illinois' first lieutenant governor. Trivia tip: the town of Kaskaskia was Illinois' first capital, though its tenure barely lasted a year.

THE DRIVE: About 6 miles down Hwy 3 you'll roll through Chester. It's the hometown of EC Segar, creator of the cartoon character Popeye – hence the statues of the spinach-eating sailor and pals Wimpy, Olive Oyl and Swee'Pea throughout town. Continue south on Hwy 3 for 85 miles until it ends at Cairo.

15 Cairo

It's the end of the line for the northern half of the Great River Road. The town – pronounced kay-ro – has seen better days, as the abandoned buildings attest. But it's compelling to see two mammoth waterways come together, as the Mississippi and Ohio Rivers do in dramatic fashion here.

For those continuing on the thoroughfare, Cairo is roughly the halfway point. The next 1000 miles meander past blues joints and barbecue shacks, steamboats and plantations, en route to New Orleans.

DETOUR

Cypress Creek National Wildlife Refuge

Start: 15 Cairo

You certainly don't expect to find Southern-style swampland, complete with moss-draped cypress trees and croaking bullfrogs, in Illinois. But it's here at **Cypress Creek National Wildlife Refuge** *(fws.gov/refuge/cypress_creek)*. For River Road–trippers who aren't going on to Louisiana, this is an opportunity to see the eerie swamp ecosystem in action. From Cairo drive north 25 miles on Hwy 37 to Cypress, and stop in at the **Cache River Wetlands Center** *(friendsofthecache.org)*. Staff can sort you out with hiking and canoeing information.

STAY AWHILE

MINNEAPOLIS

BY MARGOT BIGG

Few American cities have surprised me more than Minneapolis. While the largest city in Minnesota has a reputation for its friendly (if stoic) residents, it's not the first destination people consider visiting while on vacation in the US. This means that this under-the-radar city is an exceptional place to get a feel for life in America, without any of the gloss-over found in more touristy locales.

Before I visited Minneapolis, I assumed it was gritty and industrial, and while parts of the city do have a concrete-jungle feel, it's incredibly green (when it's not blanketed in snow, at least). The city is designed so that no matter where you are, you're never more than six blocks away from a park. Some of my favorites include the **Theodore Wirth Regional Park** *(minneapolisparks.org)*, a 740-acre expanse of gardens, waterways, and hiking and mountain-biking trails. The park's Eloise ButlerWildflower Garden and its Quaking Bog offer excellent bird-watching opportunities.

The Minneapolis art scene is equally impressive, and I could easily spend days checking out its cultural institutions. The **Weisman Art Museum** *(wam.umn.edu)* is as known for its funky architecture as it is for its massive permanent art collection, while the **Walker Art Center** *(walkerart.org)* has a solid collection of modern and contemporary works, plus a stellar sculpture garden. If I could only visit one spot, however, it would be **Paisley Park** *(paisleypark.com)*, the private estate of late musical legend Prince. It's about a 20-minute drive from town and operates as a sort of cultural museum dedicated to the artist and his musical legacy.

LINK YOUR TRIP

Close to the start of the 23 **Great River Road** (p194), Minneapolis is a great place to stop for a few days.

Left: Weisman Art Museum, Minneapolis, Minnesota; Right: Mississippi River, Minnesota

LEFT TO RIGHT: KEN WOLTER/SHUTTERSTOCK, RUDY BALASKO/SHUTTERSTOCK

PLACES TO STAY

New Victorian Mansion Bed & Breakfast
Occupying an 1881 mansion crowned with gables, dormers and even a half-turret, this fairy-tale B&B offers elegant rooms with plenty of mod-cons. Romancing couples are particularly well catered for, with optional add-ons ranging from roses and champagne to breakfast in bed.
newvictorianbb.com

Hotel Landing
Although this Scandi-style hotel is only about a 20-minute drive west of downtown Minneapolis, it feels worlds apart, especially if you nab one of the sleek rooms with views of Lake Minnetonka's Wayzata Bay. The Nordic treatments at Läka Spa offer a great way to relax after a long stint behind the wheel.
thehotellanding.com

24

★ BEST FOR

WILDLIFE

Drive the Gunflint Trail and watch for moose.

GREAT LAKES

HIGHWAY 61

DURATION: 2–3 DAYS

DISTANCE: 150 MILES / 241KM

GREAT FOR: NATURE, FAMILIES

BEST TIME TO GO: JULY TO MID-OCTOBER FOR PLEASANT WEATHER AND FALL COLORS.

Gunflint Trail (p205), Grand Marais, Minnesota

Mention Hwy 61 and many folks hum Bob Dylan. But this North Shore road is not about murder, poverty or any other mean-street mumblings from his 1965 album *Highway 61 Revisited*. Instead it's a journey dominated by water, where ore-toting freighters ply the ports, little fishing fleets haul in the day's catch, and wave-bashed cliffs offer Superior views if you're willing to trek.

LINK YOUR TRIP

01 Route 66
It's a haul to Chicago – 470 miles – but the payoff is a slowpoke ride on America's Main St.

23 The Great River Road
Pick up the Mississippi River–edged route in Grand Rapids, about 83 miles east via Hwy 2.

01 Duluth

Duluth is a brawny shot-and-a-beer port town that immerses visitors in its storied history as a major shipping center. Start downtown at the **Aerial Lift Bridge**, Duluth's landmark that raises its mighty arm to let horn-bellowing freighters into the harbor. About 1000 vessels per year glide through. The screens inside the **Maritime Visitor Center** *(lsmma.com)* tell what time the behemoths come and go. Cool model boats and exhibits on Great Lakes shipwrecks add to the museum's top marks.

Duluth is also the birthplace of Bob Dylan, though the town is pretty laid-back about its famous son. Dylan's first home (519 N 3rd Ave E) lies up a hill a few blocks northeast of downtown. He lived on the upper floor until age six, when his family moved inland to Hibbing. A small plaque over the front porch marks the spot.

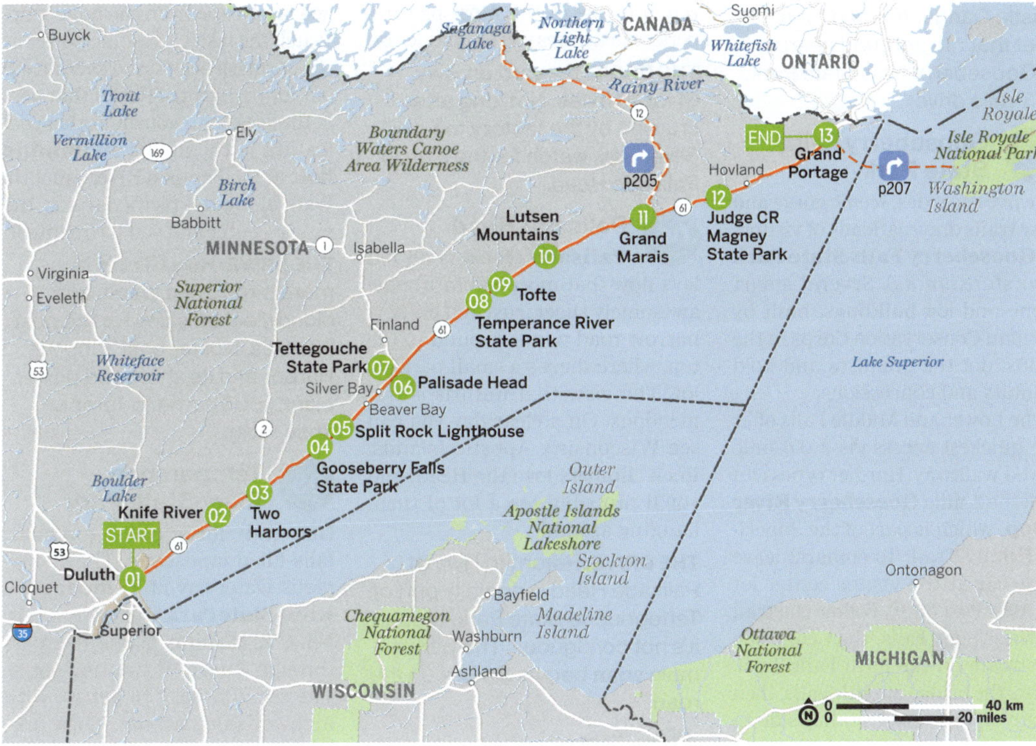

DAN THORNBERG/SHUTTERSTOCK

For a hip scene of indie breweries, cider makers and restaurants, ramble through the **Lincoln Park Craft District**, west of downtown.

THE DRIVE: Take London Rd, aka Hwy 61, heading northeast out of town. Follow the signs for the North Shore Scenic Dr (also called Scenic 61 or Old Hwy 61). There's a Hwy 61 expressway that also covers the next 20 miles, but steer clear and dawdle on the original, curvy, two-lane route instead.

02 Knife River

Unspoiled shoreline and fisherfolk casting at river mouths are your companions along the way until you reach **Russ Kendall's Smoke House** *(facebook.com/russkendalls)* in Knife River. A groovy neon sign beckons you in. Four generations of Kendall folk have cooked up the locally plucked trout and line-caught Alaskan salmon. Buy a brown-sugar-cured slab (staff will wrap it in newspaper) and you'll be set for picnics for miles to come.

THE DRIVE: Continue northeast on Hwy 61 through the pines. In about 9 miles you'll reach Two Harbors.

03 Two Harbors

Industry prevails in Two Harbors, the biggest town you'll encounter for the rest of the route. Watch iron-ore freighters maneuvering around the huge docks that jut into Agate Bay, and check out Minnesota's only operating **lighthouse** *(lakecountyhistoricalsociety.org/lighthouse)*, a 1892 redbrick fog-buster that doubles as a B&B. In case you're wondering: the other harbor that gives the town its name is Burlington Bay, around the point to the north.

Hikers should stop at the **Superior Hiking Trail Office** *(superiorhiking.org)* for information on the pristine, 300-mile footpath that follows the ridgeline above Lake Superior between Duluth and the Canadian border. Trailheads with parking lots pop up every 5 to 10 miles, making it ideal for day hikes. Overnight hikers will find 94 backcountry campsites and several lodges along the way.

THE DRIVE: Motor onward on Hwy 61, past the hamlet of

Castle Danger (named for a boat that ran aground nearby), to Gooseberry Falls State Park, a 13-mile drive.

04 Gooseberry Falls State Park

The five cascades, scenic gorge and easy trails draw carloads of visitors to **Gooseberry Falls State Park** *(dnr.state.mn.us)*. Several smart stone and log buildings, built by Civilian Conservation Corps in the 1930s, dot the premises and hold exhibits and concessions.

The Lower and Middle Falls offer the quickest access via a 0.6-mile paved walkway. Hardier types can trek the 2-mile **Gooseberry River Loop**, which is part of the Superior Hiking Trail. To embark, leave your car at the visitor center lot (at Mile Post 38.9). Follow the trail to the Upper Falls, then continue upstream on the Fifth Falls Trail. Cross the bridge at Fifth Falls, then return on the river's other side to where you started. Voila! It's one of the simplest Superior trail jaunts you'll find.

THE DRIVE: Yep, it's back to Hwy 61 heading northeast, this time for 7 miles.

05 Split Rock Lighthouse

Split Rock Lighthouse State Park *(mnhs.org/splitrock)* is the most visited spot on the entire North Shore. The shiner itself is a state historic site with a separate admission fee to the grounds. If you don't mind stairs, say 170 or so each way, tramp down the cliff to the beach for incredible views of the lighthouse and surrounding shore.

The lighthouse was built after a whopping storm in November 1905 battered 29 ships in the area. Modern navigation equipment rendered it obsolete by 1969. No matter. It remains one of the most picture-perfect structures you'll come across.

THE DRIVE: Onward on Hwy 61 for 10 miles. Not long after cruising by the factory town of Silver Bay, watch for the sign to Palisade Head.

06 Palisade Head

Palisade Head is an old lava flow that morphed into some awesomely sheer, rust-red cliffs. A narrow road winds around to the top, where there's a small parking lot. The view that unfurls is tremendous. On a clear day you can see Wisconsin's Apostle Islands. Rock climbers love the Head, and you'll probably see a lot of them hanging around.

THE DRIVE: Return to Hwy 61. Palisade Head is actually part of Tettegouche State Park, though it's not contiguous. The park's main span begins 2 miles up the road.

07 Tettegouche State Park

Like most of the parks dotting the North Shore, **Tettegouche State Park** *(dnr.state.mn.us)* offers fishing, camping, paddling and hiking trails to waterfalls and little lakes, plus skiing and snowshoe trails in winter.

There are two worthy to-dos, both accessed near the park entrance (Mile 58.5). Leave your car in the parking lot by the visitor center, then hit the trail to **Shovel Point**. It's a 1.5-mile round-trip jaunt over lots of steps and boardwalks. It pays off with sublime views of the rugged landscape from the point's tip. Watch the lake's awesome power as waves smash below. And keep an eye out for peregrine falcons that nest in the area. Tettegouche's other cool feature is the idyllic **swimming hole** at the Baptism River's mouth. Walk along the picnic area by the visitor center and you'll run into it.

THE DRIVE: Hwy 61 rolls by more birch trees, parks and cloud-flecked skies for the next 22 miles. Not far past Taconite Harbor and its shuttered power plant, you'll come to Temperance River.

08 Temperance River State Park

Get ready for another gorgeous, falls-filled landscape. The eponymous waterway at **Temperance River State Park** *(dnr.state.mn.us)* belies its moderate name and roars through a narrow, twisting gorge. The scene is easy to get to, with highway-side parking. Then hike over footbridges and around rock pools to see the action.

THE DRIVE: It's a quick 2 miles up Hwy 61 to Tofte.

09 Tofte

The teeny town of Tofte is worth a stop to browse the **North Shore Commercial Fishing Museum** *(commercialfishingmuseum.org)*. The twin-gabled red building holds fishing nets, a fishing boat and other tools of the trade, as well as intriguing photos, most of them from the original Norwegian families who settled and fished here in the late 1800s.

Nearby **Sawtooth Outfitters** *(sawtoothoutfitters.com)* offers guided kayaking tours for all levels of paddling. It has trips on the Temperance River and out on Lake Superior, as well as easier jaunts on wildlife-rich inland lakes. Sawtooth

PHOTO OPPORTUNITY

Split Rock Lighthouse on its perfect clifftop.

AMB-MD PHOTOGRAPHY/SHUTTERSTOCK

Palisade Head, Minnesota

also rents mountain bikes to pedal over the many trails in the area, including the popular **Gitchi Gami State Bike Trail**.

THE DRIVE: Get back on Hwy 61 and head 7 piney miles northeast. Turn left on Ski Hill Rd.

10 Lutsen Mountains

Lutsen *(lutsen.com)* is a ski resort – the biggest alpine ski area in the Midwest, in fact. So it bustles in winter when skiers and snowboarders pile in for the 95 runs on four mountains.

In summer, visitors come for the scenic aerial gondola to the top of **Moose Mountain**. The cars glide at treetop level into the valley and over the Poplar River before reaching the mountaintop 1000ft later.

Gape at the view from the chalet and hike the paths. The **Superior Hiking Trail** cuts through and you can take it plus a spur for the 4.5-mile trek back down the mountain.

Kids go crazy for the alpine slide on **Eagle Mountain**; it's accessed by chairlift. The resort also arranges family-friendly canoe trips in voyageur-style vessels on the Poplar River.

THE DRIVE: It's back to Hwy 61, past maple- and birch-rich Cascade River State Park (particularly lovely in fall), for 20 miles to Grand Marais.

11 Grand Marais

Home to an art colony since 1947, pretty Grand Marais makes an excellent base to explore the region. Stroll the waterfront and take advantage of the downtown filled with bars, restaurants, galleries and antique shops. Do-it-yourself enthusiasts can learn to build boats, tie flies or harvest wild rice at the **North House Folk School** *(northhouse.org)*. The course list is phenomenal – including a day-long class on sailing aboard the Viking ship *Hjordis*. Reserve in advance.

THE DRIVE: On Hwy 61 beyond Grand Marais, the traffic thins and the lake reveals itself more. After 14 miles, you'll arrive at Judge CR Magney State Park.

DETOUR

Gunflint Trail

Start: 11 Grand Marais

The Gunflint Trail, aka County Rd 12, slices inland from Grand Marais to Saganaga Lake. The paved, 57-mile-long byway dips into the **Boundary Waters Canoe Area Wilderness**, the legendarily remote paddlers' paradise. The

Gunflint Ranger Station, just southwest of Grand Marais, has permits and information.

Even if you're not canoeing, the road presents exceptional hiking, picnicking and moose-viewing opportunities. It takes 1½ hours to drive one way, but you'll want longer to commune with your new antlered friends. There aren't any towns along the route, but several lodges are tucked in the woods where you can grab a meal or snack.

12 Judge CR Magney State Park

Magney State Park *(dnr.state.mn.us)* – named after the Minnesota Supreme Court Justice who helped preserve the area – is a beauty. See it by hiking to **Devil's Kettle**, the famous falls where the Brule River splits around a huge rock. Half of the flow drops 50ft in a typically gorgeous North Shore gush, but the other half disappears down a hole and flows underground. Where it goes is a mystery – scientists have never been able to determine the water's outlet. It's a moderately breath-sapping 1.1-mile walk each way.

A short distance beyond the park entrance is **Naniboujou Lodge** *(naniboujou.com)*. The 1920s property was once a private club for Babe Ruth and his contemporaries. You're welcome to walk in and look at the Great Hall (now the lodge's dining room), where mind-blowing, psychedelic-colored Cree Indian designs are painted on the domed ceiling.

THE DRIVE: For the next 20 miles trees and rivers flash by, and Hwy 61 passes through the Grand Portage Reservation. Turn right on County Rd 17 (Mile Creek Rd) near the Trading Post.

13 Grand Portage

Grand Portage National Monument *(nps.gov/grpo)* is where the early voyageurs had to carry their canoes around the Pigeon River rapids. It was the center of a far-flung fur-trading empire, and the reconstructed 1788 trading post and Ojibwe village show how the little community lived in the harsh environment. Learn how the original inhabitants prepared wild rice and pressed beaver pelts as you wander through the Great Hall, kitchen, canoe warehouse and other buildings with costumed interpreters.

The half-mile paved path that goes to **Mt Rose** rewards with killer views. Or make like a voyageur and walk the 17-mile round-trip **Grand Portage Trail** that traces the early fur men's route.

Grand Portage is impressively lonely and windblown – fitting for the end of the road. Because with that, Hwy 61 concludes at the Canadian border 6 miles later.

DETOUR

Isle Royale National Park

Start: 13 Grand Portage

Isle Royale National Park is technically part of Michigan, but it's easily accessed from Grand Portage. ***Ferries*** *(isleroyaleboats.com)* sail to the park in Lake Superior three to five days per week. The 210-sq-mile island is totally free of vehicles and roads, and gets fewer visitors in a year than Yellowstone National Park gets in a day. Wilderness buffs love it for backcountry hiking, moose-spotting, camping and kayaking.

High Falls, Pigeon River, Grand Portage National Monument, Minnesota

JRTWYNAM/SHUTTERSTOCK

MANITOBA
Winnipeg
ONTARIO
Thunder Bay
Lake Superior
MONTANA
Williston
Minot
NORTH DAKOTA
Devils Lake
Grand Forks
Theodore Roosevelt National Park
Lake Sakakawea
Washburn
Bismarck
Jamestown
Fargo
MINNESOTA
Superior
MICHIGAN
Little Missouri National Grassland
Brainerd
WISCONSIN
Ellendale
Alexandria
SOUTH DAKOTA
Aberdeen
28
27
Willmar
St Paul
Eau Claire
Green Bay
Spearfish
Rapid City
Pierre
Redfield
Watertown
Brookings
Mitchell
Sioux Falls
Madison
WYOMING
Hot Springs
Missouri River
Chadron
Valentine
Yankton
Crawford
NEBRASKA
Sioux City
Waterloo
Cedar Rapids
Dubuque
Rockford
ILLINOIS
Chicago
Alliance
O'Neill
Norfolk
IOWA
Marshalltown
Iowa City/Coralville
Scottsbluff
North Platte
Columbus
Des Moines
Des Moines River
Grand Island
Omaha
Burlington
Sidney
Ogallala
Lincoln
Fort Morgan
Platte River
Hastings
Auburn
Mississippi River
McCook
Beatrice
St Joseph
Springfield
Norton
26
28
Burlington
Topeka
Columbia
COLORADO
Wa Keeney
Salina
Kansas City
Jefferson City
St Louis
KANSAS
Great Bend
Emporia
Lamar
Dodge City
Newton
Iola
Cape Girardeau
Arkansas River
Pratt
Wichita
MISSOURI
Springfield
Boise City
Joplin
Mark Twain National Forest
Guymon
Alva
Bartlesville
OKLAHOMA
Enid
Dalhart
Canadian River
Tulsa
TENNESSEE
25
Clinton
Muskogee
Pampa
Oklahoma City
ARKANSAS
Memphis
Amarillo
NEW MEXICO
Wichita Mountains
Lawton
Little Rock
Frederick
Ardmore
Wichita Falls
Durant
Lubbock
Texarkana
TEXAS
Brazos River
MISSISSIPPI
Dallas
Shreveport
Jackson
0 200 km
0 100 miles

SL - PHOTOGRAPHY/SHUTTERSTOCK

Badlands National Park (p225), South Dakota

GREAT PLAINS

EXPLORE

GREAT PLAINS

The Great Plains transition you between east and west. Along the way, you'll encounter some of the country's finest history, scenery and adventure yarns. And you'll hear the stories of outlaws, pioneers and the likes of Geronimo, Crazy Horse and the Five Civilized Tribes, as well as explorer duo Lewis and Clark.

Then there's Gateway Arch, Mt Rushmore and Scotts Bluff. One required stop? The prairie. Vaulting grasshoppers, scratchy blue stems, unabashed birdsong, the smell of cut grass. By stimulating the senses, it reinvigorates the soul. Pull over, get out of the car, breathe deep. You'll see what we mean.

Oklahoma City

Oklahoma City is everything about the state writ large and in one place. Here you'll find a city proud of the state's cowboy heritage but just as eager to shrug off any perceived lack of sophistication with cutting-edge museums, the trendy Paseo Arts District, Route 66 kitsch and Native American history. Somehow it all hangs together. But some of the best things here are the traditional ones – the city has always been known for its top-notch hamburgers and steaks, and it's a mighty fine place to buy that ten-gallon hat you've always craved before heading out to sample the country-and-western music scene. It's a terrific example of the urban American West. As a base, it's a top place to begin so many Oklahoma journeys.

Omaha

Omaha is one of the loveliest cities anywhere in the Great Plains. It owes its appeal in part to its brick-and-cobblestoned Old Market neighborhood, a booming riverfront, and a lively music scene. Although very much a city of the Plains with some fabulous museums that tell the region's story, Omaha is also an oasis of urban charm and sophistication in the midst of all that vastness. There's outstanding

WHEN TO GO

The best time to travel the Great Plains is from April or May to September–October. This is when the weather is lovely and wildflowers are in bloom. Expect most attractions to be open and, although it's the busiest time of year, it's less likely to be overwhelmed with visitors than many other areas of the country.

dining to be had, too, all across the city, but especially in Old Market, Benson and Midtown Crossing. It's a good starting point for (and resting place between) at least two of the Great Plains routes.

Rapid City

Compact enough to have a walkable downtown, Rapid City is perfect for exploring the Black Hills and the rest of South Dakota. It's a cosmopolitan place with good restaurants and places to stay, and there's an unpretentious authenticity to the city that makes it feel very much at home here out west. As you walk around town, tick off the statues of America's 43 presidents, then drive 8 miles south of town to look for bears.

Kansas City

They say that the American West begins on the west bank of the Missouri River, just across the water from Kansas City, but not everyone agrees. Culturally, it's very much a Great Plains city, known for its fiery barbecue joints, nearly 200 fountains, and a jazz scene to rival the best. It's certainly a don't-miss Great Plains highlight with world-class museums and quirky art-filled neighborhoods with lots of cafes and restaurants that jostle for your attention. In short, Kansas City is one of America's most appealing cities, and many first-time visitors find it irresistible. Most residents would agree.

TRANSPORTATION

All of the gateway or hub towns – including Rapid City, Omaha, Oklahoma City, St Louis and Kansas City – have air services from all across the US, and each of these airports has multiple car-rental possibilities. **Greyhound** *(greyhound.com)* and **Jefferson Lines** *(jeffersonlines.com)* have the widest range of bus services in and out of the region.

WHERE TO STAY

The Great Plains and surrounding areas specialise in friendly B&Bs and historic hotels that blend the pioneering history with a respectful nod to Native American history and culture. Examples of the former include **Blue Fern B&B** in Tahlequah, while the latter can be experienced in the **Hotel Alex Johnson** in Rapid City, South Dakota. Omaha, Oklahoma City and Tulsa, in particular, have fine examples of the historic-hotel genre. You'll never be without somewhere to stay, and for every historic hotel, you'll find 10 roadside motels and a handful of casino hotels.

RESOURCES

- **Black Hills & Badlands**
  Outstanding portal on South Dakota's most interesting corner. *blackhillsbadlands.com*
- **Visit Cherokee Nation**
  A fine resource for learning more about (and from) the Cherokee and their Oklahoma homeland. *visitcherokeenation.com*
- **WWF**
  The Great Plains are a fascinating natural realm – learn all about them here. *worldwildlife.org/places/great-plains*

WHAT'S ON

- **Taste of Omaha**
  Discover one of America's best food festivals showcasing Omaha's excellent culinary scene in early June.
- **Sturgis Motorcycle Rally**
  Over 500,000 visitors take over Sturgis for the Sturgis Motorcycle Rally in early August.
- **NCAA College World Series**
  For over seven decades, the top college baseball teams have come to Omaha to see which one is the best. Supporters fill the city over 12 days in June.

25

★ BEST FOR

HISTORY

Unmissable Tahlequah, the Cherokee capital.

GREAT PLAINS

OKLAHOMA'S TRIBAL TRAILS

DURATION: 4–5 DAYS

DISTANCE: 453 MILES / 729KM

GREAT FOR: HISTORY & CULTURE, OUTDOORS, FAMILIES

BEST TIME TO GO: ENJOY THIS TRIP APRIL TO OCTOBER, WHEN THE WEATHER CAN BE LOVELY.

Fort Gibson, Oklahoma

There's no soft-pedaling the Trail of Tears, the forced removal and march of five Indian tribes from the southeastern US to what was then called the Indian Territory in present-day eastern Oklahoma. The tales of death, deception and duplicity are sobering. You can visit sites connected to these tragedies (and others) across Oklahoma. In addition you can learn about the vital role of Native Americans in the state today.

LINK YOUR TRIP

01 Route 66
Already one of the richest states for Route 66 sites, the Native American heritage of Oklahoma makes an excellent add-on.

26 On the Pioneer Trails
See yet more ways people spread out across the US, for better and worse. Take I-49 and I-29 430 miles north to Omaha, NE.

01 Tahlequah

Subtle, forested hills interspersed with lakes and iconic red dirt cover Oklahoma's northeast corner, aka **Green Country** *(greencountryok.com)*, which includes Tahlequah, the Cherokee capital since 1839.

Of the tragedies visited on Indian tribes, perhaps none is more tragic than the relocation of the Cherokees. The history and horror behind the forced march comprises key events, including court battles and stockade imprisonment, that preceded the forced removal culminating in army-commanded marches between 1838 and 1839. Disease, starvation and the cold killed scores on the 800-mile journey.

THE DRIVE: From the south side of Tahlequah it is a short drive (1 mile) south on South Keeler Dr to your next stop.

GEMSTOCKSY/SHUTTERSTOCK

02 Hunter's Home

A large estate from the mid-19th century, this **historic house** *(okhistory.org/sites/huntershome)* belies some of the images of the Cherokees as downtrodden. George Murrell, who was of European descent, was married to Minerva Ross, a member of a prominent Cherokee family (her uncle was principal chief of the tribe from 1828 to 1866). He moved with his family at the time of the forced removals and built this estate, which offers a look at the more genteel aspects of life in the early days of the Indian Territory.

THE DRIVE: The third stop on the tour is an easy 18 miles southwest along US 62. Enjoy the gently rolling countryside and iconic red Oklahoma earth.

03 Fort Gibson

Built as a frontier fort in 1824, **Fort Gibson** *(okhistory.org/sites/fortgibson)* came to play an integral – and notorious – role in the Trail of Tears. It was home to the removal commission in the 1830s and is where surviving Creek and Seminole people were brought after the forced march. From here they were dispatched around the Indian Territory. You can get a good sense of military life 200 years ago at the restored grounds and buildings. Fort Gibson is a National Historic Landmark managed by the Oklahoma Historical Society.

Washington Irving wrote his landmark *A Tour of the Prairies* in 1835 based on trips he took with Fort Gibson troops in 1832 and 1833 looking for local bands of Native Americans.

THE DRIVE: Continue southwest on US 62 to Muskogee, 9 miles away.

04 Muskogee

The namesake of Merle Haggard's 1969 hit 'Okie from Muskogee,' this place is a bit different from the rest of Oklahoma. It is deep in the Arkansas River Valley and there are hints of humid air from the Gulf of Mexico.

Here you can learn more about the relocated tribes at the small but engaging **Five Civilized Tribes Museum** *(fivetribes.org)*. The museum is located in an 1875 former Indian Agency office that was used as a meeting place for the leaders

THE CHOCTAWS & OKLAHOMA'S IDENTITY

The Choctaws were skilled farmers living in brick and stone homes in Mississippi and Alabama in the early 1800s. They were relocated to Oklahoma in the 1830s – after 16 broken treaties with the US. Oklahoma's name derives from the Choctaw words for 'red man,' and the state flag is derived in part from a flag carried by Choctaw soldiers fighting for the Confederacy during the Civil War.

of the five tribes. It dedicates one wall to each tribe; displays cover an eclectic array of topics from Choctaw code talkers in WWI to variations in lacrosse sticks. The gift shop sells pottery, painting and jewelry made by members of the five tribes.

THE DRIVE: Skip the tolls and monotony of the Muskogee Turnpike and opt instead for US 64, which wanders through classic small towns such as Haskell that give a timeless sense of rural Oklahoma. The 60-mile drive to Tulsa will take about 90 minutes.

05 Tulsa

Self-billed as the 'Oil Capital of the World,' Tulsa is home to scores of energy companies that make their living drilling for oil, selling it or supplying those who do. The wealth this provides once helped create Tulsa's richly detailed art-deco downtown and has funded some excellent museums that give the state's Native American heritage its due.

South of town you can visit a former oil magnate's property, a converted Italianate villa ringed by fabulous foliage. It houses some fine Native American works at the **Philbrook Museum of Art** *(philbrook.org)*.

THE DRIVE: Link Oklahoma's two largest cities via the quick route of I-44, otherwise known as the Turner Turnpike. In return for the tolls, you'll minimize your time between the big-name attractions as you zip along slightly more than 100 miles.

Philbrook Museum of Art, Tulsa, Oklahoma

KIT LEONG/SHUTTERSTOCK

06 Oklahoma City

At the impressive **Oklahoma History Center** *(okhistory.org/historycenter)* you can explore the heritage of the 39 tribes headquartered in the state. Artifacts include an 1890 cradleboard, a Kiowa pictorial calendar and an original letter from Thomas Jefferson that Lewis and Clark gave to the Otoe tribe. In it, Jefferson invites the tribe to the nation's capital. Be sure to look up before you leave – there's a Pawnee star chart on the ceiling.

You can experience the frontier in a manner more familiar to anyone who has seen an old Western movie at the **National Cowboy & Western Heritage Museum** *(nationalcowboymuseum.org)*.

THE DRIVE: A 40-mile drive southwest on I-44 (the Bailey Turnpike toll road) leads to Chickasha at exit 83. Head 20 miles west on US 62 through Native American lands to Anadarko.

07 Anadarko

Eight tribal lands are located in this area, and students from many more tribes are enrolled in Anadarko schools. The town regularly hosts powwows and Native American events.

To mix a little shopping with your learning, visit **Oklahoma Indian Arts & Crafts Cooperative**, which sells museum-quality crafts, including jewelry, dolls and beadwork items (barrettes, purses and moccasins). About 85% of the store's customers are Native American.

You can also visit the **Southern Plains Indian Museum** *(doi.gov/iacb/southern-plains-indian-museum)*, which houses a small but diverse collection of Plains Indian clothing, weaponry and musical instruments. Just east is the **National Hall of Fame for Famous American Indians** *(americanindianhof.com)*. A short outdoor walk leads past the bronze busts of well-known Native Americans including Pocahontas, Geronimo and Sitting Bull. The visitor center has a good selection of books on Oklahoma Indians.

THE DRIVE: US 62 continues to figure prominently in this tour as you drive 35 miles south to Fort Sill. The historic portion is just west of US 62 on the edge of this very active military base.

08 Fort Sill

Oklahoma isn't just home to eastern tribes. Numerous western and Plains tribes, including the Apache, Comanche, Kiowa and Wichita, were also forced here as the US expanded west. The US Army built Fort Sill in 1869 in Kiowa and Comanche territory to prevent raids into settlements in Texas and Kansas. By the 1880s and 1890s its role had changed, and the fort was serving as a protective sanctuary for many tribes.

The **Fort Sill National Historic Landmark & Museum** *(sill-www.army.mil/fs-museum)*, which fills several original stone buildings, explores the history of the fort. Another highlight is the 1872 **Post Guardhouse**, the center of law enforcement for the Indian Territory. Step inside to see where Apache leader Geronimo was detained on three separate occasions. Geronimo's grave is on fort grounds a few miles from the guardhouse.

Fort Sill remains an active army base. You'll need to register at the Visitors Control Center before passing through the gates to view the historic sites.

THE DRIVE: Leave booming artillery in your wake as you roll west on Hwy 62 to state Hwy 115 north. Black-eyed Susans, scrubby trees and barbed-wire

TRAIL OF TEARS ACROSS THE US

From Alabama to Oklahoma, across nine states, the National Park Service administers the **Trail of Tears National Historic Trail** *(nps.gov/trte)*, which features important sites from the tragedy. Among the highlights:

Alabama – Fort Payne Cabin Site. Dates to 1837, when federal troops arrived to force the Cherokee to Oklahoma.

Georgia – Rockdale Plantation. An 18th-century plantation building once owned by a Cherokee enslaver.

Tennessee – Brainerd Mission Cemetery. The remains of a mission for the Cherokees near Chattanooga. Most of the missionaries accompanied the tribe's removal to Oklahoma.

Kentucky – Trail of Tears Commemorative Park. Used as a cemetery for chiefs who died during the removals.

Illinois – Shawnee National Forest. A bleak forest with a marked trail where hundreds of Native Americans died during the horrible winter of 1838–39.

Missouri – Trail of Tears State Park. Another natural area that commemorates the horrible events of the removals.

fences line the two-lane byway as it unfurls from tiny Cache toward the hill-dappled Wichita Mountains Wildlife Refuge.

09 Wichita Mountains Wildlife Refuge

Southwest Oklahoma opens into expansive prairie fields all the way to Texas. Beautiful mountains provide texture.

The 59,020-acre **Wichita Mountains Wildlife Refuge** *(fws.gov/refuge/wichita_mountains)* protects bison, elk, longhorn cattle and a super-active prairie dog town. Wildlife is abundant; observant drivers might even see a spindly, palm-sized tarantula tiptoeing across the road. At the visitor center, informative displays highlight the refuge's flora and fauna. A massive glass window yields inspiring views of prairie grasslands. For a short but scenic hike, try the creek-hugging **Kite Trail** to the waterfalls and rocks at the Forty Foot Hole. It starts at the Lost Lake Picnic Area.

THE DRIVE: After 15 miles on Hwy 49, turn north on Hwy 54, which runs through tribal lands. Look for schools, tiny towns and small farms on the 38.5 miles. At Hwy 152, just north of Cloud Chief village, turn west for 44 miles to US 283. Go north for 24 miles to Cheyenne and follow the signs to the Washita site.

10 Washita Battlefield National Historic Site

Marking the place where George Custer's troops launched a dawn attack on November 27, 1868, on the peaceful village of Chief Black Kettle, is **Washita Battlefield National Historic Site** *(nps.gov/waba)*. It was a slaughter of men, women, children and domestic animals, an act some would say led to karmic revenge on Custer eight years later. Among those who died was the peace-promoting chief, Black Kettle. Even today, you may encounter current members of the US military studying what exactly transpired here that cold, pre-winter morning.

Self-guiding trails traverse the site of the killings, which is remarkably unchanged. A visitor center 0.7 miles away contains a good museum. Seasonal tours and talks are very worthwhile.

A small garden shows how traditional plants were grown for medicine, spiritual rituals and food.

FIVE CIVILIZED TRIBES

Two of eastern Oklahoma's earliest known tribes, the Osage and the Quapaw, ceded millions of acres to the US government in the 1820s. The US then gave the land to five East-Coast tribes: the Cherokee, Chickasaw, Choctaw, Creek and Seminole. Because these five tribes had implemented formal governmental and agricultural practices in their communities, they were collectively called the Five Civilized Tribes.

The Five Civilized Tribes were forced to move to the Oklahoma area, known then as the Indian Territory, after settlers in the southern states decided they wanted the tribes' fertile farmlands for themselves. Between 1830 and 1850, the five tribes were forcibly relocated; their routes are collectively known as the Trail of Tears. How many people died in this forced march is unknown; however, records suggest deaths were in the tens of thousands. Often overlooked are the thousands of African Americans who were enslaved by the Native Americans. Scores died during the removals.

As for their new homes in the Indian Territory, the US government said the land would belong to the five tribes as long as the stars shine and rivers flow. The reality? More like 70 years. In the mid-1800s the country was quickly expanding west, and white settlers wanted the land. Through legislative maneuvering, certain Indian-owned lands were deemed 'unassigned,' opening them up for settlement. The Oklahoma Land Rush began on April 22, 1889, when 50,000 would-be settlers made a mad dash for their own 160-acre allotment.

Wichita Mountains Wildlife Refuge, Oklahoma
VREYER43/SHUTTERSTOCK

26

GREAT PLAINS

ON THE PIONEER TRAILS

★ BEST FOR

EXPLORING

Off-the-beaten-path explorations of a land many blithely whiz through.

Homestead National Monument of America, Beatrice, Nebraska

DURATION: 5–7 DAYS

DISTANCE: 802 MILES / 1290KM

GREAT FOR: HISTORY & CULTURE, NATURE, FAMILIES

BEST TIME TO GO: MAY TO SEPTEMBER, WHEN EVERYTHING IS OPEN AND THE WILDFLOWERS ARE IN BLOOM.

Balmy days driving through lush green valleys and barren buttes; nights hanging outside a small-town ice-cream stand recalling the day's adventures to the background sound of crickets. These are just some of the charms of exploring the back roads of Nebraska, which, like the ubiquitous state plant, corn, when left on the fire, pops with attractions. Eschew I-80 and be a modern-day pioneer.

LINK YOUR TRIP

27 Black Hills Loop
A trip of icons, colorful history and natural beauty. Take US 20, then US 18 west, then go north on scenic US 385.

28 The Mighty Mo
Follow in the tracks of famous explorers Lewis and Clark along America's longest river. Join the trip right in Omaha.

01 Omaha

Omaha's location on the Missouri River and proximity to the Platte made it an important stop on the Oregon, California and Mormon Trails. Many heading west paused here before plunging into Nebraska and you should do the same. Learn tales from these pioneer trails at the beautiful **Durham Museum** *(durhammuseum.org)*, housed in the once-bustling Union Station.

THE DRIVE: Scoot along US 6 with its old drive-ins still peddling soft-serve cones and other pleasures for the 57 miles to Lincoln.

DETOUR

Independence, MO

Start: 01 Omaha

Long associated with colorful US president Harry S Truman, Independence, MO, was also a popular jumping-off point for pioneers

preparing to follow the Oregon and California Trails. For an enjoyable history of these two trails and others, spend an hour or two at the city's National Frontier Trails Museum *(nps.gov/places/000/national-frontier-trails-museum.htm)*. Exhibits include a wall-sized map of the major trail routes, a mock general store and diary entries from the pioneers. Independence is near Kansas City, 200 miles south of Omaha off I-29.

02 Lincoln

Home to the historic Haymarket District and the huge downtown campus of the University of Nebraska, the capital city is a good place to get the big picture of the state's story. You can almost hear the wagon wheels creaking and the sound of sod busting at the **Nebraska History Museum** *(history.nebraska.gov/museum)*.

THE DRIVE: Drive 35 miles south of Lincoln on Hwy 77 to Beatrice.

03 Homestead National Monument of America

The **Homestead National Monument** *(nps.gov/home)* just west of Beatrice is on the site of the very first homestead granted under the landmark Homestead Act of 1862, which opened much of the US to settlers who received land for free if they made it productive. The pioneering Freeman family is buried here and you can see their reconstructed log house and hike the site. The heritage center is a striking building with good displays.

THE DRIVE: An even 100 miles west on US 136 takes you through near-ghost towns, where the solitary gas stations serve as town centers and quaint brick downtowns slowly crumble. Head north at Red Cloud and drive for 68 miles on US 281.

04 Grand Island

For a wide-ranging introduction to pioneer life, spend a few hours at the 200-acre **Stuhr Museum of the Prairie Pioneer** *(stuhrmuseum.org)* in Grand Island. In summer, period reenactors go about their business in an 1890s railroad town, answering questions about their jobs and home life. Also on view is an 1860s log-cabin settlement, a one-room schoolhouse and a Pawnee earth lodge.

On the 2nd floor of the museum's Stuhr Building, a covered wagon overflows with furniture and clothes – an inspiring symbol of the pioneers' can-do optimism. A few steps away, a display of black-and-white photos of a primitive sod house and a prairie funeral depict the darker, harsher realities lurking behind the romance of the pioneer dream. Interesting fact? In 1880, 20% of Nebraska's population was foreign born, with most settlers emigrating from Germany, Sweden and Ireland.

THE DRIVE: The leaves of cottonwoods shimmer in the sunlight on this lonely yet lush 42 miles of US 30.

05 Kearney

A shimmering brown arch sweeps across four lanes of I-80 like an imposing medieval drawbridge. This horizon-breaking distraction – it depicts a setting Nebraska sun – is the **Great Platte River Road Archway Monument** *(archway.org)*. A little bit hokey, a little bit history, it's a relentlessly cheery ode to the West that puts a high-tech, glossy spin on the pioneer journey, sweeping in everything from stampeding buffalo to the gold-seeking forty-niners. Afterwards drive 10 minutes southeast to **Fort Kearny State Historical Park** *(outdoornebraska.gov/fortkearny)*, which preserves the fort that protected travelers on the Oregon and California Trails.

Pony Express Station, Gothenburg, Nebraska

MR PRIVACY/SHUTTERSTOCK

Kearney's compact, cute and walkable downtown, near US 30 and the busy Union Pacific (UP) main line, has good cafes and craft breweries.

THE DRIVE: Count the grain silos and see if they outnumber the passing trains along the next 60 miles of US 30.

06 Gothenburg

The Pony Express (1860–61) was the FedEx of its day, using a fleet of young riders and swift horses to carry letters between Missouri and California in an astounding 10 days. Each horseman rode full-bore for almost six hours – changing horses every 10 miles – before passing the mail to the next rider. Their route through Nebraska generally followed the Oregon Trail.

In Gothenburg, step inside what some researchers think is an original **Pony Express Station** *(ponyexpressstation.org)*, one of just a few still in existence.

The engaging array of artifacts includes a mochila, the rider's mail-holding saddlebag. Afterwards, wander a few of the streets downtown lined with beautiful old Victorian houses.

THE DRIVE: A never-ending procession of UP trains zips along the world's busiest freight line for the next 36 miles of US 30.

07 North Platte

North Platte, a rail-fan mecca, is home to the **Buffalo Bill Ranch State Historical Park** *(outdoornebraska.gov/buffalobillranch)*, 2 miles north of US 30. Once the home of Bill Cody – an iconic figure of the American West and the father of rodeo and the famed Wild West show – it has a fun museum that reflects his colorful life.

Enjoy sweeping views of UP's Bailey Yard, the world's largest railroad classification yard, from the **Golden Spike Tower** *(goldenspiketower.com),* an eight-story observation tower with indoor and outdoor decks.

THE DRIVE: Set the cruise control on 'chill' as you drive a straight line 52 miles due west on US 30.

08 Ogallala

Adjust your clocks to mountain time just west of Sutherland. Ogallala was once known as the 'Gomorrah of the Cattle Trail.' It now has all the salacious charm of a motel's nightstand Bible.

The Oregon and California Trails turn north near here, following the Platte River toward Wyoming and the wild blue yonder.

THE DRIVE: Cornfields give way to untamed prairie grasses and desolate bluffs on two-lane US 26, known as Nebraska's Western Trails Historic & Scenic Byway. Look right soon after leaving Ogallala to glimpse sparkling Lake McConaughy through the low hills. Otherwise, cattle herds, passing trains with coal from Wyoming and tumbleweed towns are the biggest distractions for the next 101 miles.

09 Chimney Rock National Historic Site

Heading west, centuries-old bluff formations rise up from the horizon, their striking presence a visual link connecting modern-day travelers (and Oregon Trail gamers) with their pioneer forebears. One of these links is **Chimney Rock**, located inside the Chimney Rock National Historic Site. It's visible 12 miles after Bridgeport off Hwy 92. Chimney Rock's fragile 120ft spire was an inspiring landmark for pioneers, and it was mentioned in hundreds of journals. It also marked the end of the first leg of the journey and the beginning of the tough – but final – push to the coast.

THE DRIVE: Stay on Hwy 92 for 21 miles west after Chimney Rock. As you enter Gering, just south of the city of Scottsbluff, continue straight onto M St, which leads to the Old Oregon Trail Rd. It follows the actual route of the trail and leads straight to Scotts Bluff National Monument after just 3 miles.

10 Scotts Bluff National Monument

Spend a few minutes in the visitor center of this picturesque monument *(nps.gov/scbl)* run by the National Park Service – there's a nice collection of Western art in the William Henry Jackson Gallery – then hit the trail. You can hike the 1.6-mile (one way) **Saddle Rock Trail** or drive the same distance up to the **South Overlook** for bird's-eye views of Mitchell Pass.

Before you leave, spend a few moments hiking the trail through Mitchell Pass itself. The covered wagons on display here look unnervingly frail as you peer through the bluff-flanked gateway, a narrow channel that spills onto the Rocky Mountain-bumping plains. For pioneers, reaching this pass was a significant milestone; it marked the completion of 600 miles of Great Plains trekking.

THE DRIVE: From Scottsbluff, leave the Great Platte River Rd and head north to a historic military fort and a lonely trading post, important bastions that paved the way for long-term settlers. Along the way, revel in Nebraska's prairie, which is aptly described as a 'sea of grass.' This analogy proves true on the 52-mile drive north on Hwy 71.

> ☑ TOP TIP
>
> **AVOID I-80**
>
> I-80 zips across Nebraska for 455 miles. But while it speeds travelers on their way, it does the state no favors. Here are some fine alternatives: take US 6 out of Omaha to Lincoln, US 34 on to Grand Island and then historic US 30 – the original Lincoln Hwy – all the way to Wyoming.

11 Sioux County

Prairie grasses bend and bob as strong winds sweep over low-rolling hills, punctuated by the occasional wooden windmill or lonely cell-phone tower as you drive through Sioux County, named for the Plains tribe that hunted and traveled throughout Nebraska.

Enjoy the drive: this is roll-down-your-window-and-breathe-in-America country.

THE DRIVE: Like bristles on the visage of a trail-weary pioneer, trees begin appearing amid the rolling grasslands as you head north for 27 miles on Hwy 2.

12 Fort Robinson State Park

Sioux warrior Crazy Horse was fatally stabbed on the grounds of Fort Robinson, now **Fort Robinson State Park** *(outdoornebraska.gov/fortrobinson),* on September 5, 1877, at the age of 35. The fort – in operation between 1874 and 1948 – was the area's most important military post during the Indian Wars.

In summer, visitors descend on the 22,000-acre park for stagecoach rides, steak cookouts, trout fishing and hiking. There are two museums on the grounds – the Fort Robinson Museum and the Trailside Museum – as well as the reconstructed Guardhouse where Crazy Horse spent his final hours.

THE DRIVE: If you prefer your historic digs in an urban setting, drive 20 miles east to Chadron.

13 Chadron

Chadron's **Museum of the Fur Trade** *(furtrade.org)* is a well-curated tribute to the mountain men and trappers who paved the way for the pioneers. It holds a fascinating array of artifacts: from 1820s mountain-man leggings and hand-forged animal traps to blankets, pelts and liquor bottles. Kit Carson's shotgun is displayed beside the world's largest collection of Native American trade guns.

Out back, there's a reproduction of the Bordeaux Trading Post; it was in operation here from 1837 to 1876. The harsh reality of life on the plains is evident the moment you step inside the unnervingly cramped building. Though it's not the original structure, the reproduction is so precisely done it's listed on the National Register of Historic Places.

> **PHOTO OPPORTUNITY**
>
> The postcard-worthy buttes of Scotts Bluff.

THE DRIVE: Continue east to the Sandhills for 77 miles on US 20, known as the Bridges to Buttes Byway. The little towns along here are just hanging on amid the buttes, canyons and rolling hills of the often-dramatic landscape.

14 Arthur Bowring Sandhills Ranch State Historical Park

The hardscrabble lives of Nebraskan ranchers are faithfully recalled at this 1920s ranch near the South Dakota border. Owned by the Bowring clan, it includes an early sod house that makes it clear that any farmhouse was a major step up. Still, you'll find comforts here as Eva Bowring, who lived here for much of her long life, collected fine crystal, china and antique furniture.

THE DRIVE: Keep the camera ready for moody shots of lonely windmills amid the sandy bluffs on the 60 miles east on US 20 to Valentine.

15 Valentine

What better way to literally immerse yourself in a timeless Nebraska from before the pioneer days than floating down a scenic river – especially on a steamy summer day.

Valentine sits on the edge of the Sandhills and is a great base for canoeing, kayaking and inner-tubing the winding canyons of **Niobrara National Scenic River** *(nps.gov/niob)*. The river crosses the **Fort Niobrara National Wildlife Refuge** *(fws.gov/refuge/Fort_Niobrara)*. Driving tours take you past bison, elk and more.

Floating down the river draws scores of people through the summer. Sheer limestone bluffs, lush forests and spring-fed waterfalls along the banks shatter any 'flat Nebraska' stereotypes. Most float tours are based in **Valentine** *(visitvalentine.com)*.

GO WEST

An estimated 400,000 people trekked west across America between 1840 and 1860, lured by tales of gold, promises of religious freedom and visions of fertile farmland. They were also inspired by the expansionist credo of President James Polk and the rallying cry of New York editor John O'Sullivan, who urged Americans in 1845 to 'overspread the continent allotted by Providence for the free development of our yearly multiplying millions.'

These starry-eyed pioneers became the foot soldiers of Manifest Destiny, eager to pursue their own dreams while furthering America's expansionist goals. The movement's success depended on the safe, reliable passage of these foot soldiers through the Great Plains and beyond. The California, Oregon and Mormon pioneer trails served this purpose well, successfully channeling the travelers and their prairie schooners on defined routes across the country.

Scotts Bluff National Monument (p221), Nebraska
ZACK FRANK/SHUTTERSTOCK

27

GREAT PLAINS

BLACK HILLS LOOP

★ BEST FOR

OUTDOORS

Where buffalo roam is just the start of critter-filled days amid beautiful scenery.

Bison, Custer State Park (p226), South Dakota

DURATION: 2–3 DAYS

DISTANCE: 265 MILES / 426 KM

GREAT FOR: HISTORY & CULTURE, NATURE, FAMILIES

BEST TIME TO GO: MAY TO SEPTEMBER, WHEN ALL SIGHTS ARE OPEN.

In the early 1800s, 60 million buffalo roamed the plains. Rampant overhunting decimated their ranks and by 1889 fewer than 1000 remained. Today, their numbers have climbed to 500,000; several Black Hills parks manage healthy herds. On this tour you'll see the iconic buffalo and other legendary sights, including the Badlands, Mt Rushmore, the Crazy Horse Memorial, sprawling parks and the town made famous for having no law: Deadwood.

LINK YOUR TRIP

28 The Mighty Mo
Follow North America's longest river through magnificent wilderness and great cities. Join the route in Pierre, SD, a 170-mile trip east of Rapid City via I-90 plus a scenic leg on US 14.

29 Grand Teton to Yellowstone
More great American parks are west through Montana.

01 Rapid City

A worthy capital to the region, 'Rapid' has an intriguing, lively and walkable downtown. Well-preserved brick buildings, filled with quality shops and places to dine, make it a good urban base and hub for your looping tour. Get a walking-tour brochure of Rapid's historic buildings and public art from the visitor center. Check out the watery fun on **Main St Square**.

While strolling, don't miss the **Presidential Statues** on downtown street corners. From a shifty-eyed Nixon in repose to a triumphant Harry Truman, lifelike statues dot corners throughout the center. Collect all 43.

Learn about how dramatic natural underground events over the eons have produced some spectacular rocks. See these plus dinosaur bones and some stellar fossils at the **Museum of Geology** *(museum.sdsmt.edu)*, located at the South Dakota School of Mines & Technology.

THE DRIVE: Choose from the commercial charms on Hwys 16 and 16A on the 21-mile drive to Keystone.

DETOUR

Badlands National Park

Start: 01 Rapid City

More than 600 buffalo, also known as North American bison, roam **Badlands National Park** *(nps.gov/badl)*. The name originated with French trappers and the Lakota Sioux, who described the park's jagged spires and crumbling buttes as 'bad lands.' Today, this crumbling former floodplain is visually compelling, its corrugated hillsides enlivened by an ever-changing palette.

You can see the eroding rocks up close on the **Notch Trail**, a 1.5-mile (round-trip) leg stretcher that twists through a canyon, scampers up a wooden ladder, then curves along a crumbly ridgeline to an expansive view of grasslands and more serrated walls. At the **Ben Reifel Visitor Center** just down the road, a visually stunning film captures the park's natural diversity with jaw-dropping close-ups of the plants and animals that thrive in the mixed-grass prairie.

From Rapid City, head about 50 miles east on I-90, where Badlands Loop Rd (Hwy 240) links with I-90 at exits 131 and 110. The loop stretches west from the visitor center into the park's north unit, curving along a narrow ridge of buttes known as the **Badlands Wall**. It can be driven in an hour, but stopping at the numerous overlooks can easily fill a morning. Exit 110 off I-90 also serves Wall, home to the eponymous **Wall Drug Store** *(walldrug.com)*, one of the world's great – and unmissable – tourist traps.

To avoid I-90 back to Rapid City, pick up Hwy 44, which can be accessed at several points from Badlands. Jagged bluffs give way to rolling prairie on this made-for-convertibles byway that swings through the Buffalo Gap National Grassland on its way west.

02 Keystone

One indisputable fact about the Black Hills? It will always, always, always take longer than you think to reach a key attraction. Trust us. Slow-moving Winnebagos, serpentine byways and kitschy roadside distractions will deaden your pace. And the distractions start early on Hwy 16 where family-friendly and delightfully hokey tourist attractions vie for dollars on the way to Mt Rushmore, including the animal-happy **Bear Country USA** *(bearcountryusa.com)* and **Reptile Gardens** *(reptilegardens.com)*.

Kitsch reigns supreme in Keystone, a gaudy town bursting with rah-rah patriotism, Old West spirit and too many fudgeries. The fuss is directly attributable to its proximity to Mt Rushmore, 3 miles west.

THE DRIVE: It's a mere 3-mile jaunt uphill to Mt Rushmore. Keep your eyes peeled for the first glimpse of a president.

03 Mt Rushmore National Memorial

Glimpses of Washington's nose from the roads leading to this hugely popular monument never cease to surprise and are but harbingers of the full impact of this mountainside sculpture once you're up close (and past the less impressive parking area and entrance walk). George Washington, Thomas Jefferson, Abraham Lincoln and Theodore Roosevelt each iconically stare into the distance in 60ft-tall granite glory.

Though it's hugely popular, you can easily escape the crowds and fully appreciate **Mt Rushmore** *(nps.gov/moru)* while marveling at the artistry of sculptor Gutzon Borglum and the immense labor of the workers who created the memorial between 1927 and 1941.

> PHOTO OPPORTUNITY
>
> Find a new angle on the four mugs at Mt Rushmore.

The **Presidential Trail** loop passes right below the monument for some fine nostril views and gives you access to the worthwhile **Sculptor's Studio**. Start clockwise and you're right under Washington's nose in less than five minutes. The nature trail to the right as you face the entrance connects the viewing and parking areas, passing through a pine forest and avoiding the crowds and commercialism.

The official **National Park Service Information Center** has an excellent bookstore whose proceeds go to the park. Avoid the schlocky gift shop and the disappointing Carvers Cafe, which looked much better in the scene where Cary Grant gets plugged in *North by Northwest*. The main museum is far from comprehensive but the fascinating Sculptor's Studio conveys the drama of how the monument came to be.

THE DRIVE: Backtrack slightly from Mt Rushmore and head southwest for 16 miles of thrills on Iron Mountain Rd.

04 Peter Norbeck Scenic Byway

Driving the 66-mile Peter Norbeck Scenic Byway is like flirting with a brand-new crush: always exhilarating, occasionally challenging, and sometimes you get a few butterflies. Named for the South Dakota senator who pushed for its creation in 1919, the oval-shaped byway is broken into four roads linking the most memorable destinations in the Black Hills (drivers of large RVs should call Custer State Park for tunnel measurements).

Iron Mountain Rd (Hwy 16A) is the real star, beloved for its pigtailing loops, Mt Rushmore–framing tunnels and one gorgeous glide through sun-dappled pines. It's a 16-mile roller coaster of wooden bridges, virtual loop-the-loops, narrow tunnels and stunning vistas. Expect lots of drivers going even slower than you are.

The 14-mile Needles Hwy (Hwy 87) swoops below granite spires, careens past rocky overlooks and slings through a super-narrow tunnel.

THE DRIVE: Once past Iron Mountain Rd, other Peter Norbeck Scenic Byway options aside, it is only 3 miles along Hwy 16 west to the Custer State Park visitor center.

05 Custer State Park

The only reason 111-sq-mile **Custer State Park** *(gfp.sd.gov/parks/detail/custer-state-park)* isn't a national park is that the state grabbed it first. It boasts one of the largest free-roaming bison herds in the world (about 1500), the famous 'begging burros' (donkeys seeking handouts) and more than 200 bird species. Other wildlife include elk, pronghorns, mountain goats, bighorn sheep, coyotes, prairie dogs, mountain lions and bobcats. Meandering over awesome stone bridges and across sublime alpine meadows, the 18-mile **Wildlife Loop Rd** allows plenty of spotting.

The **Custer State Park Visitor Center** *(gfp.sd.gov/csp-visitor-center)*, situated on the eastern side of the park, contains good exhibits and offers guided nature walks. The nearby **Black Hills Playhouse** *(blackhillsplayhouse.com)* hosts summer theater.

Mt Rushmore, South Dakota
GARY YIM/SHUTTERSTOCK

Hiking through the pine-covered hills and prairie grassland is a great way to see wildlife and rock formations. Trails through Sylvan Lake Shore, Sunday Gulch, Cathedral Spires and French Creek Natural Area are all highly recommended.

The park is named for the notorious George A Custer, who led a scientific expedition into the Black Hills in 1874. The expedition's discovery of gold drew so many new settlers that an 1868 treaty granting the Sioux a 60-million-acre reservation in the area was eventually broken. Crazy Horse and the Lakotas retaliated, killing Custer and 265 of his men at Montana's Battle of the Little Big Horn in 1876.

THE DRIVE: Near the western edge of Custer State Park, head due south on Hwy 87 for 19 miles from US 16. It's a beautiful ride through a long swath of wilderness and park.

06 Wind Cave National Park

This park *(nps.gov/wica)*, protecting 44 sq miles of grassland and forest, sits just south of Custer State Park. The central feature is, of course, the cave, which contains 147 miles of mapped passages. The cave's foremost feature is its 'boxwork' calcite formations (95% of all that are known exist here), which look like honeycomb and date back 60 to 100 million years. The strong gusts of wind that are felt at the entrance, but not inside, give the cave its name. Tours run from April to early January, and Wind Cave's above-ground acres abound with bison and prairie dogs.

THE DRIVE: Scenic drives continue as you go from one big hole in the ground to another.

Sylvan Lake, Custer State Park
MARYGAVANPHOTOS/SHUTTERSTOCK

Jewel Cave is 38 miles northwest on US 385 and US 16.

07 Jewel Cave National Monument

Another of the Black Hills' many fascinating caves is **Jewel Cave** *(nps.gov/jeca)*, 13 miles west of Custer on US 16, so named because calcite crystals line many of its walls. Currently 187 miles have been surveyed (3% of the estimated total), making it the third-longest known cave in the world. Entry is by ranger-guided tour only, and self-guided trails depart right outside of the center.

THE DRIVE: Retrace your route for 13 miles until US 385 joins US 16 and then go north for |5 miles.

08 Crazy Horse Memorial

The world's largest monument, the **Crazy Horse Memorial** *(crazyhorsememorial.org)* is a 563ft-tall work in progress. When finished, it will depict the Sioux leader astride his horse, pointing to the horizon and saying, 'My lands are where my dead lie buried.'

Never photographed or persuaded to sign a meaningless treaty, Crazy Horse was chosen for a monument that Lakota Sioux elders hoped would balance the presidential focus of Mt Rushmore. In 1948 a Boston-born sculptor, the indefatigable Korczak Ziółkowski, started blasting granite. His family have continued the work since his death in 1982. (It should be noted that many Native Americans oppose the monument as desecration of sacred land.)

No one is predicting when the sculpture will be complete (the face was dedicated in 1998). A rather thrilling laser-light show tells the tales of the monument on summer evenings.

♥ WHY I LOVE THIS TRIP

MARK JOHANSON, WRITER

Ride the roller-coaster roads into the pine-covered Black Hills, and the golden plains of the American heartland seem a world away. Iconic Mt Rushmore lures most visitors to this remote region, but it's the prismatic caves, herds of bison and Wild West tales of Deadwood's larger-than-life characters that leave lasting memories. Hike or bike near attractive resort towns, then laze away an afternoon in a bubbling thermal spring.

The visitor center complex includes a Native American museum, a cultural center, cafes and Ziółkowski's studio.

THE DRIVE: It's a short 10-mile drive north on US 16/385 to the refreshments of Hill City.

09 Hill City

One of the most appealing towns up in the hills, **Hill City** *(hillcitysd.org)* is less frenzied than places such as Keystone. Its main drag has cafes and galleries.

The **1880 Train** *(1880train.com)* is a classic steam train running through rugged country to and from Keystone. An interesting train museum is next door.

THE DRIVE: Lakes, rivers, meadows and a few low-key tourist traps enliven the 42 miles on US 385 to Deadwood through the heart of the Black Hills.

10 Deadwood

Fans of the iconic HBO TV series may recall that Deadwood was the epitome of lawlessness in the 1870s. Today things have changed, although the 80 gambling halls, big and small, would no doubt put a sly grin on the faces of the hard characters who founded the town.

Deadwood's atmospheric streets are lined with gold-rush-era buildings lavishly restored with gambling dollars. Its storied past is easy to find at its museums and cemeteries. There's eternal devotion to Wild Bill Hickok, who was shot in the back of the head here in 1876 while gambling.

Actors reenact famous shootouts on Main St during summer, including the 1877 saloon fight between Tom Smith and David Lunt (who lived for 67 days relatively unbothered by the bullet in his head before finally dropping dead).

THE DRIVE: Lead is just 4 miles uphill from Deadwood, through land scarred by generations hunting for gold.

11 Lead

Lead (pronounced 'leed') has slowly gentrifying charm but still bears plenty of scars from the mining era. Gape at the 1250ft-deep open-pit mine from the **Sanford Lab Homestake Visitor Center** *(sanfordlab.org/slhvc)* to see what open-pit mining can do to a mountain. Nearby are the same mine's shafts, which plunge more than 1.5 miles below the surface and are now being used for physics research.

THE DRIVE: Climb out of steep canyons for 11 miles on US 14A until you plunge back down into Spearfish Canyon.

12 Spearfish

Spearfish Canyon Scenic Byway *(spearfishcanyon.com/scenicbyway)* is a waterfall-lined, curvaceous 20-mile road that cleaves from the heart of the hills into Spearfish. There's a sight worth stopping for around every bend; pause for longer than a minute and you'll hear beavers hard at work.

THE DRIVE: It's a quick 22 miles east on I-90 to Sturgis. That solitary headlight in the rear-view mirror is a hog hoping to blow past. From Sturgis back to Rapid City is only 36 miles.

13 Sturgis

Neon-lit tattoo parlors, Christian iconography and billboards for ribald biker bars featuring dolled-up models are just some of the cacophony of images in this loud and proud biker town. Shop for leather on Main St, don your American flag bandana and sidle up to the saloon bar to give a toast to the stars and stripes.

Things get even louder for the annual **Sturgis Motorcycle Rally** *(sturgismotorcyclerally.com)*, when over 500,000 riders, fans and curious onlookers take over the town.

Deadwood Main Street, Deadwood, South Dakota

RAINER GROSSKOPF/GETTY IMAGEST

STEAKHOUSE
SALOON
BERG
JEWELRY
GOLD
GIFTS

28

GREAT PLAINS

THE MIGHTY MO

★ BEST FOR

HISTORY

Much of the USA's 19th-century sense of self was formed by events along the river.

DURATION: 7 DAYS

DISTANCE: 1388 MILES / 2234KM

GREAT FOR: HISTORY & CULTURE, OUTDOORS, FAMILIES

BEST TIME TO GO: MAY TO SEPTEMBER, WHEN ALL THE SIGHTS ARE OPEN.

Mark Twain Boyhood Home & Museum, Hannibal, Missouri

In 1804–05, Lewis and Clark followed the Missouri River during the first stages of their legendary journey west. With their Corps of Discovery, they canoed up the river, meeting Native Americans – some friendly, others hostile – and discovering vast expanses of land, untouched for eons and teeming with wildlife. Exploring the river today, you can make your very own discoveries.

LINK YOUR TRIP

27 Black Hills Loop
Great sights, including Mt Rushmore, await in South Dakota's beautiful Black Hills. Start in Rapid City, SD, a 170-mile trip west of Pierre.

23 The Great River Road
Link up with the more famous – yet shorter – Mississippi River north of St Louis to see America's two greatest rivers.

01 St Louis

Fur-trapper Pierre Laclede knew prime real estate when he saw it, putting down stakes at the junction of the Mississippi and Missouri Rivers in 1764. The hustle picked up considerably when prospectors discovered gold in California in 1848 and St Louis became the jumping-off point first for get-rich-quick dreamers and later for waves of settlers. Its unique position made it the 'Gateway to the West.'

As a symbol for the city, the **Gateway Arch** *(gatewayarch.com)* has soared above any expectations its backers could have had in 1965 when it opened. The centerpiece of this National Park Service complex, the silvery, shimmering 630ft-high arch is the Great Plains' own Eiffel Tower. A tram ride takes you to the tight confines at the top.

The arch sits atop a revitalized museum *(nps.gov/jeff)* that explains the vision of Thomas Jefferson, who sponsored the Lewis and Clark expedition. It began here on May 14, 1804, and followed the Missouri

MIHAI_ANDRITOIU/SHUTTERSTOCK

River, much as you'll do on this tour. It offers a balanced view of what western expansion meant for the Native Americans living on the lands and the newly arrived pioneers.

THE DRIVE: To use a cliché, from the arch, go west (about 24 miles on busy I-70).

02 St Charles

This Missouri River town, founded in 1769, has a cobblestoned Main St. Within the well-preserved downtown you can visit the **First Missouri State Capitol** *(mostateparks.com)*. Ask at the visitor center *(discoverstcharles.com)* about tours, which pass some rare French colonial architecture in the Frenchtown neighborhood just north.

Clark joined Lewis here and they began their epic journey on May 21, 1804. Their encampment is reenacted annually on that date. The **Lewis & Clark Boat House and Museum** *(lewisandclarkboathouse.org)* has displays about the duo and replicas of their boats.

THE DRIVE: Skip the elusive charms of I-70 and instead stay close to the river, taking first Hwy 94 and then cutting north via Columbia (which has good cafes downtown) on US 63. From here take Hwy 740, Hwy 240, US 40 and Hwy 41 in that order for a total journey of 190 miles.

DETOUR

Hannibal

Start: 02 St Charles

Hannibal is on that other river, the Mississippi. When the air is sultry in this old river town, you almost expect to hear the whistle of a paddle steamer. Mark Twain's boyhood home, 100 miles northwest of St Louis, has some authentically vintage areas and plenty of sites where you can get a sense of the writer and his creations, Tom Sawyer and Huck Finn.

The **Mark Twain Boyhood Home & Museum** *(marktwainmuseum.org)* presents eight buildings, including two homes Twain lived in and that of Laura Hawkins, the real-life inspiration for Becky Thatcher. Afterward, float down the Mississippi on the **Mark Twain Riverboat** *(marktwainriverboat.com)*. **National Tom Sawyer Days** *(hannibaljaycees.org)* feature frog-jumping and fence-painting contests and much more.

From St Charles, Hannibal is 95 miles northwest through low, rolling hills via US 61.

03 Arrow Rock

Perched just above and west of the Missouri River, **Arrow Rock State Historic Site** *(mostateparks.com/park/arrow-rock-state-historic-site)* is a small preserved town that feels little changed since the 1830s when it was on the main stagecoach route west.

THE DRIVE: Hwy 41 followed by US 65 and US 24 takes you through rolling Missouri countryside and after 95 miles right into the heart of Kansas City.

04 Kansas City

Kansas City (KC) began life in 1821 as a trading post but really came into its own once westward expansion began. The Oregon, California and Santa Fe Trails all met steamboats loaded with pioneers here.

KC is famed for its barbecues (100-plus joints smoke it up), fountains (more than 200; on par with Rome) and jazz.

Neighborhoods not to miss include: **River Market**, home to hipster spots, immediately north of downtown; and **Westport**, located on Westport Rd, just west of Main St, filled with alluring locally owned restaurants and bars. Hit the **Kaw Point Park** *(kawpointpark.org)* at the confluence of the Missouri and Kansas Rivers where Lewis and Clark passed in 1804.

The unpredictable Missouri River claimed hundreds of riverboats. At the **Arabia Steamboat Museum** *(1856.com)* you can see 200 tons of salvaged 'treasure' from an 1856 victim. In nearby Independence, don't miss the **National Frontier Trails Museum**, which details the hardships on a wagon train.

THE DRIVE: Quickly escape KC's endless suburbs by darting north 55 miles on I-29.

05 St Joseph

The first Pony Express set out in 1860, carrying mail from 'St Jo' 2000 miles west to California and taking just eight days. The service lasted 18 months before

Paddle steamer, Hannibal, Missouri

PHOTOS BRIANSCANTLEBURY/SHUTTERSTOCK

telegraph lines made it redundant. The **Pony Express National Museum** *(ponyexpress.org)* tells the story of the dangerous Express and its riders.

St Jo, just east of the Missouri River, was home to outlaw Jesse James. He was killed at what is now the **Patee House Museum** *(ponyexpressjessejames.com)*. The fateful bullet hole is still in the wall.

Housed in the former 'State Lunatic Asylum No 2,' the **Glore Psychiatric Museum** *(stjosephmuseum.org)* gives a frightening and fascinating look at lobotomies, the 'bath of surprise' and other discredited treatments.

THE DRIVE: Cross west to Nebraska on US 36 and then head north on US 75. While on this 157-mile-long leg, look for views of the Missouri from old river towns like Nebraska City.

APN PHOTOGRAPHY/SHUTTERSTOCK

Patee House Museum, St. Joseph, Missouri

06 Omaha

Home to the brick-and-cobblestoned Old Market neighborhood downtown, a lively music scene and several quality museums, Omaha can turn a few hours into a few days.

Omaha's location on the Missouri River and proximity to the Platte made it an important stop on the Oregon, California and Mormon Trails. Later, the first transcontinental railroad to California stretched west from here. Its history is recounted at the **Union Pacific Railroad Museum** *(uprrmuseum.org)* in nearby Council Bluffs.

The downtown riverfront (8th St & Riverfront Dr) offers many walking routes and sights. Among the highlights: the architecturally stunning **Bob Kerrey Pedestrian Bridge** (705 Riverfront Dr), which soars over to Iowa; the **Heartland of America Park** (800 Douglas St), with fountains and lush gardens; and **Lewis & Clark Landing** (345 Riverfront Dr), where the explorers did just that in 1804. It's home to the **Lewis & Clark National Historic Trail Visitor Center** *(nps.gov/lecl)*, where you can get information and advice for following in their footsteps.

THE DRIVE: Just beyond the outer reaches of ever-growing Omaha, Fort Calhoun is 16 miles north on US 75.

07 Fort Calhoun

The small town of Fort Calhoun has a sight that takes you back to days long gone on the Missouri. **Fort Atkinson State Historical Park** *(fortatkinsononline.org)* preserves the first US military fort built west of the Missouri River. It was built in 1820 on a recommendation of Lewis and Clark, who, besides being explorers, were keen military officers.

THE DRIVE: Farm towns hoping to be remembered by time dot the 84 miles of US 75 north from Fort Calhoun. The road's general route gently bends with the overall course of the Missouri River to the east.

08 Sioux City

On a high bluff, the modest Sioux City, IA, has grand views looking west over the Missouri River. There's a good overlook at the corner of W Fourth and Burton Sts.

On August 20, 1804, Sergeant Charles Floyd became the only person to die on the Lewis and Clark expedition team, probably from appendicitis. You can learn much more about this and other aspects of the journey at the beautiful **Lewis & Clark Interpretive Center** *(siouxcitylcic.com)*, which is right on the river.

THE DRIVE: Enjoy the smallest of rural two-laners to reach the first capitol of the Dakota states. Angle out of Sioux City on Hwy 12, then cross over to South Dakota at Westfield and pick up the alternately sinuous and angular Hwy 50, which closely follows the river. The final 64 miles of this 306-mile-long leg are on Hwy 34.

DETOUR

Mitchell

Start: 08 Sioux City

Why not honor the starch you'll see growing in profusion in vibrant green fields all along the Missouri? Every year, half a million people pull off I-90 (exit 332) to see the Taj Mahal of agriculture, the all-time-ultimate roadside attraction, the **Corn Palace** *(cornpalace.com)*. Close to 300,000 ears of corn are used each year to create a tableaux of murals on the outside of the building. Ponder the scenes and you may find a kernel of truth or just say 'aw shucks.' Head inside to see photos of how the facade has evolved over the years.

Mitchell is 150 miles northwest of Sioux City via I-29 and I-90. Rejoin the drive at Pierre, 150 miles northwest via I-90 and US 83.

09 Pierre

Pierre (pronounced 'peer'), SD, is just too small (population 14,100) and ordinary to feel like a seat of power. Small-town Victorian homes overlook the imposing 1910 **State Capitol** *(boa.sd.gov/capitol)* with its black copper dome.

Hard by the Missouri River, it lies along the Native American Scenic Byway and lonely, stark US 14. Imagine this area when it was rich with bison, beavers, elk and much more.

At a bend on the river, **Framboise Island** has several hiking trails and plentiful wildlife. It's across from where the Lewis and Clark expedition spent four days in late September, 1804. The expedition was nearly derailed when they inadvertently offended members of the local Brule tribe.

THE DRIVE: Dams cause the Missouri to look like a lake for much of the 208 miles you'll drive north along US 83 to the other Dakota capitol.

10 Bismarck

Compared with the sylvan charms of Pierre, the stark 1930s State Capitol in Bismarck, ND, is often referred to as the 'skyscraper of the prairie' and looks like a Stalinist school of dentistry.

Behind the statue of Sacajawea (a Native American woman whose friendship proved invaluable to Lewis and Clark), the huge **North Dakota Heritage Center** *(statemuseum.nd.gov)* has details on everything from Norwegian bachelor farmers to the scores of nuclear bombs perched on missiles in silos across the state.

Fort Abraham Lincoln State Park *(parkrec.nd.gov/fort-abraham-lincoln-state-park)*, 7 miles south of nearby Mandan on SR 1806, is well worth the detour. Its On-a-Slant Indian Village has five recreated Mandan earth lodges, while the fort, with several replica buildings, was Custer's last stop before the Battle of Little Bighorn.

THE DRIVE: Maybe pancakes are popular in North Dakota because that's how flat much of the land is. See for yourself on this 40-mile drive north on US 83.

11 Washburn

There are several worthwhile attractions near the spot where Lewis and Clark wintered with the Mandan in 1804–05. Learn about the duo's expedition and

Knife River Indian Villages National Historical Site, Stanton, North Dakota

TRAVELLER70/SHUTTERSTOCK

JOSEPH SOHM/SHUTTERSTOCK

PHOTO OPPORTUNITY

Any shot that shows the Missouri River's impressive girth.

Missouri–Yellowstone Rivers confluence, Missouri

the Native Americans who helped them at the **Lewis & Clark Interpretive Center** *(parkrec.nd.gov/lewis-clark-interpretive-center)*.

Fort Mandan, a replica of the fort built by Lewis and Clark, is 2.5 miles west (10 miles downstream from the flooded original site). It sits on a lonely stretch of the Missouri River marked by a monument to Seaman, the expedition's dog.

THE DRIVE: Head 22 miles west of Washburn through verdant rolling prairie on Hwy 200 to just north of the small town of Stanton, ND.

12 Stanton

At **Knife River Indian Villages National Historical Site** *(nps.gov/knri)* you can still see the mounds left by three earthen villages of the Hidastas, who lived on the Knife River, a narrow tributary of the Missouri, for more than 900 years. The National Park Service has recreated one of the earthen lodges. A stroll through the mostly wide-open and wild site leads to the village where Lewis and Clark met Sacajawea.

THE DRIVE: More dams cause the Missouri to balloon out into a tangle of waters that look like a couple of lizards doing a mating dance. Hwy 200 takes you for most of the 169 miles of your final leg.

13 Williston

Twenty-two miles southwest of Williston along SR 1804, **Fort Buford State Historic Site** *(history.nd.gov/historicsites/buford)* preserves the bleak army outpost where Sitting Bull surrendered. The adjacent **Missouri-Yellowstone Confluence Interpretive Center** includes the fort's visitor center and has good views of where the Yellowstone River joins the Missouri.

About 2 miles west, on the Montana–North Dakota border, the moody and evocative **Fort Union Trading Post** *(nps.gov/fous)* is a reconstruction of the American Fur Company post built in 1828.

Over the border in Montana, the Missouri frays out into myriad tributaries. Lewis and Clark had numerous portages as they continued their epic journey west.

STAY AWHILE

ST LOUIS

BY MARGOT BIGG

Like many Americans, my introduction to St Louis came from a computer game called *Oregon Trail*, based on the Emigrant Trail that brought hundreds of thousands of settlers west in the 1840s. The goal of the game was to get an ox-driven wagon full of family members and housewares from Missouri to Oregon, a feat that involved crossing rivers and mountains, hunting animals, and trying not to die of dysentery. While the game positioned Independence as the city where it all began, most of us who grew up playing it have misremembered the starting point as St Louis. This is possibly because the city's landmark **Gateway Arch** *(gatewayarch.com)* – the world's largest archway – has long been touted as the 'gateway to the west.'

The St Louis of today is a quintessential US heartland city, and it's a great place to linger if you're looking for an all-American metropolis with a surprisingly large variety of local culinary specialties. I'd suggest sampling toasted ravioli right where it was invented at **Mama's on the Hill** *(mamasonthehill.com)* before popping over to **Ruma's Deli** *(rumasdeli.com)*, the birthplace of the Gerber sandwich – an open-faced toastie topped with ham and St Louis' own Provel cheese. Make sure to also save room for some gooey butter cake; this rich, Depression-era dessert is widely available – **McArthur's Bakery** *(mcarthurs.com)* is a popular option. Then grab a nightcap at one of the many bars in the **Delmar Loop** *(visittheloop.com)*, an entertainment district that offers the best people-watching.

LINK YOUR TRIP

28 The Mighty Mo (p232) road trip begins in the Gateway to the West, St Louis.

Left: Downtown, St Louis, Missouri; Right: Gateway Arch, St Louis, Missouri

LEFT TO RIGHT: SEAN PAVONE/SHUTTERSTOCK, JOSEPH HENDRICKSON/SHUTTERSTOCK

PLACES TO STAY

The Cheshire
Unabashedly Anglophilic but not exactly authentic, this hotel attempts to evoke Old Blighty with faux-Tudor exteriors, a Union Jack on the outside and some curious decor choices (including a taxidermied bear). Still, prices are great, and the on-site Fox and Hounds Tavern offers a cozy spot for a pint. *cheshirestl.com*

Moonrise Hotel
In the heart of the Delmar Loop, this pet-friendly midrange modern hotel has plenty of creative touches, from technicolor stairs to lunar decor in the rooms and common areas. The rooftop bar is a particularly fun place to chill, with great city views and its own giant replica of the moon. *moonrisehotel.com*

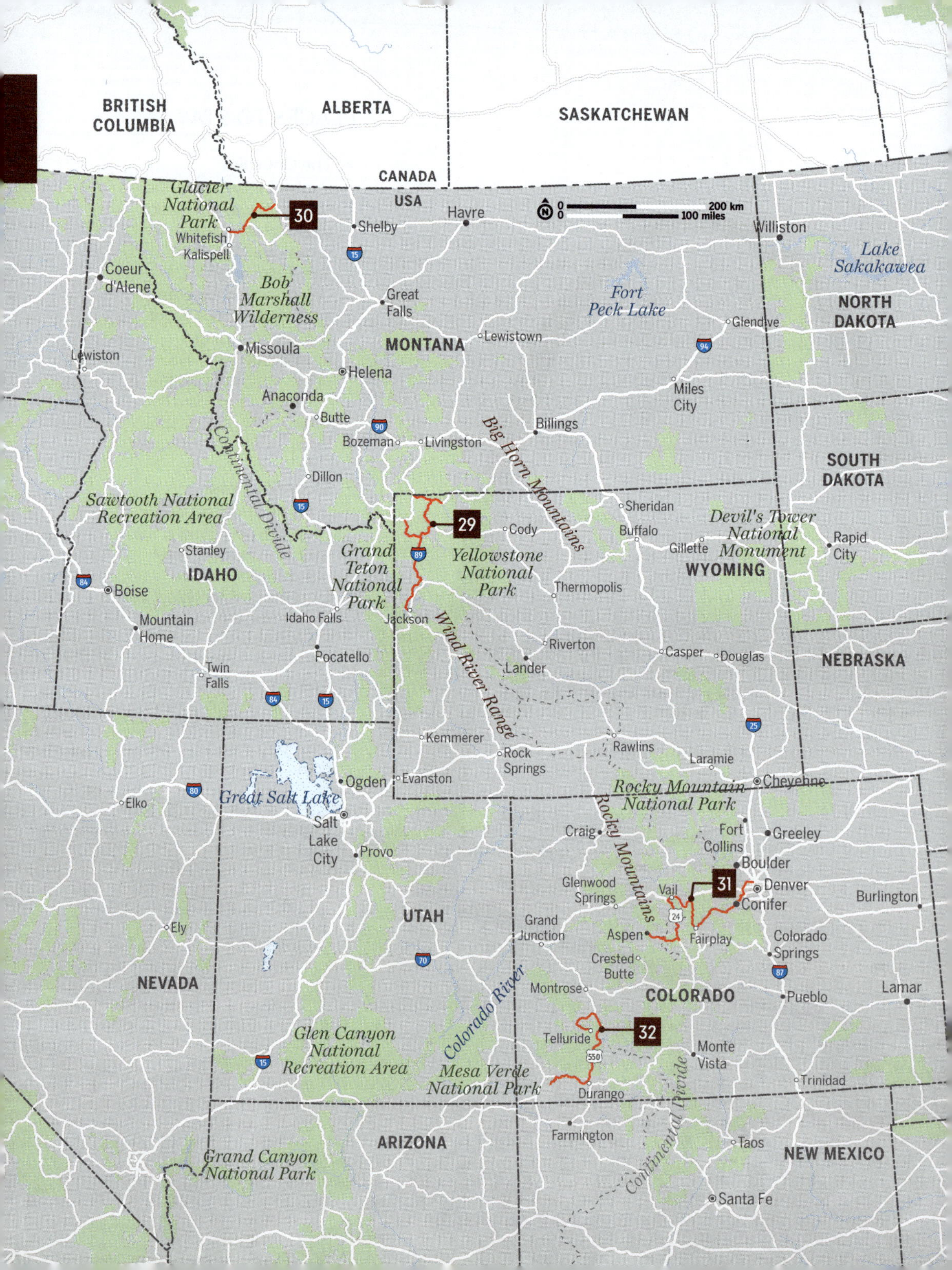
BRITISH COLUMBIA
ALBERTA
SASKATCHEWAN
CANADA
USA
Glacier National Park
30
Whitefish
Kalispell
Shelby
Havre
200 km
100 miles
Williston
Lake Sakakawea
Coeur d'Alene
Bob Marshall Wilderness
Great Falls
Fort Peck Lake
NORTH DAKOTA
Glendive
Lewistown
MONTANA
Missoula
Lewiston
Helena
Miles City
Anaconda
Butte
Billings
Bozeman
Livingston
Big Horn Mountains
Continental Divide
SOUTH DAKOTA
Dillon
Sawtooth National Recreation Area
Sheridan
29
Cody
Buffalo
Devil's Tower National Monument
Gillette
Rapid City
Stanley
Grand Teton National Park
Yellowstone National Park
WYOMING
IDAHO
Boise
Thermopolis
Mountain Home
Idaho Falls
Jackson
Wind River Range
Riverton
Pocatello
Casper
Douglas
NEBRASKA
Lander
Twin Falls
Kemmerer
Rock Springs
Rawlins
Laramie
Ogden
Evanston
Rocky Mountain National Park
Cheyenne
Elko
Great Salt Lake
Salt Lake City
Craig
Rocky Mountains
Fort Collins
Greeley
Provo
Boulder
Glenwood Springs
Vail
31
Denver
Conifer
Burlington
UTAH
Grand Junction
Aspen
Fairplay
Colorado Springs
Ely
Crested Butte
NEVADA
Montrose
COLORADO
Pueblo
Lamar
Colorado River
32
Telluride
Glen Canyon National Recreation Area
Monte Vista
Mesa Verde National Park
Trinidad
Durango
Farmington
ARIZONA
Taos
NEW MEXICO
Grand Canyon National Park
Continental Divide
Santa Fe

GESTALT IMAGERY/SHUTTERSTOCK

San Juan Skyway (p266), Colorado

ROCKY MOUNTAINS

EXPLORE

ROCKY MOUNTAINS

Combine America's love of cars with the majesty of the Rockies' imposing purple mountains and you get a road-tripper's playlist second to none.

An endless network of lonely highways snakes between snowcapped peaks, follows crystal-clear rivers and penetrates rugged canyons. You'll drive for hours through forests thick with bear, deer and elk without passing a town.

A growing flood of young adventure-seekers has brought an urban edge to the Wild West, and with them an emphasis on farm-to-fork food and microbrew beer. They're also blazing trails that provide new options for exploring the Rockies beyond the asphalt.

Jackson

Jackson (also known as Jackson Hole) effortlessly spans the seasons, offering everything you could need without ever feeling like a big town. It's a ski resort and a summer starting point for exploring Grand Teton and Yellowstone. It's Wyoming's craft-beer capital, yet they do love a good rodeo. And if you throw in a rich array of restaurants, cafes and hotels of every stripe for every budget, then Jackson's the kind of place you'll want to stay awhile. Oh, and Jackson has looks to go with its well-rounded personality: the setting is simply superb.

Whitefish

At a little over 3000ft above sea level, Whitefish is an easygoing mountain town that'll get you sorted on your way to and from Glacier National Park's Going-to-the-Sun Road. It has just enough to prepare you for what lies ahead, with an agreeable feel added to the mix: there are good restaurants, cool cafes, a historic railway station and an underrated ski resort, as well as excellent biking and hiking on a rapidly growing network of trails. There's even a fur-lined playground that probably just tips Whitefish's balance away from the Old West and toward a New West sensibility.

WHEN TO GO

Unless you're a skier, driving through the Rockies is only possible most years in late spring, summer and early fall; in years with high spring snowfall, you can only make these drives from June to August. Roads are closed, often under many feet of snow, the rest of the year. Summer is also when you're most likely to see wildlife.

Denver

So much that's good about the gorgeous state of Colorado begins in Denver. It has beautiful weather and beautiful people, and you'll find the latter enjoying the city's good restaurants, even better bars, and a lively arts and music scene. Denver is the kind of city that rewards those who stay for a few days, with each neighborhood showcasing a different side to the city's personality. And its extensive transportation connections put almost everywhere in Colorado within reach of just about anywhere else in the US.

Durango

Everyone loves Durango. It feels like the Wild West, thanks to its streets lined with Old West architecture. But this is one happening place: a historic mining town transformed and offering the perfect combination of easy access to adventures by river, by bike and by ski; super-cool locals; a fun nightlife scene powered by the local college kids; and plenty of great eateries, brewpubs, boutiques and more. It also has unmistakable small-town appeal and a pleasantly cool climate thanks to its 6850ft-above-sea-level perch. And when you're done with Durango, it's the perfect base for trips to Telluride, Mesa Verde National Park and even neighboring Utah and New Mexico.

TRANSPORTATION

Denver is your major air and rail hub for entering the region: it's one of America's busiest (and best-connected airports) and it lies along the Chicago–San Francisco Amtrak line. You can also fly to Whitefish, Jackson and Durango, although flight frequency can vary with the seasons. The scenic Empire Builder Amtrak service passes right through Whitefish.

WHERE TO STAY

From one end of the Rockies to the other, you'll find cozy and comfortable mountain lodges, friendly B&Bs, boutique luxury hotels, and a few historic hotels that nod with respect to the region's Wild West heritage. In places like Durango, Jackson, Whitefish and in the larger cities, most places to stay are open year-round; this may not be the case in smaller, summer-loving towns away from the main highways. As a general rule (although there are exceptions), the best accommodations are likely to be either downtown or out in the surrounding hills, with roadside motels all too often filling the land in between.

RESOURCES

- **National Park Service**
  Both inspirational and practical information about Yellowstone, Glacier, Mesa Verde and Grand Teton National Parks. *nps.gov*
- **Colorado Tourism**
  Your go-to for every corner of the state, from urban cool to the Wild West. *colorado.com*
- **Jackson Hole Vacation Planner**
  Local lowdown on the Rockies' coolest base for exploring. *jacksonholenet.com*

WHAT'S ON

- **Grand Teton Music Festival**
  A near-continuous program of classical music in a fantastic summer venue.
- **Jackson Hole Rodeo**
  This popular rodeo saddles up 8pm Wednesday and Saturday June through August.
- **Denver March Powow**
  Nearly 100 Native American peoples come together to celebrate through song and dance.
- **San Juan Brewfest**
  Showcases 30-odd specialist brewers from Durango and further afield. Expect bands, food and carnival fun.

29

ROCKY MOUNTAINS

GRAND TETON TO YELLOWSTONE

DURATION: 7 DAYS

DISTANCE: 263 MILES / 423KM

GREAT FOR: OUTDOORS

BEST TIME TO GO: JUNE THROUGH SEPTEMBER IS USUALLY SNOW-FREE AND FULL OF WILDLIFE.

As if having the world's highest concentration of geysers wasn't enough, Yellowstone also excels when it comes to landscape and wildlife. You've a good chance of spotting herds of bison, lumbering grizzlies and packs of wolves as you drive past the country's largest alpine lake and countless gushing waterfalls. Approach from the south and you'll be overwhelmed by the craggy peaks of the Tetons towering above pristine Snake River Valley.

LINK YOUR TRIP

30 Going-to-the-Sun Road
From Mammoth, take Hwy 89 north to I-90, then Hwy 93 north at Missoula – a seven-hour trip to even more spectacular mountain grandeur.

31 Top of the Rockies
From Jackson take US 191 south to I-80 east, then I-25 south to Denver – an eight-hour trip to Colorado high country.

01 Jackson

Just south of Grand Teton National Park, the rustic-haute saloon town of Jackson is much more than a park gateway. A destination on its own, this world-class skier magnet is also a summer stunner, with plentiful outdoor activities, galleries and a shopping scene that reaches beyond trinketry into the realm of cool boutiques and tailored outdoor gear.

Don't skip the **National Museum of Wildlife Art** *(wildlifeart.org)*, where major works by Remington and Bierstadt offer perspectives on nature that will make your skin prickle. Across the street, elk herds, bison and bighorn sheep congregate in winter at the **National Elk Refuge** *(fws.gov/refuge/national_elk_refuge)*, though it's mostly a visual feast for birders in summer.

Finally, take advantage of a foodie scene that's among the best in the West, with renowned chefs and an emphasis on local, farm-raised food.

DANITA DELIMONT/SHUTTERSTOCK

Yellowstone National Park (p246), Wyoming

THE DRIVE: Rather than shoot straight north from Jackson on Hwy 26/89/191, take Hwy 22 to the Moose–Wilson Rd (Hwy 390) past Teton Village through the Granite Canyon entrance to Grand Teton National Park ($35 fee per car). The narrow road is closed to trucks and trailers, and grizzly sightings are not uncommon. Turn into the Laurance S Rockefeller Preserve, 18 miles from Jackson.

DETOUR

Wilson, WY

Start: 01 Jackson

Big barns and the open range make this outpost 13 miles from Jackson feel more like Marlboro country – even though the median home price averages a cool $3 million. Don't miss the **Stagecoach Bar** *(stagecoachbar.net)*, where fun bands have ranch hands mingling with rhinestone cowgirls, hippies and hikers. Thursday is disco night and on Sundays the popular house country band croons until 10pm. Local institution **Nora's Fish Creek Inn** *(norasfishcreekinn.com)* dishes up heaping country breakfasts, fresh trout and homemade cobbler.

02 Laurance S Rockefeller Preserve

In contrast to conventional visitor centers, the **Laurance S Rockefeller Preserve Center** *(nps.gov/grte/planyourvisit/lsrpvc.htm)* aims to provide a more contemplative experience. Sparsely furnished, it sets the scene for your foray into nature with inspiring quotes from naturalists etched into the walls and a gorgeous conservation library with titles best enjoyed in the leather armchairs.

Oil tycoon John D Rockefeller secretly purchased this land – and much of the Snake River Valley – when fears of a 'massive government land grab' made Grand Teton National Park an unpopular idea among avaricious developers and self-interested locals. He donated it all to the park in the 1930s, save for this ranch which his son handed over in 1990.

From here, you might take an easy stroll to **Phelps Lake**. Any part of the 7-mile loop is spectacular, but a

30ft plunge off **Jumping Rock** at the far end of the lake is thrilling.

THE DRIVE: The road ends in 4 miles at Teton Park Rd. Ultimately you want to go left, but first turn right for the Craig Thomas Discovery & Visitor Center before backtracking. In 16 miles, turn left for String and Leigh Lake trailheads as well as the scenic one-way loop along Jenny Lake that will return you back south a short distance.

03 String & Leigh Lakes

In **Grand Teton** *(nps.gov/grte)* the drive-by views are so dramatic it's hard to keep your eyes on the road. Each turnout affords a better photo-op than the last – no matter which direction you're going.

Prepare for adventure in Moose, where you can rent a canoe or paddleboard and head for **String Lake** and **Leigh Lake** trailhead. This adventure involves a mellow paddle through rocky String Lake to a short portage to Leigh Lake, which opens up considerably. Float, swim and enjoy views of the craggy peaks from your own beach. Better yet, reserve a waterfront backcountry campsite.

These shores also make for a great, gentle hike, apt for all ages. **String Lake Trail** is 3.3 miles round trip on foot.

THE DRIVE: Take a left out of the Jenny or String Lake areas to Teton Park Rd. As you head 13 miles north the landscape turns from sagebrush to pine forest, climbing near densely forested Signal Mt Rd (a worthy side trip). At the Jackson Lake Junction go right to Oxbow Bend, almost immediately after the turn on your right.

04 Oxbow Bend

Located 1.2 miles east of the Jackson Lake Junction, Oxbow Bend is one of the most scenic views in the valley, with the stunning backdrop of Mt Moran reflecting off the placid Snake River. The oxbow was created as the river's faster water eroded the outer bank while the slower inner flow deposited the sediment. During many sunsets the banks will be lined with photographers looking for their next masterpiece by nature.

Families enjoy rafting the mellow section of **Snake River** that runs through the park, with views of sharp snowbound peaks and the occasional wading moose. Contact a Jackson outfitter to book a half-day trip.

These wet lowlands are also prime wildlife habitat, so bring binoculars. Early morning and dusk are ideal for spotting moose, elk, sandhill cranes, ospreys, bald eagles, trumpeter swans and other birds.

THE DRIVE: From Oxbow Bend, backtrack toward Jackson Lake Lodge before continuing north 65 beautiful but slow miles on Hwy 89/191/287 past Jackson Lake to Yellowstone. After entering Yellowstone National Park, the straight road climbs to the Continental Divide (7988ft). At West Thumb junction, continue straight. This will take you over Craig Pass (8262ft) toward Old Faithful.

05 Old Faithful

Yellowstone National Park *(nps.gov/yell),* America's first – and arguably its most diverse – national park, covers an astounding 3472 sq miles. You could spend a year here and not see it all.

Make a quick stop at **Grant Visitor Center** to put the 1988 fires that burned one-third of the park into

YELLOWSTONE SAFARI

Lamar Valley evokes the wildlife of the Serengeti, with its large herds of bison, elk and the occasional grizzly or coyote. It's the best place to spot wolves, particularly in spring. Wolf-watchers should ask visitor center staff for the wolf-observation sheet, which differentiates the various packs and individual members.

The central **Hayden Valley** is the other solid wildlife-watching area, where spotters crowd the pullouts around dusk. It's a good place to view large predators such as wolves and grizzlies, especially in spring when thawing winter carcasses offer almost-guaranteed sightings. Coyotes, elk and bison are all common. The tree line is a good place to scan for wildlife. The more you know about animals' habitats and habits, the more likely you are to catch a glimpse of them.

In general, spring and fall are the best times to view wildlife, but each season has its own highlight. Elk calves and baby bison are adorable in late spring, while bugling bull elk come out in the fall rut. Most animals withdraw to the forests to avoid the midday heat, so plan your observations around dawn or dusk.

It's worth having good binoculars or even renting a spotting scope. A high-end telephoto lens will also help you capture that prize-winning grizzly shot at a grizzly-safe distance.

Mt Moran, Oxbow Bend, Wyoming
OLEG SHABUNIN/SHUTTERSTOCK

PHOTO OPPORTUNITY

Mt Moran reflecting off the placid water of Oxbow Bend.

perspective, before heading west on the loop road to the **Old Faithful Visitor Education Center** *(nps.gov/yell)*, which demystifies geyser plumbing and has predicted times for famous eruptions.

Spouting some 8000 gallons of water over 180ft high, **Old Faithful** pleases the crowds roughly every 90 minutes. If you just missed a show, fill the wait with a 1.1-mile walk to **Observation Hill** for an overview of the entire basin. Loop back via **Solitary Geyser** (whose sudden bursts come every four to eight minutes) before rejoining the boardwalk.

Another prime viewing spot is the porch of the historic **Old Faithful Inn**. Even if you're not staying over, treat yourself to a cocktail in the cavernous log lobby.

THE DRIVE: From Old Faithful overpass it's only 16 miles to Madison Junction, but these are action-packed. If driving out and back (to loop back to Yellowstone Lake), you might consider taking all the easterly right-hand turnouts first, and following with the west-side turnouts while heading south the following day after camping at Madison.

06 Grand Prismatic Spring

Exploring Geyser Country can take the better part of a day. Unlike the wildlife, these spurting geysers, multihued springs and bubbling mud pots are nearly guaranteed to show up for the picture.

Leaving Madison Campground, backtrack 2 miles south and take Firehole Canyon drive on your right past rhyolite cliffs to **Firehole Falls** and swimming area.

Five miles south, a pullout offers fine views of the smoking geysers and pools of **Midway Geyser Basin** to the right and **Firehole Lake Basin** to the left, with bison making it a classic Yellowstone vista.

One mile on, take a right for **Fountain Paint Pot**, a huge pool of plopping goop and assorted geysers. Try to stop at Midway Geyser Basin with breathtaking rainbow-hued **Grand Prismatic Spring** – Yellowstone's most photogenic pool. If parking is full, consider driving south 1.5 miles to the **Fairy Falls** trailhead and hiking 1 mile in to a new overlook that gives an elevated view of Grand Prismatic Spring.

THE DRIVE: From Grand Prismatic Spring, drive south

toward Old Faithful. The road curves west to climb back over Craig Pass (8262ft) before descending to West Thumb. Go left on the shoreline road to Lake Village approximately 45 miles away.

07 Yellowstone Lake

At 7733ft above sea level, shimmering Yellowstone Lake is the largest high-elevation lake in the US. Despite having a number of thermal features under it, however, the temperature remains bitterly cold at 41°F (5°C), and is not great for swimming.

Grand Loop Rd hugs the western shore. Stop to picnic at **Sand Point**, where it's worth taking a short walk to the lagoon and black-sand beach, looking beyond to the rugged Absaroka Range.

Continue north and have a rest at the 1891 **Lake Yellowstone Hotel**, the park's oldest building. Enjoy classical concerts and cocktail hour in the sprawling sunroom of this buttercup-yellow colonial mansion – you may want to return at the day's end.

At the intersection, Hwy 14/16/20 heads east past Fishing Bridge (closed to fishing), toward Cody over what Theodore Roosevelt once called the '50 most beautiful miles in America,' but for the time being, continue north to Hayden Valley.

THE DRIVE: Drive along Yellowstone Lake to Lake Village, and 10 miles north to Hayden Valley. Bear jams are frequent here; drive slowly and stop only at turnouts.

08 Hayden Valley

Flowing from Yellowstone Lake, the Yellowstone River is broad and shallow as it meanders gently through the grasslands of Hayden Valley. This is the heart of the **Yellowstone Plateau**, the largest valley in the park and a premier wildlife-watching spot.

A former lake bed, the valley's fine silt and clay keeps shrubs and grasses thriving, attracting elk by the herd. Watch for coyotes, springtime grizzlies and bison that turn out in the fall for the largest rut in the country. Early morning or near dusk are the best times to spot critters.

Also check out the mud pots and sulfur pits at **Mud Volcano**, a thermal area 6 miles north of Fishing Bridge Junction. Earthquakes in 1979 generated enough heat and

Grand Prismatic Spring, Yellowstone National Park, Wyoming

MIHAI ANDRITOIU/SHUTTERSTOCK

♥ WHY I LOVE THIS TRIP

LOREN BELL, WRITER

Watching the bubbling mud pits is one of my first childhood memories. That early Yellowstone road trip infected me with a passion for travel and the outdoors. Every time I drive or bike these roads, I never fail to see something that surprises or amazes me.

gases in the mud pots to cook nearby lodgepole pines. Follow the 2.3-mile loop boardwalk to see the sights.

THE DRIVE: The road runs for 5 miles north along the Yellowstone River to the Grand Canyon of the Yellowstone. This is another spot famous for bear jams (though the offender is usually bison). After the open valley changes to densely forested terrain, keep watch for the right-hand South Rim Dr with sublime views of the upper and lower falls.

09 Grand Canyon of the Yellowstone

Here the Yellowstone River takes a dive over the **Upper Falls** (109ft) and **Lower Falls** (308ft) before raging through the 1000ft Grand Canyon of the Yellowstone.

Heading north on Grand Loop Rd, take the right-hand turn to South Rim Dr. A steep 500ft descent, **Uncle Tom's Trail** offers the best view of both falls (though note the trail closes at times due to poor conditions). Hop in the car again to continue to **Artist Point** (South Rim Dr, Canyon). Canyon walls shaded salmon pink, chalk white, ochre and pale green make this a masterpiece. A short 1-mile trail continues here to **Point Sublime**, which is worth following just to bask in the landscape.

Returning to the Grand Loop, go north and turn right on North Rim Dr, a 2.5-mile one-way with overlooks. **Lookout Point** offers the best views of the Lower Falls. Hike the steep 500ft trail for closer action. This is where landscape artist Thomas Moran sketched for his famous canyon painting, supposedly weeping over his comparatively poor palette.

THE DRIVE: After leaving Lookout Point, stay on North Rim Dr, which winds to Canyon Village. Take a right turn on the Grand Loop to head north here for Dunraven Pass. This section is narrow and curvy with huge drops. It descends to Tower-Roosevelt junction, where you can head right (east) for Lamar Valley a total of 35 miles away. Before setting out though, check *nps.gov/yell/planyourvisit/parkroads.htm*, as road construction around Tower-Roosevelt may call for a detour.

☑ TOP TIP

BEAT THE CROWDS

To avoid crowds, visit in May or October. Services may be limited, and some roads may be closed, but the scenery is no less spectacular. Plan your movements around dawn and dusk, which increases your chances of seeing wildlife and decreases the crowds. Pitch your tent in the wild (permit required) – less than 1% of visitors overnight in Yellowstone's backcountry.

10 Lamar Valley

Take the winding road to Tower-Roosevelt, stopping at **Washburn Hot Springs Overlook** for views of the Yellowstone Caldera. On clear days you can even see the Teton range. The road climbs Dunraven Pass (8859ft), surrounded by fir and whitebark pines.

At the Tower-Roosevelt junction, head east through Lamar Valley (Tower-Roosevelt), a hot spot for wolves, bears, foxes, bison and coyotes. Watching a wolf pack stalk and take down an elk in a matter of seconds is truly one of the most powerful sights in the world, though without the aid of a spotting scope you may have a hard time following the action. Along this road, Buffalo Ranch hosts **Yellowstone Forever Institute** *(yellowstone.org)* courses, with biologist-led wildlife-watching. The wolf-watching course is particularly fascinating.

THE DRIVE: To continue to Mammoth, turn around at Pebble Creek campground and return to Tower-Roosevelt. From here it's 18 miles to Mammoth Hot Springs, where there's a visitor center and full services. Turn left for parking for the upper and lower terraces of Mammoth Hot Springs.

11 Mammoth Hot Springs

At over 115,000 years old, Mammoth Hot Springs is North America's oldest and most volatile continuously active thermal area. Here the mountain is actually turning itself

IV-OLGA/SHUTTERSTOCK

Lower Falls, Grand Canyon of the Yellowstone, Yellowstone National Park, Wyoming

inside-out, depositing dissolved subterranean limestone that builds up in white sculpted ledges. There are no geysers here as the limestone substrate dissolves too readily to build up the necessary pressure.

Take the one-way loop around the **Upper Terraces** for views, but it's best to park at the **Lower Terraces** to walk the hour's-worth of boardwalks, so you can descend back to your car.

End your trip with a dip in the **Boiling River**, a hot-spring swimming hole, reached via an easy 0.5-mile footpath from on the eastern side of the road 2.3 miles north of Mammoth. The hot springs here tumble over travertine rocks into the cool Gardner River. Though usually crowded, soaking here is still a treat.

Leave the park via the north entrance and Gardiner at the Montana state line.

30

ROCKY MOUNTAINS

GOING-TO-THE-SUN ROAD

★ BEST FOR

WILDLIFE

Spy on elk herds and roaming coyotes at Two Dog Flats.

DURATION: 2–3 DAYS

DISTANCE: 76 MILES / 122KM

GREAT FOR: NATURE

BEST TIME TO GO: JULY THROUGH SEPTEMBER ONCE THE ROAD HAS BEEN PLOWED.

Going-to-the-Sun Road, Glacier National Park, Montana

Few national parks are as magnificent and pristine as Glacier, where grizzly bears roam free in a wilderness that's both easily accessible to humans and authentically wild. It's renowned for its historic 'parkitecture' lodges, intact pre-Columbian ecosystem and the spectacular Going-to-the-Sun Rd. This 53-mile mountain route is a National Historic Landmark, purpose-built for you to drive into this wild country.

LINK YOUR TRIP

29 Grand Teton to Yellowstone
From Whitefish, it's 400 miles to Yellowstone via Hwy 93 to I-90 before cutting south through Paradise Valley on Hwy 89 to Mammoth.

31 Top of the Rockies
For a Rocky Mountain epic, head south through Yellowstone cutting over to Lander, WY, and on to Denver, CO.

01 Whitefish

This charismatic and caffeinated New West ski town would merit a long-distance trip itself. It's 1 sq mile of rustic Western chic, with welcoming shops and restaurants surrounded by the great outdoors.

Summer at **Whitefish Mountain Resort** *(skiwhitefish.com)* has intrepid explorers touring the treetops via ziplines, mountain-biking white-knuckle trails and finishing with beers at the resort's **Summit House**.

THE DRIVE: From Whitefish, head south on Hwy 93 and go left on MT 40 East, which runs into Hwy 2. While early travelers had to lower their wagons down the steep walls of Badrock Canyon just west of Columbia Falls, where the Flathead River slices like a knife through the Swan Range, it's now an easy 26-mile trip to West Glacier.

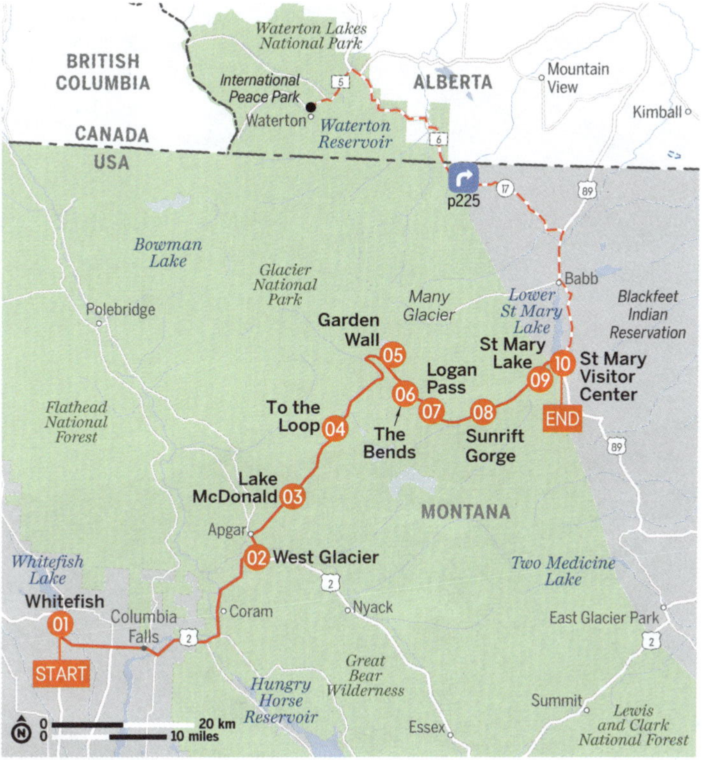

AMEHIME/SHUTTERSTOCK

02 West Glacier

West Glacier is little more than a rail depot and an entryway to Glacier National Park, albeit a busy one. Services, including a visitor center and backcountry permit office, are found in the nearby hub of Apgar.

In Apgar, you can also ditch your car and travel the rest of this route on the park's free hop-on hop-off **shuttle** *(nps.gov/glac)* that stops at all major trailheads and sights.

Mind-boggling amounts of snow must be plowed off **Going-to-the-Sun Rd** *(nps.gov/glac/planyourvisit/goingtothesunroad.htm)*, and opening times vary. If the road is closed, don't fret: it means you have an excellent opportunity to cycle one of America's most scenic routes car-free.

THE DRIVE: Apgar is 2.5 miles north of West Glacier on the paved Going-to-the-Sun Rd. Services and lodging are left at the intersection, the visitor center is straight ahead and Going-to-the-Sun Rd is to the right. There is a large campground just beyond.

03 Lake McDonald

The lush, verdant glacier-carved valley of Lake McDonald boasts some of the park's oldest temperate rainforest. Paddling your rowboat over the glassy surface of the largest lake in the park may be the best way to experience serenity on a super scale. Rent a boat from **Glacier Park Boat Co** *(glacierparkboats.com)* at the lodge dock.

Shrug off the crowds and sleep under the fragrant pines at **Sprague Creek**, our favorite lakeside campground. There's only tent camping allowed, and with just 25 sites you'll feel like the lake belongs to you.

Reaching the eastern end of the shore, rustic **Lake McDonald Lodge** *(glaciernationalparklodges.com)* was first built in 1895, though it was replaced with Swiss-style architecture in 1913. Enter via the back door, which faces the lake to welcome the guests who historically arrived by boat.

THE DRIVE: Rimmed by pines, this 11-mile section skirts Lake McDonald's eastern shore, serving up views of Mt Stanton beyond the northern shore. Both Sprague Creek and Lake McDonald Lodge are to the left. Note: vehicles over 21ft long, 8ft wide or 10ft tall are not permitted on Going-to-the-Sun Rd beyond Avalanche Creek at the north end of Lake McDonald.

04 To the Loop

The road runs parallel to blue-green McDonald Creek and McDonald Falls, a seemingly endless cascade gushing through rock chasms along the longest river in the park.

Though it's often crowded, make the stop to appreciate the old-growth cedars and hemlocks – the easternmost outpost of this decidedly Pacific Northwest forest type – of **Avalanche Creek** (north of Lake McDonald) and consider hiking the pleasant and popular trail to snow-fed **Avalanche Lake** for superior views for little effort.

The 192ft West Tunnel took two years to drill in 1926. An interior sidewalk accesses the view of Heaven's Peak through observation windows.

The sharp hairpin turn known as the Loop is an elegant engineering

PHOTO OPPORTUNITY

The view of Bird Woman Falls from the flanks of Haystack Butte.

solution to one very vertical climb. Instead of making a proposed 15 switchbacks to Logan Pass, this routing allowed a more subtle line that would be easier to plow. The road has a maximum slope of 6%, the grade at which 1920s automobiles could climb without down-shifting to second gear.

THE DRIVE: At The Loop, the road breaks from McDonald Creek to angle sharply toward the Garden Wall, a 9000ft spine of the Continental Divide 14 miles beyond McDonald Falls. In early summer, there may be standing water on the road from the Weeping Wall.

05 Garden Wall

Powerful glaciers carved this dramatic arête running parallel to Going-to-the-Sun Rd millions of years ago. The steep western slopes of Garden Wall feature lush wildflower meadows traversed by the Highline Trail.

Located below the Garden Wall, the glistening **Weeping Wall** features seasonal waterfalls, formed when drilling during road construction unleashed a series of mountain springs. Water falls over the lip of a 30ft artificial cliff and frequently gives westbound car passengers a good soaking in early summer. By early August, the torrent reverts to its more gentle aspect: weeping.

For a more natural waterfall, look across the valley to the distant **Bird Woman Falls**, a spectacular 500ft spray emerging from a hanging valley between Mt Oberlin and Mt Cannon. This phenomenon was created when a small glacier from above the falls fed into a larger glacier along Logan Creek. The Logan Glacier had significantly more mass, gouging deeper into the rocks as it flowed down Lake McDonald valley.

Bird Woman Falls, Glacier National Park, Wyoming
DANITA DELIMONT/SHUTTERSTOCK

THE DRIVE: The next section of roadway provides ample evidence of why Going-to-the-Sun Rd is renowned as a marvel of civil engineering. Highlights include Haystack Creek Culvert and Triple Arches, which blend almost seamlessly with the landscape. Stop at designated pullouts along this 3-mile stretch for both Big Bend and Oberlin Bend. Wildlife may get close here.

06 The Bends

Just beyond the Weeping Wall, **Big Bend** features magnificent views of Mt Oberlin, Heaven's Peak and Mt Cannon amid blooming beargrass and fireweed. It's midway between The Loop and Logan Pass, and is a good spot for a break. Bighorn sheep blend well into the cliffs – grab your binoculars to find them.

Just west of Logan Pass, **Oberlin Bend** sits below the cascading waterfalls of Mt Oberlin. Take the short boardwalk for breathtaking views of hanging valleys and Going-to-the-Sun Rd itself. On a clear day, views extend all the way to Canada. It may also be the best spot to see the park's signature mountain goats hanging out on steep rock ledges.

THE DRIVE: Continue the ascent to Logan Pass, about a mile beyond Oberlin Bend.

07 Logan Pass

The highest point of Going-to-the-Sun Rd, panoramic Logan Pass (6646ft) also marks the Continental Divide. Stop at **Logan Pass Visitor Center** with interesting

NICK FOX/SHUTTERSTOCK

natural-history displays and a browse-worthy bookstore. Take the 1.5-mile boardwalk trail behind it to the wildflower meadows of **Hidden Lake Overlook**.

Across the way, the **Highline Trail** is lauded as one of America's best hikes and is a highlight for trekkers. Cutting daringly across the famous Garden Wall, this rugged path traces mountain-goat terrain along the Continental Divide with huge vistas of glaciated valleys and jagged peaks. Though it isn't difficult (there's minimal elevation change), the trail is quite exposed. For a classic romp, turn back at **Granite Park Chalet**, 7.6 miles one way.

Five hikers' express shuttles run from Apgar to Logan Pass, leaving between 7am and 7:36am. Many people start here, hike the Highline Trail to The Loop and catch the return shuttle from there.

THE DRIVE: Descend Going-to-the-Sun Rd heading east. From here the road makes a relatively straightforward descent, passing through 408ft East Side Tunnel and Siyeh Bend switchbacks on its way to St Mary Lake. The Jackson Glacier overlook comes up on the right 4.7 miles from the pass.

08 Sunrift Gorge

Pull out near Gunsight Pass Trailhead for telescopic views of **Jackson Glacier**. It's a short walk to the overlook of the park's fifth-largest glacier. As it has melted over the years, it has actually split into two glaciers called Jackson and Blackfoot. In 1850 the park had 150 glaciers. Today there are a scant 26, and scientists predict they will completely disappear by 2030.

Just off the road and adjacent to a shuttle stop to your left, **Sunrift Gorge** is a narrow canyon that's 80ft deep and 800ft long. The picturesque **Baring Bridge** is considered the most beautiful artificial feature on the road. Follow the short 0.25-mile wooded trail here to **Baring Falls**.

THE DRIVE: The road skirts north of St Mary Lake for the remainder of the drive and has a few pull-offs to let other drivers pass. Sun Point is approximately 3.5 miles beyond Jackson Glacier overlook.

09 St Mary Lake

Located on the park's drier eastern side, St Mary Lake fills a deep, glacier-carved valley famous for its astounding views and ferocious winds. Known to the Blackfeet as the Walled-in Lake, its long shoreline features numerous trailheads and viewpoints.

Logan Pass (p255), Glacier National Park, Montana

Windy and spectacular, **Sun Point** is a rocky promontory overlooking the lake. Take in views of the magnificent Going-to-the-Sun Mountain (9642ft) to the north. You will also see Wild Goose Island, a tiny stub in the middle of St Mary Lake. Lace up your boots if you want to take the trails linking to **Baring Falls** and **St Mary Falls**.

THE DRIVE: Services at Rising Sun are 4 miles beyond Sun Point and St Mary Visitor Center is 6 miles further. Note: if you're traveling this route east to west, vehicles over 21ft long, 8ft wide or 10ft tall are not permitted on Going-to-the-Sun Rd beyond Sun Point. Park at Sun Point and take the free park shuttle.

10 St Mary Visitor Center

Handy shuttle stop **Rising Sun Motor Inn** *(glaciernationalparklodges.com)* has a lovely backdrop, hotel, campground and services. A 1½-hour lake cruise can be combined with a 3-mile hike to St Mary Falls with **Glacier Park Boat Co**. The amazing biological diversity at **Two Dog Flats** is a result of the eastern prairies butting against massive mountains.

The restored 1950s **St Mary Visitor Center** has classic lines that imitate mountain silhouettes. Rangers present evening programs here throughout the summer.

DETOUR

International Peace Park

Start: 10 St Mary Visitor Center

Hello, Canada! This overnight detour takes Hwy 89 north from St Mary Visitor Center to Hwy 17, which becomes Canada's Hwy 6 at Chief Mountain border crossing. Hook a left at Hwy 5 to Waterton Lakes National Park, Glacier's sister park in Alberta, Canada. Together, these two stunners compose the Waterton Glacier International Peace Park, declared a World Heritage Site in 1995. From the northern end, the mountains of the Waterton Glacier are arguably even more dramatic than along Going-to-the-Sun Rd, and can be enjoyed from daily boat cruises, or the charmingly pretentious but venerable **Prince of Wales Hotel** *(glacierparkcollection.com)*, perched on a hill above the lake. You also can take in the majestic cross-border landscape on a free **International Peace Park Hike**. Check at the St Mary or Waterton Visitor Center to see when the hikes are happening and reserve a spot up to three days in advance.

31

ROCKY MOUNTAINS

TOP OF THE ROCKIES

★ BEST TWO DAYS

Head from Breckenridge to Aspen to hit the highlights; Vail is optional.

DURATION: 4–5 DAYS

DISTANCE: 242 MILES / 389KM

GREAT FOR: NATURE

BEST TIME TO GO: JUNE TO OCTOBER FOR THE SKY-HIGH DRIVE OVER INDEPENDENCE PASS.

Skiers, Vail (p261), Colorado

This high-altitude adventure follows Colorado's back roads from one spectacular mountain pass to the next. Along the way you'll get a glimpse of countless jagged peaks (including the two tallest in the state, Mt Elbert and Mt Massive), rich veins of Wild West history, and skiing and mountain resorts such as Breckenridge, Vail and Aspen. Come here to hike, bike, ski, ride rivers or spot wildlife – for lovers of the great outdoors, this here's paradise.

LINK YOUR TRIP

32 San Juan Skyway & the Million Dollar Highway
Follow a string of gorgeous back roads 250 miles south to the peaks and cliff houses of Telluride and Mesa Verde.

36 High & Low Roads to Taos
Take Hwy 285 south to enchanted New Mexico and Santa Fe (300 miles), passing Salida and the Great Sand Dunes.

01 Denver

While Denver has its moments, it won't be long before you feel the urge to head up into those alluring snowcapped peaks west of town. But while everyone else will be leaving via the interstate, this trip will introduce you to the Rockies' prettiest backdoor secret: **Hwy 285**.

THE DRIVE: Kenosha Pass is 65 miles southwest of downtown Denver on Hwy 285.

02 Kenosha Pass

The climb out of Denver is pretty enough, but it's not until you reach **Kenosha Pass** (10,000ft) that you really start to feel that Rocky Mountain magic. This is also the best place to see fall colors close to Denver. Although there's a scenic overlook at the pass, the best views, ironically, are not at the overlook at all, but after you round the bend on the way down. Suddenly, you'll find yourself looking out over the distant

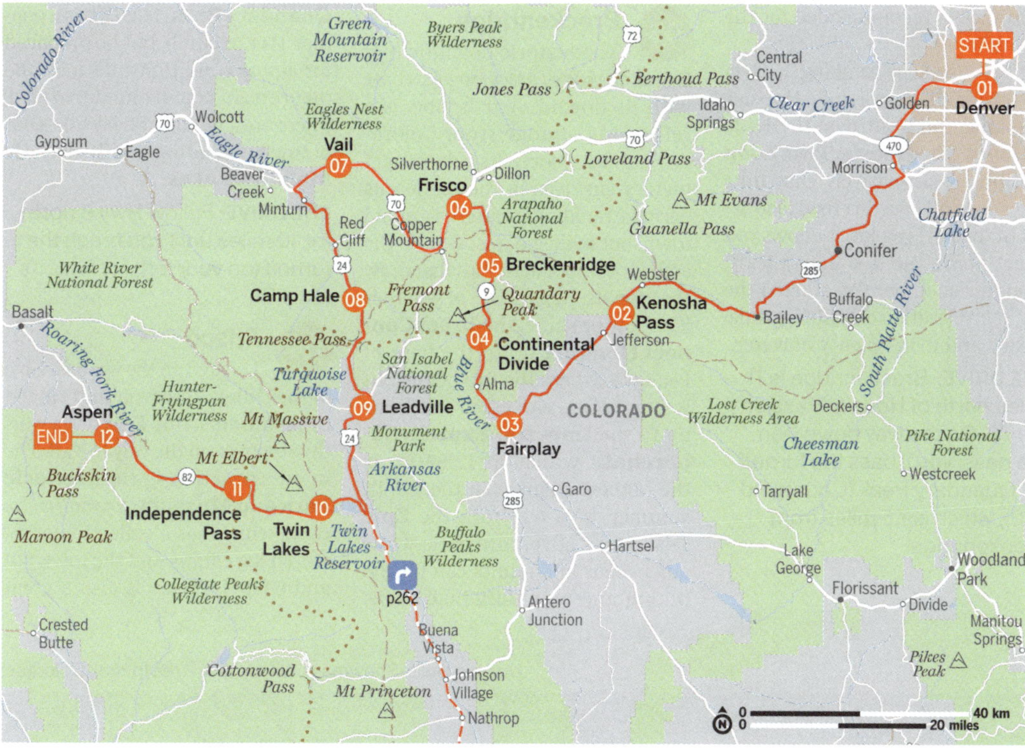

peaks of the Mosquito Range, rising mightily above the high-altitude prairie of the South Park basin. Inspired? You're not the first. Walt Whitman wrote about this same view on a trip west in 1879.

THE DRIVE: Fairplay is 21 miles southwest of Kenosha Pass on Hwy 285. When you reach town, turn north onto Hwy 9 to access Main St. Much of the highway between here and Denver follows an old stagecoach road – originally an 18-hour-long journey, broken up over two days.

03 Fairplay

Tiny Fairplay was originally a mining settlement and supply town for Leadville (pack burros used to clop back and forth over 13,000ft-Mosquito Pass to the west), and you can stop here to visit **South Park City** *(southparkcity.org)*, a recreated 19th-century Colorado boomtown. Get a taste of life back in the good-old, bad-old days of the gold rush through the 40 restored buildings on display, which range from the general store and saloon to a dentist's office and morgue. And yes, *South Park* fans, Fairplay does bear more than a passing resemblance to the hometown of Kyle, Cartman and Stan.

THE DRIVE: Hoosier Pass and the Continental Divide are 11 miles north of Fairplay on Hwy 9. The pass is hemmed in by Mt Lincoln (14,286ft) to the west and Mt Silverheels (13,822ft) to the east. The latter is named after a dancer who stayed behind to care for the ill during a smallpox epidemic in Alma, eventually succumbing to the disease herself.

04 Continental Divide

The stunning climb up to the Continental Divide begins just north of Fairplay. A mere 5.5-mile drive will bring you to Alma, the highest incorporated town in the US, at an elevation of 10,578ft. It's surrounded by four '14ers' (mountains over 14,000ft), thousand-year-old bristlecone pines and scores of old mining claims.

If you want to explore, follow the unpaved Buckskin Rd 6 miles west toward Kite Lake – 4WD and high clearance is recommended for the last mile.

Otherwise, keep climbing up Hwy 9 and you'll soon reach Hoosier Pass and the Continental Divide (11,539ft). The **Hoosier Pass Loop** (3 miles) is a relatively easy hike that starts off on a dirt road leading out of the parking lot. It allows you to get above the tree line quickly, though remember you started the day at an elevation of 5280ft, so take it easy and drink plenty of water.

THE DRIVE: Breckenridge is 11 miles north of Hoosier Pass on Hwy 9. On the way down from the pass, you'll pass the turnoff for Quandary Peak (County Rd 850), which is 7.5 miles from Breckenridge.

05 Breckenridge

The historic downtown of **Breckenridge** *(breckenridge.com)*, with its down-to-earth vibe, is a refreshing change from Colorado's glitzier resorts. Its gold-nugget history survives in the numerous heritage buildings scattered around town, but make no mistake, it's the endless outdoor activities that draw the crowds. Regardless of whether it's snow or shine, the **BreckConnect Gondola** up to the base of Peak 8 is where the fun begins. In winter, skiers can catch the T-bar up to the **Imperial Express Superchair**, which, at 12,840ft, is the highest chairlift in the US. In summer, kids will rock the **Epic Discovery** adventure park, while older teens and adults can hit the hiking and mountain-bike trails. **Quandary Peak** (14,265ft) is a popular 14er to climb, but be prepared for alpine conditions; it's a 6-mile (figure eight hours) round-trip hike. There are a number of day hikes out of town, including family-friendly **Mohawk Lakes**.

THE DRIVE: Follow Hwy 9 north for 10 miles until you reach the turnoff (on your left) for Frisco's Main St.

06 Frisco

Located on the western edge of the Dillon Reservoir and ringed by mountains, tiny Frisco is a worthy stopover on the way to Vail. The main attraction is the **Historic Park and Museum** *(townoffrisco.com)*, which has a collection of restored log cabins and the town jail and chapel. Frisco is also a great

Maroon Bells-Snowmass Wilderness Area (p263), Colorado

ZHUKOVA VALENTYNA/SHUTTERSTOCK

PHOTO OPPORTUNITY

Maroon Bells, Colorado's most iconic peaks.

place to get on two wheels and exercise your lungs – **Summit County's** *(summitbiking.org)* paved bike lanes extend around the reservoir all the way from Vail to Keystone to Breck. Get the scoop on local trails and rent a bike at **Pioneer Sports** *(pioneersportscolorado.com)*.

THE DRIVE: From Frisco, take I-70 west 27 miles to exit 176 and follow signs to either Vail Village (the main town) or Lionshead further west. Either way, look for the public parking garages ($35 per day in winter, free in summer) – they're the only places to park, unless you're spending the night. Bikers can also ride this section on an off-road paved trail.

07 Vail

Vail Mountain Resort *(vail.com)* is Eagle County's legendary winter playground. This is where the movie stars and tycoons ski, and it's not unusual to see Texans in ten-gallon hats and women in mink coats zipping down the slopes. Whether you're here for the powdery back bowls or it's your first time on a snowboard, the largest ski resort in the US rarely disappoints – so long as you're prepared for the price tag. There's plenty of action in summer too. For mountain-bike rental see **Bike Valet** *(bikevalet.com)*, and for horseback riding **Bearcat Stables** *(bearcatstables.com)*. Book ahead if you plan on teeing off at the **Vail Golf Club** *(vailrec.com)*, and check out the **Holy Cross Ranger Office** *(fs.usda.gov/whiteriver)* for hiking and camping info. Families stay occupied at **Epic Discovery**, which features a plethora of activities 10,000ft up at the top of Eagle Bahn Gondola.

THE DRIVE: From Vail, take I-70 west for 4.5 miles to exit 171, and then turn onto Hwy 24 east. After you pass through the town of Minturn, the road begins to wind up along a cliff face, with impressive views of Notch Mountain (13,237ft) and the Holy Cross Wilderness on your right. After 17 miles you'll reach the turnoff for Camp Hale – now no more than a grassy meadow.

08 Camp Hale

Established in 1942, Camp Hale was created specifically for the purpose of training the 10th Mountain Division, the US Army's only battalion on skis. At its height during WWII, there were over 1000 buildings and some 14,000 soldiers housed in the meadow here.

After the war Camp Hale was decommissioned, only to be brought back to life again in 1958, this time by the CIA. Over the next six years, CIA agents trained Tibetan freedom fighters in guerrilla warfare, with the goal of driving the communist Chinese out of Tibet.

In 1965 Camp Hale was officially dismantled, and the land returned to the US Forest Service. Many vets from the 10th Mountain Division returned to Colorado to become involved in the burgeoning ski industry, including Pete Seibert, who co-founded Vail Resort in 1962.

> ☑ TOP TIP
>
> **TRIP ESSENTIALS**
>
> Much of this drive is above 9000ft: don't underestimate the altitude. Essential gear includes sunglasses, sunscreen, a hat, a windbreaker, a fleece and ibuprofen (known to decrease the likelihood of altitude sickness). Staying hydrated is crucial.

THE DRIVE: Hwy 24 is known as the 'Top of the Rockies Scenic Byway.' On the way down from Tennessee Pass you'll be treated to a panorama of Colorado's two highest peaks – Mt Massive and Mt Elbert – stretching away to the south. All told, it's 16 miles from Camp Hale to Leadville.

09 Leadville

Originally known as Cloud City, Leadville was once Colorado's second-largest municipality. It was silver, not gold, that made the fortunes of many here; the best place to learn about the town's mineral-rich history is at the surprisingly interesting **National Mining Hall of Fame and Museum** *(mininghalloffame.org)*, which can be combined with a visit to the Matchless Mine exterior in summer. The historic downtown area makes for a pleasant stroll; check out landmarks such as the **Healy House Museum** *(healyhousemuseum.org)* and the **Tabor Opera House** *(taboroperahouse.org)*, where the likes of Houdini and Oscar Wilde once appeared.

THE DRIVE: From Leadville, take Hwy 24 south for 14 miles, following the Arkansas River until you reach the turnoff for Hwy 82. Follow Hwy 82 west for 6.5 miles until you reach Twin Lakes. Along the way you will find marked turnoffs for the Mt Elbert and Interlaken trailheads.

10 Twin Lakes

A short drive from Leadville is Twin Lakes, the two largest glacial lakes in the state and an excellent spot to spend a night. A few cabins are all that's left of Dayton, the original town, but the scenery is fabulous and there are plenty of opportunities to get out and hike or fish. On the south shore of the main lake is Interlaken, the vestiges of what was once Colorado's largest resort, built in 1889. You can get here along the **Colorado and Continental Divide trails**; it's about 5 miles round-trip with little elevation gain.

If you're up for something quite a bit more challenging, Colorado's tallest peak, **Mt Elbert** (14,433ft), is also a possibility. This is a 9-mile round-trip hike with nearly 5000ft of elevation gain, so figure on spending the entire day.

THE DRIVE: It's 17 miles from Twin Lakes to the top of Independence Pass along Hwy 82. The ghost town of Independence is roughly 3 miles west of the summit.

DETOUR

Salida

Start: 10 Twin Lakes

If you're on the road from November to May, chances are Independence Pass will be closed. If this is the case, don't fret – simply follow Hwy 24 and the Arkansas River south for 50 miles until you reach the town of Salida. Home to one of the largest historic downtown areas in the state, funky Salida is Colorado's white-water rafting hub and a great base from which to explore the Collegiate Peaks, whether you're on foot, bike or skis. A favorite with Coloradans, Salida is nevertheless less well-known than the big ski towns and has a much more local, small-town feel.

Alternatively, if you simply can't miss Aspen, retrace your steps from Twin Lakes back to I-70 with a back-road route to Minturn, before you head west to Glenwood Springs, then follow Hwy 82 east up the Roaring Fork Valley until you reach town. It's roughly 150 miles or three hours of driving.

11 Independence Pass

Looming at 12,095ft, Independence Pass (open June to October) is one of the more high-profile passes along the Continental Divide. The views along the narrow ribbon of road range from pretty to stunning to downright cinematic, and by the time you glimpse swatches of glacier just below the knife edge of the peaks, you'll be living in your own IMAX film. A paved nature trail leaves the parking area at the top of the pass – you're above the tree line here, so dress warmly. On your way down into Aspen, don't miss the ghost town of **Independence** *(aspenhistory.org)*, operated and preserved by the Aspen Historical Society. You can see the remains of the old livery, general store and a few cabins here.

THE DRIVE: Aspen is 20 miles west of Independence Pass on

Hikers, Aspen, Colorado

CSNAFZGER/SHUTTERSTOCK

VICTORIA DITKOVSKY / SHUTTERSTOCK

Independence Pass, Colorado

Hwy 82. Although in theory you can find metered street parking, it's simplest to park in the public garage ($12 per day) next to the Aspen Visitor Center on Rio Grande Pl.

12 Aspen

A cocktail of cowboy grit, Hollywood glam, Ivy League brains and fresh powder, Aspen is a town unlike any place else in the American West. And whatever the season, you'll find plenty here to keep you occupied. The **Aspen Skiing Company** *(aspensnowmass.com)* runs the area's four resorts – **Aspen**, **Snowmass**, **Buttermilk** and **Highlands** – while the historic redbrick downtown has some of Colorado's best restaurants, a great **art museum** *(aspenartmuseum.org)*, plenty of galleries and boutiques, and the noteworthy **Aspen Center for Environmental Studies** *(aspen nature.org)*. Whether you go on a tour or venture out on your own, the backcountry here is simply spectacular: hikers and bikers have a range of trails to choose from, including several in the iconic **Maroon Bells-Snowmass Wilderness Area**. Go to the **Aspen ranger office** *(fs.usda.gov/white river)* for maps and hiking tips.

STAY AWHILE

DENVER

BY MARGOT BIGG

I almost always gasp – and not for want of air – when I drive into Denver from the east. While the Colorado capital's 5280ft elevation has earned it the 'Mile High City' moniker, it's the almost overpowering view of the immense Rocky Mountains that has me catching my breath. While peaks so majestic may have you itching to keep on driving through the range and over the **Continental Divide** (p259), I'd suggest slowing down for a few days to get a sense of life in this mountain city before continuing your journey.

First, head to the historic Lower Downtown ('LoDo') neighborhood, or the Larimer Square area for shopping, dining and people-watching. **Comedy Works** *(comedyworks.com)* is my favorite place to check out stand-up comedy. Try to make time to visit **Meow Wolf Denver's Convergence Station** *(meowwolf.com)*, an unabashedly trippy immersive experience that's as fun for grown-ups as it is for little ones.

While there's enough in Denver to keep you busy for a few days, it's well worth driving over to **Red Rocks Park and Amphitheatre** *(redrocksonline.com)*, about 15 miles west of downtown. The naturally formed open-air amphitheater attracts top-name talent from around the world, and I highly recommend checking out a concert if you can get tickets. If you come on a non-event day, you can roam the venue and the park surrounding it free of charge; it's open from an hour before sunrise to an hour after sunset.

LINK YOUR TRIP

Denver is the kick-off point for the **31 Top of the Rockies** (p258) road trip.

Left: Continental Divide, Colorado; Right: Red Rocks Park and Amphitheatre, Colorado

LEFT TO RIGHT: SEAN XU/SHUTTERSTOCK, EQROY/SHUTTERSTOCK

PLACES TO STAY

Crawford Hotel
If you're coming to Denver by train, you won't find a more convenient option than this chic spot, located right inside Union Station. Rooms and common areas feature lovely art-deco interiors paired with decorative nods to the golden era of rail travel. *thecrawfordhotel.com*

The Curtis
This playful Theatre District hotel offers a mix of regular lodgings with intentionally kitschy, kiddish touches and 'hyper-themed' rooms based on concepts such as summer camp, underwater adventures and '70s game shows. *thecurtis.com*

Queen Anne Urban Bed & Breakfast
Housed in a lovely Victorian mansion, this unfussy spot offers well-maintained rooms and a compact garden. *queenannebnb.com*

32

ROCKY MOUNTAINS

★ BEST FOR

FOODIES

The farm-to-table options in Mancos and Durango.

SAN JUAN SKYWAY & MILLION DOLLAR HIGHWAY

DURATION: 6–8 DAYS

DISTANCE: 157 MILES / 253KM

GREAT FOR: HISTORY & CULTURE, NATURE, FAMILIES

BEST TIME TO GO: FROM JUNE TO OCTOBER FOR CLEAR ROADS AND SUMMER FUN.

Million Dollar Highway, Silverton (p268), Colorado

This is the West at its most rugged: a landscape of twisting mountain passes and ancient ruins, with burly peaks and gusty high desert plateaus – a land of unbroken spirit. Beyond the thrills of outdoor adventure and the rough charm of old plank saloons, there remains the lingering mystery of the region's earliest inhabitants whose awe-inspiring cliff dwellings are explored in Mesa Verde National Park.

LINK YOUR TRIP

03 Four Corners Cruise
Join the super-sized Four Corners drive on US 160 at Durango.

31 Top of the Rockies
Head north from Ridgway on US 550 to Grand Junction. Turn right to join I-70 toward Glenwood Springs, then take Hwy 82 to Aspen.

01 Mesa Verde

More than 700 years after Ancestral Puebloans left, the mystery behind their last known home remains at **Mesa Verde** *(nps.gov/meve)*. Amateur anthropologists love it: the incredible cultural heritage makes it unique among American national parks. Ancestral Puebloan sites are scattered throughout the canyons and mesas, and perched on a high plateau south of Mancos, though many remain off-limits to visitors.

If you only have a few hours, stop at **Mesa Verde Visitor & Research Center** and drive around Chapin Mesa where you can take a ranger-led tour to **Balcony House** *(recreation.gov)*, climbing to a well-preserved, hidden cliff dwelling via an exposed ladder. Purchase

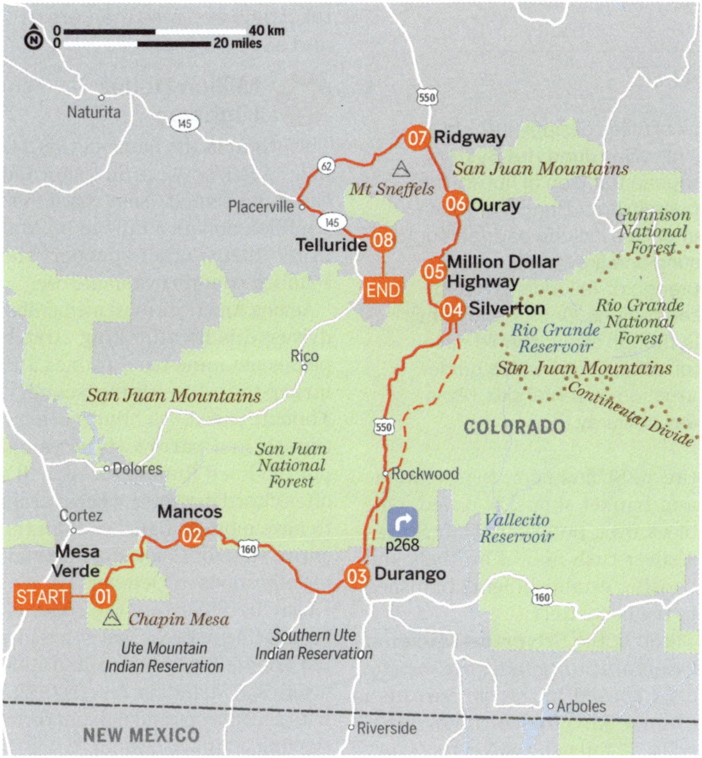

KYLEBSMITH/SHUTTERSTOCK

your ticket a day in advance at the visitor center.

If you have more time, buy tickets in advance for popular ranger-led tours of **Cliff Palace** or hike the scenic trails around the campground. Cliff-dwelling visits involve climbing rung ladders and scooting through ancient passages. The heat in summer is brutal – go early if you want to hike or cool off at the informative **Chapin Mesa Museum** *(nps.gov/meve)* near Spruce Tree House.

THE DRIVE: Entering Mesa Verde, go immediately left for the visitor center. Return to the main access road. It takes 45 minutes to reach the main attractions on Wetherill Mesa and the road is steep and narrow in places. Leaving the park, head east on US 160 for Mancos, exit right for Main St and follow to the intersection with Grand Ave.

02 Mancos

Blink and you'll miss this hamlet embracing the offbeat, earthy and slightly strange (witness the puppets dangling through the roof of the local coffee shop). With a vibrant arts community and love for locavore food, Mancos is the perfect rest stop. You will find most points of interest in a three-block radius. These include galleries and good cooking. During the last Friday of each month, the **Arts Walk** fires up what locals deem 'downtown.'

The area's oddest accommodations is **Jersey Jim Lookout Tower** *(jerseyjimfoundation.org)*, a watchtower standing 55ft high with panoramic views. This sought-after lodging is 14 miles north of Mancos at 9800ft. It comes with an Osborne Fire Finder and topographic map.

THE DRIVE: Drive east on US 160. On reaching Durango turn left onto Camino del Rio and right onto W 11th St in half a mile. Main Ave is your second right.

03 Durango

A regional darling, Durango's style straddles its ragtime past and a cool, cutting-edge future where townie bikes, caffeine and farmers markets rule.

Outdoor enthusiasts, get ready to be smitten. The **Animas River** floats right through town – float it or fly-fish it – while hundreds of mountain-bike rides range from scenic dirt roads to steep singletrack. When you've gotten your kicks, you can join the summer crowds strolling Main Ave, stopping at bookstores, boutiques and breweries.

You'll want to fuel up for the adventure, so hit up **Carver Brewing Company** *(carverbrewing.com)* followed by a quick 10-mile mountain bike loop at the **Overend Mountain Park** before hitting the road.

Leave town heading north on the San Juan Skyway, which passes farms and stables as it starts the scenic climb toward Silverton.

THE DRIVE: Take Main Ave heading north. Leaving Durango it becomes US 550, also part of the San Juan Skyway. Along the way, you can stop at Purgatory Resort for skiing in winter and mountain biking in summer. Before Silverton the road climbs both Coal Banks Pass (10,640ft) and Molas Pass (10,910ft).

LOCAL KNOWLEDGE

COLORADO'S HAUTE ROUTE

An exceptional way to enjoy hundreds of miles of singletrack in summer or virgin powder slopes in winter, **San Juan Hut System** *(sanjuanhuts.com)* continues the European tradition of hut-to-hut adventures with five backcountry mountain huts. Bring just your food, flashlight and sleeping bag – amenities include padded bunks, propane stoves, wood stoves for heating and firewood.

Mountain-biking routes go from Durango or Telluride to Moab, winding through high alpine and desert regions. Or pick one hut as your base. There's terrain for all levels, though skiers should have knowledge of snow and avalanche conditions or go with a guide. The website has helpful tips and information on rental skis, bikes and (optional) guides based in Ridgway or Ouray.

DETOUR

Narrow Gauge Railroad

Start: 03 Durango

Climb aboard the steam driven **Durango & Silverton Narrow Gauge Railroad** *(durangotrain.com)* for the train ride of the summer. The train, running between Durango and Silverton, has been in continuous operation since 1881, and the scenic 45-mile journey north to Silverton, a National Historic Landmark, takes 3½ hours one way. Most locals recommend taking it one way and returning from Silverton via bus, as it's faster. It's most glorious in late September and early October when the Aspens go golden.

04 Silverton

Ringed by snowy peaks and proudly steeped in tawdry mining-town lore, Silverton would seem more at home in Alaska than the lower 48. At 9318ft the air is thin, but that discourages no one from hitting the bar stool.

Explore it all and don't shy away from the mere 500 locals – they're happy to see a fresh face. It's a two-street town, but only respectable Greene St, now home to restaurants and trinket shops, is paved. One block over, notorious Blair St was a silver-rush hub of brothels and boozing establishments banished to the backstreet.

Stop at the **Silverton Museum** *(sanjuancountyhistoricalsociety.org)*, housed in the old San Juan County Jail, to see the original cells. It tells the Silverton story from terrible mining accidents to sex work, drinking, gambling and robbery, showing the many ways to meet a grisly end in the West.

Most visitors use Silverton as a hub for jeep tours – sketchy mining roads climbing in all directions offer unreal views. In winter, **Silverton Mountain** *(silvertonmountain.com)* offers experts the best in untamed, ungroomed terrain.

THE DRIVE: Leaving Silverton head north on US 550, the Million Dollar Hwy. It starts with a gentle climb but becomes steeper. Hairpin turns slow traffic at Molas Pass to 25mph. The most hair-raising sections follow, with 15mph speed limits in places. The road lacks guardrails and drops are huge, so stay attentive. Pullouts provide relief between mile markers 91 and 93.

05 Million Dollar Highway

The origin of the name of this 24-mile stretch between Silverton and Ouray is disputed – some say it took a million dollars a mile to build it in the 1920s; others purport the roadbed contains valuable ore.

Among America's most memorable drives, this breathtaking stretch passes old mine head frames and larger-than-life alpine scenery. Though paved, its blind corners, tunnels and narrow turns would put the Road Runner on edge. It's often closed in winter, when it's said to have more avalanches than the entire state of Colorado. Snowfall usually starts in October.

Leaving Silverton, the road ascends Mineral Creek Valley, passing the Longfellow mine ruins 1 mile before Red Mountain Pass (11,018ft), with sheer drops and hairpin turns slowing traffic to 25mph.

Descending toward Ouray, visit **Bear Creek Falls**, a large turnout with a daring viewing platform over the crashing several-hundred-foot falls. A difficult 8-mile trail here switchbacks to even greater views – not for vertigo sufferers.

Stop at the lookout over Ouray at mile marker 92. Turn right for the lovely **Amphitheater Campground** *(recreation.gov)*.

THE DRIVE: The Million Dollar Hwy makes a steep descent into Ouray and becomes Main St.

06 Ouray

A well-preserved mining village snug beneath imposing peaks, Ouray breeds enchantment. It's named after the legendary Ute

Bear Creek Falls, Ouray, Colorado

ANDTHEYTRAVEL/SHUTTERSTOCK

chief who kept the peace between the white settlers and the crush of miners invading the San Juan Mountains in the early 1870s, by relinquishing the Ute tribal lands. The area is rife with hot springs. One cool cave spring, now located underneath the **Wiesbaden** *(wiesbadenhotsprings.com)* hotel was favored by Chief Ouray. Now you can soak there by the hour.

The annual **Ouray Ice Festival** *(ourayicepark.com)* draws elite climbers for a four-day competition. But the town also lends thrills to hikers and 4WD fans. If you're skittish about driving yourself, San Juan **Scenic Jeep Tours** *(sanjuanjeeptours.com)* takes open-air Jeeps into the high country, offering special wildflower or ghost-town trips. It's worth hiking up to **Box Canyon Falls** from the west end of 3rd Ave. A suspension bridge leads you into the belly of this 285ft waterfall. The surrounding area is rich in birdlife – look for the protected black swift, which nests in the rock face.

THE DRIVE: Leave Ouray heading north via Main St, which becomes US 550 N. It's a flat 10-mile drive to Ridgway's only traffic light. Turn left onto Sherman St. The center of town is spread over the next half-mile.

07 Ridgway

Wide-open meadows backed by the snow-covered San Juans and stellar Mt Sneffels, Ridgway is an inviting blip of a burg. The backdrop of John Wayne's 1969 cowboy classic *True Grit,* today it sports a sort of neo-Western charm.

TELLURIDE FESTIVALS

Telluride is mountain magic in the summer when bluebird skies converge with stellar festival opportunities. For more information, see *telluride.com/festivals-events/festivals.*

Mountainfilm (late May) A four-day screening of high-caliber outdoor adventure and environmental films.

Telluride Bluegrass Festival (late June) Thousands enjoy a weekend of top-notch rollicking alfresco bluegrass going well into the night.

Telluride Film Festival (early September) National and international films are premiered throughout town, and the event attracts big-name stars.

Sunny rock pools at **Orvis Hot Springs** *(orvishotsprings.com)* make this clothing-optional hot spring hard to resist. Though it gets its fair share of exhibitionists, a variety of soaking areas, ranging from 100°F (37°C) to 114°F (45°C), mean you can probably scout out the perfect quiet spot. Less appealing are the private indoor pools lacking fresh air. It's 9 miles north of Ouray, outside Ridgway.

THE DRIVE: Leaving town heading west, Sherman St becomes CO62. Take this easy drive 23 miles with spectacular views to the south. At the crossroads go left onto CO145 S for Telluride. Approaching town there's a traffic circle; take the second exit onto W Colorado Ave. The center of Telluride is in half a mile.

08 Telluride

Surrounded on three sides by mastodon peaks, exclusive Telluride was once a rough mining town. Today it's dirtbag-meets-diva – where glitterati mix with ski bums, and renowned music and film festivals create a frolicking summer atmosphere.

The very renovated center still has palpable old-time charm. Stop into the plush **New Sheridan Bar** *(newsheridan.com)* to find out the story of those old bullet holes in the wall and the plucky survival of the bar itself, even as the adjoining hotel sold off chandeliers to pay the heating bills during waning mining fortunes.

Touring downtown, check out the free box where you can swap unwanted items; the tradition is a point of civic pride. Then take a free 15-minute gondola ride up to the **Telluride Mountain Village** *(telluride.com)* where you can rent a mountain bike, dine or just bask in the panoramas.

If you are planning on attending a festival, book your tickets and lodging months in advance.

Ice climber, near Ouray, Colorado
DANITA DELIMONT/SHUTTERSTOCK

NEVADA
UTAH
COLORADO
KANSAS
OKLAHOMA
ARIZONA
NEW MEXICO
TEXAS
CALIFORNIA
BAJA CALIFORNIA
MEXICO
CHIHUAHUA
COAHUILA
0 250 km
0 150 miles
Great Salt Lake
Ogden
Salt Lake City
Provo
Nephi
Ely
Cheyenne
Denver
Grand Junction
Green River
Manti-La Sal National Forest
Moab
Monticello
Cannonville
Dixie National Forest
Grand Staircase-Escalante National Monument
Caliente
Cedar City
Pueblo
Lamar
Kansas City
Topeka
Wichita
Bartlesville
Tulsa
Durango
Raton
Farmington
Page
Kaibab National Forest
Lake Mead
Las Vegas
Grand Canyon National Park
Kingman
Flagstaff
Prescott
Tonto National Forest
Phoenix
Casa Grande
Tucson
Sonoyta
Nogales
Mexicali
Golfo de California
Hermosillo
Gallup
Taos
Santa Fe National Forest
Santa Fe
Albuquerque
Socorro
Rio Grande
Gila National Forest
Roswell
Alamogordo
Las Cruces
El Paso
Aguas Temales
Dalhart
Canadian River
Amarillo
Oklahoma City
Lawton
Lake Texoma
Lubbock
Possum Kingdom Lake
Dallas
Abilene
Waco
Odessa
Colorado River
Van Horn
Fort Stockton
Sonora
Alpine
Big Bend National Park
Fredericksburg
Austin
Houston
San Antonio
Rio Grande
Nuevo Laredo
Corpus Christi
Gulf of Mexico
33
34
35
36
37
38

JIM MALLOUK/SHUTTERSTOCK

Colorado River, Grand Canyon (p282), Arizona

THE SOUTHWEST

EXPLORE

THE SOUTHWEST

Mother Nature had some fun in the Southwest. Red-rock canyons ripple across ancient plateaus. Whisper-light sand dunes shimmer on distant horizons. And wildflowers, saguaros and ponderosa pines lure you in for a closer look.

Our trips across the Southwest swoop from scrubby deserts to the majestic Grand Canyon, from sandstone buttresses sculpted by desert winds to the shimmering lights of Las Vegas. En-route, dramatic landscapes and movie locations unfold – this is the road trip as it was meant to be driven. Fill your tank, don your Ray-Bans and set off in search of the Southwest.

Flagstaff

Deep in the heart of Arizona, America's largest ponderosa forest surrounds Flagstaff with its historic core, arboretum, museums and restless spirit. Everyone here seems to want to head out hiking or cycling. Then they all return to town for great coffee, craft beer and a surprisingly cosmopolitan culinary scene. Accommodations here run the full gamut of possibilities, from B&Bs and historic hotels to ubiquitous motels. Oh, and the Grand Canyon is not far away, either.

Cedar City

Quiet little Cedar City, in Utah's southwest, has a fabulous collection of B&Bs, as well as a 6000ft-above-sea-level location that offers respite from the heat of the deserts on the plains down below. These would be reason enough to base yourself here. But there are state parks, dramatic landforms and a hearty pizza-and-steak gastronomic sensibility, all before you set out to explore Zion, Bryce and beyond.

Bluff

Bluff is a blink-and-you'll-miss-it kinda place. This is even more likely because of the jaw-dropping red-rock scenery that will capture your attention as you approach town. But stay awhile and you'll find campgrounds, motels and B&Bs, as well as a handful of restaurants and cafes. Best of all, you're perfectly placed for exploring a whole slew of natural wonders, among them Moki Dugway (30 miles), Hovenweep National Monument (40 miles), Monument

WHEN TO GO

Most of these routes pass through scorching desert country, with some of the hottest summer temperatures in the country. Summer can also feel like a procession as half the country takes to the road and heads for the Grand Canyon. Fall and spring are ideal for fewer crowds, milder temperatures and, in places, blooming wildflowers in spring.

Valley (47 miles) and Natural Bridges National Monument (61 miles).

Santa Fe

Santa Fe has a beguiling character all its own. Part of that comes from its historical story and the adobe architecture of its neighborhoods. Or the full calendar of fun festivals. Or Santa Fe's famously artsy inclinations. Or its cooling altitude at over 7000ft above sea level. Or the eclectic museums. Then there's the extraordinary array of activities you can join, accommodations for every budget and from every genre, and simply fabulous restaurants. What's not to like?

El Paso

Big-city El Paso is very much a city on the up. The city has had a facelift in recent years, and it can now boast some excellent museums, a fistful of new hotels, a restored streetcar line, the Chihuahuas baseball team and even its very own crop of microbreweries. It's a fun, unashamedly multicultural place with a culinary scene that draws inspiration from its Mexican near-neighbors just across the border.

San Antonio

Much the most attractive of Texas' major cities – and much the oldest, too, having celebrated its 300th birthday in 2018 – San Antonio is a rather pleasurable Texas base. It has the legendary Alamo, symbol of Texan independence, at the very heart of the city, while the River Walk, a glorious network of waterside pathways tucked below street level and lined with bars and restaurants, offers leisurely strolling through downtown and beyond. Start your Big Bend excursion here, but you'll long to return at journey's end.

TRANSPORTATION

El Paso, San Antonio and Santa Fe have major airports with excellent flight connections across the US. That makes Texas and New Mexico ideal places to begin many Southwestern explorations. Thereafter it's a sliding scale: Flagstaff has buses, Amtrak and automobile access; Cedar City has buses and cars; and Bluff – well, you'll need your own vehicle to reach Bluff.

WHERE TO STAY

As with many US towns out West, historic hotels are a recurring theme. Some lean towards the kitsch, others exude a faded elegance, while others still are just downright luxurious. All take their Wild West history serious, just as you'd hope they would. More intimate are the B&Bs, which are the real repositories of that age-old Western hospitality. You'll find them everywhere across the region, but they're at their best in Cedar City, Utah. For out-of-the-way, or stunningly sited campgrounds, try **Cottonwood** (Big Bend), **North Rim**, **Indian Garden** or **Bright Angel** (Grand Canyon), or **View** (Monument Valley).

RESOURCES

- **National Park Service**
  Essential resource for national parks like Bryce Canyon, Zion and Big Bend. *nps.gov*
- **Arizona Trail**
  Good resource covering the 800-odd-mile Arizona National Scenic Trail. *aztrail.org*
- **Utah State Parks & Recreation Department**
  Info about 40-plus state parks, many of them beautiful and little known. *stateparks.utah.gov*

WHAT'S ON

- **Utah Shakespeare Festival**
  Well-regarded Shakespeare plays and fun associated events in Cedar City from June to October.
- **Astronomy Festival**
  Bryce Canyon's four-day Astronomy Festival celebrates the exceptionally clear night skies at Bryce with walks, talks and stargazing with experts in late June.
- **International Chili Championship**
  Three days of chili-making contests in November in Terlingua, Texas.
- **Fiestas de Taos**
  New Mexican music, parades and dance fill the streets of Taos, in late July.

33

SOUTHWEST

GRAND CANYON VOYAGE

★ BEST FOR

HISTORY

Push through the swinging doors of the past in Wickenburg, Prescott and Jerome.

DURATION: 4–5 DAYS

DISTANCE: 235 MILES / 378KM

GREAT FOR: HISTORY & CULTURE, NATURE, FOOD

BEST TIME TO GO: VISIT IN FALL AND SPRING, TO BEAT THE HEAT AND SUMMER CROWDS.

Jerome (p278), Arizona

This road trip steers you through the greatest hits of Central Arizona, en route to the incomparable Grand Canyon. It's pretty, it's wild and it carries a decent whack of Arizona's rough-and-tumble history. Scenic trails wind past sandstone buttes and ponderosa pines. Wild West adventures include horseback rides, saloons and mine shafts. But this route isn't all about the past: a burgeoning wine scene and contemporary dining add 21st-century allure.

LINK YOUR TRIP

03 Four Corners Cruise
Trade natural wonders for Sin City wows by driving west on I-40 to Hwy 93 north.

43 Palm Springs & Joshua Tree Oases
From Wickenburg, take Hwy 60 west to I-10 for lush desert getaways and outdoor fun.

01 Wickenburg

With its saddle shops and Old West storefronts, Wickenburg looks like it fell out of the sky – directly from the 1890s. At the ever-popular **Sigler Western Museum** *(westernmuseum.org)*, the artwork celebrates the West and the lives of those that won it. The Hays' Spirit of the Cowboy collection examines the raw materials behind the cowboy myth, showcasing rifles, ropes and saddles. The *Cowgirl Up!* exhibit and sale each March and April is a fun and impressive annual tribute to an eclectic array of Western women artists.

Scattered across downtown are statues of the town's founders and colorful characters. One of the latter was George Sayers, a 'bibulous reprobate' who was chained to the **Jail Tree** on Tegner St in the late 1800s. Press the button to hear his tale, then head over the road to the locally loved **Nana's Sandwich Shoppe** for a feed.

CAVAN-IMAGES/SHUTTERSTOCK

Wickenburg is pleasant anytime but summer, when temperatures regularly top 110°F (43°C).

THE DRIVE: Head west on Hwy 60, then turn left onto Vulture Mine Rd. Saguaros and cattle guards mark the lonely 14-mile drive to the mine.

02 Vulture Mine Road

At the remote and dusty **Vulture City** *(vultureminetours.com)*, Austrian immigrant Henry Wickenburg staked his claim and made his fortune. The ghost town holds the main shaft (where $30 million worth of gold was mined), the blacksmith shop and other decrepit old buildings, and the **Hanging Tree**.

On the way back into town, consider spending the night at rustically posh **Rancho de los Caballeros** *(ranchodeloscaballeros.com)*, where guests can sign up for small-group trail rides or private riding lessons.

THE DRIVE: From downtown Wickenburg, pick up Hwy 93 north and drive 5 miles to 89N. Continuing north, the route leaves the Sonoran Desert and tackles the Weaver Mountains, climbing 2500ft in 4 miles. It's 59 miles to Prescott.

03 Prescott

Fire raged through Whiskey Row in downtown Prescott (presskit) on July 14, 1900. Quick-thinking locals saved the town's most prized possession: the 24ft-long Brunswick Bar that anchored the **Palace Restaurant and Saloon** *(thepalacerestaurantandsaloon.com)*. After lugging the solid oak bar onto Courthouse Plaza, they grabbed their drinks and continued the party. Prescott's cooperative spirit lives on, infusing the city with a welcoming vibe.

The Palace is at the center of Prescott's Historic Downtown and Whiskey Row, where 40 drinking establishments once supplied suds and sour mash to rough-hewn cowboys, miners and wastrels.

To learn more about Prescott, which was Arizona's first territorial capital, visit the engaging **Sharlot Hall Museum** *(sharlothallmuseum.org)*, named for its 1928 founder, pioneer woman Sharlot Hall. The city is also home to the **World's Oldest Rodeo** *(worldsoldestrodeo.com)*, which dates to 1888 and is held the week before July 4.

THE DRIVE: From the County Courthouse downtown, drive west on Gurley St, which turns into Thumb Butte Rd, an overall drive of just 4 miles.

04 Thumb Butte

Prescott sits in the middle of the Prescott National Forest, a 1.2-million-acre playground bursting with scenic slopes, lakes and ponderosa pines. The **Prescott National Forest Office** *(fs.usda.gov/prescott)* has information about local hikes, drives, picnic areas and campgrounds. A $5 day-use fee is required – and payable – at many area trailheads. Intra-agency passes, including the America the Beautiful pass, cover this fee.

For a short hike, head to the hard-to-miss **Thumb Butte**. The 1.75-mile **Thumb Butte Trail #33** is a moderate workout and offers nice views of the town and mountains. Leashed dogs are permitted.

THE DRIVE: Follow Hwy 89N out of Prescott, passing the Granite Dells rock formations on the

11-mile drive. Granite Dells Rd leads to a trail through the granite boulders on the Mile High Trail System.

05 Phippen Museum

Strutting its stuff like a rodeo champ, the thoroughly engaging **Phippen Museum** *(phippenartmuseum.org)* ropes in visitors with an entertaining mix of special exhibits spotlighting cowboy and Western art. Named for the late George Phippen, a local self-taught artist who helped put Western art on the map, it's worth a stop to see what's brewing. As you'll discover, Western art is broader than oil paintings of weather-beaten faces under broad hat brims – although you might see some of those, too.

THE DRIVE: Just north of the museum, leave Hwy 89 for Hwy 89A. This 27-mile serpentine road brooks no distraction as it approaches hillside Jerome, tucked in the Mingus Mountains. If you dare, glance east for stunning glimpses of the Verde Valley.

06 Jerome

As the road snakes down steep Cleopatra Hill, it can be hard to tell whether the buildings are winning or losing their battle with gravity. Just take the Sliding Jail – it's waaaay down there at the bottom of town.

Now shabbily chic, this resurrected ghost town was known as the 'Wickedest Town in the West' during its late-1800s copper-mining heyday. In those days it teemed with brothels, saloons and opium dens. When the mines petered out in 1953, Jerome's population plummeted. Then came the '60s, when scores of hippies snapped up crumbling, atmospheric buildings for pennies, more or less restored them and injected the town with a groovy joie de vivre.

Join the party with a stroll past the galleries, indie shops, old buildings and wine-tasting rooms that are scattered up and down the hillside. Local artists sell their work at the **Jerome Artists Cooperative Gallery** *(jeromecoop.com)* while burly but friendly-enough bikers gather at the **Spirit Room** *(spiritroom.com)* bar.

THE DRIVE: Follow Main St/Hwy 89A out of downtown, then turn left onto Douglas Rd.

07 Audrey Headframe Park & Jerome State Historic Park

Jerome's darkly humorous embrace of its industrial past is clear at this former minehead, which boasts the largest surviving timber headframe in the state. The glass platform covering the mining shaft at **Audrey Headframe Park** *(jeromehistoricalsociety.com)* isn't your everyday roadside attraction: it's death staring you in the face. If the cover shattered, the drop is 1910ft – a mere 650ft longer than from atop the Empire State Building.

Sufficiently disturbed? Chill out next door at the excellent **Jerome State Historic Park** *(azstateparks.com/jerome)*, which explores the town's mining past. The museum is inside the 1916 mansion of eccentric mining mogul Jimmy 'Rawhide' Douglas. The folksy video is worth watching before you tour the museum.

THE DRIVE: Hwy 89A drops to tranquil Clarkdale. At the traffic circle, take the second exit onto the Clarkdale Pkwy and into town. Follow Main St east to S

Mather Point (p282), Grand Canyon, Arizona
JAY YUAN/SHUTTERSTOCK

PHOTO OPPORTUNITY

The Grand Canyon from Mather Point.

Broadway then turn left onto Tuzigoot Rd, a total drive of just 7 miles.

08 Tuzigoot National Monument

Squatting atop a ridge east of Clarkdale, **Tuzigoot National Monument** *(nps.gov/tuzi)*, a pueblo built by the prehistoric Sinaguan people (Spanish for 'without water'), is believed to have been inhabited from 1000 to 1400 CE. At its peak, as many as 225 people lived in its 110 rooms. Stop by the informative visitor center to examine tools, pottery and arrowheads, then climb a short, steep trail (not suitable for wheelchairs) for memorable views of the Verde River Valley.

THE DRIVE: Return to S Broadway and follow it south into Old Town Cottonwood, just 3 miles south of Tuzigoot.

09 Cottonwood

Cottonwood has kicked up its cool quotient, particularly around the pedestrian-friendly **Old Town District**. On this low-key strip there are loads of good restaurants and wine-tasting rooms, and several interesting indie stores. The inviting tasting room **Arizona Stronghold** *(azstronghold.com)* has welcoming staff, comfy couches, and live music on Friday nights. Enjoy a few more wine samples across the street at the chocolate-and-wine pairing **Pillsbury Wine Company** *(pillsburywine.com)*. For wet-and-wild wine tasting in Cottonwood, join a Water to Wine kayak tour with **Sedona Adventure Tours** *(sedonaadventuretours.com)* on the Verde River to **Alcantara Vineyards** *(alcantaravineyard.com)*.

THE DRIVE: Follow Main St south to reconnect with Hwy 89A, then drive a further 20 miles to Sedona. At the roundabout at the junction of Hwy 89A and Hwy 179, called the Y, continue into uptown Sedona. The main visitor center sits at the junction of Hwy 89A and Forest Rd.

10 Sedona

The stunning red rocks here have an intensely spiritual pull for many visitors, who believe that certain sandstone formations are the sites of vortexes that radiate the earth's energy. Judge for yourself atop **Airport Mesa**, the vortex most convenient to downtown.

Tuzigoot National Monument, Arizona

KENNETH KEIFER/SHUTTERSTOCK

Here, a short scramble leads to a lofty view of the surrounding sandstone monoliths, which blaze a psychedelic red and orange at sunset. To get to the viewpoint, drive up Airport Rd for half a mile and look for a small parking area on the left.

Another arresting site is the **Chapel of the Holy Cross** *(chapel oftheholycross.com),* a church tucked between spectacular red rock columns 3 miles south of town. This modern Catholic chapel was built by Marguerite Brunwig Staude in the tradition of Frank Lloyd Wright.

THE DRIVE: Follow Hwy 179 9 miles south, past Bell Rock, through the village of Oak Creek to the Red Rock Country Visitor Center.

11 Red Rock Country Visitor Center

Outdoor adventurers love the super-scenic hiking and biking trails in and around Sedona. The US Forest Service provides the helpful and free Recreation Guide to Your National Forest, which has brief descriptions of popular trails and a map pinpointing their routes and trailheads. Pick one up at the **Red Rock Country Visitor Center** *(fs.usda.gov/coconino),* just south of the village of Oak Creek. Staff can guide you to less-populated trails, or those best suited to your interests.

THE DRIVE: Hwy 89A rolls north through the riparian greenery of scenic Oak Creek Canyon, where red cliffs and pine forest rear spectacularly from either side of the road. Once out of the canyon pick up I-17 north. The total drive to Flagstaff is 39 miles.

12 Flagstaff

Flagstaff's charms are myriad, from its pedestrian-friendly historic downtown to high-altitude pursuits like skiing and hiking. **Humphreys Peak** *(fs.usda.gov/coconino),* the highest point in the state, provides an inspiring backdrop. Start at the downtown **visitor center** *(flagstaffarizona.org),* which has free brochures for walking tours, including a guide to Flagstaff's haunted places.

The fascinating **Lowell Observatory** *(lowell.edu),* built in 1894 and site of the first official sighting of Pluto (in 1930), sits on a hill just outside downtown. During the day you can take a guided tour, while at night, weather permitting, there's stargazing. Flagstaff's microbreweries are the stars on the 1-mile **Flagstaff Brewery Trail** *(craft beerflg.com).* But if walking seems too pedestrian, climb aboard the **Alpine Pedaler** *(alpinepedaler.com),* a 14-passenger 'party on wheels' that brakes for bars and breweries.

THE DRIVE: The next morning – and mornings are best for the 90-mile trip – take Hwy 180 west and enjoy the views of the San Francisco Peaks through the treetops. When you reach Hwy 64 at the town of Valle, turn right and drive the remainder of the journey north on the broad uplands of the Coconino Plateau.

13 Tusayan

This little town, sitting 1 mile south of the Grand Canyon's South Entrance on Hwy 64, is basically a half-mile strip of canyon-focused hotels and restaurants. Stop at the **Grand Canyon Visitor Center & IMAX Theater** *(explorethe canyon.com)* to pre-pay the park fee and save yourself what could be a long wait at the entrance. Always screening in the IMAX theater is the terrific 34-minute film *Grand Canyon: The Hidden Secrets.* With exhilarating river-running scenes and virtual-reality drops off canyon rims, the film plunges you into the history and geology of the canyon through the eyes of ancient American Indians, explorer John Wesley Powell and a soaring eagle.

In summer, you can leave your car here and catch the Tusayan shuttle into the park.

THE DRIVE: Follow Hwy 64 for 1 mile north to the park entrance. Admission to the national park is $35 per vehicle and is good for seven days. All told, it's a serene 7 miles to Mather Point.

♥ WHY I LOVE THIS TRIP

CHRISTOPHER PITTS, WRITER

Yes, you could drive straight from Phoenix to the Grand Canyon in a mere four hours, but then you'd miss all the good stuff: the ghosts that haunt improbable cliffside Jerome, the undiscovered vineyards of Cottonwood and, of course, the ever-present allure of Sedona's red rock sunsets. And don't forget the mountain town of Flagstaff, the perfect combination of epicurean delights and outdoorsy adventures.

BILLY MCDONALD/ SHUTTERSTOCK

14 Mather Point & Grand Canyon Visitor Center

Park at the visitor center *(nps.gov/grca/planyourvisit/visitorcenters.htm)* but don't go inside. Not yet. Walk (or run) directly to **Mather Point**, the first overlook after the South Entrance. It's usually packed elbow-to-elbow with a global array of tourists, all snapping away in ecstasy, but even with the crowds there's a sense of communal wonder that keeps things civil. The sheer immensity of the canyon grabs you, then holds you as you scan the endless details: rugged mesas, sculpted spires and an almost overwhelming sense of scale.

Once your sense of wonder is surfeited, head back to the main visitor center, with its theater and bookstore. On the plaza, bulletin boards and kiosks display information about ranger programs, the weather, tours and hikes. Inside is a ranger-staffed information desk and a lecture hall, where rangers offer daily talks on a variety of subjects. The theater screens a 20-minute movie, *Grand Canyon: A Journey of Wonder*, on the hour and half-hour.

From here, explore the park via park shuttle, a bike *(bikegrandcanyon.com)*, or your own four wheels. In summer, parking can be a challenge in Grand Canyon Village.

THE DRIVE: The Village Loop Rd leads into Grand Canyon Village. Pass El Tovar and Kachina & Thunderbird lodges on the 2-mile drive to Bright Angel Lodge. The Bright Angel Trailhead is just west of the lodge.

DETOUR

Desert View Drive

Start: 14 Mather Point & Grand Canyon Visitor Center

This scenic road meanders 25 miles to the East Entrance on Hwy 64, passing some of the park's finest viewpoints, picnic areas and historic sites. **Grand View Point** marks the trailhead where miner Peter Berry opened

Bright Angel Trail Grand Canyon, Arizona

the aptly named Grand View Hotel, in 1897 – it really is one of the Grand Canyon's most stunning viewpoints. Another captivating view awaits at **Moran Point**, named for the landscape painter whose work helped secure the Grand Canyon national monument status, in 1908. Further along is **Tusayan Museum & Ruin**, where you can walk around the remains of an excavated Ancestral Puebloan village dating to 1185. At the end of the road is the **Desert View Watchtower**, designed by Mary Jane Colter and inspired by ancient Ancestral Puebloan structures – the terrace provides panoramic views of the canyon and river. The circular staircase inside leads past Hopi murals to 360-degree views on the top floor.

15 Grand Canyon Village

The **Bright Angel Trail** *(nps.gov/grca)* is the most popular of the South Rim corridor trails, and its steep and scenic 8-mile descent to the Colorado River has four logical turnaround points: **Mile-and-a-Half Resthouse**, **Three-Mile Resthouse**, **Indian Garden** and **Plateau Point**. Summer heat can be crippling and the climb is steep. Day hikers should turn around at one of the two resthouses (a 3- to 6-mile round trip).

If you're more interested in history and geography than strenuous hiking, follow the easy **Rim Trail** east from here. If you opt for the western direction, the Rim Trail passes every overlook on the way to Hermits Rest, offering spectacular views. The **Hermits Rest** shuttle runs parallel to the trail, so hike until you're tired, then hop aboard to continue or return. But be sure to hop off for the sunset, which is best at **Hopi Point**, which draws crowds, or Pima Point.

34

SOUTHWEST

★ BEST FOR

HIKING

Zion Canyon has easy river walks to strenuous, canyon-climbing hikes.

ZION & BRYCE NATIONAL PARKS

DURATION: 6 DAYS

DISTANCE: 178 MILES / 286KM

GREAT FOR: NATURE

BEST TIME TO GO: IN APRIL AND SEPTEMBER YOU'LL LIKELY HAVE WARM WEATHER AT LOW AND HIGH ELEVATIONS.

Zion Canyon, Utah

Meet red-rock country in all its heart-soaring, sculpted splendor. From the sheer wall of Zion to the pastel sentinels of hoodoos that form Bryce Canyon, these are the landscapes that no one traveling in the Southwest should miss. This trip takes in the parks' classic highlights as well as tiny Western towns and off-the-beaten-path nature sanctuaries where the screech of a hawk breaks the silence of the trail.

LINK YOUR TRIP

03 Four Corners Cruise
Twist east from Zion on Hwy 9, then follow Hwys 89 and 89A south to the Grand Canyon North Rim.

35 Monument Valley & Trail of the Ancients
For majestic monoliths, take Hwy 9 and then Hwy 89 southeast to Page, then follow Hwys 98 and 160 east to Hwy 163 north.

01 Kolob Canyons

Start your visit at the **Kolob Canyons Visitor Center** *(nps.gov/zion)*, gateway to the less-visited, higher-elevation section of Zion National Park off I-15. Even in peak season you'll see relatively few cars on the scenic 5-mile Kolob Canyons Rd, a high-plateau route where striking canyon and rangeland views alternate. The road terminates at Kolob Canyons Overlook (6200ft); from there the **Timber Creek Trail** (1-mile round trip) follows a 100ft ascent to a small peak with great views of the Pine Valley Mountains beyond. In early summer the trail area is covered with wildflowers. Note that the upper section of the road may be closed due to snow from November through May.

The best longer hike in this section of the park is the **Taylor Creek Trail** (5-mile round trip), which passes pioneer ruins and criss-crosses a creek, with little elevation change.

AARON KATO/SHUTTERSTOCK

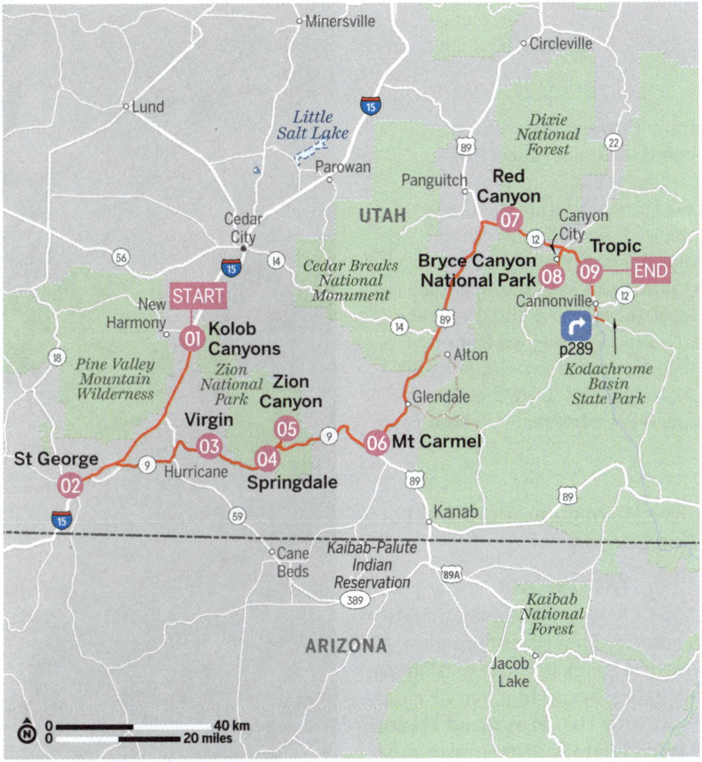

THE DRIVE: Distant rock formations zoom by as you cruise along at 70-plus mph on I-15. St George is 33 miles south.

02 St George

A spacious Mormon town with an eye-catching temple and a few pioneer buildings, St George sits about equidistant between the two halves of Zion. The **Chamber of Commerce** *(stgeorgechamber.com)* can provide information on the historic downtown. Otherwise, use this time to stock up on food and fuel in this trip's only real city (population around 100,000). **Snow Canyon State Park** *(stateparks.utah.gov/parks/snow-canyon),* 11 miles north of town, is a 7400-acre sampler of southwest Utah's famous land features. Easy trails that are perfect for kids lead to tiny slot canyons, cinder cones, lava tubes and fields of undulating slickrock.

THE DRIVE: Off the interstate, Hwy 9 leads you into canyon country. You'll pass the town of Hurricane before sweeping curves give way to tighter turns (and slower traffic). Virgin is 28 miles east of St George.

03 Virgin

The tiny town of Virgin, named after the river (what else?), has an odd claim to fame – in 2000 the city council passed a largely symbolic law requiring every resident (about 600 of them) to own a gun. You can't miss **Fort Zion**, which sells homemade fudge, ice cream and every Western knick-knack known to the free world. Stop and have your picture taken in the 'Virgin Jail' or 'Wild Ass Saloon' in the replica Old West village here. It's pure, kitschy fun.

THE DRIVE: Springdale is 13 miles further along Hwy 9 (55 minutes from St George).

04 Springdale

Stunning orangish-red mountains, including the Watchman (6555ft), form the backdrop for a perfect little park town. Here eclectic cafes and restaurants are big on locally sourced ingredients. Galleries and artisan shops line the long main drag, interspersed with indie motels, lodges and a few B&Bs. Make this your base for three nights while exploring Zion Canyon and surrounds. Outfitters **Zion Guru** *(zionguru.com)* and **Zion Adventure Company** *(zionadventures.com)* lead canyoneering and climbing outside the park; the latter also offers bicycle rentals and tours. They both outfit for backcountry hikes through the Narrows.

THE DRIVE: The entrance to the Zion Canyon section of Zion National Park is only 2 miles east of Springdale. Note that here you're at about 3900ft, the lowest (and hottest) part of your trip.

05 Zion Canyon

More than 100 miles of trails cut through the surprisingly well-watered, deciduous-tree-covered Virgin River canyon section of Zion National Park. Map out your routes at the **Zion Canyon Visitor Center** *(nps.gov/zion).* Your first activity should be the 6-mile Scenic Drive, which pierces the heart of the park. From March through November, using the free shuttle is mandatory, but you can hop off and on at any of the scenic stops and trailheads along the way.

LOCAL KNOWLEDGE

EAST MESA TRAIL

It feels deliciously like cheating to wander through open stands of tall ponderosa pines and then descend to **Observation Point** instead of hiking more than 2100ft uphill from the Zion Canyon floor. On **East Mesa Trail** (6.4-mile round trip, moderate difficulty) you can do just that, because your vehicle does all the climbing. North Fork Rd is about 2.5 miles beyond the park's east entrance; follow it 5 miles north up Hwy 9 from there. Getting to the trailhead in some seasons requires 4WD; ask about conditions and maps at the **Zion Canyon Visitor Center**. Nearby **Zion Ponderosa Ranch Resort** *(zionponderosa.com)*, which also has accommodations and activities, can provide hiker shuttles. Note that at 6500ft, these roads and the trail may be closed due to snow November through May.

The paved, mile-long one-way **Riverside Walk** at the end of the road is an easy stroll. When the trail ends, you can continue hiking along in the Virgin River for 5 miles. Alternatively, a half-mile one-way trail leads up to the lower of the **Emerald Pools**.

The strenuous, 5.4-mile round-trip **Angels Landing Trail** (four hours, 1400ft elevation gain) is a vertigo-inducer with narrow ridges and 2000ft sheer drop-offs. Succeed and the exhilaration is unsurpassed.

For the 16-mile one-way trip down through the Narrows, spectacular slot canyons of the Virgin River, you need to plan ahead. An outfitter shuttle and gear plus a backcountry permit from the park are required; make advance reservations via the park website.

THE DRIVE: Driving east, Hwy 9 winds over bridges and up 3.5 miles of tight switchbacks before reaching the impressive gallery-dotted Zion–Mt Carmel Tunnel. From there until the east park entrance, the canyon walls are made of etched, light-colored slickrock, including Checkerboard Mesa. Mt Carmel lies 27 miles (45 minutes) northwest of Zion Canyon.

06 Mt Carmel

Several little towns line Hwy 89 north of the Hwy 9 junction. As you drive, look for little rock shops, art galleries and home-style cafes. Stop into the **Maynard Dixon Living History Museum** *(thunderbirdfoundation.com)*, 2 miles north of the Mt Carmel junction, to explore the rustic retreat of this seminal Western painter. The Great Depression–era painter created breathtaking, light-infused landscapes and scenes of social struggle. Guides lead visitors through the log home and studio where solitude fueled the artist's imaginative drive.

THE DRIVE: Hwy 89 is a fairly straight shot through pastoral lands; turn off from there onto Scenic Byway 12 where the red rock meets the road. Red Canyon is 45 miles northeast of Mt Carmel.

Virgin River and the Narrows, Zion Canyon, Utah

TOMASZ WOZNIAK/SHUTTERSTOCK

PHOTO OPPORTUNITY

The amphitheater's color at sunrise on Fairyland Point.

07 Red Canyon

Impossibly red monoliths rise up roadside as you reach **Red Canyon** *(fs.usda.gov/recarea/dixie)*. These parklands provide super-easy access to eerie, intensely colored formations. Check out the excellent geologic displays and pick up maps at the visitor center, where several moderate hiking trails begin. The 0.7-mile one-way **Arches Trail** passes 15 arches as it winds through a canyon. Legend has it that outlaw Butch Cassidy once rode in the area; a tough 8.9-mile hiking route, **Cassidy Trail**, bears his name.

THE DRIVE: Stop to take the requisite photo before you drive through two blasted-rock arches to continue on. Bryce Canyon National Park is only 12 miles down the road.

08 Bryce Canyon National Park

The pastel-colored, sandcastle-like spires of **Bryce Canyon National Park** *(nps.gov/brca)* look like something straight out of Dr Seuss' imagination. The 'canyon' is actually an amphitheater of formations eroded from the cliffs. Rim Road Scenic Drive (18 miles one way) roughly follows the canyon rim past the visitor center (8000ft), the lodge, incredible overlooks and trailheads, ending at **Rainbow Point** (9115ft). From mid-April through late October, an optional free shuttle bus departs from a staging area just north of the park.

The easiest walk would be to follow the **Rim Trail** that outlines Bryce Amphitheater from Fairyland Point to Bryce Point (up to 5.5 miles one way). Several sections are paved and wheelchair accessible, the most level being the half-mile between Sunrise and Sunset Points.

A number of moderate trails descend below the rim to the maze of fragrant juniper and undulating high-mountain desert. The **Navajo Loop** drops 521ft from Sunset Point. To avoid a super-steep ascent, follow the **Queen's Garden Trail** on the desert floor and hike up 320ft to Sunrise Point. From there take the shuttle, or follow the Rim Trail back to your car (2.9-mile round trip).

THE DRIVE: Only 11 miles east of Bryce Canyon, the town of Tropic is 2000ft lower in elevation – so expect it to be 10 degrees warmer.

09 Tropic

A farming community at heart, Tropic does provide services for park goers. There's a grocery store, several restaurants and a decent range of motels. Basing yourself here for two nights is less expensive than staying in the park. Note that the town is entirely seasonal: many businesses shut their doors tight from October through March.

DETOUR

Kodachrome Basin State Park

Start: 09 Tropic

Dozens of red, pink and white sandstone chimneys punctuate **Kodachrome Basin State Park** *(stateparks.utah.gov/parks/kodachrome-basin)*, named for its photogenic landscape by the National Geographic Society in 1948. The moderately easy, 3-mile round-trip **Panorama Trail** provides an overview of the otherworldly formations. Be sure to take the side trails to **Indian Cave**, where you can check out the handprints on the wall (cowboys' or Indians'?), and **Secret Passage**, a short spur through a narrow slot canyon.

The park lies 24 miles southeast of Bryce Canyon National Park, off Cottonwood Canyon Rd, south of Cannonville.

Fairyland Point, Bryce Canyon National Park, Utah
CHRISTOPHER MOSWITZER/SHUTTERSTOCK

35

SOUTHWEST

MONUMENT VALLEY & TRAIL OF THE ANCIENTS

★ BEST FOR

ANCIENT SITES

Hire a guide in Bluff or Monument Valley to help you see amazing rock art and ruins.

Petroglyph, Bears Ears, Bluff, Utah

DURATION: 5 DAYS

DISTANCE: 262 MILES / 422KM

GREAT FOR: NATURE, HISTORY & CULTURE

BEST TIME TO GO: OCTOBER THROUGH APRIL TO AVOID SCORCHING DESERT HEAT.

The red-rock beauty found here is no exception to southern Utah, but those who come this way want something more. Ancestral Puebloan history courses through the veins of these dusty-hued canyons, pocked with ruins of cliff dwellings and granaries, and marked with rock art. Photo highlights include the Valley of the Gods and Goosenecks State Park. Much of this area is protected in the Bears Ears National Monument.

LINK YOUR TRIP

32 San Juan Skyway & Million Dollar Highway
Swap Utah's ancient wonders for Colorado cliff dwellings via Hwy 162 southeast and Hwy 160E.

03 Four Corners Cruise
With the Mittens Buttes in the rearview mirror, pick up US 163 south to Hwy 160E.

01 Monument Valley

Don't worry if you feel like you've seen this place before. Monument Valley's monolithic chocolate-red buttes and colossal, colorful mesas have starred in countless films, TV shows and commercials. The most famous formations are conveniently visible from the 17-mile, rough-dirt scenic drive looping through **Monument Valley Navajo Tribal Park** *(navajonationparks.org)*, down a 4-mile spur road south of **Goulding's Lodge** *(gouldings.com)*, which has a small museum and also offers tours. Note that the park and scenery straddle the Utah–Arizona state line.

The only way to get into the backcountry to see rock art, natural arches and coves is by taking a Navajo-led tour on foot, on horseback or by vehicle. Easygoing guides have booths set up in the parking lot at the visitor center. Tours are

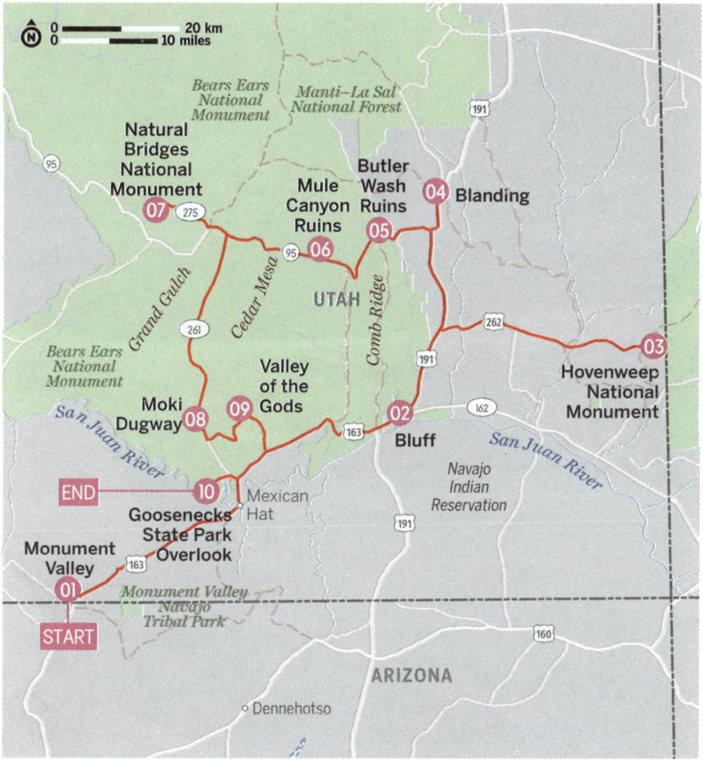

COLIN D. YOUNG/SHUTTERSTOCK

peppered with details about Diné culture, life on the reservation, movie trivia and whatever else comes to mind.

THE DRIVE: The monument's mesas diminish and then disappear in your rearview mirror as you head north, crossing the San Juan River and continuing along its valley for the 45 miles to Bluff, UT.

02 Bluff

Tiny tot Bluff (population 224) isn't much, but several good motels and a handful of restaurants – surrounded by stunning red rock – make it a cool little base for exploring. We've set up the trip for two nights in Monument Valley, two here in Bluff and one in Mexican Hat or back in the Valley. But distances are short enough that you could spend every night in Bluff and take daily forays to area sights.

Descendants of the town's pioneers recreated a tourable log-cabin settlement called **Bluff Fort** *(blufffort.org)*. Three miles west of town on public lands, the accessible **Sand Island Petroglyphs** *(blm.gov)* were created between 800 and 2500 years ago.

A few outfitters in town lead backcountry excursions that access rock art and ruins. History- and geology-minded outfit **Wild Expeditions** *(riversandruins.com)* takes rafts out along the San Juan. For more on area highlights, drop by **Bears Ears Education Center** *(bearsearspartnership.org/education-center)*.

THE DRIVE: The best route to Hovenweep is paved Hwy 262 (off Hwy 191), then follow the signs along Reservation Rd. From Bluff to the monument's main entrance is a slow, 42-mile drive (1¼ hours).

03 Hovenweep National Monument

Meaning 'deserted valley' in the Ute language, the archaeological sites of **Hovenweep National Monument** *(nps.gov/hove)* exist in splendid isolation. Most of the eight towers and unit houses you'll see in the Square Towers Group, accessed near the visitor center, were built from 1230 to 1275 CE. Imagine stacking each clay-formed block to create such tall structures on tiny ledges. You could easily spend a half-day or more hiking around the gorge's ruins. Other sites, which lie across the border in Colorado, require long hikes.

THE DRIVE: Bluff is the closest base in the area, so you'll have to drive to Hovenweep and back in one day. Moving onto Blanding, 26 miles north of Bluff, Hwy 191 is a rural road unimpeded by too many twists or turns.

04 Blanding

A special museum elevates small, agriculturally oriented Blanding a little above its totally drab name. The **Edge of the Cedars State Park Museum** *(stateparks.utah.gov/parks/edge-of-the-cedars)* is where you can learn more about the area's cultures, with its trove of archaeological treasures that have been gathered from across southeastern Utah. Outside, climb down the rickety ladder into a dark, earthy-smelling ceremonial kiva (an Ancestral Puebloan ceremonial structure) c 1100 CE. Can you feel a power to the place? (Just ignore the encroaching subdivision noise.)

Hunt's Trading Post sells handmade jewelry, Native American tribal music and books on Navajo teachings.

THE DRIVE: Heading west on Hwy 95, the scenery gets up close and personal. Butler Wash is only 14 miles along on free public lands; look for the signs.

05 Butler Wash Ruins

No need to hike for days into the backcountry here: it's only a half-mile tramp to views of the freely accessible **Butler Wash Ruins**, a 20-room cliff dwelling on public lands. Scramble over the slickrock boulders (follow the cairns) to see the sacred kivas, habitation and storage rooms associated with the Ancestral Puebloan (or Anasazi) Kayenta group of northern Arizona c 1300 CE.

THE DRIVE: Continue west on Hwy 95. After the road veers north, look for a sign announcing more ruins – about 14 miles along.

06 Mule Canyon Ruins

Though not particularly well preserved or evocative, the base of the tower, kiva and 12-room **Mule Canyon Ruins** sit almost roadside. Pottery found here links the population (c 1000 to 1150 CE) to the Mesa Verde group in southern Colorado. Nearby your eyes will play tricks on you at the wonderfully weird **House on Fire Ruin**.

THE DRIVE: Continue along through the cliffs and canyons of Hwy 95 until you branch off onto the even smaller Hwy 275. The monument is 18 miles west of Mule Canyon.

Owachomo Bridge, Natural Bridges National Monument, Utah

NATURE'S CHARM/SHUTTERSTOCK

FROM LEFT: NATURE'S CHARM/SHUTTERSTOCK, DANITA DELIMONT/SHUTTERSTOCK

House of Fire Ruins, Mule Canyon, Utah

TAKE ONLY PICTURES

Sadly enough, many invaluable archaeological sites in the area have been vandalized by thieves. Even casual visitors do irreparable damage by climbing on old dwelling walls or picking up 'just one' little pot shard. The old maxim 'take only pictures' bears repeating. Do not touch, move or remove any artifacts; it's against the law. The best way to explore ancient backcountry sites is with a well-informed, responsible guide.

07 Natural Bridges National Monument

The views at **Natural Bridges** *(nps.gov/nabr)* are of a white sandstone canyon (it's not red!). All three impressive and easily accessible bridges are visible from a 9-mile winding Scenic Drive loop with overlooks. The oldest is also the closest: take a half-mile hike to the beautifully delicate **Owachomo Bridge**, spanning 180ft at only 9ft thick. Note that trails to **Kachina** and **Siapu** bridges are not long, but they require navigating super-steep sections or ladders. Near the end of the drive, don't skip the 0.3-mile trail to the **Horsecollar Ruin** cliff-dwelling overlook.

THE DRIVE: Ocher-yellow to reddish-orange sandstone canyons surround you as you wend your way south on Rte 261. To your right is Cedar Mesa–Grand Gulch primitive area, a seriously challenging wilderness environment once part of the Bears

Ears National Monument. Driving the 38 miles to Moki Dugway will take at least an hour.

08 Moki Dugway

Along a roughly paved, hairpin-turn-filled section of road, Moki Dugway descends 1100ft in just 3 miles. Miners 'dug out' the extreme switchbacks in the 1950s to transport uranium ore. Note that the road is far from wide by today's standards, but there are places to pull out. You can't always see what's around the next bend, but you can see down the sheer drop-offs. Those afraid of heights (or in trailers over 24ft long), steer clear.

THE DRIVE: At the bottom of the dugway, prepare yourself for another wild ride. The turnoff for Valley of the Gods is about 2 miles ahead on your left.

09 Valley of the Gods

Think of the gravel road through the freely accessible **Valley of the Gods** *(blm.gov)* as a do-it-yourself roller coaster, with sharp, steep hills and quick turns around some amazing scenery. Locals call it 'mini–Monument Valley.' Download the brochure *(blm.gov/documents/utah/public-room/brochure/valley-gods-brochure)* to identify the strangely shaped sandstone monoliths and pinnacles (Seven Sailors, Lady on a Tub, Rooster Butte...) Allow an hour-plus for the 17 miles between Hwys 261 and 163. Do not attempt it without a 4WD if it has rained recently.

THE DRIVE: Once you emerge from the valley, follow Hwy 163 back west and take the little jog up Hwy 261 to the Goosenecks State Park spur, a total of 8 miles away.

10 Goosenecks State Park Overlook

Following the 4-mile spur to **Goosenecks State Park** *(stateparks.utah.gov/parks/goosenecks)* brings you to a mesmerizing view. From 1000ft above you can see how the San Juan River's path carved tight turns through sediment, leaving gooseneck-shaped spits of land untouched. The dusty park itself doesn't have much to speak of besides pit toilets and picnic tables.

Monument Valley (p290), Monument Valley Navajo Tribal Park, Arizona
F11PHOTO/SHUTTERSTOCK

PHOTO OPPORTUNITY

Monument Valley's monolithic buttes at sunrise or sunset.

36

★ BEST FOR

CULTURE

The 'miracle church' and arts and crafts in Chimayó.

SOUTHWEST

HIGH & LOW ROADS TO TAOS

DURATION: 1–4 DAYS

DISTANCE: 150 MILES / 241KM

GREAT FOR: HISTORY & CULTURE, FOOD & DRINK

BEST TIME TO GO: JUNE TO MARCH, WHEN TEMPERATURES ARE NOT TOO HOT.

El Santuario de Chimayó, Chimayó, New Mexico

Kick off in hip and historic Santa Fe, then rise from scrub-and-sandstone desert into ponderosa forests, snaking between the villages at the base of the 13,000ft Sangre de Cristos, until you reach the Taos Plateau. After checking out this little place that's lured artists, writers and hippies for the past century, dive south through the ruggedly sculpted Rio Grande Gorge, with the river coursing alongside you.

LINK YOUR TRIP

32 San Juan Skyway & Million Dollar Highway
The landscape becomes the art after leaving Española on US 84 north to US 160 east to Mesa Verde.

01 Route 66
From Santa Fe drive south on I-25 to Albuquerque for green chili specialties on Route 66.

01 Santa Fe

A destination for traders, artists and adventurers for more than 400 years, Santa Fe could have rested on its laurels for another 100 years without even trying. But change is afoot, and it's revving up the city in an utterly appealing way, from the mysteries of **Meow Wolf** *(meowwolf.com)* to innovations at the **Railyard District** to the revamp of facilities and exhibits at the venerable **Palace of the Governors** *(nmhistorymuseum.org/about/campus/the-palace-of-the-governors.html)*. But don't worry, the beloved historic buildings and local traditions are still there. In fact, walking among the historic adobe neighborhoods, and even around the tourist-filled plaza, there's no denying that 400-year-old Santa Fe has a timeless, earthy soul. Known as 'the city different,' it seamlessly blends historical and contemporary styles and casts a spell that's hard to resist: it's the second-oldest city in the US, the

NAGEL PHOTOGRAPHY/SHUTTERSTOCK

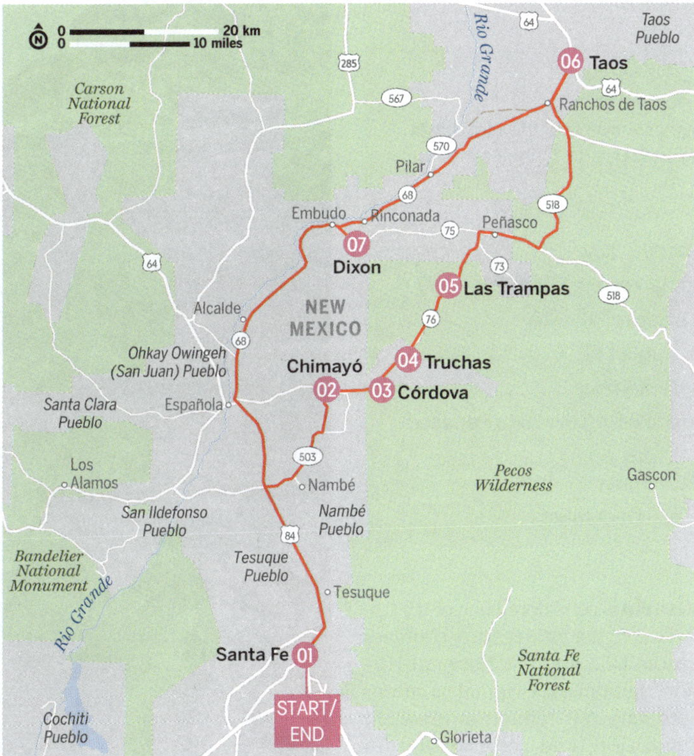

oldest state capital, and throws one of the oldest annual parties *(santafefiesta.org)*. The city is also considered the third-largest art market in the nation, and you'll find gourmet restaurants, world-class museums, opera, spas and more.

At 7000ft above sea level, Santa Fe is the highest state capital in the US, and a fantastic base for hiking, mountain biking, backpacking and skiing. The plaza area has the highest concentration of sights but it's worth a trip to Museum Hill, where you'll find the fantastic **Museum of International Folk Art** *(internationalfolkart.org)* and the excellent **Museum of Indian Arts & Culture** *(indianartsandculture.org)*, among others.

THE DRIVE: For this 28-mile leg, take Hwy 84/285 north, then exit right onto Hwy 503 toward Nambé. Turn left onto Juan Medina Rd, toward El Santuario de Chimayó.

02 Chimayó

Tucked into this little village is **El Santuario de Chimayó** *(holychimayo.us)*, one of the most important cultural sites in New Mexico. In 1816 this two-towered adobe chapel was built over a spot of earth said to have miraculous healing properties. Even today, the faithful come to rub the *tierra bendita* (holy dirt) from a small pit inside the church on whatever hurts; some mix it with water and drink it. The baked-mud walls are lined with crutches left behind by those healed by the dirt. During Holy Week, about 30,000 pilgrims walk to Chimayó from Santa Fe, Albuquerque and beyond in the largest Catholic pilgrimage in the US. The artwork in the *santuario* is worth a trip on its own.

Chimayó also has a centuries-old tradition of producing some of the finest weavings in the area and there are a handful of family-run galleries. Irvin Trujillo, a seventh-generation weaver whose carpets can be seen at the Smithsonian in Washington DC, works out of his gallery **Centinela Traditional Arts** *(chimayoweavers.com)*. Naturally dyed blankets, vests and pillows are sold, and you can watch the artists weaving on handlooms. Just up the road, the Oviedo family has been carving native woods since 1739. Today the **Oviedo Gallery** *(oviedoart.us)*, housed in the centuries-old family farm, also sells carvings and a wide range of bronze sculptures made in the on-site foundry.

THE DRIVE: Follow Hwy 76 north for a few miles, and take the right-side turnoff to Córdova. The Sabinita López Ortiz shop will be on your right, not very far down the road.

03 Córdova

Down in the Rio Quemado Valley, this little town is best known for its unpainted, austere santos (saints) carvings created by local masters such as George López, José Dolores López and Sabinita López Ortiz – all members of the same artistic family. Stop and see their work at the **Sabinita López Ortiz shop** – one of a few galleries in town. Cash or check only for this one.

THE DRIVE: Hop back on Hwy 76 north, and climb higher into the Sangre de Cristo Mountains, for about 4 miles.

LOCAL KNOWLEDGE

LOW ROAD FESTIVALS

Try to catch – or avoid, if you hate crowds – some of the highlights from around the year on the High and Low Roads. Check websites for exact dates each year:

Easter (Chimayó) – March/April

Taos Pueblo Pow-Wow *(taos.org/events)* – July

International Folk Art Market (*folkartmarket.org*; Santa Fe) – July

Spanish Market (*spanishcolonial.org*; Santa Fe) – July

Santa Fe Indian Market *(swaia.org)* – August

Santa Fe Fiesta *(santafefiesta.org)* – September

High Road Art Tour (*highroadnewmexico.com*; Hwy 76 to Peñasco) – September

Dixon Studio Tour *(dixonarts.org)* – November

Christmas on Canyon Road (Santa Fe) – December

04 Truchas

Rural New Mexico at its most sincere is showcased in Truchas, originally established by the Spaniards in the 18th century. Robert Redford's *The Milagro Beanfield War* was filmed here (but don't bother with the movie – the book it's based on, by John Nichols, is waaaay better). Narrow roads, many unpaved, wend between century-old adobes. Fields of grass and alfalfa spread toward the sheer walls and plunging ridges that define the western flank of the Truchas Peaks. Between the run-down homes are some wonderful art galleries, which double as workshops for local weavers, painters, sculptors and other artists.

THE DRIVE: Continue north on Hwy 76 for around 8 miles, transecting the little valleys of Ojo Sarco and Cañada de los Alamos.

05 Las Trampas

Completed in 1780 and constantly defended against Apache raids, the **Church of San José de Gracia** is considered one of the finest surviving 18th-century churches in the USA and is a National Historic Landmark. Original paintings and carvings remain in excellent condition, and self-flagellation bloodstains from Los Hermanos Penitentes (a 19th-century religious order with a strong following in the northern mountains of New Mexico) are still visible. On your way out of town, look right to see the amazing irrigation aqueduct, carved from tree trunks!

If you're skipping Taos for now and returning to Santa Fe, take a fun chutes-and-ladders-style shortcut and turn left onto Hwy 75 in Las Trampas for a gorgeous drop to Dixon, a nice stop for lunch or a glass of wine.

THE DRIVE: Continue north on Hwy 76, through lovely Chamisal. At the T, turn right onto Hwy 75 and stay on it through

Rio Grande Gorge, Taos (p300), New Mexico

TAMARA STANALAND/SHUTTERSTOCK

PHOTO OPPORTUNITY

Capture the gorge and mountains at once, from Hwy 68 near Taos.

WINTER CALLS

One of the biggest winter draws to this part of New Mexico is the skiing and snowboarding, and **Taos Ski Valley** *(skitaos.org)* is the premier place to hit the slopes. There's just something about the abundant powder, wicked steeps and laid-back atmosphere that makes this mountain a wintry heaven-on-Earth – if heaven has a 3274ft vertical drop, that is.

Offering some of the most difficult terrain in the US, the Taos Ski Valley is a fantastic place to zip down steep tree glades into untouched powder bowls. Seasoned skiers luck out, with just over half of the 110 trails ranked expert, but there's also an award-winning ski school, so complete beginners thrive here too. The resort has a peak elevation of 12,481ft and gets an average of 300in of snowfall annually. There is also a skier-cross obstacle course at its popular terrain park.

That said, **Ski Santa Fe** *(skisantafe.com)* is no slouch. Less than 30 minutes from the Santa Fe plaza, it boasts the same fluffy powder (though usually a little less), with an even higher base elevation (10,350ft). Briefly admire the awesome desert and mountain vistas, then fly down chutes, steep bump runs or long groomers. The resort caters to families and expert skiers alike with its varied terrain. The quality and length of the ski season can vary wildly from year to year depending on how much snow the mountain gets (you can almost always count on a good storm in late March).

Peñasco and Vadito. At Hwy 518, turn left toward Taos. At the end of the road, turn right on Paseo del Pueblo Sur/Hwy 68 and take it on into Taos – around 32 miles in total.

06 Taos

Taos is a place undeniably dominated by the power of its landscape: 12,300ft often-snowcapped peaks rise behind town, while a sage-speckled plateau unrolls to the west before plunging 800ft straight down into the **Rio Grande Gorge**. The sky can be a searing sapphire blue or an ominous parade of rumbling thunderheads. And then there are the sunsets...

The pueblo here is one of the oldest continuously inhabited communities in the US and it roots the town in a long history with a rich cultural legacy – which also includes conquistadors, Catholicism and cowboys.

Skilift, Santa Fe (p296), New Mexico

ROSCHETZKY PHOTOGRAPHY/SHUTTERSTOCK

Taos remains a relaxed and eccentric place, with classic mud-brick buildings, quirky cafes and excellent restaurants. It's both rural and worldly, and a little otherworldly.

The best thing to do is walk around the plaza area soaking in the aura of the place. But you also won't want to miss **Taos Pueblo** *(taospueblo.com)*. Built around 1450 and continuously inhabited ever since, it's the largest existing multistoried pueblo structure in the USA and one of the best surviving examples of traditional adobe construction. Also well worth a visit is the **Millicent Rogers Museum** *(millicentrogers.org),* filled with pottery, jewelry, baskets and textiles from the private collection of a model and oil heiress who moved to Taos in 1947 and acquired one of the best collections of Native American and Spanish Colonial art in the USA.

THE DRIVE: On this 26-mile leg, cruise the Low Road back toward Santa Fe by taking Hwy 68 south. Just before the road drops downhill, there's a large pullout with huge views, so hop out and see what you're leaving behind. Then head down into the Rio Grande Gorge. Go left on Hwy 75 to Dixon.

RAISA NASTUKOVA/SHUTTERSTOCK

Wheeler Peak, Taos, New Mexico

NATURE CALLS

Want to see the scenery without a pane of glass in front of your face? Off the High Road, take a stroll on the **Santa Barbara Trail**, which follows a trout-filled creek through mixed forest into the Pecos Wilderness; it's pretty flat and easygoing. To reach the trailhead, take Hwy 73 from Peñasco and follow the signs.

Off the Low Road, turn onto Hwy 570 at Pilar and check out the **Orilla Verde Recreation Area** *(blm.gov),* where you can hang out or camp along the Rio Grande (or tube or fish in it). Hike up to the rim on Old 570, a dirt road blocked by a landslide, with expansive vistas of the Taos Plateau and the Sangre de Cristos.

Some of the best views in the state are from the top of **Lake Peak** (12,409ft), which can be reached on a day hike starting at the Santa Fe Ski Basin.

From Taos Ski Valley, you can day-hike to the top of **Wheeler Peak** (13,161ft), New Mexico's highest summit (the views are pretty good up there, too). For trail maps and more information, go to the **Travel Bug** *(mapsofnewmexico.com)* bookstore in Santa Fe or check *taos.org*.

07 Dixon

This small agricultural and artistic community is spread along the gorgeous Rio Embudo Valley. It's famous for its apples but plenty of other crops are grown here too, including some of the grapes used by two award-winning local wineries, **Vivác** *(vivacwinery.com)* and **La Chiripada** *(lachiripada.com),* both of which have tasting rooms. In summer and fall, there's a farmers market on Wednesday mornings, with food fresh from the fields.

On the first weekend in November, local artists open their homes and studios to the public in New Mexico's oldest **studio tour** *(dixonarts.org).*

Our favorite art gallery is actually on Hwy 68, in Rinconada, just north of Hwy 75: **Rift Gallery** *(riftgallery.com)* features masterful ceramics and stonework.

In summer, ask at the local food co-op and some kind soul might point you to the waterfalls, up a nearby dirt road.

THE DRIVE: Back on Hwy 68, head south along the river, through Embudo (a great lunch stop) and out of the gorge. Continue through Española, where you'll meet Hwy 84/285, which you can take back to Santa Fe. This leg is around 47 miles.

STAY AWHILE

SANTA FE

BY MARGOT BIGG

Driving from the sparse New Mexico desert into Santa Fe feels like crossing into another dimension. Arid expanses give way to single-story strip malls, a last nod to all-American sprawl before you enter the Santa Fe Historic District, where the buildings adhere to strict architectural guidelines. In other words, they have to resemble the earth-toned pueblo-revival and territorial architectural styles that give the nation's oldest state capital its distinct look. It's this beautiful architecture that made me fall in love with Santa Fe, and it's what keeps me coming back.

While there are certainly some great attractions to check out, from the **Georgia O'Keeffe Museum** *(okeeffemuseum.org)* to the **San Miguel Chapel** *(sanmiguelchapelsantafe.org)* – the oldest church in the country – I find that the best way to spend time in Santa Fe is to simply wander around and soak it all in. A good place to start is at the Santa Fe Plaza, where you can window-shop at art galleries before heading up to the Cross of the Martyrs, a hilltop cross and popular spot to take in one of Santa Fe's famous technicolor sunsets.

Don't miss the chance to try some authentic New Mexican dishes, many of which are local takes on Mexican and Tex-Mex classics, but with the addition of roasted Hatch chili sauce. When you order, you'll be asked if you want red or green sauce – ask for it 'Christmas style' to get half of each.

LINK YOUR TRIP

Spend a few days in Santa Fe at the beginning or end of the 36 **High & Low Roads to Taos** (p296) road trip.

Left: Pueblo-revival stores, Santa Fe, New Mexico; Right: San Miguel Chapel, Santa Fe, New Mexico

FROM LEFT: LYNDA MCFAUL/SHUTTERSTOCK, LIZ COUGHLAN/SHUTTERSTOCK

PLACES TO STAY

Inn of the Turquoise Bear
Housed in a mud adobe home dating to 1886, this cozy inn near the Santa Fe Plaza features only nine rooms, all with kiva fireplaces. An included breakfast is served in a plant-filled courtyard (or indoors on cold days), and includes a mix of Santa Fe specialties and continental classics. *turquoisebear.com*

Ojo Santa Fe
Road-weary travelers can soak away their aches and pains in the warm, spring-fed pools and tubs before retiring to a spacious room or casita for a solid night's sleep at this spa resort just outside the city. *ojosparesorts.com*

37

★ BEST FOR

OUTDOORS

McDonald Observatory's nighttime star parties.

SOUTHWEST

BIG BEND SCENIC LOOP

DURATION: 5–7 DAYS

DISTANCE: 702 MILES / 1130KM

GREAT FOR: NATURE

BEST TIME TO GO: BEST BETWEEN FEBRUARY AND APRIL – BEFORE THE HEAT SETS IN.

McDonald Observatory, Fort Davis, Texas

Getting to visit Big Bend National Park and experience endless vistas straight out of an old Western would be reason enough to make this trip. But you'll also have plenty of fun along the way, exploring quirky small towns that are definitive road-trip material. Unforgettable experiences in West Texas include minimalist art installations, nighttime astronomy parties and thriving ghost towns.

LINK YOUR TRIP

03 Four Corners Cruise
Leave the Marfa Lights for super-sized wonders in the Southwest via I-10 west to I-25 north.

38 Hill Country
Honky-tonks and wildflowers? Yep, just take I-10 south to start in San Antonio.

01 El Paso

Start your trip in El Paso, a border city that's wedged into a remote corner of West Texas. While here, take advantage of the great Mexican food you can find all over the city – it's right across the river from Mexico – and enjoy El Paso's many free museums. Downtown, the **El Paso Museum of Art** *(epma.art)* has a terrific Southwestern collection.

Don't miss the **El Paso Holocaust Museum** *(elpasoholocaustmuseum.org)*, which hosts amazingly thoughtful and moving exhibits that are imaginatively presented for maximum impact.

To the west, you'll find several good restaurants and watering holes in the new and developing Montecillo commercial and residential district.

THE DRIVE: Head southeast on I-10 for just over two hours, then turn south onto TX 118 toward Fort Davis. The area belongs to both the Chihuahuan Desert

KRIS DAVIDSON/LONELY PLANET

and the Davis Mountains, resulting in a compelling landscape where the endless horizons are suddenly interrupted by rock formations springing from the earth.

02 Fort Davis

Here's why you'll want to plan on being in Fort Davis on either a Tuesday, Friday or Saturday: to go to an evening star party at **McDonald Observatory** *(mcdonaldobservatory.org)*. The observatory has some of the clearest and darkest skies in North America, not to mention some of the most powerful telescopes.

Besides that, nature lovers will enjoy **Davis Mountains State Park** *(tpwd.texas.gov)*, and history buffs can immerse themselves at the 1854 **Fort Davis National Historic Site** *(nps.gov/foda)*, a well-preserved frontier military post that's impressively situated at the foot of Sleeping Lion Mountain.

THE DRIVE: Marfa is just 20 minutes south on TX 17, a two-lane country road where tumbleweeds bounce slowly by and lazily congregate around the barbed-wire fences.

03 Marfa

Marfa got its first taste of fame when Rock Hudson, Elizabeth Taylor and James Dean came to town to film *Giant* (1956).

But these days, this tiny town with one stoplight draws visitors from around the world for a different reason: its art scene. Donald Judd single-handedly put Marfa on the art-world map in the 1980s when he used a bunch of abandoned military buildings to create one of the world's largest permanent installations of minimalist art at the **Chinati Foundation** *(chinati.org)*.

Art galleries are sprinkled around town, exploring everything from photography to sculpture to modern art. **Ballroom Marfa** *(ballroommarfa.org)* is a great gallery to catch the vibe. Try not to visit on a Monday or Tuesday, when many businesses are closed.

THE DRIVE: Alpine is about 30 minutes east of Marfa on Hwy 90/67.

04 Alpine

The biggest little town in the area, Alpine is the county seat, a college town (Sul Ross University is here) and the best place to stock up on whatever you need before you head down into the Chihuahuan Desert.

Stop by the **Museum of the Big Bend** *(museumofthebigbend.com)* to brush up on the history of the Big Bend region. But don't expect it to be dry and dusty. The multimedia exhibits are big and eye-catching, and display-reading is kept to a minimum. Most impressive? The enormous replica wing bone of the Texas pterosaur found in Big Bend – the largest flying creature ever found, with an estimated wing span of almost 40ft.

THE DRIVE: Keep heading east. In 15 miles, look south for the guerilla art installation *Target Marathon*, a fun nod to *Prada Marfa*. In another 15 miles you'll reach the seriously small town of Marathon. The views aren't much during this stretch of the drive, but Big Bend will make up for all that.

05 Marathon

This tiny railroad town has two claims to fame. It's the closest town to Big Bend's north entrance – providing a last chance to fill up your car and your stomach – and it's got the **Gage Hotel** (*gagehotel.com*), a true Texas treasure that's worth a peek even if you can't manage an overnight stay.

THE DRIVE: Heading south on US 385, it's 40 miles to the northern edge of Big Bend, and 40 more to reach the Chisos Basin, the heart of the park. For most of the way, the flat road affords miles and miles of views.

06 Big Bend National Park

At 1252 sq miles, this national park is almost the size of Rhode Island. Some people duck in for an afternoon, hike a quick trail and leave, but we recommend staying at least two nights to hit the highlights. A park entrance pass costs $30 per vehicle, and it's valid for seven days.

Seventeen miles south of the Persimmon Gap Visitor Center, pull over for the **Fossil Discovery Exhibit** (*nps.gov/bibe*), which spotlights the dinosaurs and other creatures that inhabited this region beginning 130 million years ago.

With more than 200 miles of trails to explore, it's no wonder hiking is one of the most popular activities, with many of the best hikes leaving from the **Chisos Basin**. Hit the short, paved **Window View Trail** at sunset, then hike the 4.4-mile **Window Trail** the next morning before it gets too hot. Spend the afternoon hiking the shady 4.8-mile **Lost Mine Trail**, or take a scenic drive to see the eerily abandoned **Sam Nail Ranch** or the scenic **Santa Elena Canyon**.

THE DRIVE: From the west park entrance, turn left after 3 miles, then follow signs for Terlingua Ghost Town, just past Terlingua proper. It's about a 45-minute drive from the middle of the park.

07 Terlingua

Terlingua is a unique combination: it's both a ghost town and a social hub. When the local cinnabar mines closed down in the 1940s, the town dried up and blew away like a tumbleweed, leaving buildings that fell into ruins.

But the area has slowly repopulated, businesses have been built on top of the ruins, and locals gather here for two daily rituals. In the late afternoon, everyone drinks beer on the porch of **Terlingua Trading Company** (*facebook.com/terlinguatradingcompany*). And after the sun goes down, the party moves next door to **Starlight Theater**, where there's live music most nights.

THE DRIVE: Continue west on Rte 170, also known as the River Road, for a gorgeous drive along the Rio Grande through Big Bend Ranch State Park. In 60 miles or so you'll reach Presidio. Head north on US 67 to return to Marfa, then cut west on US 90.

08 Prada Marfa

So you're driving along a two-lane highway out in the middle of nowhere, when suddenly a small building appears in the distance like a mirage. You glance over and see…a Prada store? Known as the *Prada Marfa* (although it's really closer to Valentine) this art installation set against the backdrop of dusty West Texas is a tongue-in cheek commentary on consumerism.

THE DRIVE: Take US 90 back to I-10 and head west back to El Paso.

MARFA LIGHTS VIEWING AREA

Flickering beneath the Chinati Mountains, the Marfa Lights have been capturing travelers' imaginations for over a century. The first account of mysterious lights appearing and disappearing on the horizon came from a cowboy in 1883, who thought they were Apache signal fires. Numerous studies have attempted to explain the apparition, but the only thing scientists agree on is that they have no idea what causes it.

The **Marfa Lights Viewing Area**, on the south side of the highway 9 miles east of Marfa, holds benches, binoculars and restrooms, plus a placard explaining the lights are 'an unusual phenomenon similar to a miracle.' From the platform, look south to find the red blinking light (that one's real). Just to the right, just maybe, you'll see the Marfa Lights doing their ghostly thing.

Santa Elena Canyon, Big Bend National Park, Texas

YGGDRASILL/SHUTTERSTOCK

38

★ BEST FOR

CULTURE

Two-stepping at Texas' oldest dance hall in Gruene.

SOUTHWEST

HILL COUNTRY

Gruene Hall (p313), Gruene, Texas

DURATION: 2–5 DAYS

DISTANCE: 229 MILES / 369KM

GREAT FOR: NATURE, FAMILIES

BEST TIME TO GO: IN MARCH AND APRIL FOR WILDFLOWER SEASON.

In March and early April especially, when wildflowers are blooming, this is one of the prettiest drives in all of Texas – perfect for a day trip or a meandering, low-stress vacation. En route, you can rummage through antique stores, listen to live music, dig in to a plate of barbecue, and learn about the US president who called the Hill Country home.

LINK YOUR TRIP

07 Cajun Country
For po'boys and crawfish, take I-10 east to Lafayette, then head south on US 90, with a left to Thibodaux.

37 Big Bend Scenic Loop
West Texas? Breathtaking, quirky and big. Head northwest on I-10 to El Paso.

01 San Antonio

While sprawling San Antonio isn't part of the Hill Country, it's a great launching point for your trip. Don't miss the lovely, European-style **River Walk**, a paved canal that winds its way through downtown and is lined with colorful cafes, hotel gardens and stone footbridges. It stretches north to the museum district and south to the missions, adding pretty mileage for walking and cycling. For the best overview, hop on a **Rio San Antonio** *(goriocruises.com)* cruise.

Whatever you do, pay your respects at the **Alamo** *(thealamo.org)*, the beloved historic site where revolutionaries fought for Texas' independence from Mexico.

THE DRIVE: Ready to get out of town? Head 50 miles northwest on I-10 to reach Comfort, less than an hour's drive from downtown San Antonio. When the wildflowers are blooming, detouring north on Waring-Welfare Rd then back on TX 473 makes a nice scenic drive.

02 Comfort

Somehow, remarkably, under the tourist radar, the 19th-century German settlement of Comfort is perhaps the Hill Country's most idyllic town. The rough-hewn limestone homes in its beautifully restored historic center, focused around High and 8th Sts, date from the late 1800s.

Shopping for antiques is the number-one activity here, but you'll also find a few good restaurants, a couple of wineries and, as the town's name suggests, an easy way of life. Start at the **Comfort Antique Mall** *(facebook.com/ComfortAntiqueMall)*, where you can pick up a map of antique stores, or discover your options by checking out the website of the **Chamber of Commerce** *(comfortchamber.com)*.

THE DRIVE: The interstate is a straight shot for the 18-mile drive northwest to Kerrville, but we prefer TX 27, a back road through serene farmland.

03 Kerrville

The Hill Country can feel a bit fussy at times, but not Kerrville. What it lacks in historic charm, it makes up for in size, offering plenty of services for travelers, as well as easy access to kayaking, canoeing and swimming on the Guadalupe River. Stretch your legs on the **River Trail** *(kerrvilletx.gov)*, which runs alongside the Guadalupe River for several miles. The best place to hop in the water is **Kerrville-Schreiner Park**.

Check out an eye-catching collection of cowboy art at the **Museum of Western Art** *(museumofwesternart.com)*. The building itself is beautiful, with hand-made mesquite parquet floors and unique vaulted domes overhead.

THE DRIVE: Take TX 16 northeast of town for half an hour (25 miles) to get to Fredericksburg.

04 Fredericksburg

The unofficial capital of the Hill Country, Fredericksburg is a 19th-century German settlement that packs a lot of charm into a relatively small area. Its street signs proclaim 'Willkommen,' and you'll be welcome indeed along its main street, lined with historic buildings that house German restaurants, beer gardens, antique stores and wine-tasting rooms. Admiral Chester Nimitz, Commander of the US Pacific Fleet during WWII, grew up here, and the town now holds the only US museum devoted to the conflict, the fascinating, multi-part **National Museum of the Pacific War** *(pacificwarmuseum.org)*.

Many of the shops are typical tourist-town offerings, but there are enough interesting stores to make it fun to wander, while Fredericksburg also makes a great base for checking out the local peach orchards and vineyards. A few miles east, **Wildseed Farms** *(wildseedfarms.com)* holds cultivated fields of wildflowers, as well as its own winery, and sells seeds along with wildflower-related gifts.

THE DRIVE: Five miles southeast of Fredericksburg on US 290, turn right, and follow Ranch Rd 1376 for another 4.5 miles. Luckenbach only holds a handful of buildings, so don't panic that you've missed it.

05 Luckenbach

It's hard to imagine a more laid-back place than little Luckenbach, a beguiling mix of genuine Wild West village and themed outlaw-music enclave. All visitors leave their vehicles at the edge of town; there's paid admission for larger events, but normally you can simply stroll in.

The original 1849 trading post, now the **Luckenbach General Store** *(luckenbachtexas.com)*, serves as the local post office, saloon and community center; there's usually live music out on the lawns (no cover) or in the **Dance Hall** nearby. Pick up some barbecue or bratwurst from the 'Feed Lot,' settle down at one of the plentiful picnic tables beneath the trees, and bask in the small-town atmosphere.

THE DRIVE: Take Luckenbach Rd 4.5 miles back north to US 290. The LBJ Ranch is now just 7 miles east, entered right off the highway.

06 LBJ Ranch

You don't have to be a history buff to appreciate the **LBJ Ranch** *(nps.gov/lyjo)*, the family home of the 36th president of the United States. This beautiful piece of Texas land is where Lyndon B Johnson was born, lived and died.

The park includes the Johnson birthplace, the one-room schoolhouse where he briefly attended school and a neighboring farm that now serves as a living history museum. The centerpiece of the park is the ranch house where LBJ and Lady Bird lived and where he spent so much time during his presidency that it became known as the 'Texas White House.'

You can also see the Johnson family cemetery, where LBJ and Lady Bird are both buried under sprawling oak trees.

Stop by the state-run visitor center at the entrance to get your free park permit and a map.

THE DRIVE: LBJ's childhood home is just 15 minutes (14 miles) east on US 290.

07 Johnson City

You might assume Johnson City was named after President Johnson, but the bragging rights go to James Polk Johnson, a town settler back in the late 1800s. The fact that James Johnson's nephew went on to become president of the United States was just pure luck.

Here you'll find **Lyndon Johnson's Boyhood Home** *(nps.gov/lyjo)*, which Johnson himself had restored for personal posterity. Park rangers from the visitor center – where you can also find local information and exhibits on the president and first lady – offer free guided tours that meet on the front porch. On the surface, it's just an old Texas house, but it's fascinating when you think about the boy who grew up there.

THE DRIVE: Follow US 290 6 miles south, and then another 19 miles east, to reach Dripping Springs. Turn south there, on Ranch Rd 12, to reach Wimberley after a total 45-minute drive of 39 miles.

DETOUR

Austin

Start: 07 Johnson City

Since this trip is all about winding your way through the Hill Country, we didn't list Austin as a stop. After all, with its great restaurants, legendary nightlife and fine museums – not to mention the mid-March **South by Southwest** *(sxsw.com)* – Austin warrants a whole trip to itself.

However, we'd be remiss if we didn't mention that when you get to Dripping Springs, you only have to continue another half-hour east on US 290 (24 miles) to reach the Texas state capital. To rejoin the route, return to Dripping Springs, or drive for 50 minutes (37 miles) southwest to the next stop, Wimberley.

08 Wimberley

A popular weekend escape for Austinites, this artists' community gets absolutely bonkers during summer weekends – and especially on the first Saturday of each month from March to December, when local art galleries, shops and craftspeople set up booths for **Wimberley Market Days** *(wimberleymarketday.com)*, a bustling collection of live music, food and around 500 vendors at Lion's Field on RR 2325. Keep an eye out, too, for the **48 painted cowboy boots** *(bootifulwimberley.com)* scattered around town.

For superb scenic views of the surrounding limestone hills, take a drive along FM 32, otherwise known as the Devil's Backbone. From Wimberley, head south on RR 12 to FM 32, then turn right toward Canyon Lake. The road gets steeper, then winds out onto a craggy ridge – the 'backbone' – with a 360-degree vista.

Afterwards, cool off at Wimberley's famous **Blue Hole** *(wimberleyparksandrec.com/blue-hole-regional-park)*, one of the Hill Country's best-loved swimming holes, in the calm, shady and crystal-clear waters of Cypress Creek.

THE DRIVE: Keep going south on Ranch Rd 12; San Marcos is about 20 minutes southeast, through 15 more miles of (mostly) undeveloped countryside.

Luckenbach General Store
Luckenbach, Texas
CIRE NOTREVO/SHUTTERSTOCK

U. S. POST-OFFICE
1850 LUCKENBACH, TX, 1971
OPEN 9AM
LIVE MUSIC DAILY
HONDO

PHOTO OPPORTUNITY

Bluebonnets – pose in a field full of wildflowers.

SCENIC DRIVE: WILDFLOWER TRAILS

You know spring has arrived in Texas when you see cars pulling up roadside and families climbing out to take the requisite picture of their kids surrounded by bluebonnets, Texas' state flower. From March to April in Hill Country, Indian paintbrushes, wine-cups and bluebonnets are at their peak.

Taking Rte 16 and FM 1323, north from Fredericksburg and east to Willow City, is usually a good route.

09 San Marcos

Around central Texas, 'San Marcos' is practically synonymous with 'outlet malls.' Bargain shoppers can make a full day of it at two side-by-side shopping extravaganzas. It's not exactly in keeping with the spirit of the Hill Country, but it's a popular enough activity that we had to point it out.

The fashion-oriented **San Marcos Premium Outlets** *(outlets.com)* is enormous – and enormously popular – with 150 name-brand outlets. Across the street, **Tanger Outlets** *(tanger.com/sanmarcos)* has more modest offerings, with brands that aren't that expensive to start with, but it's still fun to hunt for deals.

THE DRIVE: Shoot 12 miles southwest down I-35 to the turnoff for Canyon Lake. Gruene is just a couple of miles west of the highway.

DETOUR

Lockhart

Start: 09 San Marcos

People travel from all over the state to dig into brisket, sausage and ribs in Lockhart, officially designated the Barbecue Capital of Texas. Lucky for you, you only have to detour 18 miles to experience the smoky goodness. You can eat very well for less than $20 at the following places:

Black's Barbecue *(blacksbbq.com)* A Lockhart favorite since 1932, with sausage so good Lyndon Johnson had them cater a party at the nation's capital.

Kreuz Market *(kreuzmarket.com)* Serving Lockhart since 1900, the barn-like Kreuz Market uses a dry rub, which means you shouldn't insult them by asking for barbecue sauce – they don't serve it, and the meat doesn't need it.

Smitty's Market *(smittysmarket.com)* The blackened pit room and homely dining room are all original (they used to have knives chained to the tables). Choose from a succulent array of barbecued meats – and feel free to ask them to trim the fat off the brisket.

10 Gruene

Founded in the 1840s, the endearing little village of Gruene was wiped out during the Depression a century later. All except **Gruene Hall** *(gruenehall.com)*, that is. This legendary 1878 dance hall never closed, making it the oldest in Texas. It now attracts a constant flow of day-trippers, meaning the nearby streets are filled with antique stores, cafes, and shops selling housewares, gifts and souvenirs. Come if you can for **Old Gruene Market Days** *(gruenemarketdays.com)*, held the third weekend of the month, February through November, and the first weekend of December.

Gruene Hall itself opens early, so you can stop by any time to toss back a longneck, two-step on the well-worn wooden dance floor or play horseshoes out in the yard. There's only a cover on weekend nights and when big acts are playing, so at least stroll through and soak up the vibe.

THE DRIVE: You don't even have to get back on the interstate; New Braunfels is just 3 miles south.

11 New Braunfels

The historic town of New Braunfels was the first German settlement in Texas. In summer, visitors flock here to float down the Guadalupe River in an inner tube – a Texas tradition. There are plenty of outfitters in town, including **Rockin' R River Rides** *(rockinr.com)*. Their tube rentals include shuttle service, while for an additional fee they'll hook you up with an ice chest – to keep your drinks cold – and a tube to float it on.

THE DRIVE: From New Braunfels it's a 32-mile drive southeast back to San Antonio on I-35.

Bluebonnets
E_COTNER/GETTY IMAGES

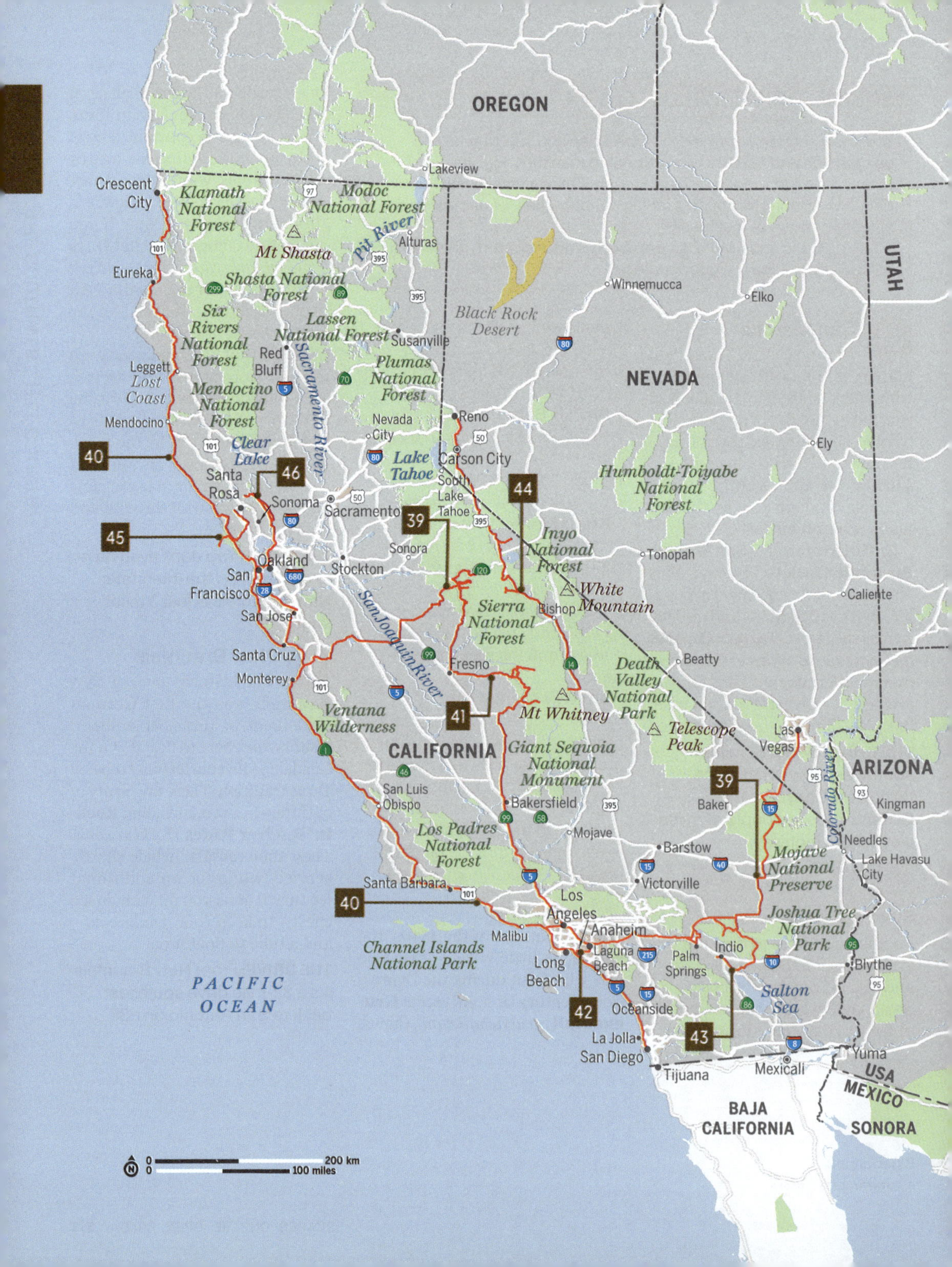
OREGON
NEVADA
UTAH
ARIZONA
CALIFORNIA
BAJA CALIFORNIA
SONORA
USA
MEXICO
PACIFIC OCEAN
Crescent City
Eureka
Leggett
Lost Coast
Mendocino
Klamath National Forest
Modoc National Forest
Mt Shasta
Pit River
Shasta National Forest
Six Rivers National Forest
Lassen National Forest
Plumas National Forest
Mendocino National Forest
Clear Lake
Sacramento River
Red Bluff
Susanville
Alturas
Lakeview
Black Rock Desert
Winnemucca
Elko
Ely
Reno
Carson City
Nevada City
Lake Tahoe
South Lake Tahoe
Humboldt-Toiyabe National Forest
Santa Rosa
Sonoma
Sacramento
Oakland
San Francisco
San Jose
Stockton
Sonora
Santa Cruz
Monterey
San Joaquin River
Inyo National Forest
White Mountain
Tonopah
Caliente
Bishop
Sierra National Forest
Fresno
Mt Whitney
Death Valley National Park
Beatty
Telescope Peak
Las Vegas
Ventana Wilderness
Giant Sequoia National Monument
San Luis Obispo
Bakersfield
Mojave
Baker
Kingman
Colorado River
Needles
Lake Havasu City
Barstow
Victorville
Mojave National Preserve
Los Padres National Forest
Santa Barbara
Los Angeles
Anaheim
Malibu
Long Beach
Laguna Beach
Palm Springs
Indio
Joshua Tree National Park
Blythe
Channel Islands National Park
Salton Sea
Oceanside
La Jolla
San Diego
Tijuana
Mexicali
Yuma
40
46
45
39
44
41
42
43
0 200 km
0 100 miles

YAYA ERNST/SHUTTERSTOCK

Redwood National Park (p333), California

CALIFORNIA & NEVADA

EXPLORE

CALIFORNIA & NEVADA

California and Nevada have long enticed travelers dreaming of fame and fortune. Ever since Spanish conquistadors and gold-rush pioneers stalked the region, the quest for riches and new beginnings has led to the desert expanses and glitzy cities of these neighboring states. But even gold seems overrated alongside the platinum glint of the Pacific, and no movie star is ever as big as California's giant sequoias.

Hang tight around curves that hug the coastline on legendary Hwy 1. Follow country lanes to Napa and Sonoma Valley vineyards. And take a head-spinning trip on Sierra Nevada byways past jagged peaks and glacial lakes. Or test your luck in Las Vegas, where you'll quickly see that there's more to Sin City than casinos and neon lights.

Las Vegas

The irresistible allure of Vegas is much more nuanced than it first appears. Incredible festivals and live events lie at the heart of its appeal, but it also has a spectacular culinary scene, fabulous accommodations and the kind of shopping that makes you hope you win big in the casino. When it all gets to be too much, Las Vegas lies amid a world of dramatic natural beauty that will tempt your inner explorer and adventurer.

San Francisco

Somewhere close to the midpoint of the Californian coast, San Francisco is a special city. For one thing, it's convenient for just about anywhere, whether you're heading north, south or inland. It's also the kind of city that captures the freedom-loving spirit of America in the best possible way, with amazing food, stunning natural surrounds, and a patchwork of neighborhoods, each with its own magical, zany, anything-is-possible spirit.

Fresno

Fresno wouldn't win a beauty contest, but it doesn't have to. This Central Valley city lies just an hour and a half from four world-class national parks (Yosemite, Sierra, Kings

WHEN TO GO

For the beach and the coastal hinterland, summer has the best beach weather and everything's open. Summer is also when high-altitude roads should be snow-free. Also great is April–May (for Yosemite waterfalls), February–April for spring wildflowers and cooler desert temperatures around Palm Springs and Joshua Tree, and early fall (September and October) for Napa Valley's wine harvest.

Canyon and Sequoia), allowing you to come and go and enjoy the best of all possible worlds. You could stay in the parks themselves, but the food scene (in Tower District, for example) is reason enough to base yourself here, with fine delis (including one in an old mortuary), brewpubs and farmers markets.

San Diego

Down south in California, close to where the United States runs out of space and becomes Mexico, San Diego is a sunny, breezy, surf-loving city. Everyone seems so laid back here, and why wouldn't you be? San Diego has more than 60 beaches, fantastic museums and festivals, hundreds of possible activities, great accommodations and a food scene that seems to span the entire globe. You may like it so much that you decide never to leave.

Mendocino

When you arrive in Mendocino, you could be forgiven for wondering if you haven't somehow crossed the country to New England. This is a charming world of white-picket fences, rose gardens and redwood water towers. Almost as soon as you leave the village center, you find yourself amid wildflowers, cypress trees, cliffs and a stunning headland reaching out into the Pacific. Good festivals, lots of activities, and fine accommodations and restaurants all help make Mendocino a terrific base for California's north coast.

TRANSPORTATION

You're following a fine Californian (even American) tradition if you fly into San Francisco and drive out on a journey of discovery. San Francisco is a major domestic and international air hub and from SF, domestic flights, Amtrak trains and Greyhound buses (among others) fan out across the state; Amtrak alone has over 75 Californian stations.

RESOURCES

- **National Park Service**
  Info on Yosemite, Sequoia, Kings Canyon, Joshua Tree and more. *nps.gov*
- **California's High Sierra**
  Visitor information for California's beautiful mountain region. *californiahighsierra.com*
- **Napa Valley**
  Lodging assistance, wine-tasting passes, spa deals and comprehensive winery maps. *visitnapavalley.com*

WHAT'S ON

- **Coachella Valley Music and Arts Festival**
  One of the biggest music festivals in America, held in California's Coachella Valley in April.
- **BottleRock**
  Three-day music, food and wine festival at the end of May in Napa Valley.
- **Dana Point Festival of Whales**
  Watch whales and enjoy all manner of live events during the first weekend in March.
- **Festival of the Swallows**
  The famous swallows return to nest in the walls of Mission San Juan Capistrano around March 19.

WHERE TO STAY

The choice of where to stay in California requires careful planning, not because there aren't many places, but because there are so many places to rest your head. Especially in smaller towns, always check for local festivals during your trip as prices go sky-high, the best places fill up quickly, and you may need to book months in advance. All of the national parks, especially Yosemite, Joshua Tree, Kings Canyon and Sequoia have numerous campgrounds to choose from, but they're very often overcrowded in summer; visit at another time if you can.

39

CALIFORNIA & NEVADA

CALIFORNIA'S GREATEST HITS & LAS VEGAS

★ BEST FOR

FOOD & DRINK

Napa Valley wineries and star chefs' tables.

Vineyard, St Helena, California

DURATION: 12–15 DAYS

DISTANCE: 1600 MILES / 2575KM

GREAT FOR: FOOD & DRINK, HISTORY & CULTURE, OUTDOORS

BEST TIME TO GO: JUNE TO SEPTEMBER FOR SUNNY DAYS AND SNOW-FREE MOUNTAIN ROADS.

California is big, so seeing its most famous places all in one trip could mean resigning yourself to driving boring multilane freeways for hours on end. But forget that. Instead, this super-sized drive connects the dots on scenic state highways and local back roads, with a minimum of mind-numbing empty miles between San Francisco, Yosemite National Park, Los Angeles and Las Vegas.

LINK YOUR TRIP

40 Coastal California
California's most famous driving route hugs the Pacific Ocean from Mexico to Oregon. Join up in San Francisco, Big Sur or LA.

01 San Francisco

In two action-packed days, explore **Golden Gate Park** *(sfrecpark.org/770/Golden-Gate-Park)*, spy on sea lions lolling around **Pier 39** *(pier39.com)* at Fisherman's Wharf and saunter through the streets of busy Chinatown to the Italian sidewalk cafes of North Beach. Feast on an overstuffed burrito in the Mission District after wandering its mural-splashed alleys. Queue up at Powell and Market Sts for a ride on a bell-clanging cable car and then cruise to the infamous prison island of **Alcatraz** *(nps.gov/alca)* out in the bay. Book Alcatraz tickets online at least two weeks ahead. At the foot of Market St, indulge your inner epicurean at the food stalls of the **Ferry Building** *(ferrybuildingmarketplace.com)*, and stop by its **farmers market** *(foodwise.org)* year-round to wallow in the bounty of California-grown produce and gourmet prepared foods. Inside the historic **Castro**

Theatre *(castrotheatre.com)*, the crowd goes wild when the great organ rises from the floor and pumps out show tunes until the movie starts, and the sumptuous chandelier complements a repertory of silver-screen classics.

THE DRIVE: Without traffic jams, it's an hour's drive from San Francisco to Napa, the nexus of Wine Country. Take Hwy 101 north over the soaring Golden Gate Bridge, stopping at the Vista Point on the far side of the bridge, and into Marin County. Zigzag northeast on Hwys 37, 121, 12 and 29 to reach downtown Napa.

02 Napa Valley

The Napa Valley is famous for regal cabernet sauvignon, château-like wineries and fabulous food. The city of Napa anchors the valley, but the real work happens up-valley. Scenic towns along Hwy 29 include St Helena, Yountville and Calistoga – the last more famous for its natural hot-springs water than its wine.

Start by the river in downtown Napa, where the **Oxbow Public Market** *(oxbowpublicmarket.com)* showcases all things culinary – produce stalls, kitchen shops, and everywhere something to taste – with emphasis on seasonal eating and sustainability. Come hungry.

A dozen miles north of Napa, tour buses flock to the corporate-owned winery **Robert Mondavi** *(robertmondaviwinery.com)*; if you know nothing about wine and can cope with crowds, the worthwhile tours provide excellent insight into winemaking. Driving back down-valley, follow the bucolic Silverado Trail, which passes several other landmark, over-the-top wineries, including **Robert Sinskey Vineyards** *(robertsinskey.com)*, where a dramatic hilltop tasting room resembles a small cathedral.

THE DRIVE: From Napa, it's a four-hour drive of nearly 200 miles to the dramatic Big Sur coast. Head south over the Carquinez Bridge to Berkeley, then sail over the Bay Bridge into San Francisco, taking Hwy 101 south toward Silicon Valley.

Detour on Hwy 17 over the mountains to Santa Cruz, then join Hwy 1 south past Monterey and Carmel-by-the-Sea.

03 Big Sur

Hwy 1 along Big Sur coast may be the most famous stretch of highway in the entire state. The road twists and turns a thousand feet above the vast blue Pacific, hugging the skirts of mile-high sea cliffs, above which California condors fly.

In the 1950s and '60s, Big Sur – so named by Spanish settlers who referred to the wilderness as *el país grande del sur* (the big country to the south) – became a bohemian retreat for artists and writers, including Henry Miller and the Beat Generation. Today it attracts new-age mystics, hippies and city slickers seeking to unplug on this emerald-green edge of the continent.

All along Hwy 1 in Big Sur's state parks *(parks.ca.gov)*, you'll find hiking trails through forests of redwoods (incidentally, the tallest trees on Earth) and to magical waterfalls – don't miss **McWay Falls**, which picturesquely tumbles onto an ocean beach.

TOP TIP

SAFE DRIVING IN ALL WEATHER

If you plan on driving this route in winter, be prepared for snow in the Sierra Nevada; carry tire chains in your car. During summer, the deserts can be dangerously hot; avoid overheating your car by not running the air-conditioning and by traveling in the cooler morning and late-afternoon hours.

THE DRIVE: It's about a five-hour, 220-mile trip from Big Sur to Yosemite Valley. Backtrack north on coastal Hwy 1 past Monterey, then veer inland through California's agricultural valleys, taking Hwy 152 east past San Luis Reservoir and crossing I-5, then continuing east toward Hwy 99. Outside Merced, join Hwy 140 – an all-weather highway normally open year-round – to Yosemite National Park.

04 Yosemite National Park

With wild rock formations, astonishing waterfalls, vast swaths of granite and humbling Sierra Nevada peaks, **Yosemite National Park** *(nps.gov/yose)* is no less than perfect. On your way in, stop at Tunnel View to drink in views of the Yosemite Valley, with iconic Half Dome and plunging Bridalveil Fall in the distance. Go deeper into the valley to see triple-decker **Yosemite Falls** up close, or to hike the **Mist Trail**, which climbs a rocky staircase beside mighty Vernal and Nevada Falls. Drive up to Glacier Point to catch a brilliant sunset.

The next day, detour along high-elevation Tioga Rd (closed in winter and spring) to wildflower-strewn **Tuolumne Meadows**, encircled by skyscraping peaks and granite domes. Picnic beside sparkling **Tenaya Lake** and pull over at roadside Olmsted Point for panoramic views over the rooftop of the Sierra Nevada. Then backtrack down to the valley and take Hwy 41 south, exiting the park near the Mariposa Grove of giant sequoia trees.

THE DRIVE: It's a straight shot south on Hwy 41 from Yosemite's south entrance to Fresno, then head east on Hwy 180, which eventually winds uphill and gains over 6000ft in elevation to enter Kings Canyon National Park. The 120-mile trip to Grant Grove Village takes about 2½ hours, without traffic.

05 Kings Canyon National Park

From giant sequoia crowns down into one of the USA's deepest canyons, the twisting scenic drive in **Kings Canyon National Park** *(nps.gov/seki)* is an eye-popping, jaw-dropping revelation.

At the northern end of the Generals Hwy, take a walk in **General Grant Grove**, encompassing the world's second-largest living tree, then wash off all that sweat with a dip down the road at **Hume Lake**. Get back on the Kings Canyon Scenic Byway (Hwy 180; closed in winter and spring), which makes a precipitous descent, and make sure you pull over to survey the canyon depths and lofty Sierra Nevada peaks from Junction View.

At the bottom of the canyon, cruise past Cedar Grove Village. Admire striking canyon views from verdant **Zumwalt Meadow**, a wildlife-watching hot spot with a boardwalk nature trail. At truthfully named Road's End, cool off by the sandy **Kings River beach** or make an 8-mile round-trip hike to **Mist Falls**, which roars in late spring and early summer.

THE DRIVE: It's only a 60-mile drive from Cedar Grove to the Giant Forest in Sequoia National Park, but it can take nearly two hours, thanks to hairpin turns and gawking drivers. Backtrack along the Kings Canyon Scenic Byway (Hwy 180) to Grant Grove, then wind south on the Generals

Yosemite Falls, Yosemite National Park, California

LORCEL/SHUTTERSTOCK

PHOTO OPPORTUNITY

Waterfalls and iconic peaks from Tunnel View in Yosemite Valley.

♥ WHY I LOVE THIS TRIP

AMY C BALFOUR, WRITER

This jam-packed journey sweeps in the best of California – beaches, mountains, deserts, wineries, big trees and even bigger cities. It even includes the glitzy charms of Las Vegas, a casino-loving city a short hop away in Nevada and a favorite weekend getaway for Californians. The Sierra Nevada mountains are best visited in summer; spring brings wildflower blooms to the deserts.

Hwy through the sun-dappled forests of the Giant Sequoia National Monument.

06 Sequoia National Park

Big trees, deep caves and high granite domes are all on the agenda for this day-long tour of Sequoia National Park. Arriving in the **Giant Forest**, let yourself be dwarfed by the majestic **General Sherman Tree**. Learn more about giant sequoias at the **Giant Forest Museum** *(nps.gov/seki)*. Snap a photo of your car driving through the Tunnel Log, or better yet, leave your car behind and hop on the park shuttle for a wildflower walk around **Crescent Meadow** and to climb the puff-and-pant stairway up **Moro Rock**, granting bird's-eye canyon and peak views.

Picnic by the river at the **Lodgepole Market Center**, then get back in the car and make your way to the chilly underground wonderland of **Crystal Cave** *(sequoiaparksconservancy.org/crystal-cave)*, where you can marvel at delicate marble formations while easing through eerie passageways. You must book tour tickets online in advance. Before sunset, take the dizzyingly steep drive down the Generals Hwy into the Foothills area, stopping at riverside swimming holes.

THE DRIVE: After a few days in the wilderness, get ready to zoom down to California's biggest city. The fastest route to Los Angeles takes at least 3½ hours to cover 200 miles. Follow Hwy 198 west of Three Rivers to Hwy 65 south through the valley. In Bakersfield, join

Giant sequoia trees, Sequoia National Park, California

MY GOOD IMAGES/SHUTTERSTOCK

Hwy 99 south to I-5, which streams south toward LA.

07 Los Angeles

Make a pilgrimage to Hollywood, with its pink-starred sidewalks, blingy nightclubs and restored movie palaces. Long ago, the TV and movie biz (locals just call it 'the Industry') decamped over the hills to the San Fernando Valley. Peek behind the scenes on a **Warner Bros Studio Tour** *(wbstudiotour.com)*, or get a thrill along with screaming tweens at **Universal Studios Hollywood** *(universalstudioshollywood.com)*.

Downtown LA is a historical, multilayered and fascinating city within a city, known for its landmark architecture. Wander through the old district of **El Pueblo** *(elpueblo.lacity.org)*, then be awed by the **Broad** *(thebroad.org)* art museum, which is free but requires reservation, before partying at the entertainment complex **LA Live** *(lalive.com)* and worshipping at the star-spangled altar of the **Grammy Museum** *(grammymuseum.org)*.

Hitting LA's sunny beaches is also a must-do – and pretty darn fun. In laid-back **Santa Monica** and hipper **Venice**, you can mix with the surf rats, skate punks, muscled bodybuilders, yogis and street performers along a stretch of sublime coastline cradling the city.

THE DRIVE: It's a tedious 25-mile trip south on I-5 between Downtown LA and Anaheim. The drive can take well over an hour, especially in rush-hour traffic. As you approach Anaheim, follow the freeway signs and take exit 110b for Disneyland Dr.

08 Disneyland

When Walt Disney opened Disneyland on July 17, 1955, he declared it the 'Happiest Place on Earth.' More than 70 years later, it's hard to argue with the ear-to-ear grins on the faces of kiddos, grandparents, honeymooners and everyone else here in Anaheim.

If you've only got one day to spend at **Disneyland** *(disneyland.disney.go.com)*, buy tickets online in advance and arrive early. Stroll Main Street USA toward Sleeping Beauty Castle. Enter Tomorrowland to ride Space Mountain. In Fantasyland don't miss the classic 'It's a Small World' ride or racing downhill on the Matterhorn Bobsleds. Grab a Genie Pass for the Indiana Jones Adventure or the Pirates of the Caribbean before lunching in New Orleans Square. Plummet down Splash Mountain, then visit the Haunted Mansion before the *Fantasmic!* show and fireworks begin. In the Galaxy's Edge area, which celebrates the best of the Star Wars movie franchise, the thrilling Millennium Falcon: Smugglers Run hurtles you into hyperspace.

LOCAL KNOWLEDGE

HIKING HALF DOME

Just hold on, don't forget to breathe and – whatever you do – don't look down. A pinnacle so popular that hikers need a permit to scale it, **Half Dome** lives on as Yosemite Valley's must-reach-it obsession for millions. It's a day hike longer than an average workday, an elevation gain equivalent to almost 480 flights of stairs, and a final stretch of near-vertical steps that melts even the strongest legs and arms to masses of quivering jelly.

Reaching the top can only be done when the fixed cables are up, usually from late May until mid-October. To stem lengthy lines (and increasingly dangerous conditions) on the vertiginous cables, the park now requires that all day and overnight backpackers obtain an advance permit. Half Dome permits go on sale by a preseason lottery in March, with a limited number available via another daily lottery two days in advance during the hiking season. Permit regulations and prices are subject to change; check the park website *(nps.gov/yose/planyourvisit/hdpermits.htm)* for current details.

THE DRIVE: A few different routes from Anaheim to Palm Springs all eventually funnel onto I-10 eastbound from Los Angeles. It's a trip of almost 100 miles, which should take less than three hours without traffic jams. Watch for the towering wind turbines on the hillsides as you shoot through San Gorgonio Pass. Take Hwy 111 south to downtown Palm Springs.

09 Palm Springs

In the 1950s and '60s, Palm Springs was the swinging getaway of Sinatra, Elvis and dozens of other stars. Now a new generation has fallen for the city's mid-century modern charms: steel-and-glass bungalows designed by famous architects, boutique hotels with vintage decor and kidney-shaped pools, and hip bars serving perfect martinis.

North of downtown 'PS,' ride the revolving **Palm Springs Aerial Tramway** *(pstramway.com)*, which climbs 6000ft vertically in under 15 minutes. It's 30°F to 40°F (up to 22°C) cooler as you step out into pine forest at the top, so bring warm clothing – the ride up from the desert floor is said to be the equivalent (in temperature) of driving from Mexico to Canada.

Down-valley in **Rancho Mirage**, **Sunnylands** *(sunnylands.org)* was the glamorous modern estate of the Annenberg family. Explore the magnificent desert gardens or book ahead for tours of the stunning house with its art collection.

THE DRIVE: North of Palm Springs, take I-10 west to Hwy 62, which winds northeast to the high desert around Joshua Tree. The 35-mile trip goes by quickly; it should take you less than an hour to reach the park's west entrance. Fuel up first in the town of Joshua Tree – there's no gas, food or water inside the park.

DETOUR

World's Biggest Dinosaurs
Start: 09 Palm Springs

West of Palm Springs, you may do a double take when you see the **World's Biggest Dinosaurs** *(cabazondinosaurs.com)*. Claude K Bell, a sculptor for Knott's Berry Farm, spent over a decade crafting these concrete behemoths, now owned by Christian creationists who contend that God created the original dinosaurs in one day, along with the other animals, as part of his 'intelligent design.' In the gift shop you'll find the sort of dino-swag you might find at science museums.

10 Joshua Tree National Park

Taking a page from a Dr Seuss book, whimsical-looking Joshua trees (actually tree-sized yuccas) symbolize this **national park** *(nps.gov/jotr)* at the convergence of the Colorado and Mojave Deserts. Allegedly, it was Mormon settlers who named the trees because the branches stretching toward heaven reminded them of the biblical prophet pointing the way to the promised land.

Rock climbers know 'JTree' as the best place to climb in California, but kids and the young at heart also welcome the chance to scramble up, down and around the giant boulders. Hikers seek hidden, shady, desert-fan-palm oases fed by natural springs and small streams. Book ahead for fascinating guided tours of **Keys Ranch** *(nps.gov/jotr)*, built by a 20th-century desert homesteader.

Scenic drives worth taking inside the park include the side road to panoramic Keys View and the Pinto Basin Rd, which winds down to Cottonwood Spring, letting you watch nature transition from the high Mojave Desert to the low Colorado Desert. A bird's-eye view of the park is your reward at the end of the steep Ryan Mountain Trail, which is 3 miles round trip.

THE DRIVE: It's a gloriously scenic back-road adventure to Las Vegas, three hours and nearly 200 miles away. From Twentynine Palms, Amboy Rd barrels east and then north, opening up desert panoramas. At Amboy, head east on Route 66 and north on Kelbaker Rd across I-40 into the Mojave National Preserve. North of the preserve, join I-15 northbound to Las Vegas.

11 Las Vegas, Nevada

Vegas is the ultimate escape. It's the only place in the world where you can spend the night partying in ancient Rome, wake up in Egypt, brunch under the Eiffel Tower, watch an erupting volcano at sunset and get married in a pink Cadillac at midnight.

Double down with the high rollers, pick up some tacky souvenirs and sip a neon 3ft-high margarita as you stroll along the Strip. Traipse through mini versions of New York, Paris and Venice before riding the **High Roller** *(caesars.com/linq/high-roller)*. After dark, check out the projections at **The Sphere** *(thespherevegas.com)*, a giant orb that showcases the world's largest LED screen.

Do you like old-school casinos, vintage neon signs and dive bars more than celebrity chefs and clubbing? No problem. Head downtown to historic 'Glitter Gulch' along the **Fremont Street Experience** *(vegasexperience.com)*, a pedestrian-only zone with the **Slotzilla Zip Line** *(vegasexperience.com/slotzilla-zip-line)*, near the **Mob Museum** *(themobmuseum.org)*. Afterward, mingle with locals at hip hangouts in the Fremont East entertainment district.

Las Vegas sign, Las Vegas Boulevard, Las Vegas, Nevada
MINIPRODUCTION/SHUTTERSTOCK

WELCOME
TO Fabulous
LAS VEGAS
NEVADA
YESCO

40

CALIFORNIA & NEVADA

COASTAL CALIFORNIA

DURATION: 7–10 DAYS

DISTANCE: 1030 MILES / 1660KM

GREAT FOR: FOOD & DRINK, FAMILIES, NATURE

BEST TIME TO GO: YEAR-ROUND, BUT JULY TO OCTOBER FOR THE SUNNIEST SKIES.

Escape from California's tangled, traffic-jammed freeways for a breezy cruise in the slow lane. Once you get rolling, you'll never want to leave those ocean views behind. Officially, only the short, sun-loving stretch of Hwy 1 through Orange and Los Angeles Counties can legally call itself Pacific Coast Highway (PCH). But never mind those technicalities, because equally bewitching ribbons of Hwy 1 and Hwy 101 await all along this route.

LINK YOUR TRIP

42 Disneyland & Orange County Beaches
Soak up the SoCal sunshine in glam beach towns along PCH, then take the kids to Anaheim's world-famous theme parks.

01 San Diego

At the bottom of the state map, the pretty peninsular beach town of Coronado is connected to the San Diego mainland via the white-sand beaches of the Silver Strand. If you've seen Marilyn Monroe cavort in *Some Like It Hot,* you'll recognize the dapper **Hotel del Coronado** *(hoteldel.com),* which has hosted US presidents, celebrities and royalty, including the Prince of Wales who gave up his throne to marry a Coronado divorcée. Wander the turreted palace's labyrinthine corridors, then quaff tropical cocktails at ocean-view **Babcock & Story Bar**.

Hold tight driving over the 2.1-mile-long San Diego–Coronado Bridge. Detour inland to Balboa Park. Head west, then south to Point Loma's **Cabrillo National Monument** *(nps.gov/cabr)* for captivating bay panoramas from the 19th-century lighthouse and monument to the West Coast's first Spanish explorers. Roll north of

★ BEST TWO DAYS

Santa Barbara north to Monterey via Big Sur.

JON BILOUS/SHUTTERSTOCK

Pacific Coast Highway, California

Mission Beach and the old-fashioned amusement park at Pacific Beach, and suddenly you're in hoity-toity La Jolla, beyond which lie North County's beach towns.

THE DRIVE: It's a 70-mile trip from La Jolla north along coastal roads and then I-5 into Orange County (aka the 'OC'), passing Camp Pendleton Marine Corps Base and recently shuttered – but still decommissioning – San Onofre Nuclear Generating Station. Exit at San Clemente and follow Avenida del Mar downhill to the beach.

02 San Clemente

In off-the-beaten-path spots such as beautiful San Clemente, sloping steeply toward the sea, the Orange County coast feels like a trip back to the beach culture of yesteryear. Home to living surfing legends and top-notch surfboard companies, this may be the last place in the OC where you can authentically live the surf lifestyle. Ride your own board or swim at the city's main beach beside San Clemente Pier. Then head over to **Casa Romantica Cultural Center and Gardens** *(casaromantica.org)*, which features exhibits on art and history in an elegant Spanish Revival building dating to the 1920s.

THE DRIVE: Slingshot north on I-5, exiting onto Hwy 1 near Dana Point. Speed by the wealthy artist colony of Laguna Beach, wild Crystal Cove State Park, Newport Beach's yacht harbor and 'Surf City USA,' Huntington Beach. Turn west off Hwy 1 near Naples toward Long Beach, about 45 miles from San Clemente.

03 Long Beach

In Long Beach, the biggest stars are the **Queen Mary** *(queenmary.com)*, a grand (and allegedly haunted) British ocean liner permanently moored here, and the giant **Aquarium of the Pacific** *(aquariumofpacific.org)*, a high-tech romp through an underwater world in which sharks dart and jellyfish float. Often overlooked, the **Museum of Latin American Art** *(molaa.org)* shows off influential, contemporary Latinx creators from south of the border and right

♥ WHY I LOVE THIS TRIP

AMY C BALFOUR, WRITER

Rock-'em-sock-'em scenery never stops on this coastal adventure, from the gorgeous sun-kissed beaches of Southern California to soaring coastal redwoods in foggy Northern California. My travels on this route have ranged from joyous romps to reflective sojourns – and the landscape has somehow matched my mood every time. Laguna Beach, Malibu, Big Sur, north of Santa Cruz, and Jenner to Mendocino and Westport are reliable crowd-pleasers.

here in California. A mile away, vintage shoppers will be in their element on **Retro Row**, several blocks of mid-century fashion and furnishings.

THE DRIVE: Wind slowly around the ruggedly scenic Palos Verdes Peninsula. Follow Hwy 1 north past the South Bay's prime-time beaches. Curving around LAX airport and Marina del Rey, Hwy 1 continues north to Venice, Santa Monica and all the way to Malibu, almost 60 miles from Long Beach.

04 Malibu

Leaving traffic-jammed LA behind, Hwy 1 breezes northwest of Santa Monica to Malibu. You'll feel like a movie star walking around on the public beaches, fronting gated compounds owned by Hollywood celebs. One mansion you can actually explore inside – for free – is the **Getty Villa** *(getty.edu)*, a hilltop showcase of Greek, Roman and Etruscan antiquities and manicured gardens. Next to Malibu Lagoon State Beach, west of the surfers by Malibu Pier, **Adamson House** *(adamsonhouse.org)* is a Spanish-Moorish villa lavishly decorated with locally made hand-painted tiles. Motoring further west along the coast, where the Santa Monica Mountains plunge into the sea, take time out for a frolic on Malibu's mega-popular beaches such as sandy Point Dume, Zuma or Leo Carrillo.

THE DRIVE: Hwy 1 crosses into Ventura County, winding alongside the ocean and windy Point Mugu. In Oxnard join Hwy 101 northbound. Motor past Ventura, a jumping-off point for boat trips to Channel Islands National Park, to Santa Barbara, just over 90 miles from Malibu Pier.

DETOUR

Channel Islands National Park
Start: 04 Malibu

Imagine hiking, kayaking, scuba diving, camping and whale-watching, and doing it all amid a raw, end-of-the-world landscape. Rich in unique flora and fauna, tide pools and kelp forests, the islands of this national park are home to nearly 150 plant and animal species found nowhere else in the world, earning them the nickname 'California's Galápagos.' Anacapa and Santa Cruz, the most popular islands, are within an hour's boat ride of Ventura Harbor, off Hwy 101 almost 40 miles northwest of Malibu on the way to Santa Barbara. Reservations are essential for weekends, holidays and summer trips. Before you shove off from the mainland, stop by the park's visitor center (nps.gov/chis) for educational natural history exhibits, a free 25-minute nature film and family-friendly activities.

05 Santa Barbara

Seaside Santa Barbara has almost perfect weather and a string of idyllic beaches, where surfers, kite flyers and dog walkers mingle. Admire the city's iconic Spanish Colonial Revival–style architecture along State St downtown or from the **county courthouse** *(sbcourthouse.org)*, its tower rising above the red-tiled rooftops. Gaze south toward the busy harborfront and **Stearns Wharf** *(stearnswharf.org)* or north to the historic **Spanish Mission Santa Barbara** *(santabarbaramission.org)*. Santa Barbara's balmy climate is also perfect for growing grapes – its wine country, made famous by the 2004 movie *Sideways*, is a 45-minute drive northwest along Hwy 154. Hit wine-tasting rooms in Los Olivos, then take Foxen Canyon Rd north past more wineries to rejoin Hwy 101.

THE DRIVE: Keep following fast Hwy 101 northbound or detour west onto slow Hwy 1, which squiggles along the coastline past Guadalupe, gateway to North America's largest sand dunes. Both highways meet up again in Pismo Beach, 100 miles northwest of Santa Barbara.

06 Pismo Beach

A classic California beach town, Pismo Beach has a long, lazy stretch of sand for swimming, surfing and strolling onto the pier at sunset. After digging into bowls of clam chowder and baskets of fried seafood at surf-casual cafes,

Zuma Beach, Malibu, California
WIRESTOCK CREATORS/SHUTTERSTOCK

check out the retro family fun at the bowling alley, billiards halls and bars uphill from the beach, or dash 10 miles up Hwy 101 to San Luis Obispo's vintage **Sunset Drive-In** *(sunsetdriveinslo.com)*, where you can put your feet up on the dash and munch on bottomless bags of popcorn while watching Hollywood blockbuster double-features.

THE DRIVE: Follow Hwy 101 north past San Luis Obispo, exiting onto Hwy 1 west to landmark Morro Rock in Morro Bay. North of Cayucos, Hwy 1 rolls through bucolic pasturelands, only swinging back to the coast at Cambria. Ten miles further north stands Hearst Castle, about 60 miles from Pismo Beach.

07 Hearst Castle

Hilltop **Hearst Castle** *(hearstcastle.org)* is California's most famous monument to wealth and ambition. William Randolph Hearst, the early-20th-century newspaper magnate, entertained Hollywood stars and royalty at this fantasy estate furnished with European antiques, accented by shimmering pools and surrounded by flowering gardens. Try to make tour reservations in advance, especially for living-history evening programs during the Christmas holiday season and in spring.

About 4.5 miles further north along Hwy 1, park at the signposted vista point and amble the boardwalk to view the elephant seal colony that breeds, molts, sleeps, plays and fights on the beach. Seals haul out year-round, but the winter birthing and mating season peaks on Valentine's Day. Nearby, **Piedras Blancas Light Station** *(piedrasblancas.org)* is an outstandingly scenic spot.

Jellyfish, Monterey Bay Aquarium, Monterey, California
BLUESTORK/SHUTTERSTOCK

THE DRIVE: Fill your car's gas tank before plunging north into the redwood forests of the remote Big Sur coast, where precipitous cliffs dominate the seascape, and tourist services are few and far between. Hwy 1 keeps curving north to the Monterey Peninsula, approximately a three-hour, 95-mile trip from Hearst Castle.

08 Monterey

As Big Sur loosens its condor's talons on the coastal highway, Hwy 1 rolls gently downhill toward Monterey Bay. The fishing community of Monterey is the heart of Nobel Prize–winning writer John Steinbeck's country, and although Cannery Row today is touristy claptrap, it's worth strolling down to step inside the mesmerizing **Monterey Bay Aquarium** *(montereybayaquarium.org)*, which inhabits a converted sardine cannery on the shores of a national marine sanctuary. All kinds of aquatic denizens swim in the giant tanks, from sea stars to pot-bellied seahorses and comical sea otters.

THE DRIVE: It's a relatively quick 45-mile trip north to Santa Cruz. Hwy 1 traces the crescent shoreline of Monterey Bay, passing Elkhorn Slough wildlife refuge near Moss Landing boat harbor, Watsonville's strawberry and artichoke farms, and a string of tiny beach towns in Santa Cruz County.

09 Santa Cruz

Here, the flower power of the 1960s lives on, and bumper stickers on surfboard-laden woodies shout 'Keep Santa Cruz weird.' Next to the ocean, **Santa Cruz Beach Boardwalk** *(beachboardwalk.com)* has a glorious old-school Americana vibe and a 1911 Looff carousel. Its fun-for-all atmosphere is punctuated by squeals from nervous nellies on the stomach-turning Giant Dipper, a 1920s wooden roller coaster that's a national historic landmark, as seen in the vampire cult-classic movie *The Lost Boys*.

Visit **Santa Cruz' Museum of Art & History** *(santacruzmah.org)* for regular special exhibitions and excellent permanent displays on the city's history and culture. Interesting one-off exhibitions have included the history of both skateboarding and tattooing in the city. Adjacent, there's good eating and drinking at **Abbott Square Market** *(abbottsquaremarket.com)*.

THE DRIVE: It's a blissful 75-mile coastal run from Santa Cruz up to San Francisco past Pescadero, Half Moon Bay and Pacifica, where Hwy 1 passes through the tunnels at Devil's Slide. Merge with heavy freeway traffic in Daly City, staying on Hwy 1 north through the city into Golden Gate Park.

10 San Francisco

Gridlock may shock your system after hundreds of lazy miles of wide-open, rolling coast. But don't despair. Hwy 1 runs straight through the city's biggest, most breathable greenspace: **Golden Gate Park** *(sfrecpark.org/770/Golden-Gate-Park)*. You could easily spend all day in the conservatory of flowers, arboretum and botanic gardens, or perusing the **California Academy of Sciences** *(calacademy.org)* and the fine arts **de Young Museum** *(deyoung.famsf.org)*. Then follow Hwy 1 north over the **Golden Gate Bridge** *(goldengatebridge.org/visitors)*. Guarding the entry to San

PHOTO OPPORTUNITY

Golden Gate Bridge over San Francisco Bay.

LYNN YEH/SHUTTERSTOCK

Golden Gate Bridge (p331), San Francisco, California

Francisco Bay, this iconic bridge is named after the strait it spans, not for its 'International Orange' paint job. Park in the lots on the bridge's south or north side, then traipse out onto the pedestrian walkway for a photo.

THE DRIVE: Past Sausalito, leave Hwy 101 in Marin City for slow-moving, twisted Hwy 1 along the Marin County coast, passing nearby Point Reyes. Over the next 100 miles from Bodega Bay to Mendocino, revel in a remarkably uninterrupted stretch of coastal highway. More than halfway along, watch for the lighthouse road turnoff north of Point Arena town.

DETOUR

Point Reyes

Start: 10 San Francisco

A rough-hewn beauty, **Point Reyes National Seashore** *(nps.gov/pore)* lures marine mammals and birds, as well as scores of shipwrecks. It was here that Sir Francis Drake repaired his ship the *Golden Hind* in 1579 and, while he was at it, claimed the Indigenous land for England. Follow Sir Francis Drake Blvd to the point's **edge-of-the-world lighthouse** *(nps.gov/pore/planyourvisit/lighthouse.htm)*, whipped by ferocious winds, where you can observe migrating whales in winter. The lighthouse, which reopened in 2019 after a multimillion-dollar renovation, sits below the headlands and is reached via 300 descending steps. You'll find it about 20 miles west of Point Reyes Station off Hwy 1 along Marin County's coast.

11 Around Point Arena

The fishing fleets of Bodega Bay and the seal colony at Jenner's harbor are the last things you'll see before Hwy 1 dives into California's great rural northlands. The road twists and turns past the Sonoma Coast's state parks packed with hiking trails, sand dunes and beaches, as well as underwater marine reserves, rhododendron groves and a 19th-century Russian fur-trading fort. At Sea Ranch, don't let exclusive-looking vacation homes prevent you from following public-access trailhead signs and staircases down to empty beaches and across ocean bluffs. Further north, guarding an unbelievably windy point since 1908, **Point Arena Lighthouse** *(pointarenalight house.com)* is the only lighthouse in California you can actually climb to the top. Check in at the museum, then ascend the 115ft tower to inspect the Fresnel lens, and panoramas of the sea and the jagged San Andreas Fault below.

THE DRIVE: It's an hour-long, 35-mile drive north along Hwy 1 from the Point Arena Lighthouse turnoff to Mendocino, crossing the Navarro, Little and Big Rivers. Feel free to stop and stretch at wind-tossed state beaches, parklands crisscrossed by hiking trails and tiny coastal towns along the way.

12 Mendocino & Fort Bragg

Looking more like Cape Cod than California, the quaint maritime town of Mendocino has white picket fences surrounding New England–style cottages with blooming gardens and redwood-built water towers. This yesteryear timber town and shipping port with dramatic headlands jutting into the Pacific was 'discovered' by artists and bohemians in the 1950s and has served as a scenic backdrop in more than 50 movies. Once you've browsed the cute shops and art galleries selling everything from driftwood carvings to homemade fruit jams – the town is nicknamed 'Spendocino' – escape north to workaday Fort Bragg, with its simple fishing harbor and brewpub. Stop first for a short hike on the ecological staircase and pygmy forest trail at oceanfront **Jug Handle State Natural Reserve** *(parks.ca.gov)*.

TROUBLE-FREE ROAD-TRIPPING

In coastal areas, thick fog may impede driving – slow down, and if it's too soupy, get off the road. Along coastal cliffs, watch out for falling rocks and mudslides that could damage or disable your car if struck. For current highway conditions, including road closures (which aren't uncommon during the rainy winter season) and construction updates, call 800-427-7623 or visit *dot.ca.gov.*

THE DRIVE: About 25 miles north of Mendocino, Westport is the last hamlet along this rugged stretch of Hwy 1. After 28 miles, rejoin Hwy 101 northbound at Leggett for another 90 miles to Eureka, detouring along the Avenue of the Giants and, if you have more time to spare, to the Lost Coast.

13 Eureka

Highway 101 trundles alongside **Humboldt Bay National Wildlife Refuge** *(fws.gov/refuge/humboldt_bay)*, a major stopover for migratory birds on the Pacific Flyway. Next comes the sleepy railroad town of Eureka. As you wander downtown, check out the ornate **Carson Mansion** *(ingomar.org)*, built in the 1880s by a timber baron and adorned with dizzying Victorian turrets, towers, gables and gingerbread details. **Blue Ox Millworks & Historic Park** *(blueoxmill.com)* still creates Victorian detailing by hand using traditional carpentry and 19th-century equipment. Back by Eureka's harborfront, climb aboard the blue-and-white 1910 **Madaket** *(humboldtbaymaritimemuseum.com)*, docked at the foot of C St. Sunset cocktail cruises are served by California's smallest licensed bar.

THE DRIVE: Follow Hwy 101 north past the Rastafarian-hippie college town of Arcata and turnoffs for Trinidad State Beach and Patrick's Point State Park. Hwy 101 drops out of the trees beside marshy Humboldt Lagoons State Park, rolling north toward Orick, just over 40 miles from Eureka.

14 Redwood National & State Parks

At last, you'll reach **Redwood National Park** *(nps.gov/redw)*. Get oriented to the tallest trees on earth at the coastal **Thomas H Kuchel Visitor Center**, just south of the tiny town of Orick. Then commune with the coastal giants on their own mossy turf inside **Lady Bird Johnson Grove** or the majestic **Tall Trees Grove** (free drive-and-hike permit required). For more untouched redwood forests, wind along the 10-mile Newton B Drury Scenic Parkway in **Prairie Creek Redwoods State Park** *(parks.ca.gov)*, passing grassy meadows where Roosevelt elk roam. Then follow Hwy 101 all the way north to Crescent City, the last pit stop before the Oregon border.

STAY AWHILE

SANTA BARBARA

BY MARGOT BIGG

Nicknamed the American Riviera because of its coastal Mediterranean climate and decades-old reputation as a getaway for Hollywood stars, Santa Barbara is a wonderful place to slow down and take in warm California sun – without the traffic snarls of the **Los Angeles** area. This pretty city is sandwiched between the rugged Santa Ynez Mountains and the Pacific Ocean, meaning it's easy to spend the morning at the seashore and the afternoon in the hills. My favorite hike in the area is Inspiration Point, a popular 3.4-mile out-and-back route that offers panoramic sea views from its precipice.

Although Santa Barbara's beauty alone is enough to merit a day or two, it's also a top spot for culture lovers. On a 15-acre hillside overlooking the city, the **Old Mission Santa Barbara** *(santabarbaramission.org)* has beautiful architecture and a nine-room museum brimming with centuries' worth of Franciscan art and artifacts. I also love the **Santa Barbara Museum of Art** *(sbma.net)*, which showcases artworks from around the world, including many pieces that are thousands of years old.

While there's certainly an element of glitz to the city, I've always found it surprisingly easy to visit on a modest budget, especially if I stick to more casual spots such as **Buena Onda Empanadas Argentinas** *(buenaondasb.com)* and **Mony's Mexican Food** *(monyssb.com)*. If you do want a splurge, make a reservation at **Bouchon** *(bouchonsantabarbara.com)*, which pairs modern Californian cuisine with an extensive list of regional and international wines, including some fantastic Santa Barbara pinot and chardonnay from American Viticultural Areas (AVA).

LINK YOUR TRIP

Santa Barbara is the perfect spot to stop on the 40 **Coastal California** (p326) road trip.

Left: View from the Courthouse Tower, Santa Barbara, California; Right: Beach, Santa Barbara, California

LEFT TO RIGHT: L PAUL MANN/SHUTTERSTOCK, MONICAKROBLES/SHUTTERSTOCK

PLACES TO STAY

- **Inn by the Harbor**
This cozy inn embraces Santa Barbara's Spanish Mission history, with tiled roofs and common areas, a compact pool, and plenty of palm trees. The Harbor Pool Suite features a full kitchen that's ideal for cooking your own meals during an extended stay. *sbhotels.com/inn-by-the-harbor*

- **Milo Hotel by the Sea**
Soft furnishings and whimsical wallpaper adorned with seabirds add a sense of calm to the rooms at this hotel, situated just across the street from the beach. Pets are welcome, too. Two heated outdoor pools and a hot tub supplement the nearby Pacific sands. *themilo.com*

41

CALIFORNIA & NEVADA

★ BEST FOR

SCENIC DRIVES

Kings Canyon Scenic Byway to Cedar Grove.

YOSEMITE, SEQUOIA & KINGS CANYON NATIONAL PARKS

DURATION: 5–7 DAYS

DISTANCE: 450 MILES / 726KM

GREAT FOR: FAMILIES, NATURE

BEST TIME TO GO: APRIL AND MAY FOR WATERFALLS; JUNE TO SEPTEMBER FOR FULL ACCESS.

Yosemite Falls, Yosemite National Park, California

Glacier-carved valleys resting below dramatic peaks make Yosemite an all-ages playground. Witness earth-shaking waterfalls, clamber up granite domes and camp out by high-country meadows where wildflowers bloom in summer. Home to the USA's deepest canyon and the biggest tree on the planet, Sequoia and Kings Canyon National Parks justify detouring further south into the Sierra Nevada, which conservationist John Muir called 'The Range of Light.'

LINK YOUR TRIP

39 California's Greatest Hits & Las Vegas
After a few days in the wilderness, head south to LA and then across the desert to Nevada.

44 Eastern Sierra Scenic Byway
From Yosemite's Tuolumne Meadows, roll over high-elevation Tioga Pass and downhill toward Mono Lake, a 20-mile trip.

01 Tuolumne Meadows

Tuolumne Meadows makes for an impressive introduction to the Yosemite area. These are the Sierra Nevada's largest subalpine meadows, with fields of wildflowers, bubbling streams, ragged granite peaks and cooler temperatures at an elevation of 8600ft. Hikers can find a paradise of trails to tackle, or unpack a picnic basket by the stream-fed meadows.

Note that the route crossing the Sierra and passing by the meadows, Tioga Rd (a 19th-century wagon road and Native American trading route), is completely closed by snow in winter. It usually reopens in May or June and remains passable until October or November.

Nine miles west of the meadows, a sandy half-moon beach wraps around **Tenaya Lake**, tempting you to brave some of the park's

LUNAMARINA/SHUTTERSTOCK

coldest swimming. Sunbathers lie upon rocks that rim the lake's northern shore. A few minutes further west, stop at **Olmsted Point**. Overlooking a lunar-type landscape of glaciated granite, you can gaze deeply down Tenaya Canyon to Half Dome's backside.

THE DRIVE: From Tuolumne Meadows it's 50 miles to Yosemite Valley, following Tioga Rd (Hwy 120), turning south onto Big Oak Flat Rd, then east onto El Portal Rd. There's one must-do stop before entering the valley proper, Tunnel View, so follow Wawona Rd west for a few miles where it forks with Southside Dr. You'll know you've arrived when you see all the other parked cars.

02 Tunnel View

For your first, spectacular look into Yosemite Valley, pull over at **Tunnel View**, a vista that has inspired painters, poets, naturalists and adventurers for centuries. On the right, Bridalveil Fall swells with snowmelt in late spring, but by late summer it's a mere whisper, often lifted and blown aloft by the wind. Spread below you are the pine forests and meadows of the valley floor, with the sheer face of El Capitan rising on the left and, in the distance straight ahead, iconic granite Half Dome.

THE DRIVE: Merge carefully back onto eastbound Wawona Rd, which continues downhill into Yosemite Valley, full of confusingly intersecting one-way roads. Drive east along the Merced River on Southside Dr past the Bridalveil Fall turnoff. Almost 6 miles from Tunnel View, turn left and drive across Sentinel Bridge to Yosemite Village's day-use parking lots. Ride free shuttle buses that circle the valley.

03 Yosemite Valley

From the bottom looking up, this dramatic valley cut by the meandering Merced River is song-inspiring, and not just for birds: it also has rippling meadow grasses, tall pines, cool, impassive pools reflecting granite monoliths, and cascading, glacier-cold white-water ribbons.

At busy Yosemite Village, start inside the **Yosemite Valley Visitor Center** *(nps.gov/yose)*, with its thought-provoking history and nature displays and free Spirit of Yosemite film screenings. At the nearby **Yosemite Museum**, Western landscape paintings are hung beside Native American baskets and beaded clothing.

The valley's famous waterfalls are thunderous cataracts in May but mere trickles by late July. Triple-tiered **Yosemite Falls** is North America's tallest, while **Bridalveil Falls** is hardly less impressive. A strenuous, often slippery staircase beside **Vernal Falls** leads you, gasping, right to the top edge of the waterfall, where rainbows pop in clouds of mist. Keep hiking up the same Mist Trail to the top of **Nevada Falls** for a heady 5.5-mile round-trip trek.

In midsummer you can rent a raft at **Curry Village** and float down the Merced River. The serene stretch between Stoneman Bridge and Sentinel Beach is gentle enough for kids. Or take the whole family

HIKING HALF DOME & AROUND YOSEMITE VALLEY

Over 800 miles of hiking trails in Yosemite National Park fit hikers of all abilities. Take an easy half-mile stroll on the valley floor or underneath giant sequoia trees, or venture out all day on a quest for viewpoints, waterfalls and lakes in the mountainous high country.

Some of the park's most popular hikes start right in Yosemite Valley, including to the top of **Half Dome** (16-mile round trip), the most famous of all. It follows a section of the John Muir Trail and is strenuous, difficult and best tackled in two days with an overnight in Little Yosemite Valley. Reaching the top can only be done in summer after park rangers have installed fixed cables; depending on snow conditions, this may occur as early as late May and the cables usually come down in mid-October. To limit the cables' notorious human logjams, the park now requires permits for day hikers, but the route is still nerve-racking because hikers must share the cables. Advance permits go on sale by preseason lottery in early spring, with a limited number available via another daily lottery two days in advance during the hiking season. Permit regulations and prices keep changing; check the park website *(nps.gov/yose)* for current details.

The less ambitious or physically fit will still have a ball following the **Mist Trail** as far as **Vernal Fall** (2.5-mile round trip), the top of **Nevada Fall** (5.5-mile round trip) or idyllic **Little Yosemite Valley** (8-mile round trip). The **Four Mile Trail** (9-mile round trip) up to Glacier Point is a strenuous but satisfying climb to a glorious viewpoint. If you've got the kids in tow, nice and easy valley walks include to **Mirror Lake** (2-mile round trip) and viewpoints at the base of thundering **Yosemite Falls** (1-mile round trip) and lacy **Bridalveil Fall** (0.5-mile round trip).

to see the stuffed wildlife mounts at the hands-on **Happy Isles Art and Nature Center** *(nps.gov/places/000/happy-isles-art-and-nature-center.htm),* east of Curry Village.

THE DRIVE: Use Northside Dr to loop round and join Wawona Rd again. Follow Wawona Rd/Hwy 41 up out of the valley. After 9 miles, turn left onto Glacier Point Rd at the Chinquapin intersection, driving 15 more miles to Glacier Point.

04 Glacier Point

In just over an hour you can zip from Yosemite Valley up to head-spinning Glacier Point. Note that the final 10 miles of Glacier Point Rd is closed by snow in winter, usually from November through April or May. During winter the road remains open as far as the Badger Pass Ski Area, but snow tires and tire chains may be required.

Rising over 3000ft above the valley floor, dramatic **Glacier Point** (7214ft) practically puts you at eye level with Half Dome. Glimpse what John Muir and US president Teddy Roosevelt saw when they camped here in 1903: the waterfall-strewn Yosemite Valley below and the distant peaks ringing Tuolumne Meadows. To get away from the crowds, hike a little way down the **Panorama Trail**, just south of the crowded main viewpoint.

On your way back from Glacier Point, take time out for a 2-mile hike up **Sentinel Dome** or out to **Taft Point** for incredible 360-degree valley views.

THE DRIVE: Drive back downhill past Badger Pass Ski Area, turning left at the Chinquapin intersection and winding south through thick forest on Wawona Rd/Hwy 41. After almost 13 curvy miles you'll reach Wawona, with its lodge, visitor center, general store and gas station, all on your left.

05 Wawona

At Wawona, a 45-minute drive south of the valley, drop by the **Pioneer Yosemite History Center** *(nps.gov/places/000/pioneer-yosemite-history-center.htm),* with its covered bridge, pioneer-era buildings and historic Wells Fargo office. In summer you can take a short, bumpy stagecoach ride and really feel like you're living in the past. Peek inside the **Wawona Visitor Center** at the recreated studio of 19th-century artist Thomas Hill, hung with romantic Sierra Nevada landscape paintings. On summer evenings, imbibe a civilized cocktail in the lobby lounge of the **Wawona Hotel**, where pianist Tom Bopp often plays tunes from Yosemite's bygone days.

THE DRIVE: Follow Wawona Rd/Hwy 41 south for 4.5 miles to the park's south entrance, where you must leave your car at the new parking lot. A free shuttle will take you to Mariposa Grove.

06 Mariposa Grove

Wander giddily around the Mariposa Grove, home of the

PHOTO OPPORTUNITY

Yosemite Valley from panoramic Tunnel View.

Yosemite Valley (p337), Yosemite National Park, California

1800-year-old Grizzly Giant and 500 other monumental sequoias that tower above your head. Nature trails wind through this popular grove, but you can only hear yourself think above the noise of vacationing crowds during the early morning or evening. Notwithstanding a cruel hack job back in 1895, the walk-through **California Tunnel Tree** continues to survive, so pose your family in front and snap away. If you've got the energy, make a round-trip pilgrimage on foot to the fallen **Wawona Tunnel Tree** in the upper grove.

THE DRIVE: From Yosemite's south entrance station, it's a 115-mile, three-hour trip to Kings Canyon National Park. Follow Hwy 41 south 60 miles to Fresno, then slingshot east on Hwy 180 for another 50 miles, climbing out of the Central Valley back into the mountains. Keep left at the Hwy 198 intersection, staying on Hwy 180 toward Grant Grove.

07 Grant Grove

Through **Sequoia and Kings Canyon National Parks** *(nps.gov/seki)*, roads seem barely to scratch the surface of the twin parks' beauty. To see real treasures, you'll need to get out and stretch your legs. North of Big Stump entrance station in **Grant Grove Village**, turn left and wind downhill to General Grant Grove, where you'll see some of the park's landmark giant sequoia trees along a paved path. You can walk right through the **Fallen Monarch**, a massive, fire-hollowed trunk that's done duty as cabin, hotel, saloon and horse stable. For views of Kings Canyon and the peaks of the Great Western Divide, follow a narrow, winding side road (closed in winter; no RVs or trailers) starting behind the John Muir Lodge for over 2 miles up to **Panoramic Point**.

THE DRIVE: Kings Canyon National Park's main visitor areas, Grant Grove and Cedar Grove, are linked by the narrow, twisting Kings Canyon Scenic Byway (Hwy 180), which dramatically descends into the canyon. Expect spectacular views all along this outstandingly scenic 30-mile drive. Note: Hwy 180 from the Hume Lake turnoff to Cedar Grove is closed during winter (usually mid-November through mid-April).

CHECUBUS/SHUTTERSTOCK

Moro Rock, California

08 Cedar Grove

Serpentining past chiseled rock walls laced with waterfalls, Hwy 180 plunges down to the Kings River, where roaring white water ricochets off the granite cliffs of North America's deepest canyon, technically speaking. Pull over partway down at Junction View overlook for an eyeful, then keep rolling down along the river to Cedar Grove Village. East of the village, **Zumwalt Meadow** is the place for spotting birds, mule deer and black bears. If the day is hot and your swimming gear is handy, stroll from **Road's End** to **Muir Rock**, a large flat-top river boulder where John Muir once gave outdoor talks that's now a popular summer swimming hole. Starting from Road's End, a very popular day hike climbs 4 miles each way to **Mist Falls**, which thunders in late spring.

THE DRIVE: Backtrack from Road's End nearly 30 miles up Hwy 180. Turn left onto Hume Lake Rd. Curve around the lake past swimming beaches and campgrounds, turning right onto 10 Mile Rd. At Hwy 198, turn left and follow the Generals Hwy (often closed from January to March) south for about 23 miles to the Wolverton Rd turnoff on your left.

WINTER WONDERLANDS

When the temperature drops and the white stuff falls, there are still tons of fun outdoor activities around the Sierra Nevada's national parks. In Yosemite, strap on some skis or a snowboard and go tubing downhill off **Glacier Point Rd**; plod around **Yosemite Valley** on a ranger-led snowshoe tour; or just try to stay upright on ice skates at **Curry Village**. Further south in Sequoia and Kings Canyon National Parks, the whole family can go snowshoeing or cross-country skiing among groves of giant sequoias. Before embarking on a winter trip to the parks, check road conditions on the official park websites or by calling ahead. Don't forget to put snow tires on your car, and always carry tire chains too.

DETOUR

Buck Rock Lookout

Start: 08 Cedar Grove

To climb one of California's most evocative fire lookouts, drive east of the Generals Hwy on Big Meadows Rd into the Sequoia National Forest between Grant Grove and the Giant Forest. Follow the signs to staffed **Buck Rock Fire Lookout** *(buckrock.org)*. Constructed in 1923, this active fire lookout allows panoramic views from a dollhouse-sized cab lording it over the horizon from 8500ft atop a granite rise, reached by 172 spindly stairs. It's not for anyone with vertigo. Opening hours may vary seasonally, and the lookout closes during lightning storms and fire emergencies.

09 Giant Forest

We dare you to try hugging the trees in Giant Forest, a 3-sq-mile grove protecting the park's most gargantuan specimens. Park off Wolverton Rd and walk downhill to reach the world's biggest living tree, the **General Sherman Tree**, which towers 275ft into the sky. With sore arms and sticky sap fingers, you can lose the crowds on any of many forested trails nearby. The trail network stretches all the way south to **Crescent Meadow**, a 5-mile one-way ramble.

By car, drive 2.5 miles south along the Generals Hwy to get schooled on sequoia ecology and fire cycles at the **Giant Forest Museum** *(nps.gov/seki)*. Starting outside the museum, Crescent Meadow Rd makes a 6-mile loop into the Giant Forest, passing right through Tunnel Log. For 360-degree views of the Great Western Divide, climb the steep quarter-mile staircase up **Moro Rock**. Note: Crescent Meadow Rd closes in the winter due to snow; during summer, ride the free shuttle buses around the loop road.

THE DRIVE: Narrowing, the Generals Hwy drops for more than 15 miles into the Sierra Nevada foothills, passing Amphitheater Point and exiting the park beyond Foothills Visitor Center. Before reaching the town of Three Rivers, turn left on Mineral King Rd, a dizzyingly scenic 25-mile road (partly unpaved, no trailers or RVs allowed and closed in winter) that switchbacks up to Mineral King Valley.

DETOUR

Crystal Cave

Start: 09 Giant Forest

Off the Generals Hwy, about 2 miles south of the Giant Forest Museum, turn right (west) onto twisting 6.5-mile-long Crystal Cave Rd for a fantastical walk inside 10,000-year-old **Crystal Cave** *(sequoiaparksconservancy.org/crystal-cave)*, carved by an underground river. Stalactites hang like daggers from the ceiling, and milky-white marble formations take the shape of ethereal curtains, domes, columns and shields. Bring a light jacket – it's 50°F (10°C) inside the cave. Buy tour tickets a month or more in advance online *(sequoiaparksconservancy.org)*; during October and November, tickets are only sold in person at the **Giant Forest Museum and Foothills Visitor Center**. Tour tickets are not available at the cave itself.

10 Mineral King Valley

Navigating over 700 hairpin turns, it's a winding 1½-hour drive up to the glacially sculpted Mineral King Valley (7500ft), a 19th-century silver-mining camp and lumber settlement, and later a mountain retreat. Trails into the high country begin at the end of **Mineral King Rd**, where historic private cabins dot the valley floor, flanked by massive mountains. Your final destination is just over a mile past the ranger station, where the valley unfolds all of its hidden beauty, and hikes to granite peaks and alpine lakes beckon.

Note that Mineral King Rd is typically open only from late May through late October. In summer, Mineral King's marmots like to chew on parked cars, so wrap the undercarriage of your vehicle with a tarp and rope (which can be bought, though not cheaply, at the hardware store in Three Rivers).

♥ WHY I LOVE THIS TRIP

MICHAEL GROSBERG, WRITER

When city life gets claustrophobic, the Sierra Nevada region beckons me. This drive takes you through scenery out of an Albert Bierstadt painting or a CGI version of the American West. Out of the car and into the wilderness, your thoughts become meditative as the rhythm of your walking pace and the challenge of the terrain are the only concerns.

42

CALIFORNIA & NEVADA

DISNEYLAND & ORANGE COUNTY BEACHES

★ BEST FOR

VIEWS

Corona del Mar's Lookout Point.

DURATION: 2–4 DAYS

DISTANCE: 65 MILES / 105KM

GREAT FOR: NATURE, FAMILIES

BEST TIME TO GO: JUNE TO SEPTEMBER FOR SUMMER BEACH SEASON.

Lookout Point (p345), Corona del Mar, California

You'll find gorgeous sunsets, prime surf breaks and just-off-the-boat seafood when road-tripping down the OC's sun-kissed coastal Hwy 1. Yet it's the unexpected, serendipitous discoveries you'll remember long after you've left these blissful 42 miles of surf and sand behind. Start with a couple days at Disneyland's theme parks, and call it a wrap for the perfect SoCal family vacation.

LINK YOUR TRIP

40 Coastal California
Orange County is California's official section of the Pacific Coast Hwy (PCH), running along Hwy 1 between Seal Beach and Dana Point.

01 Disneyland Resort

The West Coast's most popular attraction, **Disneyland** *(disneyland.disney.go.com)* has welcomed untold millions since opening in 1955. From the ghostly skeletons of Pirates of the Caribbean to the screeching monkeys of the Indiana Jones Adventure, the pure adrenalin of Space Mountain to Star Wars: Galaxy's Edge, there's magical detail everywhere. After dark, watch fireworks explode over Sleeping Beauty's Castle.

Across the plaza, Disneyland's younger neighbor, Disney California Adventure, highlights the best of the Golden State and moviedom in sections like Cars Land, Hollywoodland and Pixar Pier. Catch the World of Color special-effects show at night.

JON BILOUS/SHUTTERSTOCK

The adjacent, pedestrian Downtown Disney District is packed with souvenir shops, family restaurants, after-dark bars and entertainment venues.

THE DRIVE: Follow I-5 south, then take Hwy 22 west through inland Orange County, merging onto I-405 north. After another mile or so, exit onto Seal Beach Blvd, which crawls 3 miles toward the coast. Turn right onto Hwy 1, also known as the Pacific Coast Hwy (PCH) throughout Orange County, then take a left onto Main St in Seal Beach.

02 Seal Beach

In the SoCal beauty pageant for pint-sized beach towns, Seal Beach takes the crown as a refreshingly unhurried alternative to the more crowded Orange County coast further south. Its stoplight-free, three-block Main St bustles with mom-and-pop restaurants and indie shops that are low on 'tude and high on nostalgia. Follow barefoot surfers trotting toward the ocean where Main St ends, then walk out onto **Seal Beach Pier**. Down on the beach, you'll find families spread out on blankets, building sandcastles and playing in the water – all of them ignoring that hideous oil derrick offshore. The gentle waves make Seal Beach a great place to learn to surf. **M&M Surfing School** *(surfingschool.com)* parks its van in the lot just north of the pier, off Ocean Ave at 8th St.

THE DRIVE: Past a short bridge south along Hwy 1, drivers drop onto a mile-long spit of land known as Sunset Beach, with its biker bars and harborside kayak and stand-up paddleboarding (SUP) rental shops. Keep cruising Hwy 1 south another 6 miles past Bolsa Chica State Beach and Ecological Reserve to Huntington Beach Pier.

03 Huntington Beach

In 'Surf City USA,' SoCal's obsession with wave riding hits its frenzied peak. There's a statue of Hawaiian surfer Duke Kahanamoku at the intersection of Main St and PCH, and if you look down, you'll see names of legendary surfers in the sidewalk **Surfers' Hall of Fame** *(hsssurf.com/shof)*; find out more about them a few blocks east at the **International Surfing Museum** *(huntingtonbeachsurfingmuseum.org)*. On Huntington Beach Pier, you can catch up-close views of daredevils barreling through tubes, though newbie surfers should try elsewhere – locals can be territorial. In summer, the US Open of Surfing draws more than 600 world-class surfers and 500,000 spectators with a mini village of concerts and more. Otherwise, wide, flat **Huntington City Beach** is a perfect place to snooze on the sand on a giant beach towel. Snag a fire pit just south of the pier to build an evening bonfire with friends.

THE DRIVE: From the Huntington Beach Pier at the intersection of Main St, drive south on Hwy 1 alongside the ocean for another 4 miles to Newport Beach. Turn right onto W Balboa Blvd, which leads onto the Balboa Peninsula and is squeezed between the ocean and Balboa Island, off Newport Harbor.

04 Newport Beach

As seen on Bravo's *Real Housewives of Orange County* and Fox' *The OC* and *Arrested Development*, in glitzy Newport Beach wealthy socialites, glamorous teens and gorgeous beaches all share the spotlight. Bikini vixens strut down the sandy beach stretching between the peninsula's twin piers, while boogie boarders brave human-eating waves at the Wedge and the ballet of yachts in the harbor makes you dream of being rich and famous. From the harbor, hop aboard a ferry over to old-fashioned **Balboa Island** *(balboaisland.com)* or climb aboard the Ferris wheel at the pint-sized **Balboa Fun Zone** *(thebalboafunzone.com),* near the landmark 1906 **Balboa Pavilion**.

THE DRIVE: South of Newport Beach, prime-time ocean views are just a short detour off Hwy 1. First drive south across the bridge over Newport Channel, then after 3 miles turn right onto Marguerite Ave in Corona del Mar. Once you reach the coast, take another right onto Ocean Blvd.

05 Corona del Mar

Savor some of SoCal's most celebrated ocean views from the bluffs of Corona del Mar, a chi-chi bedroom community south of Newport Channel. Several postcard beaches, rocky coves and child-friendly tide pools beckon along this idyllic stretch of coast. One of the best viewpoints is at breezy **Lookout Point** on Ocean Blvd near Heliotrope Ave. Below the rocky cliffs to the east is half-mile-long **Main Beach** *(newportbeachca.gov),* with fire rings and volleyball courts (arrive early on weekends to get a parking spot). Stairs lead down to **Pirates Cove**, a great, waveless pocket beach for families – scenes from the classic TV show *Gilligan's Island* were shot here. Head east on Ocean Blvd to **Inspiration Point**, near the corner of Orchid Ave, for more vistas of surf, sand and sea.

Heisler Park, Laguna Beach, California

JON BILOUS/SHUTTERSTOCK

THE DRIVE: Follow Orchid Ave back north to Hwy 1, then turn right and drive southbound. Traffic thins out as ocean views become more wild and uncluttered by housing developments that head up into the hills on your left. It's just a couple of miles to the entrance of Crystal Cove State Park.

06 Crystal Cove State Park

With more than 3 miles of open beach and 2400 acres of undeveloped woodland, **Crystal Cove State Park** *(parks.ca.gov)* lets you almost forget that you're in a crowded metro area. It's also an underwater park where scuba enthusiasts can check out the wreck of a Navy Corsair fighter plane that went down in 1949. Or just go tide pooling, fishing, kayaking and surfing along Crystal Cove's exhilaratingly wild, windy shoreline. On the inland side of Hwy 1, miles of hiking and mountain-biking trails wait for landlubbers.

THE DRIVE: Drive south on Hwy 1 for another 4 miles or so. As shops, restaurants, art galleries, motels and hotels start to crowd the highway once again, you've arrived in Laguna Beach. Downtown is a maze of one-way streets just east of the Laguna Canyon Rd (Hwy 133) intersection.

♥ WHY I LOVE THIS TRIP

ANDREW BENDER, WRITER

The OC coast is a microcosm of the best of SoCal: 42 miles of gorgeous sunsets, prime surfing, just-off-the-boat seafood, secluded coves and sparkling white sands. Each town offers its own experience – surf lessons in Seal Beach, beach volleyball at Huntington Beach, boating around Newport Harbor, eclectic art in Laguna Beach, whale-spotting off Dana Point – but sometimes the best plan is no plan at all.

07 Laguna Beach

This early 20th-century artist colony's secluded coves, romantic-looking cliffs and arts-and-crafts bungalows come as a relief after miles of suburban beige-box architecture. Laguna celebrates its bohemian roots with summer arts festivals, dozens of galleries and the acclaimed **Laguna Art Museum** *(lagunaartmuseum.org).* In downtown's village, while away an afternoon browsing the chic boutiques. Along the shore, **Main Beach** is crowded with volleyball players and sunbathers. Just north atop the bluffs, **Heisler Park** winds past public art, palm trees, picnic tables and grand views of rocky shores and tide pools. Drop down to **Divers Cove**, a deep, protected inlet. Heading south, dozens of public beaches sprawl along just a few miles of coastline. Keep a sharp eye out for 'beach access' signs off Hwy 1, or pull into locals' favorite **Aliso Beach** *(lagunabeachcity.net)*.

THE DRIVE: Keep driving south of downtown Laguna Beach on Hwy 1 (PCH) for about 3 miles to Aliso Beach, then another 4 miles into the town of Dana Point. Turn right onto Green Lantern St, then left onto Cove Rd, which winds past the state beach and Ocean Institute onto Dana Point Harbor Dr.

DETOUR

Pacific Marine Mammal Center
Start: 07 Laguna Beach

About 3 miles inland from Laguna Beach is the heart-warming **Pacific Marine Mammal Center** *(pacificmmc.org)*, dedicated to rescuing and rehabilitating injured or ill marine mammals. This nonprofit center has a small staff and many volunteers who help nurse rescued pinnipeds (mostly sea lions and seals) back to health before releasing them into the wild. Stop by and take a self-guided facility tour to learn more about these marine mammals and to visit the 'patients' out back.

08 Dana Point

Dana Point is all about family fun with whale-watching and sportfishing boats departing from its harbor. Designed for kids, the **Ocean Institute** *(oceaninstitute.org)* has replicas of historic tall ships, maritime-related exhibits and a floating research lab. East of the harbor, **Doheny State Beach** *(dohenystatebeach.org)* offers picnic tables, volleyball courts, an oceanfront bike path and a sandy beach for swimming, surfing and tide pooling.

Surfers, Huntington City Beach (p343), California
VALERIA VENEZIA/SHUTTERSTOCK

PHOTO OPPORTUNITY

Surfers at Huntington Beach Pier.

43

★ BEST FOR

SOLITUDE

Hike to the Lost Palms Oasis.

CALIFORNIA & NEVADA

PALM SPRINGS & JOSHUA TREE OASES

DURATION: 2–3 DAYS

DISTANCE: 170 MILES / 274KM

GREAT FOR: HISTORY & CULTURE, NATURE

BEST TIME TO GO: FEBRUARY TO APRIL FOR SPRING WILDFLOWER BLOOMS AND COOLER TEMPERATURES.

Palm Springs California

Just a short drive from the chic resorts of Palm Springs, the vast Mojave and Sonoran Deserts are serenely spiritual places. You may find that what at first looked like desolate sands transform on foot into perfect beauty: shady palm tree and cactus gardens, tiny wildflowers pushing up from hard-baked soil in spring, natural hot-spring pools for soaking, and uncountable stars overhead in the inky dark.

LINK YOUR TRIP

42 Disneyland & Orange County Beaches
Drive 110 miles west starting on I-10 to Disney's Magic Kingdom, then cruise the OC's bodacious beach towns.

44 Eastern Sierra Scenic Byway
Head northwest via I-10, I-15 and Hwy 395 for 245 miles to Lone Pine, cinematically set beneath the majestic Sierra Nevada.

01 Palm Springs

Hollywood celebs have always counted on Palm Springs as a quick escape from LA. Today, this desert resort town is a showcase of retro-chic mid-century modern buildings. Stop at the **Palm Springs Visitor Center** *(visitpalmsprings.com)*, inside a 1965 gas station by Albert Frey, to pick up a self-guided architectural tour map. Then drive uphill to be whisked from desert floor to alpine forest on the rotating **Palm Springs Aerial Tramway** *(pstramway.com)* in just 15 minutes. Back down, drive south on Palm Canyon Dr to get your culture kicks at the excellent **Palm Springs Art Museum** *(psmuseum.org)*, followed by a hop between art galleries, cafes, cocktail bars, trendy restaurants and chic boutiques. Finally, head 10 miles downvalley for a saunter around the magnificent gardens of **Sunnylands** *(sunnylands.org)*,

CRE8 DESIGN/SHUTTERSTOCK

the desert retreat where Walter and Leonore Annenberg once welcomed US presidents, royalty and celebs.

THE DRIVE: Drive north out of downtown Palm Springs along Indian Canyon Dr for 7 miles, passing over I-10. Turn right onto Dillon Rd, then after 2.5 miles cut a left onto Palm Dr, which heads north into central Desert Hot Springs.

02 Desert Hot Springs

In 1774 Spanish explorer Juan Bautista de Anza was the first European to encounter the desert Cahuilla tribe. Afterward, the Spanish name Agua Caliente came to refer to both the Indigenous people and the natural hot springs that still bubble up restoratively from below the town of **Desert Hot Springs** *(visitdeserthotsprings.com)*. You can 'take the waters' in family-friendly resorts or stylish adult-only healing hideaways like the **Two Bunch Palms Resort & Spa** *(twobunchpalms.com/spa)* that sits atop an actual oasis. Imitate Tim Robbins who enjoyed a mud bath here in the 1992 Robert Altman film *The Player,* then bounce between pools and sunbathing areas or enjoy a massage all the while maintaining the code of silence (actually, whispers only).

THE DRIVE: Head west on Pierson Blvd back to Indian Canyon Dr. Turn right and drive northwest through the dusty outskirts of Desert Hot Springs. Turn right onto Hwy 62 eastbound toward Yucca Valley; after about 4 miles, turn right onto East Dr and look for signs for Big Morongo Canyon Preserve.

03 Big Morongo Canyon Preserve

An oasis hidden in the high desert, **Big Morongo Canyon Preserve** *(parks.sbcounty.gov)* is a riparian habitat flush with cottonwood and willow trees. Attracted by the water, mule deer, bighorn sheep, coyotes and other critters pass through this wildlife corridor linking the San Gorgonio Mountains and Joshua Tree National Park. The preserve is also an internationally recognized bird-watching hot spot; around 250 bird species have been identified here, including at least 72 that use the area as breeding grounds, such as the coral-red summer tanager and the brown-crested flycatcher. Keep an eye out (better yet, bring binoculars) as you trek along several short trails meandering through this marshy land where hummingbirds flutter and woodpeckers attack trees.

THE DRIVE: Rejoin Hwy 62 eastbound, which soon passes through Yucca Valley where you'll find some cool roadside antiques, vintage shops, art galleries and cafes. Continue east for another 16 miles to the town of Joshua Tree, which makes a handy base for the night. If necessary, fill up your gas tank at the intersection with Park Blvd before turning right and driving 5 miles to Joshua Tree National Park's west entrance.

04 Hidden Valley

It's time to jump into **Joshua Tree National Park** *(nps.gov/jotr)*, a wonderland of bulbous boulders and jumbo rocks interspersed with sandy forests of Joshua trees. Related to agave plants, Joshua trees were named by Mormon settlers who thought the twisted, spiky arms resembled a prophet's arms stretching toward God. Revel in the scenery as you drive along the winding park road for about 8 miles to Hidden Valley parking area. From here, an easy 1-mile loop trail meanders between whimsical rock clusters to a hidden valley where cattle rustlers once hid their hoard. If you enjoy history and Western lore, check with the national park office for ranger-led walking tours of nearby **Keys Ranch** *(nps.gov/jotr)* where pioneer homesteaders tried their hand at cattle ranching, mining and desert farming in the 19th century.

THE DRIVE: Backtrack to Park Blvd, turn left and head south again past jumbled rock formations and fields of spiky Joshua trees. Take the well-signed right turn toward Keys View. You'll pass several trailheads and roadside interpretive exhibits over the next 5.5 miles leading up to the viewpoint.

05 Keys View

Make sure you embark at least an hour before sunset for the drive up to Keys View (5185ft), where panoramic views look into the Coachella Valley and reach as far south as the shimmering Salton Sea or, on an unusually clear day, Mexico's Signal Mountain. Also looming in the distance are Mt San Jacinto (10,834ft) and Mt San Gorgonio (11,500ft), Southern California's highest peaks that are often snow-dusted until late spring. Down below snakes a section of the San Andreas Fault.

THE DRIVE: Head back downhill to Park Blvd. Turn right and wind through the park's Wonderland of Rocks (where boulders call out to scampering kids and serious rock jocks alike), passing more campgrounds. After 10 miles, veer left to stay on Park Blvd and drive north for 8 miles toward the town of Twentynine Palms onto Utah Trail.

06 Oasis of Mara

Drop by Joshua Tree National Park's **Oasis Visitor Center** *(nps.gov/jotr)* for its educational exhibits about Southern California's desert fan palms. These palms are often found growing along fault lines, where cracks in the earth's crust

Joshua Tree National Park, California
FOTIMAGEON/SHUTTERSTOCK

PHOTO OPPORTUNITY

Sunset from Keys View.

allow subterranean water to surface. Outside the visitor center, a gentle half-mile nature trail leads around the **Oasis of Mara** with the original 29 palm trees that gave Twentynine Palms its name. They were planted by native Serranos who named the area Mara, meaning 'the place of little springs and much grass'. Ask for directions to the trailhead off Hwy 62 for the 3-mile, round-trip hike to **49 Palms Oasis**, where a sun-exposed dirt trail marches you over a ridge, then drops you into a rocky gorge, doggedly heading down past barrel cacti toward a distant speck of green.

THE DRIVE: Drive back south on Utah Trail and re-enter the park. Follow Park Blvd south, turning left at the first major junction onto Pinto Basin Rd for a winding 30-mile drive southeast to Cottonwood Spring.

07 Cottonwood Spring

On your drive to Cottonwood Spring, you'll pass from the high Mojave Desert into the lower Sonoran Desert. Stop at the **Cholla Cactus Garden**, where a quarter-mile loop winds through a dense grove of 'teddy bear' cholla cactus and ocotillo plants that look like green octopus tentacles and are adorned with flaming scarlet flowers in spring. Turn left at the **Cottonwood Visitor Center** *(nps.gov/jotr)* for a short drive east past the campground to **Cottonwood Spring** *(nps.gov/jotr)*. Once used by the Cahuilla, who left behind archaeological evidence such as mortars and clay pots, the springs became a hotbed for gold mining in the late 19th century. The now-dry springs are the start of the moderately strenuous 7.5-mile round-trip trek out to Lost Palms Oasis, a fan-palm oasis blessed with solitude and scenery.

THE DRIVE: Head south from Cottonwood Springs and drive across I-10 to pick up scenic Box Canyon Rd, which burrows a hole through the desert, twisting its way toward the Salton Sea. Take 66th Ave west to Mecca, then turn right onto Hwy 111 and drive northwest toward Indio.

DETOUR

Salton Sea & Slab City
Start: 07 Cottonwood Spring

Driving along Hwy 111 southeast of Mecca, you soon hit a most unexpected sight: California's largest lake in the middle of its largest desert. The Salton Sea was created by accident in 1905 when spring flooding breached irrigation canals built to bring water from the Colorado River to the farmland in the Imperial Valley. As a long-time stopover along the Pacific Flyway, it's a prime birding spot. Alas, the winged creatures' survival is threatened by decreasing water levels and rising salinity from decades of agricultural run-off bloated with fertilizers.

About 10 miles east of the Salton Sea, near Niland, an even stranger sight is folk-art **Salvation Mountain** *(salvationmountaininc.org)*, an artificial hill slathered in paint and decorated with flowers, waterfalls, birds and religious messages. It's part of Slab City, an off-grid community set up atop the concrete remains of a former military base. It attracts society dropouts, drifters, retirees, snowbirds and just plain kooky folk – thousands in the winter, a few hardened souls year-round. Self-dubbed 'the last free place on earth', the Slabs is more organized than first meets the eye, with individual 'neighborhoods' and even a library and a hostel. While here, also check out the wacky installations at the East Jesus artist colony.

08 Coachella Valley

The hot but fertile Coachella Valley may be world-famous for its star-studded indie music and art festival held every April in Indio, but it's also the ideal place to find the date of your dreams – the kind that grows on trees, that is. Date farms let you sample exotic-sounding varieties like halawy, deglet noor and zahidi for free. The signature taste of the valley is a rich date shake from certified-organic **Oasis Date Gardens** *(oasisdate.com)* in Thermal or the 1920s pioneer **Shields Date Garden** *(shieldsdategarden.com)* in Indio.

Keys View (p350), over Coachella Valley, Joshua Tree National Park, Califonia
LYONSTOCK/SHUTTERSTOCK

44

CALIFORNIA & NEVADA

EASTERN SIERRA SCENIC BYWAY

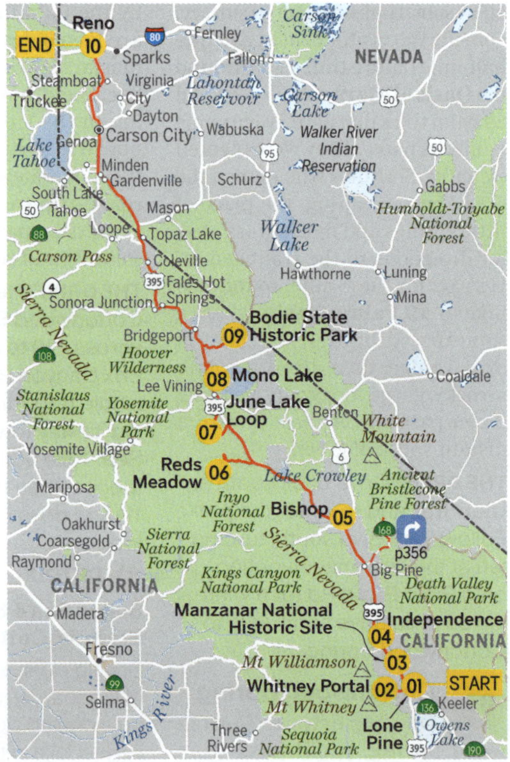

DURATION: 3–5 DAYS

DISTANCE: 360 MILES / 580KM

GREAT FOR: HISTORY & CULTURE, NATURE, FAMILIES

BEST TIME TO GO: JUNE TO SEPTEMBER FOR WARM DAYS AND (MOSTLY) SNOW-FREE MOUNTAIN RAMBLINGS.

The gateway to California's largest expanse of wilderness, Hwy 395 – also called the Eastern Sierra Scenic Byway – borders towering mountain vistas, glistening blue lakes and the seemingly endless forests of the eastern Sierra Nevada mountains. A lifetime of outdoor activities beckons beyond the asphalt (parts of which get traffic clogged in summer), and desolate Old West ghost towns, unique geological formations and burbling natural hot springs await exploration.

LINK YOUR TRIP

41 Yosemite, Sequoia & Kings Canyon National Parks
In Lee Vining, go west on Hwy 120 to enter Yosemite National Park via the 9945ft Tioga Pass.

43 Palm Springs & Joshua Tree Oases
From Lone Pine, it's a 245-mile drive southeast via Hwy 395, I-15 and I-10 to SoCal's desert playground.

01 Lone Pine

The diminutive town of Lone Pine stands as the southern gateway to the craggy jewels of the Eastern Sierra. At the southern end of town, drop by the **Museum of Western Film History** *(museumofwesternfilmhistory.org)*, which contains exhibits of paraphernalia from the over 450 movies shot in the area. Don't miss the occasional screenings in its theater or the 1928 Lincoln Camera Carin its foyer.

Just outside the center of town on Whitney Portal Rd, an otherworldly orange alpenglow makes the Alabama Hills a must for watching a slow-motion sunset. A frequent backdrop for movie Westerns and the Lone Ranger TV series, the rounded earthen-colored mounds stand out against the steely gray foothills and jagged pinnacles of the Sierra range, and a number of graceful rock arches are within easy hiking distance of the roads.

MELISSAMN/SHUTTERSTOCK

★ BEST FOR

OUTDOORS

Hike tranquil mountain trails and camp in Mammoth Lakes.

Sierra Nevada mountains, California

THE DRIVE: From Lone Pine, the jagged incisors of the Sierra surge skyward in all their raw and fierce glory. Continue west past the Alabama Hills and then brace yourself for the dizzying ascent to road's end – a total of 13 miles from Hwy 395. The White Mountains soar to the east, and the dramatic Owens Valley spreads below.

02 Whitney Portal

At 14,505ft, the celestial granite giant of **Mt Whitney** *(fs.usda.gov/inyo)* stands as the loftiest peak in the lower 48 and the obsession of thousands of high-country hikers every summer. Desperately coveted permits (assigned by advance lottery) are your only passport to the summit, though drop-in day trippers can swan up the mountain as far as **Lone Pine Lake** – about 6 miles round trip – to kick up some dust on the iconic **Whitney Trail**. Ravenous hikers can stop by the **Whitney Portal Store** *(facebook.com/WhitneyPortalStore)* for enormous burgers and plate-size pancakes.

As you get a fix on this majestic megalith cradled by scores of smaller pinnacles, remember that the country's lowest point is only 80 miles (as the crow flies) east of here: Badwater in Death Valley.

THE DRIVE: Double back to Lone Pine and drive 9 miles north on divided Hwy 395. Scrub brush and tumbleweed desert occupy the valley between the copper-colored foothills of the Sierra Nevada and the White Mountain range. Well-signed Manzanar sits along the west side of the highway.

03 Manzanar National Historic Site

A monument to one of the darkest chapters in US history, Manzanar unfolds across a barren and windy sweep of land cradled by snow-dipped peaks. During the height of WWII, the federal government interned more than 10,000 people of Japanese ancestry here following the attack on Pearl Harbor. Though little remains of the infamous war concentration camp, the camp's former high-school auditorium houses a superb interpretive center *(nps.gov/manz)*. Watch the 22-minute documentary film, then explore the thought-provoking exhibits chronicling the stories of the families that languished here yet built a vibrant community. Afterwards, take a self-guided 3.2-mile driving tour around the grounds, which include a recreated mess hall and barracks, vestiges of buildings and gardens, as well as the haunting camp cemetery.

Often mistaken for Mt Whitney, 14,375ft Mt Williamson looms above this flat, dusty plain, a lonely expanse that bursts with yellow wildflowers in spring.

THE DRIVE: Continue north 6 miles on Hwy 395 to the small town of Independence. In the center of town, look for the columned Inyo County Courthouse and turn left onto W Center St. Drive six blocks through a residential area to the end of the road.

PHOTO OPPORTUNITY

Sunrise or sunset in the Alabama Hills, framed by the snowy Sierra Nevada.

04 Independence

This sleepy highway town has been a county seat since 1866 and is home to the Eastern California Museum (inyocounty.us/ecmsite). An excellent archive of Eastern Sierra history and culture, it contains one of the most complete collections of Paiute and Shoshone baskets in the country, as well as historic photographs of local rock climbers scaling Sierra peaks – including Mt Whitney – with huge packs and no harnesses. Other highlights include artifacts from Manzanar and an exhibit about the fight to keep the region's water supply from being diverted to Los Angeles.

Fans of Mary Austin (1868–1934), renowned author of *The Land of Little Rain* and vocal foe of the desertification of the Owens Valley, can follow signs leading to her former house at 253 Market St.

THE DRIVE: Depart north along Hwy 395 as civilization again recedes amid a buffer of dreamy granite mountains, midsize foothills and (for most of the year) an expanse of bright blue sky. Tuffs of blackened volcanic rock occasionally appear roadside. Pass through the blink-and-you'll-miss-it town of Big Pine, and enter Bishop.

DETOUR

Ancient Bristlecone Pine Forest
Start: 04 Independence

For encounters with some of the earth's oldest living things, plan at least a half-day trip to the **Ancient Bristlecone Pine Forest** *(fs.usda.gov/inyo)*. These gnarled, otherworldly-looking trees thrive

Mono Lake, California

GEORGE LAMSON/SHUTTERSTOCK

above 10,000ft on the slopes of the seemingly inhospitable White Mountains, a parched and stark range that once stood even higher than the Sierra. One of the oldest trees – called Methuselah – is estimated to be over 4700 years old, beating even the Great Sphinx of Giza by about two centuries.

To reach the groves, take Hwy 168 east 12 miles from Big Pine to White Mountain Rd, then turn left (north) and climb the curvy road 10 miles to Schulman Grove, named for the scientist who first discovered the trees' biblical age in the 1950s. The entire trip takes about one hour one way from Independence. There's access to self-guided trails near the solar-powered **Schulman Grove Visitor Center** *(fs.usda.gov/inyo)*. White Mountain Rd is usually closed from November to April.

05 Bishop

The second-largest town in the Eastern Sierra and about a third of the way north from Lone Pine to Reno, Bishop is a major hub for hikers, cyclists, anglers and climbers. To get a taste of what draws them here, head to the Happy and Sad Boulders areas in the strikingly unique rocky **Volcanic Tablelands** not far north of town.

Where Hwy 395 swings west, continue northeast for 4.5 miles on Hwy 6 to reach the **Laws Railroad Museum & Historic Site** *(lawsmuseum.org)*, a remnant of the narrow-gauge Carson and Colorado rail line that closed in 1960. Train buffs will hyperventilate over the collection of antique railcars, and kids love exploring the 1883 depot and clanging the brass bell. Dozens of historic buildings from the region have been reassembled with period artifacts to create a time-capsule village.

THE DRIVE: Back on Hwy 395, continue over 40 miles north to Hwy 203, passing Lake Crowley and the southern reaches of the Long Valley Caldera seismic area. Follow Hwy 203 to The Village at Mammoth Lakes. Park and take the mandatory Reds Meadow/Devils Postpile Shuttle *(estransit.com/reds-meadow-shuttle)*. Operations vary based on seasonal snowfall and road-repair schedules.

06 Reds Meadow

One of the most beautiful and varied landscapes near Mammoth is the Reds Meadow Valley, west of Mammoth Mountain. The most fascinating attraction in Reds Meadow is the surreal 10,000-year-old volcanic formation of **Devils Postpile National Monument** *(nps.gov/depo)*. The 60ft curtains of near-vertical, six-sided basalt columns formed when rivers of molten lava slowed, cooled and cracked with perplexing symmetry. This honeycomb design is best appreciated from atop the columns, reached by a short trail. The columns are an easy half-mile hike from the **Devils Postpile Ranger Station** *(nps.gov/depo)*.

From the monument, a 2.5-mile hike passing through fire-scarred forest leads to the spectacular **Rainbow Falls**, where the San Joaquin River gushes over a 101ft basalt cliff. Chances of actually seeing a rainbow forming in the billowing mist are greatest at noon. The falls can also be reached via an easy 1.5-mile walk from the Reds Meadow shuttle stop.

THE DRIVE: Back on Hwy 395, continue north to Hwy 158 and pull out the camera for the alpine lake and peak vistas of the June Lake Loop.

07 June Lake Loop

Under the shadow of massive Carson Peak (10,909ft), the stunning 16-mile **June Lake Loop** (Hwy 158) meanders through a picture-perfect horseshoe canyon, past the relaxed resort town of June Lake and four sparkling, fish-rich lakes: Grant, Silver, Gull and June. It's especially scenic in fall when the basin is ablaze with golden aspens. Hardy ice climbers scale its frozen waterfalls in winter.

June Lake is backed by the **Ansel Adams Wilderness**, which runs into Yosemite National Park. From Silver Lake, Gem and Agnew Lakes make spectacular day hikes, and boat rentals and horseback rides are available.

THE DRIVE: Rejoin Hwy 395 heading north, where the rounded Mono Craters dot the dry and scrubby eastern landscape and the Mono Lake Basin unfolds into view.

08 Mono Lake

North America's second-oldest lake is a quiet and mysterious expanse of deep blue water, whose glassy surface reflects jagged Sierra peaks, young volcanic cones and the unearthly tufa (too-fah) towers that make the lake so distinctive. Protruding from the water like drip sand castles, tufas form when calcium bubbles up from subterranean springs and combines with carbonate in the alkaline lake waters.

The salinity and alkaline levels are unfortunately too high for a pleasant swim. Instead, paddle a kayak or canoe around the weathered towers of tufa, drink in wide-open views of the Mono Craters volcanic field, and discreetly spy on the water birds that live in this unique habitat.

EASTERN SIERRA HOT SPRINGS

Nestled between the White Mountains and the Sierra Nevada near Mammoth is a tantalizing slew of natural pools with snowcapped panoramic views. When the high-altitude summer nights turn chilly and the coyotes cry, you'll never want to towel off. About 9 miles southeast of Mammoth Lakes, Benton Crossing Rd juts east off Hwy 395, accessing a delicious bounty of hot springs.

To overnight with your very own private hot-springs tub, head to the **Inn at Benton Hot Springs** *(bentonhotsprings.org)*, a small, historic resort in a 150-year-old former silver-mining town nestled in the White Mountains.

For detailed directions and maps, pick up Matt Bischoff's excellent *Touring Hot Springs California and Nevada: A Guide to the Best Hot Springs in the Far West* for directions to a few.

The **Mono Basin Scenic Area Visitor Center** *(fs.usda.gov/inyo)*, half a mile north of Lee Vining, has interpretive displays, a bookstore and a 20-minute movie about Mono Lake.

THE DRIVE: About 10 miles north of Lee Vining, Hwy 395 arrives at its highest point, Conway Summit (8148ft). Pull off at the vista point for awe-inspiring panoramas of Mono Lake, backed by the Mono Craters and June and Mammoth Mountains. Continue approximately 8 miles north, and go 13 miles east on Hwy 270 (closed in winter); the last 3 miles are unpaved.

09 Bodie State Historic Park

For a time warp back to the gold-rush era, swing by **Bodie** *(parks.ca.gov/bodie)*, one of the West's most authentic and best-preserved ghost towns. Gold was discovered here in 1859, and the place grew from a bare-bones mining camp to a lawless boomtown of 10,000. Fights and murders occurred almost daily, fueled by liquor from 65 saloons, some of which doubled as brothels, gambling halls or opium dens.

The hills disgorged some \$35 million worth of gold and silver in the 1870s and '80s, but when production plummeted, Bodie was abandoned, and about 200 weather-beaten buildings now sit frozen in time in this cold, barren and windswept valley. Peering through dusty windows you'll see stocked stores, furnished homes, a schoolhouse with desks and books, the jail and many other buildings. The former **Miners' Union Hall** now houses a museum and visitor center, and rangers conduct free tours in summer.

THE DRIVE: Retrace your way back to Hwy 395, where you'll soon come to the big-sky settlement of Bridgeport. From here, it's approximately two hours to Reno along a lovely two-lane section of the highway that traces the bank of the snaking Walker River.

10 Reno

Nevada's second-largest city has steadily carved a non-casino niche as an all-season outdoor-recreation spot. The Truckee River bisects the heart of the mountain-ringed city, and in the heat of summer the **Truckee River Whitewater Park** *(reno.gov)* teems with urban kayakers and swimmers bobbing along on inner tubes. Two kayak courses wrap around Wingfield Park, a small river island that hosts free concerts in summertime. **Sierra Adventures** *(wildsierra.com)* offers kayak rentals, tours and lessons.

Benton Hot Springs, California
CAMPPHOTO/GETTY IMAGES

45

CALIFORNIA & NEVADA

BAY AREA CULINARY TOUR

★ BEST FOR

PICNICS

Briny oysters, local bread and cheeses, and Heidrun sparkling mead at Hog Island Oyster Company.

Cheese, Cowgirl Creamery & Cantina, Point Reyes Station, California

DURATION: 2–3 DAYS

DISTANCE: 160 MILES / 255KM

GREAT FOR: FOOD & DRINK, OUTDOOR

BEST TIME TO GO: LATE SUMMER OR EARLY FALL, WHEN FARMS DELIVER THEIR TASTIEST BOUNTY.

Making a delicious loop around the Bay Area, you'll wander through the aisles of celebrated farmers markets and drop in on artisanal food and drink producers, from Hog Island oyster farm to Cowgirl Creamery and more. A hike at Point Reyes National Seashore will work up a healthy appetite. You'll need it on this straight-from-the-source trip to foodie heaven.

LINK YOUR TRIP

46 Napa Valley
Cruise 26 miles east from Petaluma to Napa, the gateway to America's most famous wine region, home to several of California's best restaurants.

01 Sebastopol

This western Sonoma farm town was founded in the 19th century, when apples were its main cash crop. Swing by in August for the **Gravenstein Apple Fair** *(gravensteinapplefair.com)*, a lively weekend celebration of local food, wines and brews, accompanied by live music and more. In late summer and early autumn, you can pick your own apples at orchards on the outskirts of town along Sonoma **County's Farm Trails** *(farmtrails.org)*.

But Sebastopol is about so much more than apples these days. Just look at the **Barlow** *(thebarlow.net)*, a former apple-processing plant that has been repurposed into a 12-acre village of food producers, artists, wine-makers, coffee roasters and spirit distillers who showcase West County's culinary and artistic diversity. Wander shed to shed, sample everything from microbrewed beer

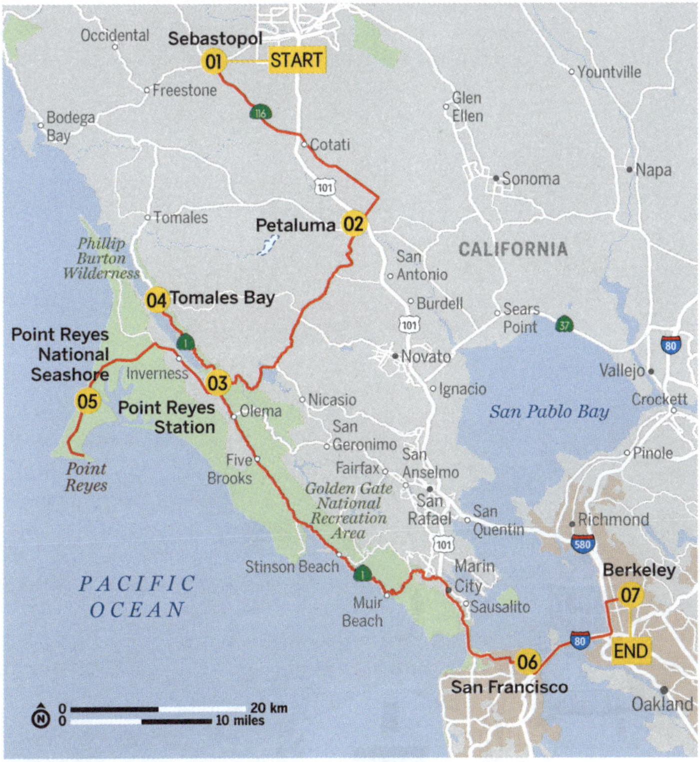

SABRINA DALBESIO/LONELY PLANET

to nitrogen flash-frozen ice-cream, and meet artisanal makers in their workshops.

THE DRIVE: Follow Hwy 116 south out of town for 8 miles to Cotati. Keep going across Hwy 101 (the speedier but more boring route to Petaluma) and turn right onto Old Redwood Hwy. After 3 miles, go left on pastoral Old Adobe Rd for 6 miles, turning left just past Petaluma Adobe State Historic Park.

02 Petaluma

'The world's egg basket' – as the agrarian town of Petaluma has long been known – is home to countless chicken farms that sell fresh eggs and dairy products. Across Hwy 101 and west of downtown, the **Petaluma Creamery** *(springhillcheese.com)* has been in business for more than a century. Stop by to sample organic cheeses or for a scoop of lavender or Meyer-lemon ice-cream from the small specialty-foods market and cafe.

More recently, Petaluma has earned a reputation for its densely foggy and wind-whipped appellation, which winegrowers have dubbed 'the Petaluma Gap.' As wineries such as **Keller Estate** *(kellerestate.com)* have become more prominent, the region's chardonnays, pinot noirs and syrahs have gained recognition for their elegance and complexity.

THE DRIVE: From downtown Petaluma, take D St southwest to Red Hill Rd and follow Point Reyes–Petaluma Rd toward the coast, turning left onto Hwy 1 for Point Reyes Station. It's a relaxing 19-mile country drive; stop en route for Camembert or Brie at the Marin French Cheese factory store.

03 Point Reyes Station

Surrounded by dairies and ranches, Point Reyes Station became a hub for artists in the 1960s. Today it offers a collection of art galleries, boutique shops and excellent food. The tour of the town's edibles begins by fighting your way through the spandex-clad crowd of weekend cyclists to grab a crusty loaf of fire-baked Brickmaiden Bread at **Bovine Bakery**. Next, step down the block to the restored barn that houses one of California's most sought-after cheesemakers, **Cowgirl Creamery & Cantina**. In spring the must-buy is its St Pat's, a smooth, mellow round wrapped in wild nettle leaves. Otherwise, the Mt Tam (available year-round) is pretty damn good, and there's a gourmet deli for picking up picnic supplies. Heading north out of town, **Heidrun Meadery** *(heidrunmeadery.com)* pours tasting sips of sparkling mead, made from aromatic small-batch honey in the style of French champagne.

THE DRIVE: Follow Hwy 1 north out of the tiny village of Point Reyes Station. Cruise for 9 miles along the east side of tranquil Tomales Bay, which flows many miles out into the Pacific. Just before the turnoff for rural Marshall–Petaluma Rd, look for the sign for bayfront Hog Island Oyster Company on your left.

04 Tomales Bay

Only 10 minutes north of Point Reyes Station, you'll find the salty turnout for the **Hog Island Oyster Company** *(hogisland oysters.com)*. There's not much to

see: just some picnic tables and BBQ grills, an outdoor cafe and a small window vending the famously silky oysters and a few other picnic provisions. While you can buy oysters to go (by the pound), for a fee you can nab a picnic table, borrow shucking tools and take a lesson on how to crack open the oysters yourself. Lunch at the waterfront farm is unforgettable – and very popular, so reserve ahead for a picnic table or for a seat at the communal tables.

THE DRIVE: Backtrack 10 miles south on Hwy 1 through Point Reyes Station. Turn right onto Sir Francis Drake Blvd, following the signs for Point Reyes National Seashore, just on the other side of Tomales Bay.

05 Point Reyes National Seashore

For another perfect picnic spot, look down the coast to **Point Reyes National Seashore** *(nps.gov/pore)*. The windswept peninsula's rough-hewn beauty lures marine mammals and migratory birds. The 110 sq miles of pristine ocean beaches also offer excellent hiking and camping opportunities. For an awe-inspiring view, follow Sir Francis Drake Blvd beside Tomales Bay all the way out toward the Point Reyes Lighthouse. Follow the signs and turn left before the lighthouse to find the trailhead for the 1.6-mile round-trip hike to **Chimney Rock**, where wildflowers bloom in spring.

THE DRIVE: Leaving the park, trace the eucalyptus-lined curves of Hwy 1 south toward Stinson Beach and past one stunning Pacific view after another. If you don't stop, you'll be back across the Golden Gate Bridge in about an hour and a half. From the bridge, follow Hwy 101 through the city to Broadway, then go east to the waterfront piers.

Point Reyes Lighthouse, Point Reyes National Seashore, California
ROBERT LEWIS 3RD/SHUTTERSTOCK

06 San Francisco

From the center of the Golden Gate Bridge, it's possible to view the clock tower of the city's **Ferry Building** *(ferrybuildingmarketplace.com)*, a transit hub turned gourmet emporium, where foodies happily miss their ferries slurping Hog Island oysters and bubbly. Star chefs are frequently spotted at the thrice-weekly **Ferry Plaza Farmers Market** *(foodwise.org)* that wraps around the building year-round. The largest market is on Saturday, when dozens of family farmers and artisanal food and flower vendors show up. From dry-farmed tomatoes to organic kimchi, the bounty may seem like an embarrassment of riches. If your trip doesn't coincide with a market day, never fear: dozens of local purveyors await indoors at the Ferry Building Marketplace. Take a taste of **McEvoy Ranch and Stonehouse** olive oils, fresh-baked loaves from **Acme Bread Company** and **Humphry Slocombe Ice Cream**.

THE DRIVE: It's a straight shot over the San Francisco–Oakland Bay Bridge and into Berkeley via I-80 eastbound. Exit at University Ave and follow it east to Shattuck Ave, then go north of downtown Berkeley to the 'Gourmet Ghetto.'

07 Berkeley

San Francisco might host a handful of banner dining rooms, but California's food revolution got started across the bay, in Berkeley. You may spot the inventor of California cuisine, famed chef Alice Waters, in her element and in raptures at the **North Berkeley Farmers Market** *(ecologycenter.org)*, run by the Ecology Center. It's in the so-called 'Gourmet Ghetto' – a neighborhood that marries the progressive 1960s ideals of Berkeley with haute-dining sensibility. The neighborhood's anchor, and an appropriate final stop, is **Chez Panisse**, Alice Waters' influential restaurant. It's unpretentious, and every mind-altering, soul-sanctifying bite of the food is emblematic of the chef's revolutionary food principles. The kitchen is even open so diners can peek behind the scenes.

ALICE WATERS' PROTÉGÉS

Operating a restaurant for 50 years, lauded chef Alice Waters of Chez Panisse fame has seen a whole lot of people come through the kitchen. Of her alumni in San Francisco, try Michael Tusk, who offers elegant, seasonally inspired Californian cuisine at **Quince** *(quincerestaurant.com)* and more rustic Italian fare at **Cotogna** *(cotognasf.com)*, or Gayle Pirie, who operates **Foreign Cinema** *(foreigncinema.com)*, a gourmet movie house in the Mission District.

More casual eateries by other Waters' protégés are found across the bay in Oakland. Tuck into grilled herby lamb and spiced king-trumpet-mushroom kebabs at Russell Moore's **The Kebabery**; and Alison Barakat serves what may be the Bay Area's best fried-chicken sandwich at **Bakesale Betty**.

46

CALIFORNIA & NEVADA

★ BEST FOR

FOODIES

Book a star chef's restaurant table in tiny Yountville or historic St Helena.

NAPA VALLEY

DURATION: 2–3 DAYS

DISTANCE: 90 MILES / 145KM

GREAT FOR: FOOD & DRINK

BEST TIME TO GO: MAY FOR THE LULL BEFORE SUMMER; SEPTEMBER AND OCTOBER TO EXPERIENCE 'THE CRUSH.'

Red wine

Wining and dining is a glorious way of life in Napa today – grapes have grown here since the gold rush. Right off Hwy 29, organic family wineries are daring to make wines besides classic cabernets, and indie winemakers have opened up shop on Napa's revitalized 1st St. Between feasts, you'll spot sous-chefs weeding organic kitchen gardens to seed farm-to-table menus. The signs are clear: you've arrived right on time for Napa's renaissance.

LINK YOUR TRIP

40 Coastal California
From Santa Rosa, head west on Hwy 12, then take 116 to the coast and point yourself north toward the quaint maritime town of Mendocino.

01 Napa

Your first stop in Napa may be the only one you need. This is where Napans come to unwind at laid-back downtown tasting rooms, historic music halls, and local gourmet **Oxbow Public Market**. Napa's revitalized 1st St is lined with indie wine-tasting rooms and world-class, California-casual bistros.

The **Napa Valley Vine Trail** *(vinetrail.org)* connecting downtown Napa to Yountville provides a welcome respite from Hwy 29 traffic, and Napa's riverbank parks help manage seasonal floods with sustainable design. Lately downtown Napa has raised its profile with the star-studded **Napa Valley Film Festival** *(napavalleyfilmfest.org)* and breakout music festival **BottleRock** *(bottlerocknapavalley.com)*.

Between events, Napa remains the sweet spot where wine flows and conversation meanders.

THE DRIVE From Napa, Yountville is 9 miles north on Hwy 29, a divided four-lane road

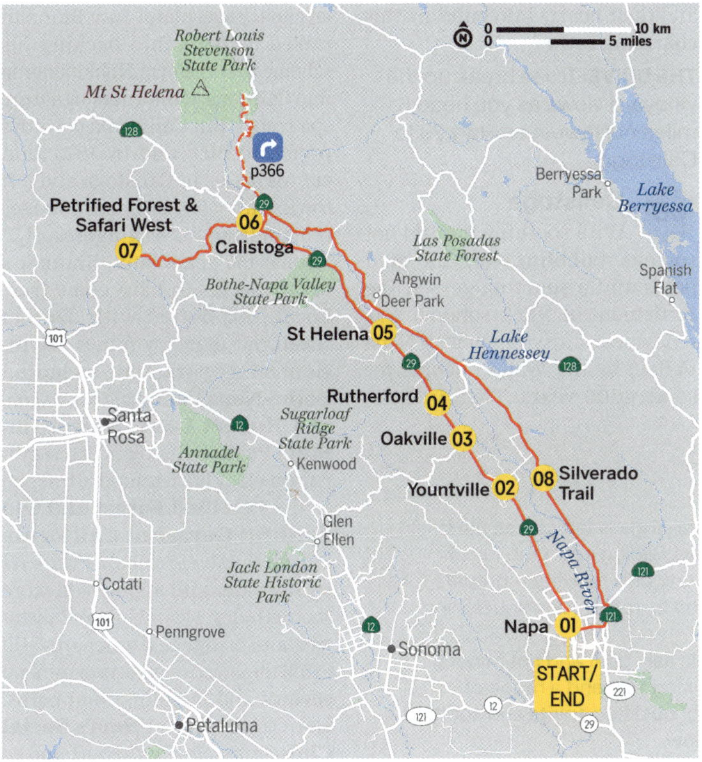

ALEXANDRU NIKA/SHUTTERSTOCK

surrounded by vineyards and framed by low hills.

02 Yountville

Planets and Michelin stars are aligned over Yountville, a tiny Western stagecoach stop that's been transformed into a global dining destination. Sounds like an urban legend – until you take a stroll down Yountville's quiet, tree-lined Washington St. Say hey to interns weeding French Laundry Gardens, chocolatiers pouring out new creations at **Kollar Chocolates** *(kollarchocolates.com)*, and trainee sommeliers grabbing lunch at **Tacos Garcia**. You've just met the talents behind Yountville's gourmet landmarks, including the legendary (but reservation-only) **French Laundry** *(thomaskeller.com/tfl)*.

THE DRIVE: Go north to Oakville via 4 miles of vineyard vistas on Hwy 29, which narrows to two lanes just outside Yountville. Tracks for the Napa Valley Wine Train line the west side of the road.

03 Oakville

Except for the famous **Oakville Grocery** *(oakville grocery.com)* and its next-door wine-history museum, you could drive through Oakville and never know you'd missed it. But when wine aficionados look at this green valley, they see red – thanks in no small part to **Robert Mondavi** *(robertmondaviwinery.com)*, the visionary vintner who knew back in the 1960s that Napa was capable of more than jug wine. His marketing savvy launched Napa's premium reds to cult status, including his own Opus One Meritage (Napa red blend).

THE DRIVE: Pass gilded signs of name-brand mega-wineries as you continue 2 miles north on Hwy 29 to Rutherford.

04 Rutherford

It's hard to believe it looking at these lush vineyards, but Napa Valley's most famous patch of cab country was once covered in wheat. Local farmers saw grape opportunity in this rich bottom land, and the rest is history in a bottle. Trailblazing winemaker **Mike Grgich** *(grgich.com)* put Napa chardonnay on the map in 1976 with his historic win in a French wine competition, dubbed the 'Judgment of Paris.'

Exit Hwy 29 onto backroads off Rutherford Rd, and you'll find idiosyncratic organic winemaking flourishing in the heart of mega-brand cab country. Meandering paths wind through fruit-bearing orchards at **Frog's Leap** *(frogsleap.com)* winery, where merlot and sauvignon blanc are produced in an 1884 barn.

THE DRIVE: St Helena is another 4 miles north on Hwy 29, though you may be slowing to a crawl before reaching downtown.

05 St Helena

Even people with places to go can't resist downtown St Helena, which looks like a Western movie set. Three blocks of Main St are a designated National Historic Site, covering 160 years of California history, including one of the oldest cinemas in America still in operation. Up the street, the 1889 **Greystone Cellars** château is home to the Culinary Institute of America.

This area was native Wappo land until it was claimed by Spain, then

Mexico – more specifically, the property of Dona Maria Ygnacia Soberanes. She gave Bale Grist Mill, still grinding flour today, to her daughter Isadora, and prime vineyards to her daughter Caroline, who married a German winemaker named Charles Krug. Together they founded the first commercial winery in Napa in 1858.

Today if you're thirsty, you're in luck: there's more than an acre of wine grapes per resident in St Helena. So raise a toast to the women who put that wine in your glass, and their hearts into building this charming town.

THE DRIVE: Trees break up the vineyard views as you head 8 miles northwest on Hwy 29 to Calistoga.

06 Calistoga

With soothing natural hot springs, bubbling volcanic mud pools and a spurting geyser, the settlement of Nilektsonoma was renowned across Talahalusi (Napa Valley) by the Wappo people for some 8000 years. Then in 1859, legendary speculator Sam Brannan talked bankers into backing his scheme to transform Nilektsonoma into Calistoga, California's signature spa resort. But California cowboys preferred dirt, and by 1873 Sam cut his losses in Calistoga and left town. Only a few Brannan cottages remain from his original resort.

Some 150 years later, Brannan's dream seems to have come true. Local hills dotted with defunct silver and mercury mines are reclaimed as parkland, including **Bothe-Napa Valley** *(parks.ca.gov)* and **Robert Louis Stevenson State Park**. Calistoga's extraordinary geology is a featured attraction at the **Petrified Forest and Old Faithful Geyser of California** *(oldfaithfulgeyser.com)* and its springwater still appears on store shelves today. Meanwhile at Calistoga's hot-spring spas, brochures still extoll the curative powers of mineral springs and bubbling mud baths. Have some wine at **Sam's Social Club** *(samssocialclub.com)*, and go with the volcanic flow.

THE DRIVE: Backtrack southeast on Hwy 128 and go 4 miles west on forested, curvy Petrified Forest Rd.

CALISTOGA SPAS

Bubbling with mineral hot springs, Calistoga is famous as the best place in the West to wallow in the mud. Sliding into a tub full of warm, silky, squishy volcanic mud is uniquely relaxing – prepare for deep muscle relaxation, accompanied by rather rude squelching sounds.

Calistoga mud is a blend of volcanic ash, peat and hot mineral springwater. Brochures promise glowing skin and a range of health benefits, including 'detoxifying,' but lifted spirits and soothed muscles are reasons enough to wallow.

Mud-bath packages take 60 to 90 minutes. You start semi-submerged in hot mud, then soak in hot mineral water – a steam bath and blanket-wrap typically follow. A massage increases the cost, and may not be strictly necessary once your muscles relax. Baths are usually solo, though some offer couples' options. Variations include thin, painted-on clay-mud wraps called 'fango' baths, good for those uncomfortable sitting in mud. Reservations are essential.

Indian Springs *(indianspringscalistoga.com)* The original Calistoga resort has kept up with the times, filling modern concrete tubs with locally sourced volcanic mud and a vast outdoor pool with hot natural springwater.

The Spa at Solage *(aubergeresorts.com/solage)* Serene top-end spa, with paint-on mud treatments and private tubs. Hang out afterwards wrapped in blankets in zero-gravity chairs, or dip into separate-gender, clothing-optional mineral pools.

Mount View Spa *(mountviewhotel.com)* Historic spa-hotel with lighter, mineral-rich mud that's easier to wash off; couples' mud baths and CBD-infused baths available.

Calistoga Spa Hot Springs *(calistogaspa.com)* Traditional mud baths and massage at a motel complex with two huge swimming pools, where you can invite one friend to join you.

DETOUR

Robert Louis Stevenson State Park
Start: 06 Calistoga

Eight miles north of Calistoga via curving Hwy 29, the extinct volcanic cone of Mt St Helena marks a dramatic end to Napa Valley at **Robert Louis Stevenson State Park** *(parks.ca.gov)*. It's a strenuous 5-mile climb to the park's 4343ft summit, but what a view – 200 miles on a clear day. For a shorter hike with views over

Calistoga, Napa Valley, California
CAMARAADICTA/SHUTTERSTOCK

❤ WHY I LOVE THIS TRIP

ALISON BING, WRITER

Napa Valley is America's fanciest stretch of farmland, with million-dollar steel sculptures in sun-drenched fields and marble bars in architect-designed barns. You'll recognize the scene from glossy magazines – but spend a day in Napa, and you'll also notice 150-plus years of hard work. No matter how early you rise, vineyard workers are already pruning grapes; even after fine-dining restaurants close, *taqueros* keep pulling carne asada off the grill. This calls for a toast: to vigilant firefighters, who protect this wondrous 30-mile stretch of dreams and dirt from increasingly regular wildfires.

valley vineyards, take **Table Rock Trail** (2.2 miles one way) from the parking-area trailhead. Check conditions before setting out.

The park also includes the old Silverado Mine site where writer Robert Louis Stevenson and artist Fanny Osbourne honeymooned in 1880 in an abandoned bunkhouse. Broke, sick and cold, they miraculously survived – and stayed married. He became famous as the author of *Treasure Island*, *Silverado Squatters*, and *The Strange Case of Dr Jekyll and Mr Hyde*, with Fanny as his editor. Robert never recovered his health and died young.

07 Petrified Forest & Safari West

Three million years ago, a volcanic eruption at Mt St Helena blew down a stand of redwoods. Their trunks gradually turned to stone, and in 1914 enterprising environmentalist Ollie Bockee preserved this land as an educational attraction. Her vision remains remarkably intact today at the **Petrified Forest** *(petrifiedforest.org)*. Wildfires struck in 2017, but the petrified redwoods were spared and the living redwoods are recovering beautifully, as you can see along two restored half-mile trails.

Four miles west, where Petrified Forest Rd curves right onto Porter Creek, you may hear some strange sounds ... yes, that was a rhino. Welcome to **Safari West** *(safariwest.com)*, a 400-acre wildlife preserve where endangered species roam free of predators and poachers. Meet rare wildlife on a guided two-hour safari in open-sided jeeps, plus a 30-minute hike. Your guide will point out areas scorched by wildfires; the owners heroically saved all 1000 animals. To maximize quality time among the giraffes, book a treehouse-style tent cabin. Stays come with continental breakfast on the deck for wildlife-watching, plus optional on-site massages.

THE DRIVE: Return east via Petrified Forest Rd and drive 1 mile south on Hwy 29/128, then 1 mile north on Lincoln Ave to take lovely, vineyard-lined Silverado Trail almost 30 miles southeast to downtown Napa.

Tasting room, Stag's Leap, Yountville, California

LEONARD ZHUKOVSKY/SHUTTERSTOCK

08 Silverado Trail

Bountiful Silverado Trail meanders from Calistoga to Napa, with tempting pit stops at three dozen wineries. Just outside Calistoga, **Joseph Phelps** *(josephphelps.com)* has been making its iconic Insignia red blend sustainably since 1974. Along with traditional tastings, Phelps offers a variety of culinary pairing programs throughout the year.

If you reserve ahead, a memorable multicourse brunch with sparkling wine awaits on the scenic balcony at **Auberge du Soleil** *(aubergeresorts.com/aubergedusoleil)*. For more bubbly still, head to **Mumm Napa** *(mummnapa.com)*, which offers tastings and tours along with a mystery tasting class that includes a blind tasting challenge. For something a bit more satiating, head to **Meadowood** *(meadowood.com)*, a 250-acre estate featuring lodging, a spa and a winery. Its onsite restaurant, Forum, serves sumptuous brunches and dinners crafted from estate-grown ingredients.

One of Napa's most prestigious growing areas is **Stag's Leap** district, east of Yountville. Turn east off Silverado and follow the signs to **Quixote** *(quixotewinery.com)*, a gold-leafed onion dome sprouting from a grassy knoll. Reserve ahead to enter the only US building by outlandish Austrian eco-architect Friedensreich Hundertwasser between crayon-colored ceramic pillars – and taste acclaimed, organically farmed Stag's Leap estate cabs and petit syrah.

ELENA KOULIK/SHUTTERSTOCK

Cabernet sauvignon grapes

NAPA VALLEY WINE

Cab is king in Napa. No varietal captures this sun-drenched valley like the fruit of the cabernet sauvignon vine, and no wine fetches a higher price. But with climate change, Napa Valley's floor is heating up, so even hardy cabernet grapes can develop highly concentrated, over-extracted flavors – resulting in fiery tannins, raisin flavors or syrupy notes. To take the edge off cabs and introduce more subtle notes, Napa winemakers are increasingly making Napa cab blends called Meritages.

Napa farmers tend to plant prestigious, pricey cabernet, so when they make an exception and grow another red grape, like merlot, it's because they believe it will be exceptional. California zinfandel grows extremely well in many of the same sunny Napa Valley blocks as cabernet – so it's a time-honored specialty at many Napa wineries. Zin blends are versatile, food-friendly, and often more affordable than Napa estate-grown zins.

Lately, more unusual varietals and blends are gracing Napa tasting-room shelves. A new crop of winemakers called 'garagistes' are buying grapes from across Northern California, and fermenting them in downtown Napa warehouse facilities. So even in the heart of Napa Valley, tasting rooms are pouring coastal chardonnay, Russian River sauvignon blanc, white picpoul from the Sierra foothills and cool-climate Sonoma pinot noir – and crafty Napa winemakers can turn almost any grape into a rosé with the right amount of skin contact and early pressing.

CANADA
USA
BRITISH COLUMBIA
Strait of Juan de Fuca
Victoria
San Juan Islands
Cape Flattery
Port Angeles
Bellingham
Mt Baker
Cascade Range
Glacier Peak Wilderness
Glacier Peak
Okanogan River
Colville National Forest
Lake Roosevelt
Olympic National Park
Mt Olympus
Everett
47
Chelan
Seattle
Bremerton
Leavenworth
Wenatchee
48
Tacoma
WASHINGTON
Moses Lake
Olympia
Aberdeen
Mt Rainier National Park
Mt Rainier
Ellensburg
Potholes Reservoir
Willapa Bay
Yakima
Columbia River
Cape Disappointment
Toppenish
Kennewick
Walla Walla
Tri-Cities
Astoria
Longview
Mt St Helens
Mt Adams
Cannon Beach
Mt St Helens National Volcanic Monument
PACIFIC OCEAN
Hood River
Vancouver
Pendleton
Arlington
Cape Lookout
Tillamook
Portland
Mt Hood
The Dalles
Newberg
John Day River
50
49
Salem
Dale
Mt Jefferson
Newport
Albany
Madras
Willamette River
Mitchell
Three Sisters Wilderness
Sisters
Lake Billy Chinook
John Day
Oregon Dunes National Recreation Area
Florence
Eugene
Bend
OREGON
Mt Bachelor
51
La Pine
Burns
Riley
Coos Bay
Cascade Range
Roseburg
Silver Lake
Malheur Lake
52
Crater Lake National Park
Port Orford
Summer Lake
Summer Lake
Albert Lake
Upper Klamath Lake
Valley Falls
Grants Pass
Medford
Klamath Falls
Lakeview
Ashland
Brookings
Crescent City
0 100 km
0 50 miles

MANUELA DURSON/SHUTTERSTOCK

Highway 101, Port Orford (p396) and Humbug Mountain, Oregon

THE PACIFIC NORTHWEST

EXPLORE

THE PACIFIC NORTHWEST

What's special about the Pacific Northwest? Plenty. Start with hundreds of miles of coastline and throw in a stunning natural landscape: thousands of years of geological events have dramatically shaped this region, leaving behind snow-capped mountain ranges, rocky islands, waterfalls, natural hot springs and one particularly lovely gorge.

Every drive here is a scenic one, which makes it perfect for road-tripping. Cruise along Oregon's epic coastline, explore volcanic Crater Lake, or even travel in the footsteps of Lewis and Clark. We'll help you find all the great stops along the way, from historical sites to natural wonders.

Seattle

Is this the coolest city in America? Seattle exists in a constant state of reinvention and in this sense it's as American as Amazon and Starbucks. It's known for its fine and varied foods, its cool cafe culture, and its love of the great outdoors. As a base for exploring the Pacific Northwest, Seattle is perfectly placed, whether you're exploring the Olympic Peninsula or the Cascades.

Olympia

Olympia is one just-the-right-sized town in just the right location, at the head of the Olympic Peninsula. It's known for its constant musical soundtrack, good restaurants, fun nightlife, parks and, as you'd expect for a place sited in such a beautiful position, a real outdoorsy culture. The accommodations scene is a mixed bag, but there are some good B&Bs, and you can always go camping in the great outdoors just beyond town.

Astoria

Sitting where the Columbia River empties into the sea, small-town Astoria has some lovely historical buildings (it was the first US settlement west of the Mississippi). It's an artsy sort of place with a full portfolio of museums, more about sailboats than beaches, and its appeal as a base is enhanced by its charming B&Bs and historic

WHEN TO GO

From late spring (late April or May) to early fall (September or October) you'll enjoy the best summer weather, snow-free mountain roads, and lots of festivals; everything should be open. The Pacific Northwest is known for being the wettest place in America, so rain is possible at any time, although it's more likely in winter.

hotels, as well as the varied restaurant scene and a small handful of brewpubs.

Brookings

Beloved by fisherfolk for its salmon runs, Brookings lies on the cusp of California (which is just 6 miles away). If you're here in July, you'll also love the lily fields in full bloom south of town, and there's even Oregon's only redwood forest nearby. It's only a small place, which is just the way we like it as a base for exploring the state's south. A handful of pretty parks and good museums, fine hiking trails in the state parks just beyond town and some good B&Bs seal the deal.

Bend

Bend is an outdoors center par excellence. You can ski fine powder in the morning, paddle a kayak in the afternoon and play golf into the evening. Or would you rather go mountain biking, hiking, mountaineering, stand-up paddle boarding, fly-fishing or rock climbing? You can even surf a river wave in the center of town. Plus, Bend gets nearly 300 days of sunshine each year. A full list of good places to stay, eat, drink and be entertained makes it one of the best bases for exploring Oregon's interior.

TRANSPORTATION

Seattle and Portland have good domestic flight connections with airports across the US. Amtrak trains also crisscross the northwest, as do a number of bus services such as **Flix Bus** *(flixbus.com)*. When driving around the region, keep an eye on the weather – torrential downpours are never far away, and when they arrive, their intensity can make driving perilous.

WHERE TO STAY

Seattle's downtown and neighborhoods have plenty of excellent places to stay across a range of budgets and styles, while Olympia, Brookings and Astoria are known for their charming B&Bs. Keep an eye out also for historic hotels, which are such a feature of staying in the country's west. In the parks, highlights include scenic **Sparks Lake Campground** (Cascade Lakes), **Ross Lake Resort** (North Cascades) with its floating cabins, and historic **Lake Quinault Lodge** (Olympic National Park).

RESOURCES

National Park Service
Get the lowdown on national parks like Olympia, North Cascades and Mt Rainier.
nps.gov

Washington State Tourism
Washington State Tourism's official website with extensive statewide info.
stateofwatourism.com

Travel Oregon
The official website of Oregon's tourism board with travel-focused articles and listings.
traveloregon.com

WHAT'S ON

Bend Summer Festival
On the second weekend in July, artists, street performers, live music and plenty of food take over Bend.

Leavenworth's Winter Karneval
This one goes all out for the holidays with carolers, gingerbread houses and around 500,000 twinkling lights.

Crab & Wine Festival
Astoria's biggest annual event brings hundreds of wine, seafood, clothing and crafts vendors together on the last full weekend in April.

47

THE PACIFIC NORTHWEST

CASCADE DRIVE

★ BEST FOR

HIKING

The Maple Pass Loop Trail from Rainy Pass.

Rainy Pass (p376), Washington

DURATION: 4–5 DAYS

DISTANCE: 350 MILES / 563KM

GREAT FOR: OUTDOORS

BEST TIME TO GO: JUNE TO SEPTEMBER WHEN ROADS ARE SNOW-FREE AND PASSABLE.

Nature defies modern engineering in the North Cascades, where high-altitude roads succumb to winter snow storms, and the names of the mountains – Mt Terror, Mt Fury, Forbidden Peak – whisper forebodingly. Less scary are the scattered settlements – small towns with eclectic distractions such as Bavarian Leavenworth and 'Wild West' Winthrop. Fill up the tank, put on your favorite Springsteen track and prepare for one of the rides of your life.

LINK YOUR TRIP

48 Olympic Peninsula
Drop down WA 20 and take the ferry over to Port Townsend to pick up the Olympic Peninsula Loop.

49 On the Trail of Lewis & Clark
Head southeast on Hwy 90 and Hwy 82 for 247 miles from Everett to Kennewick.

01 Everett

This drive incorporates four-fifths of the popular 'Cascade Loop.' You can complete the other fifth by taking in the second half of the trip through Whidbey Island. There's not much to detain you in Everett, the route's starting point, 30 miles north of Seattle. It's known mainly for its Boeing connections and as the genesis of countless Seattle-region traffic jams. Head directly east and don't stop until Stevens Pass.

THE DRIVE: Everett marks the starting point of US 2, a 2579-mile cross-continental road that terminates in Maine. Crossing I-5, the route, which parallels the Great Northern Railway and Skykomish River for much of its journey, passes the towns of Startup, Sultan and Index, climbing toward Stevens Pass, 66 miles away. There are a number of drive-through espresso huts en route.

LOWESTOCK/GETTY IMAGES

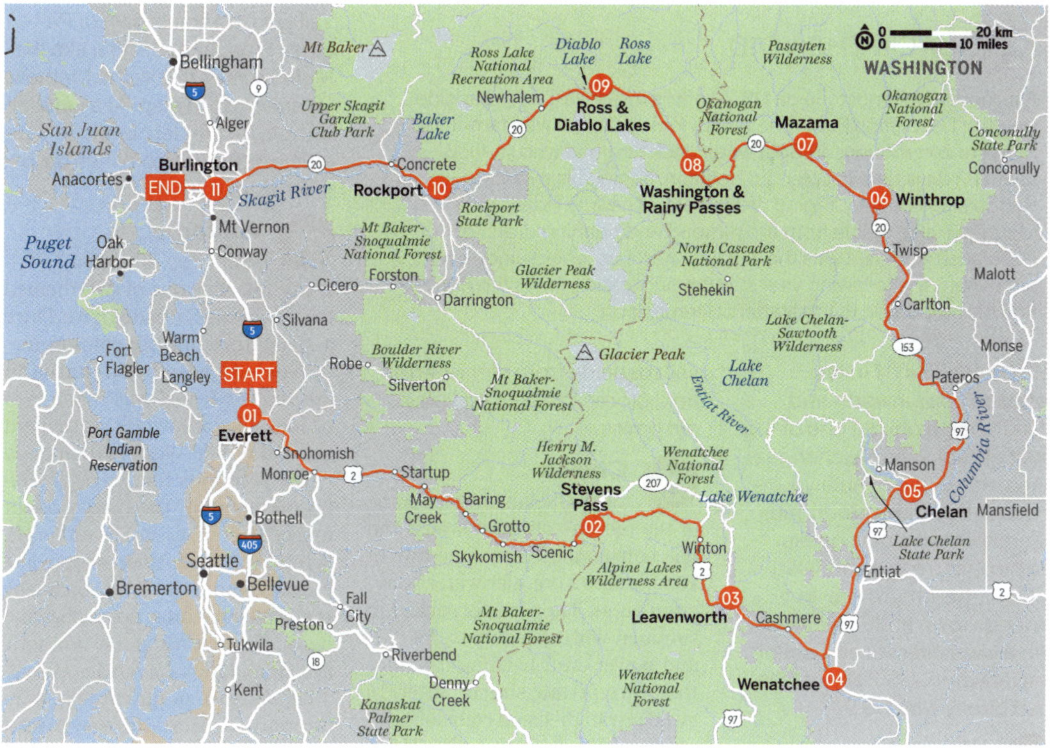

02 Stevens Pass

Accessible year-round thanks to its day-use ski area, **Stevens Pass** *(stevenspass.com)* was only 'discovered' by white settlers as recently as 1890. Despite its lofty vantage – at 4061ft it is over 1000ft higher than Snoqualmie Pass – it was chosen for the Great Northern railroad's cross-Cascade route, but you won't see any train tracks here. Instead, the railway burrows underneath the pass via the longest rail tunnel (7.8 miles) in the contiguous United States. The long-distance **Pacific Crest Trail** also crosses the highway here. Tempted?

THE DRIVE: From Stevens Pass the descent begins immediately with subtle changes in the vegetation; the cedars and hemlocks of the western slopes are gradually replaced by pine, larch and spruce. For 35 miles, the road threads through the steep-sided Tumwater canyon alongside the turbulent Wenatchee River. Suddenly, German-style houses start to appear against an eerily familiar alpine backdrop.

03 Leavenworth

Blink hard and rub your eyes. This isn't some strange Germanic hallucination. This is Leavenworth, a former lumber town that underwent a Bavarian makeover in the 1960s after the re-routing of the cross-continental railway threatened to put it permanently out of business. Swapping loggers for tourists, Leavenworth today has successfully reinvented itself as a traditional *Romantische Strasse* village, right down to the beer and bratwurst. The faux-German setting helps, as does the fact that Leavenworth serves as the main activity center for sorties into the nearby **Alpine Lakes Wilderness** *(recreation.gov/permits/233273)* and **Wenatchee National Forest**.

A surreal stroll through the gabled alpine houses of Leavenworth's Front St with its dirndl-wearing waitstaff, wandering accordionists and European cheesemongers is one of Washington state's oddest, but most endearing, experiences. For white-water rafting trips, call by **Osprey Rafting Co** *(osprey rafting.com)*.

KEROUAC & THE VOID

A turnout at milepost 135 on US 20 offers the drive's only roadside views of Desolation Peak. The peak's lookout tower was famously home to Zen-influenced Beat writer Jack Kerouac who, in 1956, spent 63 days here in splendid isolation, honing his evolving Buddhist philosophy, raging at 'the Void' of nearby Hozomeen Mountain (also visible from the turnout) and penning drafts of *Desolation Angels*. It was the last time Kerouac would enjoy such anonymity; the following year saw the publication of *On the Road*, and his propulsion to the status of literary icon.

THE DRIVE: The 22 miles between Leavenworth and Wenatchee highlight one of the most abrupt scenery changes in the state. One minute you're in quasi-Bavaria surrounded by crenellated alpine peaks, the next you're in a sprawled couldn't-be-amywhere-but-America town amid bald hills and a wide river valley. East of Leavenworth, US 2 shares the road briefly with US 97.

04 Wenatchee

Fruit stands start peppering the highway soon after you leave Leavenworth, paving your entry into Wenatchee, the self-proclaimed Apple Capital of the World. Something of an ugly sister after cute Leavenworth, Wenatchee is a place to go local and taste the apples from the nearby orchards before swinging north. The best fruit stands enliven US 2/97 on the way to Chelan.

THE DRIVE: US 2/97 plies the east side of the Columbia River for 39 miles between Wenatchee and Chelan. This is one of the best places to 'shop' at impromptu seasonal fruit outlets run by enterprising local farmers. They haul their freshly plucked produce from the nearby fields and orchards to sell roadside from semi-permanent stores, carts or just plain old boxes.

05 Chelan

Lake Chelan shelters some of the nation's cleanest water and has consequently become one of Washington's premier water recreation areas. The place is packed in summer, with speedboats, Jet Skis and power-craft battling it out for their own private slice of water. To avoid any high-speed collisions, try renting a kayak from **Lake Rider Sports** *(lakeridersportschelan.com)* and paddling up the lake to see some undiluted Cascadian nature firsthand.

There are public beaches at **Lakeside Park**, near the west side of Chelan town, and at **Lake Chelan State Park**, 9 miles west on S Lakeshore Rd.

If you have kids, don't think they'll let you sneak past **Slidewaters Water Park** *(slidewaters.com)*, located on a hill above the Lady of the Lake boat dock. If you're feeling adventerous, you can hop aboard a passenger ferry bound for remote Stehekin, a tiny vacation town on the banks of Lake Chelan that's only accessible by boat, plane or your own two feet.

THE DRIVE: Rejoin US 97 and follow it north through the grand coulees of the Columbia River Valley to the small town of Pateros. From here SR 153, aka the Methow Hwy, tracks the Methow River north to Twisp. At a junction with US 20 turn left, and continue on the highway into Winthrop, 61 miles from Chelan.

06 Winthrop

Winthrop is – along with Leavenworth – one of two themed towns on this Cascade Drive. Once a struggling mining community, it avoided ghost town status in the 1960s when it was made over to look like a cowboy settlement out of the Wild West. Although on paper it sounds like a corny Hollywood gambit, the Gary Cooper touches feel surprisingly authentic. Winthrop's High Noon shopfronts hide a genuine frontier spirit (the road ends in winter not far beyond here), along with some fantastic accommodations and places to eat.

The facades of downtown Winthrop are so realistic it's easy to miss the collection of homesteader cabins that make up the **Shafer Museum** *(shafermuseum.org)*. But best of all is the unmissable **Sun Mountain Lodge**, a sporting and relaxation dreamscape 10 miles out of town overlooking the valley.

THE DRIVE: Out of Winthrop, SR 20 enters the most bucolic and endearing stretch of the Methow Valley. Here the broad valley floor, scattered with farms, gives little hint of the jagged wilderness that lies beyond. If you thought Winthrop was small, don't blink when, in 14 miles, you reach Mazama, a small cluster of wooden buildings reminiscent of a gunslinger movie.

Maple Pass Loop Trail (p378), Washington

MASON VRANISH/SHUTTERSTOCK

07 Mazama

The last outpost before the raw, desolate, occasionally terrifying North Cascades, Mazama's half-dozen wooden abodes sit at the western end of the Methow Valley. Fuel up on brownies at the **Mazama Store** *(themazamastore.com)*, a deli/espresso bar for outdoorsy locals that's a great place to pick up trail tips.

THE DRIVE: You'll be working through your gears soon after Mazama as the North Cascade Mountains start to close in. This part of US 20 is unlike any other trans-Cascade road. Not only is the scenery more spectacular, but the road itself (closed November to May) is a major engineering feat. You have 22 miles to enjoy it before reaching Rainy Pass.

> PHOTO OPPORTUNITY
>
> View from the Sun Mountain Lodge.

08 Washington & Rainy Passes

Venture less than 100yd from your car at the Washington Pass overlook (5477ft) and you'll be rewarded with fine views of the towering Liberty Bell and its Early Winter Spires, while the highway drops below you in ribbonlike loops. By the time the highway reaches Rainy Pass (4875ft) a couple of miles further west, the air has chilled and you're well into the high country, a hop and a skip from the drive's highest hiking trails. The 6.2-mile **Maple Pass Loop Trail** is a favorite, climbing 2150ft to aerial views over jewel-like Lake Ann. The epic Pacific Crest Trail also crosses US 20 nearby, so keep an eye open for wide-eyed and bushy-bearded through-hikers popping out of the undergrowth. Perhaps the best choice if you want to shake the crowds is the excellent climb up to **Easy Pass**, hardly 'easy,' but offering spectacular views of Mt Logan and the Fisher Basin below.

THE DRIVE: Surrounded by Gothic peaks, the North Cascades Scenic Hwy makes a big swing north shadowing Granite Creek and then Ruby Creek, where it swings back west and, 20 miles from Rainy Pass, enters the Ross Lake National Recreation Area near Ruby Arm.

Liberty Bell, Washington

DANITA DELIMONT/SHUTTERSTOCK

♥ WHY I LOVE THIS TRIP

BECKY OHLSEN, WRITER

Washington's wild coastline has its defenders, but for my money, the state's crown jewel is the Cascade Range. This trip takes you into and over some of the region's most spectacular mountain scenery, from narrow, vertiginous passes to charming little alpine towns that specialize in gearing you up for adventure. Speaking of which, you should definitely stop somewhere along this route to explore on foot, too.

ROMAN KHOMLYAK/SHUTTERSTOCK

Diablo Lake, Washington

09 Ross & Diablo Lakes

The odd thing about much of the landscape on this trip is that it's unnatural, born from the construction of three huge dams that still supply Seattle with a large share of its electricity. The wilderness that surrounds it, however, is the rawest you'll get outside Alaska. Ross Lake was formed in the 1930s after the building of the eponymous dam. It stretches north 23 miles into Canada. Soon after the Ross Lake overlook, a path leads from the road to the dam. You'll see the Ross Lake Resort floating on the other side.

A classic photo op comes a couple of miles later at the **Diablo Lake** overlook. The turquoise lake is the most popular part of the park, offering beaches, gorgeous views and a boat launch at **Colonial Creek Campground** *(nps.gov)*, with nearby hikes to **Thunder Knob** and **Thunder Creek**.

THE DRIVE: From Diablo, head west alongside the sinuous Gorge Reservoir on US 20. Pass through Newhalem (where you can stop at the North Cascades Visitor Center). Look out for rafters, floaters and bald eagles along the Skagit River.

10 Rockport

As the valley widens further you'll touch down in Rockport. A 10-mile stretch of the Skagit River is a wintering ground for over 600 bald eagles who come here from November to early March to feast on spawning salmon. January is the best time to view them, ideally on a winter float trip with **Skagit River Guide Service** *(skagitriverfishingguide.com)*, whose boats use propane heat and are equipped with comfy cushioned seats. Three-hour trips run mid-November to early February.

THE DRIVE: From Rockport, head west for 37 miles on US 20 through the Cascade Mountain foothills and the ever-broadening Skagit River Valley to the small city of Burlington, which sits just east of busy I-5.

11 Burlington

The drive's end, known as the 'Hub City,' is not a 'sight' in itself (unless you like shopping malls), although the settlement's location in the heart of the Skagit River Valley means it acts as a hub for nearby attractions, including the tulip fields of **La Conner**, **Chuckanut Dr** (which officially ends here) and the **San Juan Islands**.

48

THE PACIFIC NORTHWEST

OLYMPIC PENINSULA

★ BEST FOR

WILDLIFE

Roosevelt elk at the Hoh Rainforest.

Elk, Hoh Rainforest (p382), Washington

DURATION: 4 DAYS

DISTANCE: 365 MILES / 585KM

GREAT FOR: NATURE

BEST TIME TO GO: JUNE TO SEPTEMBER, WHEN DELUGES ARE SLIGHTLY LESS LIKELY.

Imagine pine-clad beaches fused with an American Mt Olympus, with a slice of Stephenie Meyer's Twilight saga thrown in for good measure, and you've got an approximation of what a drive around the Olympic Peninsula looks like. This is wilderness of the highest order, where thick forest collides with an end-of-the-continent coastline that hasn't changed much since Juan de Fuca sailed by in 1592. Bring hiking boots – and rain gear!

LINK YOUR TRIP

47 Cascade Drive
From Port Townsend, take the ferry north, then follow WA 20 to Burlington.

50 Highway 101 Oregon Coast
Take I-5 south, then head west to the coastal town of Astoria, OR.

01 Olympia

Welcome to Olympia, city of weird contrasts, where street-side buskers belt out acoustic grunge, and stiff bureaucrats answer their ringtones on the lawns of the expansive state legislature. A quick circuit of the **Washington State Capitol** *(capitol.wa.gov)*, a huge Grecian temple of a building, will give you a last taste of civilization before you depart. Then load up the car and head swiftly for the exits.

THE DRIVE: Your basic route is due west, initially on US 101, then (briefly) on SR 8 before joining US 12 in Elma. In Grays Harbor, enter the twin cities of Aberdeen and Hoquiam, famous for producing William Boeing and the grunge group Nirvana. Here, you swing north on US 101 (again!) to leafier climes at Lake Quinault, 88 miles from Olympia.

JARRETT JAMES/SHUTTERSTOCK

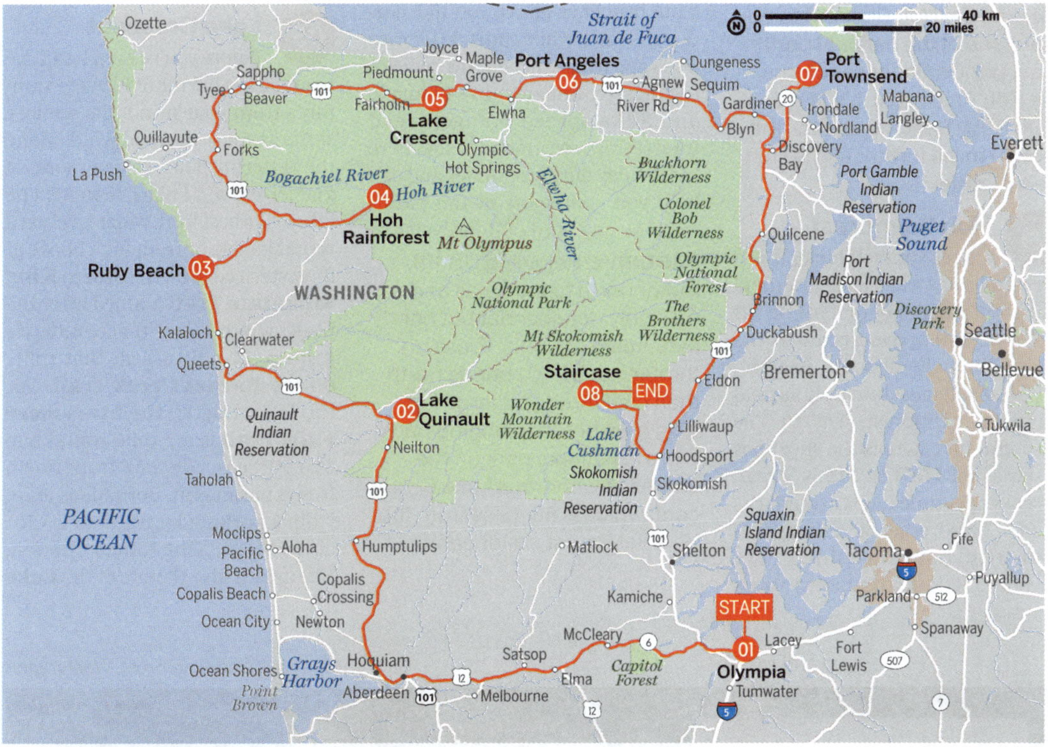

02 Lake Quinault

Situated in the extreme southwest of the **Olympic National Park** *(nps.gov/olym)*, the thickly forested Quinault River Valley is one of the park's least-crowded corners. Clustered on the south shore of deep-blue glacial Lake Quinault is the tiny village of Quinault, complete with the luscious **Lake Quinault Lodge**, a US Forest Service (USFS) office and a couple of stores.

A number of short hiking trails begin just below Lake Quinault Lodge; pick up a free map from the USFS office. The shortest of these is the **Quinault Rain Forest Nature Trail**, a half-mile walk through 500-year-old Douglas firs. This brief trail adjoins the 3-mile **Quinault Loop Trail**, which meanders through the rainforests before circling back to the lake. The Quinault region is renowned for its huge trees. Close to the village is a 191ft Sitka spruce tree (supposedly over 1000 years old), and nearby are the world's largest red cedar, Douglas fir and mountain hemlock trees.

THE DRIVE: West from Lake Quinault, US 101 continues through the Quinault Indian Reservation before entering a thin strip of national park territory that protects the beaches around Kalaloch (klay-lock). This is some of the wildest coastal scenery in the US accessible by road; various pullovers allow beach forays. After a total of 40 miles you'll reach Ruby Beach.

03 Ruby Beach

Inhabiting a thin coastal strip that was added to the national park in 1953, Ruby Beach is accessed via a short 0.2-mile path that leads down to a large expanse of windswept coast embellished by polished black stones and wantonly strewn tree trunks. To the south toward Kalaloch, other accessible beaches include unimaginatively named **Beach One** through to **Beach Six**, all of which are popular with beachcombers. At low tide, rangers give talks on tidal-pool life at **Beach Four** and on the ecosystems of the Olympic coastal strip.

THE DRIVE: North of Ruby Beach, US 101 swings sharply northeast and inland, tracking the Hoh River. Turn right off US

101 onto the Hoh River Rd to explore one of the national park's most popular inner sanctums, the Hoh Rainforest. It's 14 miles from Ruby Beach to the turnoff, then 19 miles further to the Hoh visitor center.

04 Hoh Rainforest

Count yourself lucky if you arrive on a day when it isn't raining! The most popular detour off US 101 is the 19-mile paved road to the Hoh Valley, the densest, wettest, greenest and most intensely surreal temperate rainforest on earth. The essential hike here is the short but fascinating **Hall of Moss Trail**, an easy 0.75-mile loop through the kind of weird, ethereal scenery that even JRR Tolkien couldn't have invented. Old-man's beard drips from branches above you like corduroy fringe, while trailside licorice ferns and lettuce lichens overwhelm the massive fallen trunks of maple and Sitka spruce. Rangers lead interesting free guided walks here twice a day during summer and can help you spot some of the park's 5000-strong herd of Roosevelt elk.

THE DRIVE: Rejoining US 101, motor north to the small and relatively nondescript but handy settlement of Forks. Press on through as US 101 bends north then east through a large logging area before plunging back into the national park on the shores of wondrous Lake Crescent, which is 66 miles from the Hoh Rainforest visitor center.

05 Lake Crescent

Before you've even had time to erase the horror of teenage vampires from your mind, the scenery shifts again as the road winds along the glittering pine-scented shores of glacier-carved Lake Crescent. The lake looks best from water level, on a rental kayak, or from high above at its eastern edge on the **Storm King Mountain Trail** (named after the peak's wrathful spirit), accessible via a steep, 1.7-mile ascent that splits off the **Barnes Creek Trail**. For the less athletic, the **Marymere Falls Trail** is a 2-mile round trip to a 90ft cascade that drops down over a basalt cliff. Both hikes leave from a parking lot north of US 101 at the Storm King Ranger Station. The area is also the site of the **Lake**

Hall of Moss Trail, Hoh Rainforest, Washington

PHOTO OPPORTUNITY

The Hoh Rainforest to see greens you've never imagined.

MARTINA BIRNBAUM/SHUTTERSTOCK

Crescent Lodge, the oldest of the park's trio of celebrated lodges, which opened in 1916.

THE DRIVE: From Lake Crescent take US 101 22 miles east to the town of Port Angeles, a gateway to Victoria, Canada, which is reachable by ferry.

06 Port Angeles

Up above the clouds, stormy Hurricane Ridge lives up to its name, with fickle weather and biting winds made slightly more bearable by the park's best high-altitude views. Its proximity to Port Angeles is another bonus; if you're heading up here be sure to call into the museum-like **Olympic National Park Visitor Center** *(nps.gov/olym)* in Port Angeles first. **Hurricane Hill Trail** and the **Meadow Loop Trails** network are popular and moderately easy. The first half-mile of these trails is wheelchair accessible.

THE DRIVE: Press east through the retirement community of Sequim (pronounced 'skwim'). Turn north on SR 20 to reach another, more attractive port, that of Port Townsend.

07 Port Townsend

Ease back into civilization with the cultured Victorian comforts of Port Townsend, whose period charm dates from the railroad boom of the 1890s, when the town was earmarked to become the 'New York of the West.' That never happened, but you can pick up a historic walking tour map from the visitor center *(enjoypt.com)* and wander the waterfront's collection of shops, galleries and antique malls. Don't miss the gorgeously renovated **Rose Theatre** *(rosetheatre.com)*, which has been showing movies since 1908, and the fine Victorian mansions on the bluff above town, where several charming residences have been turned into B&Bs.

THE DRIVE: From Port Townsend, head back to the junction of US 101, but this time head south, passing Quilcene, Brinnon and the Dosewallips Park entrance. You get more unbroken water views here on the park's eastern side courtesy of the Hood Canal. Track the watery beauty to Hoodsport, where signs point west off US 101 to Staircase, 67 miles from Port Townsend.

SROHDA/SHUTTERSTOCK

Forks, Oylmpic National Park, Washington

THE TWILIGHT ZONE

It would have been impossible to envisage a few decades ago: diminutive Forks, a depressed lumber town full of hard-nosed loggers, reborn as a pilgrimage site for 'tweenage' girls following in the ghostly footsteps of two fictional sweethearts named Bella and Edward. The reason for this weird metamorphosis was, of course, the Twilight saga, a four-part book series by US author Stephenie Meyer about love and vampires on the foggy Olympic Peninsula that in just a few years shifted more than 100 million books and spawned five Hollywood movies. With Forks acting as the book's main setting, the town was catapulted to international stardom, and the cachet has yet to wear off.

08 Staircase

It's drier on the park's eastern side and the mountains are closer. The Staircase park nexus, accessible via Hoodsport, has a ranger station, a campground and a decent trail system that follows the drainage of the North Fork Skokomish River and is flanked by some of the most rugged peaks in the Olympics. Nearby **Lake Cushman** has a campground and water sports opportunities.

49

THE PACIFIC NORTHWEST

★ BEST FOR

HISTORY

The Lewis & Clark Interpretive Center in Cape Disappointment State Park.

ON THE TRAIL OF LEWIS & CLARK

DURATION: 3–4 DAYS

DISTANCE: 385 MILES / 620KM

GREAT FOR: HISTORY & CULTURE, FAMILIES

BEST TIME TO GO: YEAR-ROUND. IF YOU DON'T MIND FREQUENT RAIN, THE COLUMBIA RIVER VALLEY IS ALWAYS OPEN.

Cape Disappointment State Park (p388), Washington

It would take most people their combined annual leave to follow the Lewis and Clark expedition in its entirety from St Louis, MO, to Cape Disappointment. Focusing on the final segment, this trip documents the mix of crippling exhaustion and building excitement that the two explorers felt as they struggled, worn out and weather-beaten, along the Columbia River on their way to completing the greatest overland trek in American history.

LINK YOUR TRIP

48 Olympic Peninsula
From Astoria, take Hwy 101 north 78 miles to Aberdeen to join up with this loop.

50 Highway 101 Oregon Coast
At the end of this trip, head south down the coast starting in Astoria.

01 Tri-Cities

This trip's start point has a weighty historical significance. The arrival of Lewis and Clark and the Corps of Discovery at the confluence of the Snake and Columbia Rivers on October 16, 1805, marked a milestone achievement on their quest to map a river route to the Pacific. After a greeting by 200 Native American people singing and drumming, the band camped at this spot for two days, trading clothing for dried salmon. The **Sacajawea State Park Interpretive Center** *(parks.wa.gov)*, situated at the river confluence 5 miles southeast of present-day Pasco, relates the story of the expedition through the eyes of Sacajawea, the Shoshone Native American guide and interpreter the Corps had recruited in North Dakota.

THE DRIVE: Head south on I-82 before switching west at the Columbia River on SR 14, aka

BRAM REUSEN/SHUTTERSTOCK

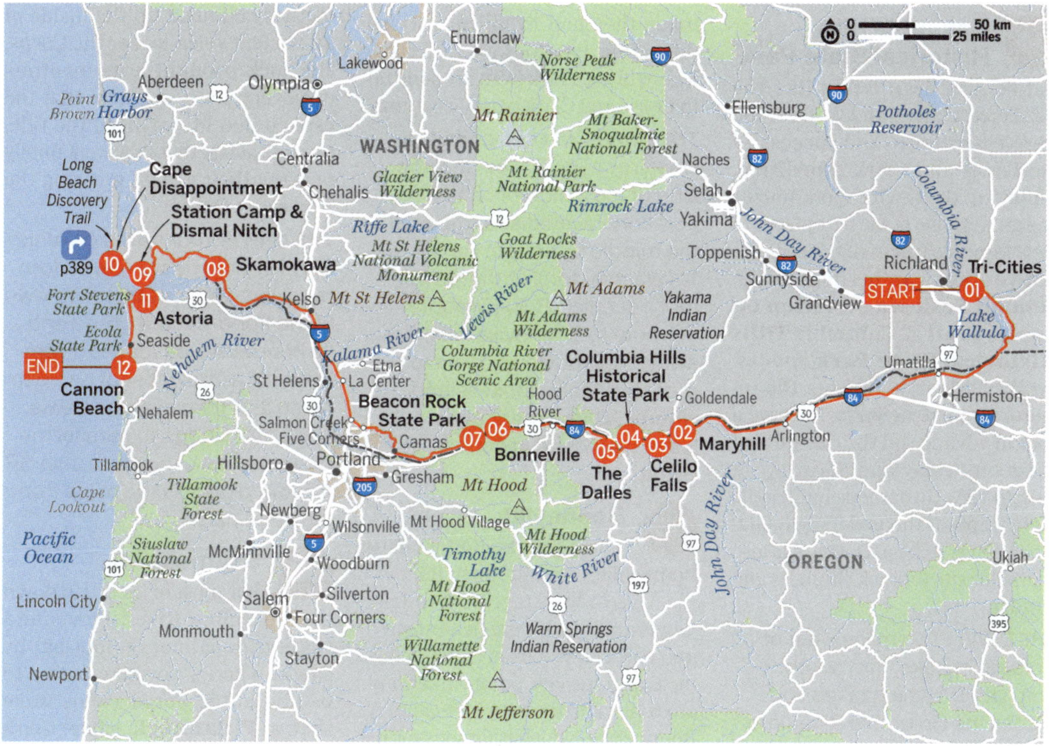

the Lewis & Clark Hwy. Here, in dusty sagebrush country, you'll pass a couple of minor sites – Wallula Gap, where the Corps first spotted Mt Hood, and the volcanic bluff of Hat Rock, first named by William Clark. Maryhill is 107 miles from Tri-Cities.

02 Maryhill

Conceived by great Northwest entrepreneur and road builder Sam Hill, the **Maryhill Museum of Art** *(maryhillmuseum.org)* occupies a mansion atop a bluff overlooking the Columbia River. Its eclectic art collection is enhanced by a small Lewis and Clark display, while its peaceful gardens are perfect for a classy picnic punctuated by exotic peacock cries. Interpretive signs point you to fine views down the Columbia Gorge to the riverside spot (now a state park) where Meriwether Lewis and William Clark camped on October 21, 1805. The park is just one of several along this trip where you can pitch a tent within a few hundred yards of the Corps' original camp.

Another of Hill's creations – a life-size, unruined replica of **Stonehenge** (US Hwy 97) – lies 2 miles to the east.

THE DRIVE: Continue west from Maryhill on SR 14 for 5 miles to the site of the now-submerged Celilo Falls.

03 Celilo Falls

A vivid imagination can be as important as sunscreen when following the 'Trail.' One example of this is the turnout 5 miles west of Maryhill that overlooks what was once the Native American salmon-fishing center of Celilo Falls. The explorers spent two days here in late October 1805, lowering their canoes down the crashing falls on elk-skin ropes. A century and a half later, the rising waters of the dammed Columbia drowned the falls – which were the sixth-most voluminous in the world – destroying a centuries-old fishing site and rendering much of Clark's description of the region unrecognizable.

THE DRIVE: Head west on SR 14, paralleling the mighty Columbia, for another 15 miles to Columbia Hills Historical State Park.

04 Columbia Hills Historical State Park

Native American tribes like the Nez Perce, Clatsop and Walla Walla were essential to the success of the Lewis and Clark expedition, supplying them with food, horses and guides. One of the best places to view tangible traces of the region's Native American heritage is the **Temani Pesh-wa (Written on Rocks) Trail** at **Columbia Hills Historical State Park** *(parks.wa.gov)*, which highlights the region's best petroglyphs. Reserve a spot in advance on the free guided tours on Friday and Saturday at 9am to view the famous but fragile pictograph of the god Tsagaglalal (She Who Watches). The park is also a popular site for rock climbers and windsurfers.

THE DRIVE: Two miles west of Horsethief Lake, turn south onto US 197, which takes you across the Columbia River into the Dalles in Oregon. Two miles upriver sits The Dalles Dam, which completely submerged the once-magnificent Celilo Falls and rapids on its completion in 1957.

05 The Dalles

Once the urban neighbor of the formidable Celilo Falls, The Dalles has a more mundane image these days. The local economy focuses on cherry-growing, computer technology and outdoor recreation. Notwithstanding, the city hosts one of the best Lewis and Clark–related museums along this stretch of the Columbia, sited in the **Columbia Gorge Discovery Center and Museum** *(gorgediscovery.org)* on the western edge of town. Displays detail the 30 tons of equipment the Corps dragged across the continent and the animals they had to kill to survive (including 190 dogs and a ferret). Kids will get a kick from dressing up in Lewis and Clark period costume.

THE DRIVE: You can continue west from The Dalles on either side of the Columbia (the expedition traveled straight down the middle by canoe) via SR 14 (Washington), or the slower, more scenic SR 30 (Oregon). En route to Bonneville, 46 miles away, look for views down to macabre Memaloose Island, where Native Americans would leave their dead in canoes of cedar.

06 Bonneville

There are two Bonnevilles: Bonneville, OR, and North Bonneville, WA. At this stage in their trip, Lewis and Clark were flea-infested and half-starved from a diet of dog meat and starchy, potato-like wapato roots. Fortunately, 21st-century Bonneville – which is famous for its Depression-era dam, completed in 1938 – has some tastier culinary offerings to contemplate.

THE DRIVE: Just west of North Bonneville on SR 14 lies Beacon Rock State Park.

07 Beacon Rock State Park

On November 2, 1805, a day after passing modern Bonneville, Clark wrote about a remarkable 848ft-tall monolith he called Beaten Rock, changing the name to **Beacon Rock** on his return. Just over a century later, Henry Biddle bought the rock for the bargain price of $1 (!) and you can still hike his snaking 1-mile trail to the top of the former lava plug in **Beacon Rock State Park** *(parks.wa.gov)*. As you enjoy the wonderful views, ponder the fact that you have effectively climbed up the inside of an ancient volcano. For the Corps, the rock brought a momentous discovery, for it was here that the excited duo first noticed the tide, proving at last that they were finally nearing their goal of crossing the American continent.

THE DRIVE: Your next stop along SR 14 should be the Cape Horn overview, with its fantastic views of the flood-carved gorge and its impressive cascades. From here, it's a straight shot on I-5 to Kelso and then over the Lewis and Clark Bridge to parallel the Columbia River westward on SR 4. Skamokawa is 103 miles from the state park.

08 Skamokawa

For most of their trip down the Columbia River, Lewis and Clark traveled not on foot but by canoe. There's nowhere better to paddle in the Corps' canoe wake than at **Pillar Rock**, where Clark wrote of his joy at finally being able to camp in view of the ocean. **Columbia River Kayaking** *(columbiariverkayaking.com)* in the town of Skamokawa offers one- and two-day kayak tours to this site, as well as **Grays Bay**.

THE DRIVE: Continue on SR 4 northwest out of Skamokawa. In Naselle, go southwest on SR 401. From Skamokawa to Dismal Nitch is 35 miles, along the north bank of the Columbia River.

09 Station Camp & Dismal Nitch

Just east of the Astoria-Megler Bridge on the north bank of the

Beacon Rock, Beacon Rock State Park, Washington
DAVIDRH/SHUTTERSTOCK

Columbia River, a turnout marks Dismal Nitch, where the drenched duo were stuck in a pounding week-long storm that Clark described as the most disagreeable time he had ever experienced. The Corps finally managed to make camp at Station Camp, 3 miles further west, now an innocuous highway pullout, where they stayed for 10 days while the two leaders, no doubt sick of each other by now, separately explored the headlands around Cape Disappointment.

THE DRIVE: You're nearly there! Contain your excitement as you breeze the last few miles west along US 101 to Ilwaco and the inappropriately named Cape Disappointment.

10 Cape Disappointment

Disappointment is probably the last thing you're likely to be feeling as you pull into blustery clifftop **Cape Disappointment State Park** *(parks.wa.gov)*. Find time to make the short ascent of **Mackenzie Hill** in Clark's footsteps and catch your first true sight of the Pacific. You can almost hear his protracted sigh of relief more than two centuries later.

Located on a high bluff inside the park not far from the Washington town of Ilwaco, the sequentially laid-out **Lewis & Clark Interpretive Center** *(parks.wa.gov)* faithfully recounts the Corps of Discovery's cross-continental journey using a level of detail the journal-writing explorers would have been proud of. Information includes everything from how to use an octant to what kind of underpants Lewis wore! A succinct 20-minute film backs up the permanent exhibits. Phone ahead and you can also tour the impressive end-of-continent **North Head Lighthouse** *(northheadlighthouse.com)* nearby.

THE DRIVE: From Ilwaco, take US 101 back east to the 4.1-mile-long Astoria–Megler Bridge, the longest continuous truss bridge in the US. On the other side, 18 miles from Cape Disappointment, lies Astoria in Oregon, the oldest US-founded settlement west of the Mississippi.

DETOUR

Long Beach Discovery Trail

Start: 10 Cape Disappointment

Soon after arriving in 'Station Camp,' the indefatigable Clark, determined to find a better winter bivouac, set out with several companions to continue the hike west along a broad sandy peninsula. They came to a halt near present-day 26th St in Long Beach, where Clark dipped his toe in the Pacific and carved his name on a cedar tree for posterity. The route of this historic three-day trudge has been recreated in the **Long Beach Discovery Trail**, a footpath that runs from the small town of Ilwaco, adjacent to Cape Disappointment, to Clark's 26th St turnaround. Officially inaugurated in September 2009, the trail has incorporated some dramatic life-size sculptures along its 8.2-mile length. One depicts a giant gray whale skeleton, another recalls Clark's recorded sighting of a washed-up sea sturgeon, while a third recreates in bronze the original cedar tree (long since uprooted by a Pacific storm).

Indian Beach, Ecola State Park, Oregon

CSNAFZGER/SHUTTERSTOCK

PHOTO OPPORTUNITY

Indian Beach, Ecola State Park: the Oregon coast epitomized.

11 Astoria

After voting on what to do next – a decision often described as the first truly democratic ballot in US history, since everyone in the party had a say – the Corps elected to make their winter bivouac across the Columbia River in present-day Oregon. A replica of the original Fort Clatsop, where the Corps spent a miserable winter in 1805–06, lies 5 miles south of Astoria. Also onsite are trails, a visitor center and buckskin-clad rangers who wander the camp between mid-June and Labor Day sewing moccasins (the Corps stockpiled an impressive 340 pairs for their return trip), tanning leather and firing their muskets.

THE DRIVE: From Fort Clatsop, take US 101, aka the Oregon Coast Hwy, south through the town of Seaside to Beach, 25 miles from Astoria.

12 Cannon Beach

Mission accomplished – or was it? Curiosity (and hunger) got the better of the Corps in early 1806 when news of a huge beached whale lured Clark and Sacajawea from a salt factory they had set up near the present-day town of Seaside down through what is now Ecola State Park to Cannon Beach.

Ecola State Park *(stateparks.oregon.gov)* is the Oregon you may have already visited in your dreams: sea stacks, crashing surf, hidden beaches and gorgeous pristine forest. Crisscrossed by paths, it lies 1.5 miles north of Cannon Beach, a gallery-filled beach town that's popular among day-tripping Portlanders.

Clark found the whale near **Haystack Rock**, a 295ft sea stack that's the most spectacular landmark on the Oregon coast and accessible from the beach. After bartering with the Tillamook tribe, he staggered away with 300lb of whale blubber – a feast for the half-starved Corps of Discovery.

LEWIS & CLARK NATIONAL HISTORICAL PARK

The so-called **Lewis & Clark National Historical Park** *(nps.gov/lewi)* combines 10 different historical sites clustered around the mouth of the Columbia River, each of which relates to important facts about the Corps of Discovery and its historic mission to map the American West. It was formed through the amalgamation of various state parks and historic sites in 2004, and is run jointly by the National Park Service and the states of Washington and Oregon. Highlights include **Cape Disappointment**, **Fort Clatsop** and the 6.5-mile **Fort to Sea** trail linking Clatsop and the ocean at Sunset Beach.

50

THE PACIFIC NORTHWEST

HIGHWAY 101 OREGON COAST

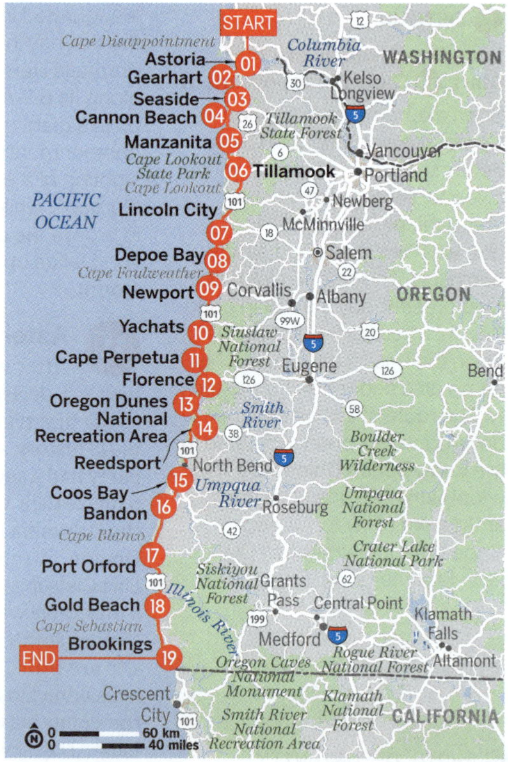

DURATION: 7 DAYS

DISTANCE: 340 MILES / 547KM

GREAT FOR: OUTDOORS, FAMILIES

BEST TIME TO GO: JULY TO OCTOBER, WHEN THE WEATHER IS MORE COOPERATIVE.

Scenic, two-lane Hwy 101 follows hundreds of miles of shoreline punctuated with charming seaside towns, exhilarating hikes, and ocean views that remind you you're on the edge of the continent. On this trip, it's not about getting from point A to point B. Instead, the route itself is the destination. And everyone from nature lovers to gourmands to families can find their dream vacation along this exceptional coastal route.

LINK YOUR TRIP

49 On the Trail of Lewis & Clark
Do the Hwy 101 trip backwards and you can pick up the trail of Lewis and Clark in Astoria.

52 Crater Lake Circuit
Continue south to Crescent City, then take US-199 northeast to Grant's Pass.

01 Astoria

We begin our coastal trek in the northwestern corner of the state, where the Columbia River meets the Pacific Ocean. Ever so slightly inland, Astoria doesn't rely on beach proximity for its character. It has a rich history, including being a stop on the Lewis and Clark trail. Because of its location, it also has a unique maritime history, which you can explore at the **Columbia River Maritime Museum** *(crmm.org)*.

Astoria has been the location of several Hollywood movies, making it a virtual Hollywood by the sea: it's best known as the setting for cult hit *The Goonies*. Fans can peek at the **Historic Clatsop County Jail** *(oregonfilmmuseum.com)*.

THE DRIVE: Head south on Hwy 101 for 14.5 miles to Gearhart.

02 Gearhart

Check your tide table and head to the beach; Gearhart is famous for its razor clamming at low

ROSS K/SHUTTERSTOCK

Cape Perpetua (p394), Oregon

tide. All you need are boots, a shovel or a clam gun, a cut-resistant glove, a license (available in Gearhart) and a bucket for your catch. Watch your fingers – the name razor clam is well earned. Boiling up a batch will likely result in the most memorable meal of your trip. For information on where, when and how to clam, visit the online guide of the **Oregon Department of Fish & Wildlife** *(myodfw.com/crabbing-clamming)*.

THE DRIVE: Don't get too comfortable yet: Seaside is just 2.4 miles further down the coast.

03 Seaside

Oregon's biggest and busiest resort town delivers exactly what you'd expect from a town called Seaside, which is wholesome, Coney Island–esque fun. The 2-mile boardwalk – known as 'the Prom' – is a kaleidoscope of seaside kitsch, with surrey rentals, saltwater taffy a 1920s-era game known as 'Fascination' often likened to a cross between Skee-Ball and bingo. It's also where you'll find the **Seaside Aquarium** *(seasideaquarium.com)*. Open since 1937, the privately owned aquarium isn't much more than a few fish tanks, a touch pool and a small indoor seal tank where you can feed the splashy critters, but it's a fun stop for inquisitive kids.

THE DRIVE: Leave the beach behind for a bit as you veer inland for the 8.8-mile drive to Cannon Beach.

04 Cannon Beach

Charming Cannon Beach is one of the most popular beach resorts on the Oregon coast. The wide sandy beach stretches for miles, and you'll find great photo opportunities and tide-pooling possibilities at glorious **Haystack Rock**, the third-tallest sea stack in the world. (What's a sea stack, you might ask? It's a vertical rock formation – in this case, one that's shaped like a haystack.) For the area's best coastal hiking, head immediately north of town to **Ecola State Park**, where you can hike to secluded beaches.

THE DRIVE: Follow the coast 14.4 miles through Oswald West State Park to reach your next stop.

PHOTO OPPORTUNITY

Silhouette of Haystack Rock in Cannon Beach.

05 Manzanita

One of the more laid-back beach resorts on Oregon's coast is the hamlet of Manzanita – much smaller and far less hyped than Cannon Beach. You can stroll along sandy beaches, or, if you're feeling more ambitious, hike on nearby **Neahkahnie Mountain**, where high cliffs rise dramatically above the Pacific's pounding waves. It's a 3.8-mile climb to the top, but the views are worth it: on a clear day, you can see 50 miles out to sea.

THE DRIVE: Drive 27 miles from Manzanita along Nehalem and Tillamook Bays to reach inland Tillamook.

06 Tillamook

Not all coastal towns are built on seafood and sand. Tillamook has an entirely different claim to fame: cheese. Thousands stop annually at the **Tillamook Cheese Factory** *(tillamook.com)* for free samples. You might choose to skip the dairy altogether and head to the two interesting museums: the **Tilamook County Pioneer Museum** *(tcpm.org)* has antique toys, a great taxidermy room (check out the polar bear) and a basement full of pioneer artifacts; and just south of town, the **Tillamook Naval Air Museum** *(tillamookair.com)* has a large collection of fighter planes and a 7-acre blimp hangar.

THE DRIVE: South of Tillamook, Hwy 101 follows the Nestucca River through pastureland and logged-off mountains 44 miles to Lincoln City.

07 Lincoln City

Lincoln City serves as the region's principal commercial center. It's also a popular getaway destination with 7.5 miles of sandy beaches, a thriving glass arts scene and plenty of annual events, from kite festivals to sandcastle contests. Throughout the year, volunteers from the Visitor and Convention Bureau hide brightly colored glass floats – which have been hand-blown by local artisans – along the beaches, making a memorable souvenir for the resourceful and diligent vacationer.

THE DRIVE: It's back to the coast for the 12-mile drive south to Depoe Bay.

08 Depoe Bay

Though edged by modern timeshare condominiums, Depoe Bay still retains some original coastal charm. It lays claim to having the 'world's smallest navigable harbor' and being the 'Oregon coast's whale-watching capital' – pretty big talk for such a pint-sized town. Whale-watching and charter fishing are the main attractions in the area, though 5 miles south of town is the **Devil's Punchbowl**, an impressive collapsed sea cave that churns with waves and offers good tide pools nearby.

THE DRIVE: Another 12.8 miles brings you to the lively tourist city of Newport.

09 Newport

Don your marine-biologist cap and head to **Yaquina Head Outstanding Natural Area** *(blm.gov/learn/interpretive-centers/yaquina)*, a giant spit of land that protrudes nearly a mile into the ocean. This headland is home to some of the best touch pools on the Oregon coast. You'll also get a good look at the tallest lighthouse in Oregon, **Yaquina Head Lighthouse** (not to be confused with Yaquina Bay Lighthouse, 3 miles south).

Also worth a stop: the cutting-edge **Oregon Coast Aquarium** *(aquarium.org)*. The seals and sea otters are cute as can be, and the jellyfish room is a near-psychedelic experience. But what really knocks this place off the charts is the deep-sea exhibit that lets you walk along a Plexiglas tunnel through sharks, rays and other fish.

THE DRIVE: It's 24 miles to Yachats along the edge of the Siuslaw National Forest.

10 Yachats

One of the Oregon coast's best-kept secrets is the friendly little town of Yachats (ya-hots), which kicks off about 20 miles of spectacular shoreline. This entire area was once a series of volcanic intrusions, which resisted the pummeling of the Pacific long enough

THREE CAPES LOOP

South of the town of Tillamook, Hwy 101 veers inland from the coast. An exhilarating alternative route is the slow, winding and sometimes bumpy **Three Capes Loop**, which hugs the shoreline for 30 miles and offers the chance to go clamming. En route you'll traverse **Cape Meares**, **Cape Lookout** and **Cape Kiwanda** – three stunning headlands that you'd otherwise miss entirely. Note that winter landslides sometimes result in lengthy road closures along the route. Check road conditions on the **Oregon Department of Transportation** website *(tripcheck.com)* before heading out.

Haystack Rock (p391), Cannon Beach, Oregon
WESTEND61/GETTY IMAGES

to rise as ocean-side peaks and promontories. Acres of tide pools are home to starfish, sea anemones and sea lions. Definitely stop in at the delicious **Yachats Brewing & Farmstore** for a bite to eat and some local flavor.

THE DRIVE: Just 3 miles down the coast, the dramatic Cape Perpetua begins.

11 Cape Perpetua

Whatever you do, don't miss the spectacular scenery of the **Cape Perpetua Scenic Area** *(fs.usda.gov)*, just 3 miles south of Yachats. You could easily spend a day or two exploring trails that take you through moss-laden, old-growth forests to rocky beaches, tide pools and blasting marine geysers.

At the very least, drive up to the **Cape Perpetua Overlook** for a colossal coastal view from 800ft above sea level – the highest point on the coast. While you're up there, check out the historic **West Shelter** observation point built by the Civilian Conservation Corps in 1933.

If you have more time to spend, stop at the visitor center *(fs.usda.gov/siuslaw)* to plan your day. High points include **Devil's Churn**, where waves shoot up a 30ft inlet to explode against the narrowing sides of the channel, and the **Giant Spruce Trail**, which leads to a 500-year-old Sitka spruce with a 10ft diameter.

THE DRIVE: It's 22 miles to Florence, but only 12 to the Sea Lion Caves.

12 Florence

Looking for a good, old-fashioned roadside attraction? North of Florence is the **Sea Lion Caves** *(sealioncaves.com)*, an enormous sea grotto that's home to hundreds of groaning sea lions. Open to the public since the 1930s, the cave is accessed by an elevator that descends 208ft to the sea lions' stinky lair.

Here's the deal: it can be fascinating, but you might feel a little taken when you realize the view is exactly the same as what was on the monitor up in the gift shop – and there's not even free fudge samples down there. But if money is no object, you'll enjoy watching the sea lions cavort, especially if you have kids in tow.

Sea Lion Caves, Florence, Oregon

DANITA DELIMONT/SHUTTERSTOCK

THE DRIVE: The Oregon Dunes start just south of Florence and continue for the next 50 miles.

13 Oregon Dunes National Recreation Area

As you drive south, you start to notice something altogether different: sand. Lots of it. Stretching 50 miles, the **Oregon Dunes** is the largest expanse of oceanfront sand dunes in the US. Sometimes topping heights of 500ft, these mountains of sand undulate inland up to 3 miles. Hikers and bird-watchers stick to the peaceful northern half of the dunes, and the southern half is dominated by dune buggies and dirt bikes.

At Mile 200.8, the **Oregon Dunes Overlook** is the easiest place to take a gander if you're just passing through. To learn more about trails and off-road vehicles, visit the **Oregon Dunes Visitors Center** *(fs.usda.gov/siuslaw)*. For the area's biggest dunes, the 6-mile **John Dellenbeck Trail** (at Mile 222.6) loops through a wilderness of massive sand peaks.

THE DRIVE: Reedsport is about halfway into the dunes area, some 22 miles south of Florence.

14 Reedsport

Reedsport's location in the middle of the Oregon Dunes makes it an ideal base for exploring the region. Check out the **Umpqua Lighthouse State Park** *(oregonstateparks.org)*, offering summer tours of a local 1894 lighthouse. Opposite is a whale-watching platform, and a nearby nature trail rings freshwater **Lake Marie**, which is popular for swimming.

Want to see how Oregon's largest land mammal spends its free time? You can spy a herd of up to 120 Roosevelt elk meandering about at the **Dean Creek Elk Viewing Area**, 3 miles east of town on Hwy 38.

THE DRIVE: Enjoy the sand for another 27.5 miles, until you reach Coos Bay and the end of the dunes.

15 Coos Bay

The no-nonsense city of Coos Bay and its modest neighbor North Bend make up the largest urban area on the Oregon coast. Coos Bay was once the largest timber port in the world. The logs are long gone, but tourists are slowly taking their place.

In a historic art-deco building downtown, the **Coos Art Museum** *(coosart.org)* provides a hub for the region's art culture with rotating exhibits from the museum's permanent collection.

Cape Arago Hwy leads 14 miles southwest of town to **Cape Arago State Park** *(stateparks.oregon.gov)*, where grassy picnic grounds make for great perches over a pounding sea. The park protects some of the best tide pools on the Oregon coast and is well worth the short detour.

THE DRIVE: Hwy 101 heads inland for a bit, then gets back to the coast 24 miles later at Bandon.

16 Bandon

Optimistically touted as Bandon-by-the-Sea, this little town sits happily at the bay of the Coquille River. Its Old Town district has been gentrified into a picturesque

FUNKYMUSICWHITE/SHUTTERSTOCK

Yaquina Head Lighthouse, Newport, Oregon

YAQUINA HEAD LIGHTHOUSE

If **Yaquina Head Lighthouse** in Newport seems a little creepier than a lighthouse ought, that's because it featured in the 2002 horror film starring Naomi Watts, *The Ring*. Built in 1873, it was originally called Cape Foulweather Lighthouse, but in the movie it was known as the Moesko Island Lighthouse. The lighthouse was also in the 1977 masterpiece by Nancy Drew, *The Mystery of Pirate's Cove*.

♥ WHY I LOVE THIS TRIP

CELESTE BRASH, WRITER

There's nowhere else on the West Coast that matches the road-tripping perfection of this curving route alongside empty beach coves and waves of evergreen forest. Pull over and find a silent patch of sandy bliss, a mountain trail to climb, or trundle along admiring the views with the windows open. I love looking for whales offshore and experiencing the changes in weather, from wild and stormy to perfect sunshine.

harborside shopping location, offering pleasant strolling and window-shopping.

Along the beach, ledges of stone rise out of the surf to provide shelter for seals, sea lions and myriad forms of life in tide pools. One of the coast's most interesting rock formations is the much-photographed **Face Rock**, a huge monolith with some uncanny facial features that does indeed look like a woman with her head thrown back – giving rise to a requisite Native American legend.

THE DRIVE: Follow the coastline another 24 miles south to Port Orford. This part of the drive isn't much to look at, but not to worry: there's more scenery to come.

17 Port Orford

Perched on a grassy headland, the hamlet of Port Orford is located on one of the most scenic stretches of coastal highway, and there are stellar views even from the center of town. If you're feeling ambitious, hike the 3-mile trail up **Humbug Mountain** *(stateparks.oregon.gov)*, which takes you up, up, up past streams and through prehistoric-looking landscapes to the top, where you'll be treated to dramatic views of Cape Sebastian and the Pacific.

Speaking of prehistoric scenery: your kids may scream at the sight of a Tyrannosaurus rex in front of **Prehistoric Gardens** *(prehistoricgardens.com)*, 12 miles south of town. Life-size replicas of the extinct beasties are set in a lush, first-growth temperate rainforest; the huge ferns and trees set the right mood for going back in time.

THE DRIVE: The scenery starts to pick up again, with unusual rock formations lining the 28-mile drive to Gold Beach.

18 Gold Beach

Passing through the tourist hub of Gold Beach, you can take a jet boat excursion up the scenic Rogue River. But the real treat lies 13 miles south of town, when you enter the 12-mile stretch of coastal splendor known as the **Samuel Boardman State Scenic Corridor**, featuring giant stands of Sitka spruce, natural rock bridges, tide pools and loads of hiking trails.

Along the highway are well over a dozen roadside turnouts and picnic areas, with short trails leading to secluded beaches and dramatic viewpoints. A 30-second walk from the parking area to the viewing platform at **Natural Bridge Viewpoint** (Mile 346, Hwy 101) offers a glorious photo op of rock arches – the remnants of collapsed sea caves – after which you can decide whether you want to commit to the hike down to China Beach.

THE DRIVE: It's just 34 miles from Gold Beach to the California border, and 28 to Brookings.

19 Brookings

Your last stop on the Oregon coast is Brookings. With some of the warmest temperatures on the coast, Brookings is a leader in Easter lily-bulb production; in July, fields south of town are filled with bright colors and a heavy scent. In May and June you'll also find magnificent displays of flowers at the hilly, 30-acre **Azalea Park**.

History buffs take note: Brookings has the distinction of being the location of the only WWII aerial bombing on the US mainland. In 1942 a Japanese seaplane succeeded in bombing nearby forests with the intent to burn them, but they failed to ignite. The Japanese pilot, Nobuo Fujita, returned to Brookings 20 years later and presented the city with a peace offering: his family's 400-year-old samurai sword, which is now displayed at the **Chetco Community Public Library** *(chetcolibrary.org)*.

WHALE-WATCHING

Each year, gray whales undertake one of the longest migrations of any animal on earth, swimming from the Bering Strait and Chukchi Sea to Baja California – and back. Look for them migrating south in winter (mid-December through mid-January) and north in spring (March through June).

Natural Bridge, Samuel Boardman State Scenic Corridor, Oregon

VICTORIA DITKOVSKY/SHUTTERSTOCK

51

THE PACIFIC NORTHWEST

OREGON CASCADES SCENIC BYWAYS

DURATION: 4 DAYS

DISTANCE: 240 MILES / 386KM

GREAT FOR: OUTDOORS, FAMILIES

BEST TIME TO GO: JUNE THROUGH SEPTEMBER TO AVOID SEASONAL ROAD CLOSURES.

★ BEST FOR

HOT SPRINGS

Terwilliger Hot Springs at Cougar Reservoir.

Terwilliger Hot Springs (p403), Oregon

The region around Oregon's Central Cascades is, without a doubt, some of the most spectacular terrain in the entire state. But one scenic byway just isn't enough to see it all. Here you have our version of an Oregon sampler platter: a loop that brings together several of the best roads to create a majestic route full of the state's best features.

LINK YOUR TRIP

50 Highway 101 Oregon Coast
Follow 58 NW to I-5 and head north to Portland. From there, follow US 30 along the south side of the Columbia River to Astoria.

52 Crater Lake Circuit
Crater Lake is a must-see, and it's just south of the Cascades. Take Hwy 97 south from Bend to join this route.

01 Westfir

Before you spend several days enjoying abundant natural wonders, start with a quick photo op of an entirely fabricated one: Oregon's longest covered bridge, the 180ft **Office Bridge**. Built in 1944, the bridge features a covered walkway to enable pedestrians to share the way with logging trucks crossing the Willamette River.

If you plan to do some exploring or mountain biking in the area, pick up a map of the Willamette National Forest at **Middle Fork Ranger Station** *(fs.usda.gov)*.

THE DRIVE: Oakridge is just a few miles to the east on either Hwy 58 or Westfir–Oakridge Rd.

02 Oakridge

Oakridge is one of Oregon's mountain-biking hot spots. There are hundreds of miles of trails around town, ranging from short, easy loops to challenging single-track routes. For novice riders, the **Warrior Fitness Trail** is a

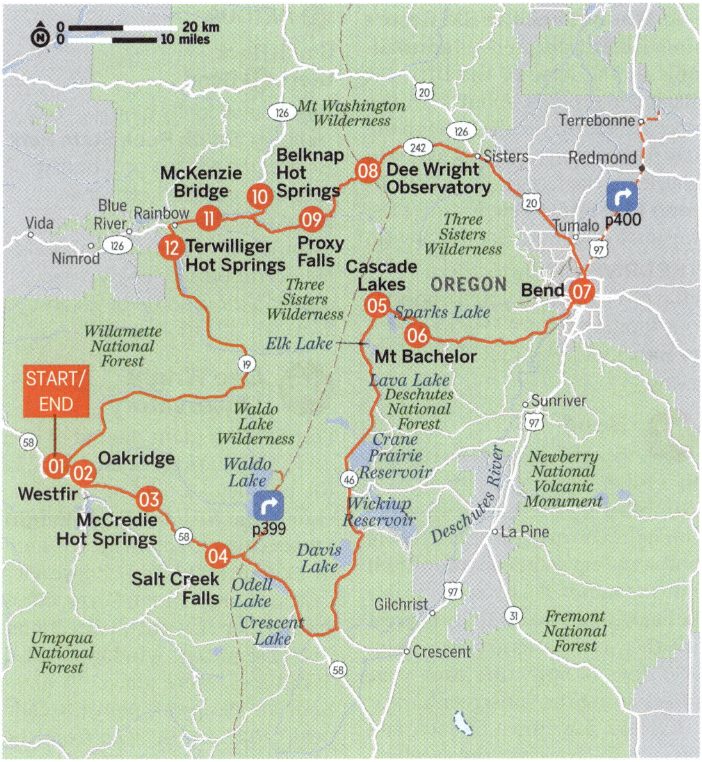

FRANCESCO VANINETTI PHOTO/GETTY IMAGES

mostly flat 12-mile loop. The **Larison Creek Trail** is a challenging ride through old-growth forests, and the 16-mile **Alpine Trail** is considered the 'crown jewel' of the local trails for its 7-mile downhill stretch.

THE DRIVE: From Oakridge, Hwy 58 climbs steadily up the Cascade Range's densely forested western slope. Your next stop is about 10 miles east of Oakridge; park on the right just past mile marker 45.

03 McCredie Hot Springs

Because **McCredie Hot Springs** *(fs.usda.gov)* lies just off the highway, it's a very popular spot for everyone from mountain bikers fresh off the trails near Oakridge to truckers plying Hwy 58. Despite this, it's worth a stop, if only because it's the site of one of the largest – and hottest – thermal pools in Oregon. If you can hit it early in the morning or late in the evening midweek, you could have the place to yourself.

There are five pools in all: two upper pools that are often dangerously hot (as in don't-even-dip-your-foot-in hot), two warm riverside pools and one smaller, murkier, but usually perfectly heated pool, tucked back into the trees. Salt Creek rushes past only steps from the springs and is ideal for splashing down with icy water.

THE DRIVE: Keep heading east another 12 miles and pull off the highway at the signed parking lot.

04 Salt Creek Falls

At 286ft, this monster of a waterfall is Oregon's second-highest. After a good snowmelt, this aqueous behemoth really roars, making for one of the most spectacular sights on the trip. Walk from the parking lot to the viewpoint and there below, in a massive basalt amphitheater hidden by the towering trees, 50,000 gallons of water pour every minute over a cliff into a giant, dark, tumultuous pool. Be sure to hike the short trail downhill toward the bottom of the falls. It's lined with rhododendrons that put on a colorful show in springtime, and the views of the falls on the way down are stunning.

Salt Creek Falls is also the starting point for some excellent short hikes, including a 1.5-mile jaunt to **Diamond Creek Falls** and a 4.75-mile walk to **Vivian Lake**.

THE DRIVE: Continue 19 miles along Hwy 58 until you reach the Cascade Lakes Scenic Byway (Hwy 46), which winds its way north through numerous tiny lakes and up to Mt Bachelor. This road is closed from November to May; as an alternative, follow Hwy 97 to Bend.

DETOUR

Waldo Lake

Start: 04 Salt Creek Falls

There's no shortage of lakes in the area, but lovely Waldo Lake stands out for its amazing clarity. Because it's at the crest of the Cascades, water doesn't flow into it from other sources; the only water that enters it is rainfall and snowfall, making it one of the purest bodies of water in the world. In fact, it's so clear that objects in the water are visible 100ft below the surface. You can swim in the summer months (it's too cold in the winter), and if you're feeling ambitious after playing 'I Spy' on the lakebed, you can hike the **Waldo Lake Trail,** a 22-mile loop that circumnavigates the lake. To get there, head 2 miles east of Salt Creek Falls on Hwy 58, and turn left at the Waldo Lake Sno-Park; follow the signs for 8 more miles to the lake.

05 Cascade Lakes

We could get all scientific and explain how lava from nearby volcanoes created the lakes around this area, or we could just tell you that Hwy 46 isn't called the Cascade Lakes Scenic Byway for nothing. The road winds past lake after beautiful lake – **Davis Lake**, **Crane Prairie Reservoir**, **Lava Lake**, **Elk Lake** – all worth a stop. Most have outstanding camping, trout fishing, boating and invigorating swimming ('invigorating' being a euphemism for cold).

We love **Sparks Lake** for its scenic beauty set against the backdrop of Mt Bachelor, and it's perfect for peaceful paddling. If you find yourself without a boat, **Wanderlust Tours** *(wanderlusttours.com)* can hook you up with a guided canoe or kayak tour.

THE DRIVE: Mt Bachelor is just a few miles past Sparks Lake. If Hwy 46 is closed for the season, you can backtrack from Bend to reach Mt Bachelor.

06 Mt Bachelor

Glorious Mt Bachelor (9065ft) provides Oregon's best skiing. Here, Central Oregon's cold, continental air meets up with the warm, wet Pacific air. The result is tons of fairly dry snow and plenty of sunshine, and with 370in of snow a year, the season begins in November and can last until May.

At **Mount Bachelor Ski Resort** *(mtbachelor.com)*, rentals are available at the base of the lifts. Mt Bachelor grooms about 35 miles of cross-country trails, though the day pass cost may prompt skiers to check out the free trails at **Dutchman Flat Sno-Park**, just past the turnoff for Mt Bachelor on Hwy 46.

THE DRIVE: Ready to add a little civilization to your rugged outdoor adventure? Head east to Bend, which is just 22 miles away.

07 Bend

Sporting gear is de rigueur in a town where you can go rock climbing in the morning, hike through lava caves in the afternoon, and stand-up paddleboard yourself into the sunset. Plus, you'll probably be enjoying all that activity in great weather, as the area gets more than 250 days of sunshine each year (don't forget the sunscreen!).

Explore downtown on foot, and be sure to check out the excellent High Desert Museum (highdesertmuseum.org). It charts the exploration and settlement of the Pacific Northwest, but it's no slog through history. The fascinating Native American exhibit shows off several wigwams' worth of impressive artifacts, and live animal exhibits and living history are sure to be hits with the kids.

THE DRIVE: Head 22 miles north to Sisters, then drive northwest along Hwy 242. This is part of the McKenzie Pass–Santiam Pass Scenic Byway – closed during the winter months. Your next stop is 15 miles from Sisters.

DETOUR
Smith Rock
Start: 07 Bend

Best known for its glorious rock climbing, **Smith Rock State Park** *(stateparks.oregon.gov)* boasts rust-colored 800ft cliffs that tower over the pretty Crooked River, just 25 miles north of Bend. Non-climbers can enjoy miles of hiking trails, some of which involve a little rock scrambling.

08 Dee Wright Observatory

Perched on a giant mound of lava rock, built entirely of lava rock, in the middle of a field of lava rock, stands the historic **Dee Wright Observatory**. The structure, built in 1935 by Franklin D Roosevelt's Civilian Conservation Corps, offers spectacular views in all directions. The observatory windows, called 'lava tubes,' were placed to highlight all the prominent Cascade peaks that can be seen from the summit, including Mt Washington, Mt Jefferson, North Sister, Middle Sister and a host of others.

THE DRIVE: Head west on Hwy 242 for 13 miles to mile marker 64 and look for the well-signed Proxy Falls trailhead.

09 Proxy Falls

With all the waterfalls around the Central Cascades – hundreds of them in Oregon alone – it's easy to feel like 'You've seen one, you've seen 'em all.' Not so fast. Grab your camera and see if you're not at least a little impressed by photogenic **Proxy Falls**. If there were a beauty contest for waterfalls, Proxy would certainly be in the running, scattering into sheer veils down a

Salt Creek Falls (p399), Oregon
LOREN L. MASSETH/SHUTTERSTOCK

PHOTO OPPORTUNITY

Salt Creek Falls, the second-highest waterfall in Oregon.

VOLCANO SIGHTS IN THE CASCADES

The Cascades are a region of immense volcanic importance. Lava fields can be seen from McKenzie Pass and along Hwy 46, and road cuts expose gray ash flows. Stratovolcanoes such as South Sister and Mt Bachelor, and shield volcanoes like Mt Washington, tower over the landscape. Although it's not instantly obvious when you drive to the center of **Newberry National Volcanic Monument** (13 miles south of Bend), you're actually inside the caldera of a 500-sq-mile volcano. What could be stranger than that? It's still active.

mossy wall of columnar basalt. It's not even like the falls make you work for it: it's an easy 1.3-mile loop from the parking area. If you want to save the best for last, take the path in the opposite direction from what the sign suggests, so you hit Upper Proxy Falls first and you can build up to the even better Lower Proxy Falls.

THE DRIVE: Nine miles from the falls, turn right on Hwy 126 (McKenzie Hwy); Belknap is just 1.4 miles away.

10 Belknap Hot Springs

Although nudity is the norm at most hot springs, **Belknap** *(belknaphotsprings.com)* is the sort of hot spring resort you can take your grandmother to and neither of you will feel out of place. Two giant swimming pools filled with 103°F (40°C) mineral water provide optimum soaking conditions in a family environment. The McKenzie River rushes by below, trees tower over everything, and everyone has a good time. An excellent alternative to camping, the resort has rooms for nearly all budgets.

THE DRIVE: Head southwest on Hwy 126 for 6 miles to reach your next stop.

11 McKenzie Bridge

Although from the road it looks like there is nothing but trees, there's actually plenty to do around here, including fishing on the McKenzie River and hiking on the nearby **McKenzie River National Recreation Trail**. To learn more about all your recreational options, stop at the **McKenzie Ranger Station**, about 2 miles east of town. The rangers are fonts of information, plus you can find everything you ever wanted to know about the McKenzie River trail, including maps and books.

THE DRIVE: About 6 miles west of McKenzie Bridge, turn left on Hwy 19 (aka Aufderheide Memorial Drive) just past Rainbow. After almost 8 miles, you'll come to the parking lot from which you'll take a 0.25-mile trail through old-growth forest.

12 Terwilliger Hot Springs

In a picturesque canyon in the Willamette National Forest is one of the state's most stunning (and clothing-optional) hot springs, **Terwilliger Hot Springs** (also known as Cougar Hot Springs). From a fern-shrouded hole, scorching water spills into a pool that maintains a steady minimum temperature of 108°F (42°C). The water then cascades into three successive pools, each one cooler than the one above it. Sitting there staring up at the trees is an utterly sublime experience. After hiking back to the car, you can even jump into **Cougar Reservoir** from the rocky shore below the parking lot.

THE DRIVE: From Terwilliger Hot Springs, take Aufderheide/Hwy 19 south 41 miles to return to Westfir.

McKenzie Bridge, McKenzie River National Recreation Trail, Oregon
CSNAFZGER/SHUTTERSTOCK

STAY AWHILE

BEND

BY MARGOT BIGG

While your windshield wipers may be doing double duty when driving through Oregon and neighboring Washington, they likely won't get much use in Bend, the largest community in Central Oregon's high desert region. While there is some rain (and winter snow) in this part of the state, you won't see much of the dank, mossy forests for which Oregon is best known. Instead, expect dry air, beautiful rock formations and famously good beer.

Though Bend is a relatively small city, you'll need to spend a couple of days here to really get a feel for local life. Devote one day to checking out local attractions such as the **High Desert Museum** *(highdesertmuseum.org)*, which has fantastic exhibits on the natural and cultural history of the area. If you're fond of beer, give yourself plenty of time to go brewery hopping. I love the 'Hopservatory' at **Worthy Brewing** *(worthybrewing.com)*, where you can gaze at the night sky through a research-grade telescope.

Spend another day getting out and exploring the surrounding area. My favorite spot to visit is **Smith Rock State Park** *(stateparks.oregon.gov)*, considered the birthplace of modern American sport climbing. While it's a great place to top-rope, it's also perfect for hiking and bird-watching – it's the first place I ever saw a bald eagle in the wild. If you're up for mountain biking, **Cog Wild** *(cogwild.com)* offers guided tours and bike rentals.

My favorite way to soothe sore muscles after a day of adventure is with a sauna session at one of the two Bend locations of **Gather Sauna House** *(gathersaunahouse.com)*.

LINK YOUR TRIP

Bend lies at the halfway point of the **51 Oregon Cascades Scenic Byways** (p398) road trip.

Left: Climbing, Smith Rock State Park, Bend, Oregon; Right: Smith Rock State Park, Bend, Oregon

LEFT TO RIHT: STEVE ESTVANIK/SHUTTERSTOCK, BLUESTORK/SHUTTERSTOCK

PLACES TO STAY

Juniper Preserve
About a half-hour drive from downtown, this golf-and-wellness resort offers lodge rooms and vacation rentals set against the backdrop of a sprawling high-desert landscape. *juniperpreserve.com*

Old St Francis School
This downtown hotel is housed in a converted Catholic school with old classrooms for guest rooms, a pub, and a glorious subterranean soaking pool. *mcmenamins.com/old-st-francis-school*

SCP Redmond
Housed in a historic brick building in neighboring Redmond, this wellness-leaning property features sleek, TV-free rooms (though they do have yoga mats and sound machines), plant-forward dining and a rooftop bar with distant views of the Three Sisters in the Cascade Range. *scphotel.com*

52

★ BEST

WATERFALL

Two-tiered Toketee Falls is our favorite.

THE PACIFIC NORTHWEST

CRATER LAKE CIRCUIT

DURATION: 2–3 DAYS

DISTANCE: 365 MILES / 587KM

GREAT FOR: NATURE, FAMILIES

BEST TIME TO GO: LATE MAY TO MID-OCTOBER, WHEN ALL THE ROADS ARE OPEN.

Toketee Falls (p408), Oregon

The star attraction of this trip is Crater Lake, considered by many to be the most beautiful spot in all of Oregon. The sight of the still, clear and ridiculously blue water that fills an ancient volcanic caldera is worth the trip alone, but the drive there is lined with beautiful hikes, dramatic waterfalls and natural hot springs, all right off the highway.

LINK YOUR TRIP

51 Oregon Cascades Scenic Byways
From Roseburg head north on I-5 and then southeast toward Westfir on Hwy 58.

01 Ashland

A favorite base for day trips to Crater Lake, Ashland is bursting at the seams with lovely places to sleep and eat (though you'll want to book your hotel room far in advance during the busy summer months). Home of the **Oregon Shakespeare Festival** *(osfashland.org)*, it has more culture than most towns its size, and is just far enough off the highway to resist becoming a chain-motel hotspot.

It's not just Shakespeare that makes Ashland the cultural heart of southern Oregon. If you like contemporary art, check out the **Schneider Museum of Art** *(sma.sou.edu)*.

Ashland's historic downtown and lovely **Lithia Park** (59 Winburn Way) make it a dandy place to go for a walk before or after your journey to Crater Lake.

THE DRIVE: Medford is 13 miles north of Ashland on I-5.

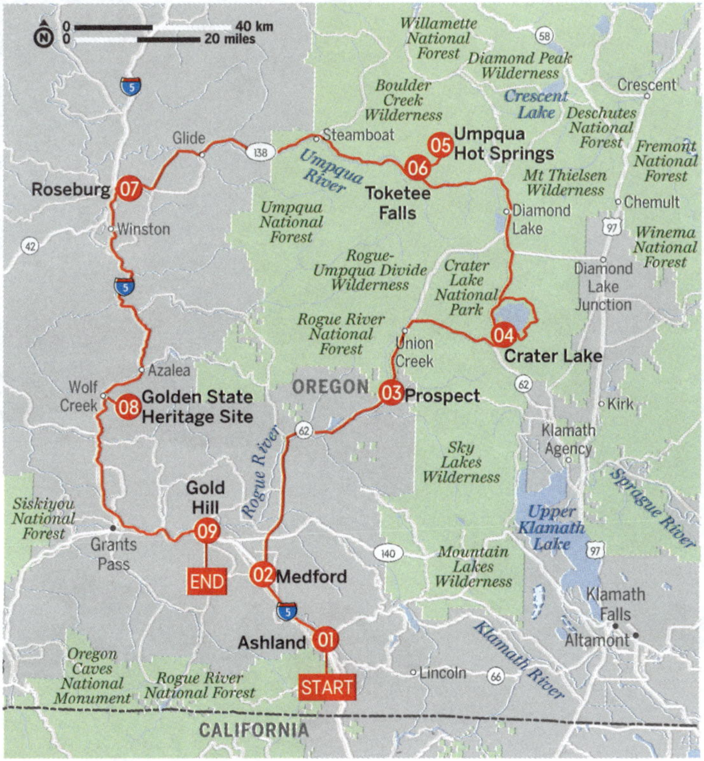

MATTL_IMAGES/SHUTTERSTOCK

02 Medford

Southern Oregon's largest metropolis is where you hop off I-5 for your trek out to Crater Lake, and it can also serve as a suitable base of operations if you want a cheap, convenient place to bunk down for the night.

On your way out, check out the **Table Rocks**, impressive 800ft mesas that speak of the area's volcanic past and are home to unique plant and animal species. Flowery spring is the best time for hiking to the flat tops, which were revered Native American sites. After **TouVelle State Park** *(stateparks.oregon.gov),* fork either left to reach the trailhead to **Lower Table Rock** (3.5-mile round-trip hike) or right for **Upper Table Rock** (2.5-mile round-trip hike).

THE DRIVE: The drive along Hwy 62 isn't much until after Shady Cove, when urban sprawl stops and forest begins. Your next stop is 45 miles northeast in Prospect.

03 Prospect

No wonder they changed the name of Mill Creek Falls Scenic Area – that implies you're just going to see another waterfall (not that there's anything wrong with that). But the real treat at **Prospect State Scenic Viewpoint** is hiking down to the **Avenue of Giant Boulders**, where the Rogue River crashes dramatically through huge chunks of rock and a little bit of scrambling offers the most rewarding views.

Take the trail from the southernmost of two parking lots on Mill Creek Dr. Keep left to get to the boulders or right for a short hike to two viewpoints for **Mill Creek Falls** and **Barr Creek Falls**. If you've got one more falls-sighting left in you, take the short hike from the upper parking lot to the lovely **Pearsony Falls**.

THE DRIVE: Follow Hwy 62 for another 28 miles to reach the Crater Lake National Park turnoff at Munson Valley Rd.

04 Crater Lake

This is it: the main highlight and reason for being of this entire trip is Oregon's most beautiful body of fresh water, **Crater Lake** *(nps.gov/crla).* This amazingly blue lake is filled with some of the clearest, purest water you can imagine – you can easily peer 100ft down – and it sits inside a 6-mile-wide caldera, created when Mt Mazama erupted nearly 8000 years ago. Protruding from the water and adding to the drama of the landscape is Wizard Island, a volcanic cinder cone topped by its own mini crater called Witches Cauldron.

Get the overview with the 33-mile Rim Drive, which offers over 30 viewpoints as it winds around the edge of Crater Lake. The gloriously still waters reflect surrounding mountain peaks like a giant dark-blue mirror, making for spectacular photographs and breathtaking panoramas.

You can also camp, ski or hike in the surrounding old-growth forests. The popular and steep mile-long **Cleetwood Cove Trail**, at the northern end of the crater, provides the only water access at the cove.

THE DRIVE: Head north on Hwy 138 for 41 miles and turn right on Rd 34.

05 Umpqua Hot Springs

Set on a mountainside overlooking the North Umpqua River, Umpqua is one of Oregon's most splendid hot springs, with a little bit of height-induced adrenalin thanks to its position atop a rocky bluff.

Springs are known for soothing weary muscles, so earn your soak at Umpqua by starting with a hike – it is in a national forest, after all – where you'll be treated to lush, old-growth forest and waterfalls punctuating the landscape. Half a mile from the parking lot is the spectacularly scenic **North Umpqua Trail** *(fs.usda.gov)*.

THE DRIVE: The turnout for Toketee Falls is right on Hwy 138, 2 miles past the Umpqua turnoff.

06 Toketee Falls

More than half a dozen waterfalls line this section of the Rogue-Umpqua Scenic Byway, but the one that truly demands a stop is the stunning, two-tiered **Toketee Falls** (USFS Rd 34). The falls' first tier drops 40ft into an upper pool behind a cliff of columnar basalt, from where the water crashes another 80ft down the rock columns into yet another gorgeous, green-blue pool below. One tiny disclaimer: although the hike is just 0.4 miles, there's a staircase of 200 steps down to the viewpoint, so climbing back up to your car is a bit of a workout.

THE DRIVE: From here, the scenery tapers back down to only moderately spectacular as you leave the Umpqua National Forest. It's just one hour to Roseburg.

> ☑ TOP TIP
>
> ### VISITING CRATER LAKE
>
> Crater Lake's popular south entrance is open year-round. In winter you can only go up to the lake's rim and back down the same way; no other roads are plowed. The north entrance is only open from early June to late October, depending on snowfall.

07 Roseburg

Sprawling Roseburg lies in a valley near the confluence of the South and North Umpqua Rivers. The city is mostly a cheap, modern sleepover for travelers headed elsewhere (such as Crater Lake), but it does have a cute, historic downtown area and is surrounded by award-winning wineries.

Don't miss the excellent **Douglas County Museum** *(umpquavalley museums.org)*, which displays the area's cultural and natural histories. Especially interesting are the railroad derailment photos and the Oregon Trail exhibit. Kids have an interactive area and taxidermy animals to look at.

THE DRIVE: Go south on I-5 for 47 miles and take the Wolf Creek exit. Follow Old State Hwy 99 to curve back under the interstate. Golden is 3.2 miles east on Coyote Creek Rd.

08 Golden State Heritage Site

Not ready to return to civilization quite yet? Stop off in the ghost town of Golden, population zero. A former mining town that had over 100 residents in the mid-1800s, Golden was built on the banks of Coyote Creek when gold was discovered there.

A handful of structures remain, as well as some newfangled interpretive signs that tell the tale of a curiously devout community that eschewed drinking and dancing, all giving a fascinating glimpse of what life was like back then. The weathered wooden buildings include a residence, the general store/post office, and a classic country church. Fun fact: the town was once used as a location for the long-running American Western TV series *Gunsmoke*.

THE DRIVE: Go south another 45 miles on I-5 and take exit 43. The Oregon Vortex is 4.2 miles north of the access road.

09 Gold Hill

Just outside the town of Gold Hill lies the **Oregon Vortex** *(oregonvortex.com)*, where the laws of physics don't seem to apply – or is it all just an optical illusion created by skewed buildings on steep hillsides? However you see it, the place is definitely bizarre: objects roll uphill, a person's height changes depending on where they stand, and brooms stand up on their own...or so it seems.

Umpqua Hot Springs, Oregon
NICHOLAS J KLEIN/SHUTTERSTOCK

TOOLKIT

Capitol Reef National Park, Utah

MARCIN MADRY/SHUTTERSTOCK

ARRIVING

Arriving in the US is usually hassle-free, provided that you have all of your documentation (visa or ESTA visa waiver) in order. Queues can, however, be long. Upon arrival, all international visitors must register with the Department of Homeland Security's Office of Biometric Identity Management program, which entails having your fingerprints scanned and a digital photo taken.

CAR RENTAL AT AIRPORTS

Car rental is a competitive business in the USA. Most rental companies require that you have a major credit card, be at least 25 years old and have a valid driver's license. Some major national companies may rent to drivers between the ages of 21 and 24 for an additional charge of around $25 per day. Except in Alabama, Alaska, Michigan and New York, those under age 21 are not permitted to rent at all.

Car-rental prices vary wildly, so shop around; you'll rarely get the best deal by simply showing up at an airport car-rental desk, quite apart from the fact that they may not have many (or any) cars available.

Most national agencies make 'unlimited mileage' standard on all cars, but independents might charge extra for this.

GETTING FROM THE AIRPORT

	NEW YORK (JFK)	LOS ANGELES	MIAMI
TRAIN	45min **$11.50–17.25**	no train	15min **$2.25**
BUS	no bus	30–50min **$12.75**	50–90min **$2.25**
TAXI	45–90min **$70**	25–50min **$55**	40–60min **$25**

MAIN AIRPORTS

Major entry airports include JFK (New York), Los Angeles, San Francisco and Miami. All have internationally enabled ATMs and currency exchange desks, and most have free wi-fi, although it's often limited to a few hours.

ESTA VISA WAIVERS

Visitors from the UK, Australia, New Zealand, Japan and many EU countries don't need visas for stays of less than 90 days, though they must get approval from the Electronic System for Travel Authorization (ESTA).

CANADIAN VISITORS

Visitors from Canada need neither a visa nor ESTA approval for stays of less than 90 days. Citizens of other nations should check *travel.state.gov*.

CUSTOMS

US and Canadian citizens, and those with ESTA visa waivers, can complete the compulsory US customs declaration electronically at an Automated Passport Control kiosk. For the question 'US Street Address', a hotel address is fine.

GETTING AROUND

PULLED OVER BY THE POLICE?

If you are pulled over by the police, do not get out of your car. Wait for the officer to approach your window. In the meantime, collect your license, proof of insurance and registration or rental agreement, and have them ready for the officer to inspect. When the officer arrives, they will usually stand a little behind your left shoulder, where they can see your hands.

DRIVING INFO

Drive on the right.

Speed limit is usually 70mph on interstates; 55–65mph on highways; 25–35mph in urban areas.

.08

Blood alcohol limit is .08mg/dL.

TAKE THE TRAIN

Amtrak *(amtrak.com)* has an extensive rail system throughout the USA. They're a relaxing, social and scenic all-American experience, especially on western routes, where double-decker Superliner trains boast spacious lounge cars with panoramic windows.

FLY TO SAVE TIME

The domestic air system is extensive and reliable, with dozens of competing airlines, hundreds of airports and thousands of flights daily. It's the way to go when you're in a hurry to get to the start of your drive.

FUELING UP

Many US gas stations have pumps with automated credit-card pay screens. Some machines ask for your ZIP code. For foreign travelers, or those with cards issued outside the US, you'll have to pay inside before fueling up.

HARLEY OR RV?

If you dream of cruising across America on a Harley, try **EagleRider** *(eaglerider.com)*. If a recreational vehicle (RV) is more your style, places such as *usarvrentals.com* and *cruiseamerica.com* can help. Rental and insurance fees for these vehicles are expensive.

TRAVEL COSTS

Petrol
Approx $3.15/gallon

EV charging
40–70¢/kWh

Train ticket from New York to Chicago
From $134 roundtrip

Greyhound bus from New York to Chicago
$92 one way

THOMAS PAJOT/SHUTTERSTOCK

ACCOMMODATIONS

HOW MUCH FOR A NIGHT IN A...

campground or hostel dorm
$30–80

double room in a midrange hotel
$100–200

double room in a resort or top-end hotel
from $300

BED & BREAKFASTS

In the USA, many B&Bs are high-end retreats in restored historic homes that are run by personable, independent innkeepers who serve gourmet breakfasts. These B&Bs often take pains to evoke a theme – Victorian, rustic, Cape Cod and so on – and amenities range from merely comfortable to indulgent. Rates normally start at $150, and the best go from $200 to $300.

CAMPGROUNDS

First-come, first-served 'primitive' campgrounds offer no facilities (free to around $15). 'Basic' sites usually provide toilets (flush or pit), drinking water, fire pits and picnic tables ($10 to $25 a night). Campgrounds in national or state parks have facilities that include showers, barbecue grills, RV sites with hookups etc ($18 to $50 a night).

B&B BOOKINGS

Some B&Bs have minimum-stay requirements, and most exclude young children. To start your search, try **Bed & Breakfast Inns Online** *(bbonline.com)*, **Savvy** *(savvy.com)*, **BnB Finder** *(bnbfinder.com)* or **Select Registry** *(selectregistry.com)*.

MOTELS

Distinguishable from hotels by having rooms that open onto a parking lot, motels tend to cluster around interstate exits and on main routes into town. Some remain smaller, less-expensive 'mom-and-pop' operations; breakfast is rarely included, and amenities might be a phone and TV (maybe with smart features); most also have free wi-fi. Motels often have a few rooms with simple kitchenettes.

THE AIRBNB EFFECT

Airbnb may have revolutionized the travel market, and generally for the better, but the impact upon local communities is a little more complicated. In many towns across the US, rental vacancies have shrunk to record levels as many property owners shift from longer-term rentals to more lucrative short-term holiday services such as Airbnb. The rise of Airbnb listings has also pushed prices higher in New York City, and the overall cost of annual rent has increased significantly due to the rise in Airbnb properties.

FEDERAL LANDS VS PRIVATE CAMPING

Camping on most federal lands, including national parks, national forests and Bureau of Land Management land, can be reserved through **Recreation.gov** *(recreation.gov)*. Private campgrounds tend to cater to RVs and families. Facilities may include playgrounds, convenience stores, wi-fi access, swimming pools and other activities. **Kampgrounds of America** *(koa.com)* is a national network of private campgrounds with a full range of facilities.

CARS

CAR RENTAL

It's not unusual to arrive to pick up your pre-booked vehicle only for the agent to try to sell you a whole list of additional services or upgrades. Make sure you know exactly what you're paying for. Tax on car rental varies by state and agency location; always ask for the total cost including all taxes and fees.

Most agencies charge more if you pick the car up in one place and drop it off in another, and usually only national agencies offer this option. Be careful about adding extra days or turning in a car early: extra days may be charged at a premium rate, or an early return may jeopardize any weekly or monthly discounts you originally arranged.

HOW MUCH TO HIRE A CAR?

a small car
$30–75 per day

a large car
$80–120 per day

an EV
$40–120 per day

ELECTRIC VEHICLES

It's still not common to rent an EV in the US, although hybrids are much easier to find. Some major national companies, including Avis, Budget and Hertz, offer 'green' fleets of hybrid or electric rental cars (eg Toyota Prius or Nissan Leafs), though you'll usually have to pay quite a bit more; remember, however, that you'll generally pay less to charge an EV than you would to fill a normal rental car's tank with gas. Because fleets are smaller, book your EV as early as possible to ensure you're not disappointed.

Some independent local agencies, especially on the West Coast, also offer hybrid-vehicle rentals. Try **Green Motion USA** *(greenmotion.com)* in Florida, California and Louisiana.

OTHER GEAR

You'll usually pay extra for everything, from child-safety seats and bike racks to GPS devices and portable fridges. Most rental agencies have limited supplies of all extra gear, so if you're after something specific, reserve as early as you can.

ONURDONGEL/GETTY IMAGES

RESPONSIBLE TRAVEL

CLIMATE CHANGE & TRAVEL

Lonely Planet urges all travelers to engage with their travel carbon footprint, which will mainly come from air travel. While there often isn't an alternative, travelers can look to minimise the number of flights they take and use cleaner ground transport, such as trains.

One proposed solution – purchasing carbon offsets – unfortunately does not cancel out the impact of individual flights. While most destinations will depend on air travel for the foreseeable future, for now, pursuing ground-based travel where possible is the best course of action.

The **UN Carbon Footprint Calculator** shows how flying impacts a household's emissions.

The **ICAO's Carbon Emissions Calculator** allows visitors to analyse the CO_2 generated by point-to-point journeys.

National Park Service
nps.gov
Gateway to America's national parks.

AAA's TripTik
triptik.aaa.com
Road-trip planning tool from the American Automobile Association.

ROADSIDE ASSISTANCE

An ecofriendly alternative is **Better World Club** *(betterworldclub.com)*, which donates 1% of revenue to assist environmental cleanup and offers ecologically sensitive choices for every service. They'll also cover you in a rental vehicle.

GREEN PORTLAND

In 1993 Portland, OR, was the first US city to implement a plan for cutting carbon. Emissions have declined 21% since 1990, while the population has grown 33%. It's also led the way in banning single-use plastics.

GO LOCAL

Support sustainable businesses, such as those committed to using locally sourced ingredients and materials, and clean energy. Using small local businesses is another way you can help support local communities.

SAFE TRAVEL

CAR BREAKDOWN

If your rental vehicle breaks down, your first call should be to the rental company (who should give you a 24-hour number to call). You should receive a replacement vehicle if your rental car is likely to be out of action for more than a few hours. The **American Automobile Association** (AAA; *aaa.com*) has reciprocal membership agreements with several international auto clubs (check with AAA and bring your membership card from home). This will only work if traveling in your own vehicle.

IN CASE OF EMERGENCY

911

Call 911 for police, fire or ambulance.

INSURANCE

Don't put the key into the ignition if you don't have insurance, which is legally required. You risk financial ruin and legal consequences if there's an accident. If you already have auto insurance, or if you buy travel insurance that covers car rentals, make sure your policy has adequate liability coverage for where you will be driving, as different states specify different minimum levels of coverage.

THEFT

For the traveler, it's not violent crime but petty theft that is the biggest concern. When possible, withdraw money from ATMs during the day, or in well-lit, busy areas at night. When driving, don't pick up hitchhikers, and lock valuables in the trunk of your car. In hotels, you can secure valuables in your room or hotel safe.

HYPOTHERMIA

If you're hiking at altitude, even in summer, weather conditions can change rapidly and without warning. Always carry waterproof garments and warm layers, and inform others of your route. Symptoms of hypothermia are exhaustion, numb skin (particularly of the toes and fingers), shivering, slurred speech, irrational or violent behavior, lethargy, stumbling, dizzy spells, muscle cramps and violent bursts of energy.

NATURAL DISASTERS

Most areas with predictable natural disturbances – tornadoes on the Great Plains and the South, hurricanes in the Gulf and Atlantic Coasts, earthquakes in California – have an emergency-siren system to alert communities to imminent danger. Hurricane season runs from June to November. Tornadoes are most likely from March to June. Wildfires are a particular peril during the summer months.

HEAT EXHAUSTION

If hiking, take it easy as you acclimatize, especially on hot summer days and in the desert. One gallon of water per person per day minimum is recommended. Dehydration (lack of water) or salt deficiency can cause heat exhaustion, often characterized by heavy sweating, pale skin, fatigue, lethargy, headaches, nausea, vomiting, dizziness, muscle cramps and rapid, shallow breathing.

NUTS & BOLTS

GOOD TO KNOW

Time zone
Four time zones ranging from GMT/UTC minus five hours to GMT/UTC minus eight hours

Country code
1

Population
343 million

CURRENCY: DOLLAR ($)

OPENING HOURS

- **Banks:** 8:30am–5pm Monday to Thursday, to 5:30pm Friday (and possibly 10am–2pm Saturday)
- **Post offices:** 9am–5pm Monday to Friday
- **Shopping malls:** 9am–9pm
- **Stores:** 10am–9pm Monday to Saturday, noon–5pm Sunday
- **Supermarkets:** 7am–10pm, some open 24 hours

TIPPING

Tipping 15–20% is expected; only withhold tips in cases of outrageously bad service.

CREDIT CARDS

Major credit cards are almost universally accepted. In fact, it's near impossible to rent a car or make hotel bookings without one.

PAYMENTS

It's normal for restaurant servers to take your card to a pay station to process. Note, too, that you may be asked to 'sign' for credit card purchases.

WEIGHTS & MEASURES

Weights are measured in ounces (oz), pounds (lb) and tons; liquids in fluid ounces (fl oz), pints (pt), quarts (qt) and gallons (gal); and distance in feet (ft), yards (yd) and miles (mi).

TOILETS

Most states have rest areas with free toilets along major highways; alternatively, as a paying customer you can seek out toilets at gas stations, coffee shops and chain restaurants.

HOW MUCH FOR A...

coffee
$2–5

local bus, subway or train
$2–5

national park entry
$15–20/person; $20–35/vehicle

museum entry
free to $40

ELECTRICITY

Type A
120V/60Hz

Type B
120V/60Hz

INDEX

Drives 000
Map pages **p000**

C

I

J

K

L

M

N

O

THE WRITERS

This is the 6th edition of Lonely Planet's Best Road Trips USA guidebook, updated with new material by Margot Bigg.

Writers on previous editions whose work also appears in this book are included below.

Margot Bigg

Margot Bigg writes about experiential travel for publications around the world. She's a huge fan of road tripping and loves taking the scenic route whenever possible. @margotbigg

Contributing writers

Kate Armstrong, Carolyn Bain, Amy C Balfour, Ray Bartlett, Loren Bell, Andrew Bender, Sara Benson, Alison Bing, Cristian Bonetto, Celeste Brash, Jade Bremner, Gregor Clark, Michael Grosberg, Anthony Ham, Ashley Harrell, Mark Johanson, Adam Karlin, Brian Kluepfel, Stephen Lioy, Vesna Maric, Carolyn McCarthy, Hugh McNaughtan, Becky Ohlsen, Christopher Pitts, Kevin Raub, Simon Richmond, Brendan Sainsbury, Andrea Schulte-Peevers, Regis St Louis, Ryan Ver Berkmoes, Mara Vorhees, Benedict Walker, Karla Zimmerman

Send us your feedback

We love to hear from travellers – your comments keep us on our toes and help make our books better. Our well-travelled team reads every word on what you loved or loathed about this book. Although we cannot reply individually to your submissions, we always guarantee that your feedback goes straight to the appropriate writers, in time for the next edition.

BEHIND THE SCENES

This book was produced by the following:

Commissioning Editor
Darren O'Connell

Coordinating Editor
Shauna Daly

Production Editor
Jeremy Toynbee

Image Researcher
Lyn Horst

Cartographer
Bohumil Ptacek

Assisting Editors
Pete Cruttenden, Maja Vatrić

Cover Researcher
Daisy Korpics

Thanks to
Sofie Andersen, Alison Killilea Charlotte Orr, Saralinda Turner, Clifton Wilkinson

Product Development
Sofie Andersen, Melinda Anderson, Marc Backwell, Alison Killilea, Darren O'Connell, James Smart, Saralinda Turner, Robin Yule

Acknowledgments

Digital Model Elevation Data
Contains public sector information licensed under the Open Government Licence v3.0 website nationalarchives.gov.uk/doc/open-government-licence/version/3/

Cover photographs
Front: Taking in the view at Glacier National Park in Montana; Ethan Gulley
Back: Monument Valley; cineuno/Shutterstock

Visit **lonelyplanet.com/contact** to submit your updates and suggestions or to ask for help. Our award-winning website also features inspirational travel stories and news.

Note: We may edit, reproduce and incorporate your comments in Lonely Planet products such as guidebooks, websites and digital products, so let us know if you are happy to have your name acknowledged. For a copy of our privacy policy visit **lonelyplanet.com/legal**

lonely planet

Published by Lonely Planet Global Limited
CRN 554153
Digital Depot, Roe Lane off Thomas Street, Dublin
D08 TCV4, Ireland (EU authorised representative)
6th edition – Sep 2026
ISBN 9781837584468

10 9 8 7 6 5 4 3 2 1
Printed in Malaysia